SCIENTIFIC PARALLEL COMPUTING

PRINCETON

Princeton University Press
Princeton and Oxford

NEW AGE

SCIENTIFIC PARALLEL COMPUTING

L. Ridgway Scott

Terry Clark

Babak Bagheri

PUBLISHING FOR ONE WORLD

NEW AGE INTERNATIONAL (P) LIMITED, PUBLISHERS

New Delhi • Bangalore • Chennai • Cochin • Guwahati • Hyderabad

Jalandhar • Kolkata • Lucknow • Mumbai • Ranchi

Visit us at **www.newagepublishers.com**

First Indian Sub-Continent Edition : 2010
by New Age International (P) Ltd., Publishers

This special low-priced edition is for sale in **India, Bangladesh, Bhutan, Myanmar (Burma), Sri Lanka, Nepal and Pakistan only.**

Originally Published by *Princeton University Press, USA.*

Branches:

- No. 37/10, 8th Cross (Near Hanuman Temple), Azad Nagar, Chamrajpet, **Bangalore**-560 018. Tel.: (080) 2675 6823, Telefax: 2675 6820, E-mail: bangalore@newagepublishers.com
- 26, Damodaran Street, T. Nagar, **Chennai**-600 017. Tel.: (044) 24353401, Telefax: 24351463, E-mail: chennai@newagepublishers.com
- CC-39/1016, Carrier Station Road, Ernakulam South, **Cochin**-682 016, Tel.: (0484) 2377004, Telefax: 4051303. E-mail: cochin@newagepublishers.com
- Hemsen Complex, Mohd. Shah Road, Paltan Bazar, Near Starline Hotel, **Guwahati**-781 008. Tel.: (0361) 2513881. Telefax: 2543669, E-mail: guwahati@newagepublishers.com
- No. 105, 1st Floor, Madhiray Kaveri Tower, 3-2-19, Azam Jahi Road, Nimboliadda, **Hyderabad**-500 027. Tel.: (040) 24652456, Telefax: 24652457, E-mail:hyderabad@newagepublishers.com
- RDB Chambers (Formerly Lotus Cinema)106A, 1st Floor, S.N. Banerjee Road, **Kolkata**-700 014. Tel.: (033) 22273773, Telefax: 22275247, E-mail:kolkata@newagepublishers.com
- 16-A, Jopling Road, **Lucknow**-226 001. Tel.: (0522) 2209578, 4045297, Telefax: 2204098, E-mail: lucknow@newagepublishers.com
- 142C, Victor House, Ground Floor, N.M. Joshi Marg, Lower Parel, **Mumbai**-400 013. Tel.: (022) 24927869. Telefax: 24915415, E-mail: mumbai@newagepublishers.com
- 22, Golden House, Daryaganj, **New Delhi**-110 002. Tel.: (011) 23262370, 23262368, Telefax: 43551305. E-mail: sales@newagepublishers.com

Printed in India at Glorious Printers, Delhi.
C-10-06-4746

ISBN: 978-81-224-3137-7
Original Edition Price: $ 64.00
Indian Edition Price: Rs. 395.00

PUBLISHING FOR ONE WORLD
NEW AGE INTERNATIONAL (P) LIMITED, PUBLISHERS
4835/24, Ansari Road, Daryaganj, New Delhi-110002
Visit us at **www.newagepublishers.com**

Dedication

To Jan, who suggested the name for the book and risked her life to take the cover photograph for the book,

To Lujia and the boys for their unwavering support, and

To the scientists and engineers who make parallel computing
a matter of practical concern.

Contents

Preface

Parallel computing may be defined as coordinated computation on independent processors devoted to a single task. As such, its roots are deep and pervasive in computer science. Modern computer arithmetic hardware exploits parallelism at the bit level. Operating systems are parallel programs which control the various components of a computer system. Web servers at major sites use collections of commodity computers to respond to requests from the worldwide web. This book does not try to survey all the possible uses of parallel computation, but rather focuses on a particular type of computation frequently used in scientific simulation, also growing in applications such as data mining and interpretation. The title reflects our primary focus, scientific computation done in parallel, but twists the usual phrasing to indicate that we are emphasizing a fundamental approach to (a large part of) parallel computing.

Parallel computing has emerged from the "pioneering" phase in which only a few utilized it, and only for "hero" calculations. Today, computing on "clusters" of PC's is as common as computing on scientific workstations was a decade ago. For economic and technical reasons discussed in Chapter 3, conventional sequential computers are no longer able to provide performance levels much beyond the desktop level. In some sense, high-performance computing has become parallel computing. Problems which require large amounts of memory or computational time can be solved today *only* with parallel computers. One prevalent application of parallel computing is to allow for all the data of the problem to fit into random-access memory.

While there are still major parallel computers packaged and sold today as a single system, the majority of computation today is done on clusters. Thus one might ask why there is a need to do more than just introduce the basics needed for "cluster computing." This book is not a short-cut to cluster computing. Rather, it represents an attempt to describe the fundamentals of parallel computing, at least those parts common to scientific computation. Computer architecture can change as design factors change, but these fundamentals will remain. Moreover, there are current computers today which are not just clusters, and a well-informed decision about which type to use must be based on a full understanding of the alternatives. On the other hand, we feel this book is an ideal introduction to the fundamentals of cluster computing, and it can be successfully used for a quarter or semester course on the subject.

One of the most compelling challenges of scientific computation today is to get good performance out of the increasingly complex commodity, desktop computer architectures. The key issues can be cast in a parallel computing framework. They include decomposing computations to exploit pipeline floating point units and restructuring code to minimize data traffic between processor and memory systems. The general approach we adopt is useful to analyze and improve performance at both the individual processor and the multi-processor level.

This book has been used in draft form at the University of Houston and the University of Chicago, with roots in courses taught at the University of Michigan and Penn State. It has been successful with a diverse audience, including typical graduate students in science and engineering, as well as advanced graduate students in mathematics and computer science. Exercises range in difficulty from those designed to help educate people with minimal computational background to ones which challenge advanced students.

The material ranges from descriptive to mathematical, and courses can be taught emphasizing either end of this spectrum. The prerequisite mathematics is not much beyond advanced calculus, so the material is accessible to advanced undergraduates.

The first three chapters are essential, as well as the beginning sections of Chapter 4. Chapter 5 is largely descriptive and should also be covered at least briefly for perspective. The important concept of reduction operation is presented in Chapter 6, and this should be covered in detail. This chapter begins the process of looking at complex parallel algorithms. After these chapters, the remaining material may be covered in a variety of orders.

There are three chapters (Chapters 8, 9, and 10) on specific high-level parallel programming languages. These have been chosen to illustrate the concepts of Chapter 5 and provide a starting point for parallel programming. It is possible to cover only one of these, or even none of these, using instead MPI or POSIX threads, both of which are introduced in Chapter 7. None of these chapters are comprehensive; it is expected that manuals for specific languages used in a course would supplement this book.

Applications begin with Chapter 11, and these can be chosen independently according to taste, based on student background and interests. In addition to Exercises, these later chapters introduce larger Projects which can be used as the basis for a term project for a course.

There is a bias in the book toward parallel computing languages based on Fortran. This may seem a bit retro to some, but there are various reasons for it. We have tried to be balanced to a certain degree between C(++) and Fortran, but there is a growing awareness of the strength of (classic) Fortran as a staticly allocated language without pointers. This makes it ideal when performance is of highest importance, as it is here. Modern scientific computation is often based on a combination of languages, with the highest level organization programmed in scripting languages such as Python. The computationally intensive code can be in another language such as C or Fortran, and it is the latter type of code that we focus on here.

We recommend that students get started with programming early. This allows an instructor to work out bugs in the system and identify students who need extra help getting going. We suggest assigning the programs associated with Section 1.3 in the first week, and a parallel computing exersise such as in Section 2.8 soon thereafter.

Many people have contributed to this book. Especially noteworthy are colleagues at the Advanced Computer Architecture Laboratory at the University of Michigan, a corresponding (but un-named) group at Penn State, the Center for Research on High-Performance Computing at Rice, the Texas Center for Advanced Molecular Computation at the University of Houston, and the Computer Science department at the University of Chicago. Courses taught at Argonne and Los Alamos National Laboratories on parallel computing gave us early experience with parallel computing and access to some of the first commercial parallel computers such as the Encore Multimax and Denelcor HEP. Collaborations with computer manufacturers such as IBM, Intel, nCUBE, NEC, and KSR also had substantial impact.

Notation

Here we collect a list of notation used in the text.

The "equal" sign gets used for many things. Here are some ways we make it more or less precise by introducing different notation for some of the different ways = can be used.

$:=$ The expression $a := b$ (or equivalently, $b =: a$) means that a is being *defined* to be the expression b. It might be written more informally just as $a = b$ in some cases, when it is clear that a definition is being made.

$\leftarrow$ In the description of an algorithm, we write $a \leftarrow b$ to mean that the value of b gets *assigned* to the memory location for a. In a code, this might be written `a=b`.

$\approx$ The expression $a \approx b$ means that a is approximately equal to the expression b, with an error which goes to zero as some parameter goes to a limit.

Here are performance measures introduced in Chapter 2.

T_P Time of execution with P processors (or processes).

S_P Speedup with P processors (or processes).

E_P Efficiency with P processors (or processes).

$T_{P,N}$ Time of execution with P processors (or processes) on a problem with data size N.

$S_{P,N}$ Speedup with P processors (or processes) on a problem with data size N.

$E_{P,N}$ Efficiency with P processors (or processes) on a problem with data size N.

Some miscellaneous mathematical notation:

$\mathcal{O}(a)$ See Section 1.3.3.

$\forall a$ For all a.

$\lceil a \rceil$ Smallest integer not less than a.

$\lfloor a \rfloor$ Largest integer not greater than a.

$\|a\|_p$ The *p-norm* of a vector a: $\|a\|_p := \left(\sum_{i=1}^{n} |a_i|^p\right)^{1/p}$.

$[a, b]$ The closed interval of real numbers x such that $a \leq x \leq b$.

(a, b) The open interval of real numbers x such that $a < x < b$.

$[a, b)$ The interval of real numbers x such that $a \leq x < b$.

$(a, b]$ The interval of real numbers x such that $a < x \leq b$.

We use some special notation in codes.

`n:m` In a code, `m:n` refers to the range of indices from `m` to `n` (inclusive).

`@` Used to describe data at a given processor (Section 6.2): `a@n` refers to the value of the variable `a` at processor `n`. Also formally defined in **P**languages codes; see Chapter 8.

$\omega\{a\}$ A **P**languages reduction operation based on the binary operator ω, e.g., $+\{a\}$, $*\{a\}$, $\texttt{AND}\{a\}$.

Chapter One
Introduction

> If you walk the footsteps of a stranger, you will learn things you never knew you never knew—*Pocahantas, by Disney*

This chapter introduces many of the basic notions of parallel computation. In Section 1.1 we give a short overview of the book, and Section 1.2 attempts to define what we mean by parallel computing. Section 1.3 introduces the critical topic of performance, which is central to the entire subject. In Section 1.4 we describe some of the motivating factors for the development of parallel computers. This is followed by some examples of parallelizing computational problems. The first two examples (Section 1.5) are quite simple, but serve to introduce many of the most important concepts. The next examples (Section 1.6) help to introduce further concepts as well as to provide some numerical applications that will be developed more in the text. Section 1.7.1 puts into context the role of parallel computation in solving technical problems, and Section 1.7.2 (also see Section 2.7) considers parallelism in a broader context.

1.1 OVERVIEW

Parallel computing enables simulation in a variety of application areas which would not be possible with sequential processing alone. To use it effectively, there are diverse subjects that must be understood. This book focuses on three main areas that contribute to overall understanding of parallel computing: algorithms, architecture, and languages. All of these are essential contributors to solving problems of interest, which we refer to as "applications" in Figure 1.1.

A basic understanding of computer architecture is needed to understand and predict the behavior of programs on different machines. A variety of fundamentally different computer architectures are commercially available today. Some differ substantially in the way they are programmed and the performance that can result. An introduction to computer architecture is presented in Chapter 3 to allow us to compare and contrast existing options. Some designs can be seen to be less appropriate for certain applications based on the simple analysis presented there.

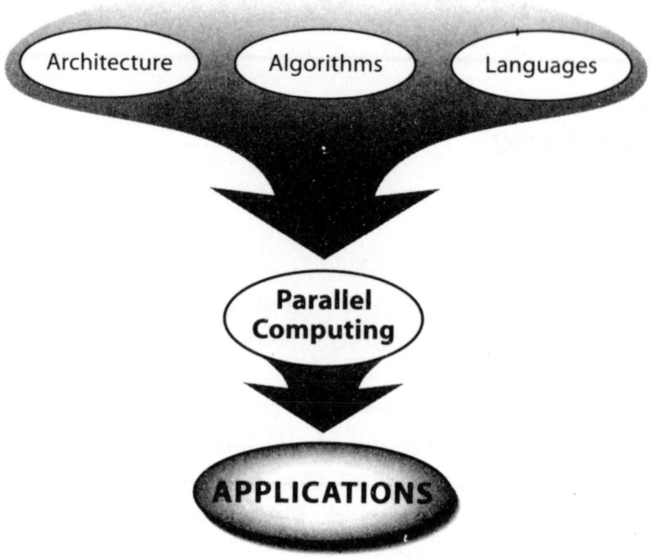

Figure 1.1 Knowledge of algorithms, architecture, and languages contributes to effective use of parallel computers in practical applications.

Central to the subject of parallel computing are algorithms. A general rule for scientific applications is that there is *no* parallelism of any significance occurring naturally. Parallelism must be created by removing *dependences* (see Chapter 4) that exist in most algorithms. Entirely new algorithms must be sought in some cases. Fortunately, the nature of scientific applications allows one to utilize a multitude of algorithms to solve the same problem, and highly efficient parallel algorithms can be found in most cases.

Several computer languages are in use today for programming parallel computers. Some languages can be used for different computer architectures with only a change at the compilation stage: the source application code does not change. Other languages are more closely aligned with a particular computer architecture. In Chapter 5, the essential features of various parallel computer languages are presented, and Chapters 8–10 introduce particular languages.

Applications are the driving force for all of computing, and much of the stimulus for parallel computing has come from scientific applications. We will introduce some simple prototypical application kernels later in this chapter as a basis for the discussion of programming languages and basic concepts of parallel computing. Once the elementary concepts are firmly established, basic algorithms of scientific computation are presented in Chapter 12. Later, more complete scientific applications will be developed and analyzed extensively, such as particle dynamics in Chapter 13. These can be used as models of projects that can be done by students as part of a course. Later chapters on mesh-based computations (Chapter 14) and on sorting (Chapter 15) are similar in approach.

1.2 WHAT IS PARALLEL COMPUTING?

We define parallel computing to be the application of two or more processing units to solve a single problem. These units can be physical processors or logical processes. A *process* is an abstraction provided by the operating system to capture the state of a program in execution. Thus, a program containing parallel units of work, or tasks, is executed by two or more cooperating processes executing on one or more processors.

In the class of parallel programs of primary interest to this book, each process executes the same program, but with different data. In fact, typically the program is viewed as processes more or less moving through the same code, but with different values according to the chunk of work assigned to the process. Although there are exceptions, this is the guiding paradigm.

Since processes calculate values that are needed by other processes, we need a way to distinguish among those data at different processes. It is useful to use a process-centric view where one process is considered with respect to all other processes. It naturally follows that the data of the one process under consideration are considered *on-process data* and all the rest are *off-process data.* We define a *processing unit* as a process executing on some processor. In using multiple processing units to solve a problem, varying degrees of coordination are required. Coordination primarily revolves around accessing off-process data required by some process to compute its tasks. Already introduced, these are referred to as dependences.

Consider a real world example of a typing pool with the job to type the chapters of this book, one typist per chapter. After completion of a chapter, typists may want to exchange chapter page counts so to sequentially number the pages of the book. If we think of each typist as a processing element, then this exchange involves somehow getting access to off-process data. Specifically, the page count of a chapter is accessed after completion of the chapter and not before. Current methods in parallel computing achieve this data exchange typically in one of two ways. In one method, the process requesting information will access the off-process information directly from memory where it was written. This requires some form of *synchronization* so that the value in memory is accessed when it is valid. In the typist example, the page count of preceding chapters is retrieved when it is complete and not before. Another method to acquire off-process information uses *messages.* In a message, the required information is packaged, somehow identified, and sent from the process that defined it to the process that requires it. Thus, in this way messages have both the *information* (page counts in our example) and *synchronization*, since the page-count message is presumably sent after the chapter has been finished. That off-process data are required and that these data may be on another physical processing unit introduces another dimension to the traditional memory hierarchy illustrated in Figure 1.2, that of off-process data. The term *communication* is often used in reference to accessing off-process data.

1.3 PERFORMANCE

The objective of the book is to help the reader achieve the best possible *performance* from parallel computers. Performance can be measured in many ways, but we will be interested primarily in the speed at which computation is done in floating point arithmetic.

Definition 1.3.1. The (floating point) **performance** of a computer code is the number of floating point operations that it can execute in a given time unit. Performance is often stated in terms of Millions of Floating Point Operations Per Second (megaFLOPS or MFLOPS), or Billions of Floating Point Operations Per Second (gigaFLOPS or GFLOPS).

Sometimes it will be necessary to refer to an amount of work in units of Floating Point OPerations (a FLOP). The plural of this will be written FLOP's to distinguish it from the performance figure FLOPS (which is a number of FLOP's per second). In particular, 10 MFLOP's means ten million floating point operations, whereas 10 MFLOPS means a performance of ten million floating point operations per second. Since this combination of units is the one most critical to describing performance, we feel it is appropriate to introduce a new unit, the Cray.[1] We define a Cray to be 10^9 floating point operations per second (one floating point operation per nanosecond), since this was the level of performance being achieved by a single processor at Seymour Cray's untimely death.

To illustrate this definition, let us begin with a very simple example. A look at a book of mathematical tables tells us that

$$\frac{\pi}{4} = 1 - \frac{1}{3} + \frac{1}{5} - \frac{1}{7} + \frac{1}{9} - \frac{1}{11} + \frac{1}{13} - \frac{1}{15} + \cdots \tag{1.3.1}$$

This is not a rapidly converging series to use to compute π, but it serves as a good example for studying the basic operation of computing the sum of a series of numbers:

$$A = \sum_{i=1}^{N} a_i. \tag{1.3.2}$$

[1] The development of the first "supercomputers" was largely the result of efforts lead by Seymour Cray (1925-1996). Seymour Cray earned a BS in engineering from the University of Minnesota in 1950. He co-founded Control Data Corporation (CDC) in 1957; the CDC 6600 is the primary candidate for the title of "first supercomputer." The series of supercomputers bearing Cray's name were produced by Cray Research. Started in 1972, this company was headquartered in Seymour's boyhood home, Chippewa Falls, Wisconsin, also home of the Jacob Leinenkugel Brewing Co.

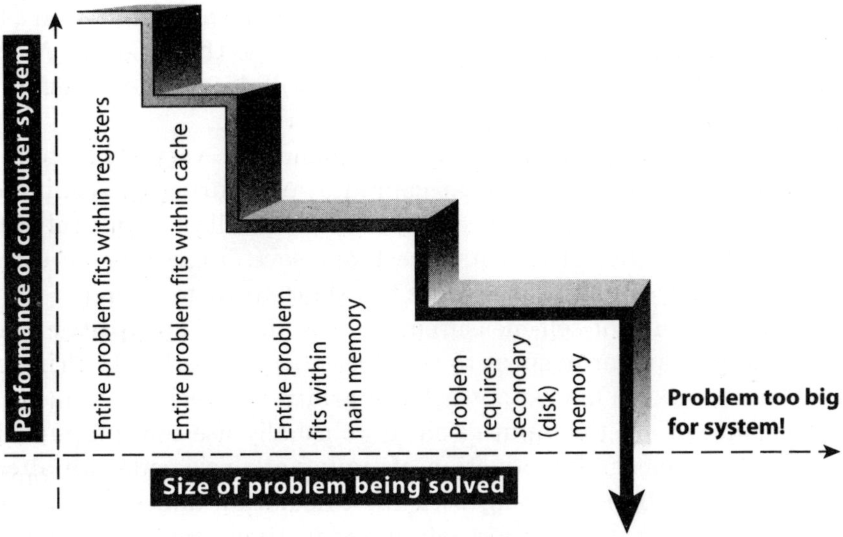

Figure 1.2 Hypothetical model of performance of a computer having a hierarchy of memory systems (registers, cache, main memory, and disk).

The computation of A requires $N-1$ floating point additions and $N+1$ memory references. If it takes T_N seconds to compute this for a given implementation (meaning for a given code compiled for a given computer), then the performance is $(N-1)/T_N$ FLOPS. Since this is likely to be a very large number, we usually say that it is either $(N-1)/(T_N \times 10^6)$ MegaFLOPS or $(N-1)/(T_N \times 10^9)$ GigaFLOPS (or Crays).

1.3.1 Performance analysis

There is often a theoretical maximum floating point performance for a given computer, and the performance of any code run on it is guaranteed not to exceed this figure. The goal of **performance analysis** is to understand not only the performance being achieved by a given code, but the reasons why this may differ from the theoretical maximum. In many cases, this is quite difficult to do with sufficient precision since computer clocks have a finite resolution. Any given operating system may have different timers available. It is crucial to understand the advertised accuracy of the timer you are using, and to compare that with your own estimate of how small a time it can measure accurately. In timing the computation of the sum in (1.3.2), this may mean that the observed time $T_N = 0$ for $N < N_c$ for a critical size N_c depends on the resolution of the timer.

Even if the timer never returns zero, it may be that it reports $T_N = 1$ time unit for all $N < N_c$, which is equally uninformative. One can estimate the minimum measurable time in various ways, but one useful way is to plot the ratio of the observed time to a predicted time based on some model of the computation. For example, we assume that the summation (1.3.2) should take an amount of time proportional to N. So the ratio T_N/N should be more or less constant. But when $T_N = 0$ it will drop to zero; before that happens, for slightly larger N, it may become erratic.

To get reliable information on performance for very short computations, it may be necessary to repeat computations during the timing cycle until the total time is large with respect to the smallest measurable time. Dividing by the number of repeats (see Exercise 1.7) can give an estimate of small times that would otherwise be too short to be measured.

Another feature of self-measurement is a kind of **computer uncertainty principle** similar in spirit to the Heisenberg Uncertainty Principle of quantum mechanics.[2] One cannot achieve arbitrary precision in measuring the performance of most computers since we usually use the computer itself to do the measurement. Introduction of timing analysis code can alter the time to completion by interfering with the calculation under measurement. In a parallel program it is important to assign time costs to sections of a program. In addition to determining the time for various procedures comprising a problem solution, it is frequently useful to separate out the costs to access remote data. The point is that timing a code can have subtle issues requiring careful engineering of a suitable timing strategy.

1.3.2 Memory effects

A critical feature of any algorithm is the relationship between the amount of work done and the amount of memory that must be accessed. In many cases, it is possible to quantify the relationship by a ratio measuring, at least in an asymptotic sense for sufficiently large problems, the number of floating point operations done per unit of memory accessed (via either a read or a write).

Definition 1.3.2. The **work/memory ratio** of an algorithm is the ratio ρ_{WM} of the number of floating point operations to the number of memory locations referenced (either reads or writes).

There is delicate wording in Definition 1.3.2. The denominator counts the *number of memory locations* referenced, L, not the *number of memory references* made, R. For example, should a program consist solely of the senseless but valid loop `for(i=0; i<1000; i++) j = i;` then $R >> L$

[2]Werner Heisenberg (1901–1976) invented matrix mechanics in 1925, the first version of quantum mechanics, and in 1932 was awarded the Nobel Prize in physics for this work. Heisenberg is best known for the Heisenberg Uncertainty Principle which he discovered in 1927. The uncertainty principle states that if you become more certain about a particle's position, then you must become less certain about its momentum, and vice versa. The uncertainty in position, δx, and in momentum, δp, are related by $2\delta x \delta p = \hbar$, a very small number equal to 1.05×10^{-34} Joule seconds, not noticeable in everyday life.

Figure 1.3 A simple memory model with a computational unit with only a small amount of local memory (not shown) separated from the main memory by a pathway with limited bandwidth μ.

since two memory locations are referenced 1000 times. The number of memory references made by a program depends on the particular implementation used to do the computation, whereas the number of memory locations used measures the total number of data (or memory locations) involved. We will see that simplified but useful definition can require quite complex analysis with the introduction of compiler optimization and additional components to the memory hierarchy. This distinction is further illustrated in Example 1.3.5 and Exercise 1.3.

Example 1.3.3. The computation of A in equation (1.3.2) requires $N-1$ floating point additions and involves $N+1$ memory locations: one for A and n for the a_i's. Therefore, the work/memory ratio for this algorithm is $\rho_{\mathrm{WM}} = (N-1)/(N+1) \approx 1$ for large N. In most cases, we will only be interested in such quantities for large data sizes, so we will loosely say that $\rho_{\mathrm{WM}} = 1$ for this algorithm. See Section 1.3.3 for a more precise way of simplifying such approximations.

It is uncommon to have ρ_{WM} much less than one, but it is not unusual to have it become arbitrarily large as a function of data size. In fact, we will see that certain computer architectures perform significantly better with algorithms having a large ρ_{WM}. One goal of this book is to help in either choosing or designing algorithms with large ρ_{WM}.

The observed performance of a computer system depends on its ability to access the memory required by a given computation. If the maximum speed that the memory system can deliver information is μ words per time unit, then the maximum performance that can be achieved is $\mu\rho_{\mathrm{WM}}$. We formalize this observation in the following theorem. We will assume that the computer system has a very simple structure as indicated in Figure 1.3: the computational unit has only a small amount of memory available locally, with the main memory accessible only via a channel of limited bandwidth.

Theorem 1.3.4. Suppose that a given algorithm has a work/memory ratio ρ_{WM}, and it is implemented on a system as depicted in Figure 1.3 with a maximum bandwidth to memory of μ million floating point words per second. Then the maximum performance that can be achieved is $\mu\rho_{\mathrm{WM}}$ MFLOPS.

Theorem 1.3.4 provides an upper bound on the number of operations p r unit time, by assuming the floating point operation blocks until data are available to the cpu. Therefore the cpu cannot proceed faster than the rat data are supplied, and it might proceed slower. Note again that ρ_{WM} measures the *amount* of memory referenced, not the *number* of memory refe ences (the same memory location could be referenced multiple times in a given algorithm).

Example 1.3.5. Consider the computation of the product of a square matrix $\mathbf{A} = (a_{ij})$ and a vector $\mathbf{V} = (v_i)$, defined by

$$(\mathbf{AV})_i := \sum_{j=1}^{n} a_{ij}v_j \quad \text{for } i = 1, \ldots, n. \tag{1.3.3}$$

Then the number n of floating point operations is n multiplies and $n - 1$ adds for each $(\mathbf{AV})_i$ for a total of $(2n - 1)n$ FLOP's to compute $\mathbf{AV}$. The number of memory locations involved is n^2 for $\mathbf{A}$, and n each for $\mathbf{V}$ and $\mathbf{AV}$. Thus the ratio ρ_{WM} of the number of floating point operations to the number of data values (i.e., number of **memory locations**) involved in the algorithm is

$$\rho_{\text{WM}} = \frac{2n^2 - n}{n^2 + 2n} \approx 2$$

for n large. Note that the number of memory **references** can be larger. If we have to read v_j from memory every time we compute $a_{ij}v_j$ (for $i = 1, \ldots, n$) then we read $\mathbf{V}$ a total of n times. In this worst case, the ratio of work to memory *references* is one instead of two, worse by a factor of two.

Theorem 1.3.4 refers to a machine with a single path to memory, but this model is too simplistic for real systems. The typical memory subsystem is a multi-component system with a *hierarchy* of components organized from fast and costly to slower and less costly. In general, the memory components closest to the cpu are fastest, with the slower memory components feeding the faster ones using various strategies to amortize the cost to pull data from a slower component into a faster one. Memory cache (Section 3.1.2) supplies resident data to the cpu in a few machine cycles, and nonresident data are obtained from slower main memory in blocks consisting of contiguous memory locations. Consequently, programs that access data in some memory locale and reuse data will get more usage of data in the cache, resulting in better performance. In terms of the previous discussion, data reuse makes the most of data fetched to the cache by accessing the same memory location multiple times. For a cpu to access a datum already in cache is called a *cache hit.* Figure 1.4 presents a simple picture of such a system. Note that to access the same memory location multiple times in a program does not guarantee a cache hit. The size of the cache is much smaller than the size of main memory, so that it follows that many locations in main memory share

Figure 1.4 A memory model with a large local data cache separated from the main memory by a pathway with limited bandwidth μ.

only a few locations in the cache; we leave this important detail aside for the present discussion.

Consider the matrix-vector multiplication algorithm (1.3.3). Let us assume that after the vector **V** has been read from memory once, it stays in cache. Then the number of memory *references* is the same as the amount of memory referenced, and the maximum performance in Theorem 1.3.4 can be achieved. That is, ρ_{WM} correctly measures the amount of memory traffic under these assumptions. Of course, this can only happen if the cache size is sufficiently large to hold all of the vector **V**.

In addition to particular analyses for particular algorithms like (1.3.3), a general model of behavior for cache systems can be developed as in the next example based on average cache hit rates. We will use notation familiar from physics such as $\frac{\text{words}}{\text{second}}$ to mean "words per second" (denoting a rate of transmission). Of course, this notation is convenient for seeing how to cancel units of time, operations, or memory.

Example 1.3.6. The performance of a two-level memory model (as depicted in Figure 1.4) consisting of a cache and a main memory can be modeled simplistically as

$$\begin{aligned}\frac{\text{average cycles}}{\text{word access}} =& \%\text{hits} \times \frac{\text{cache cycles}}{\text{word access}} \\ &+ (1 - \%\text{hits}) \times \frac{\text{main memory cycles}}{\text{word access}},\end{aligned} \tag{1.3.4}$$

where %hits is the fraction of cache hits among all memory references. For a main memory access time of 100 cycles per word and a cache access time of 2 cycles per word, the average $\frac{\text{cycles}}{\text{word}}$ for 10% and 90% hit rates are 90.2 and 11.8, respectively. The average number of words per time unit is

$$\frac{\text{words}}{\text{second}} = \left(\frac{\text{average cycles}}{\text{word access}}\right)^{-1} \times \frac{\text{cycles}}{\text{second}}.$$

On a 2 GHz processor, the corresponding average memory rates would be 22.2 and 169.5 million words per second. The performance of programs exhibiting an average memory access time of n cycles per word on a 2 GHz processor is bounded by

$$\left(n\,\frac{\text{cycles}}{\text{word access}}\right)^{-1} \times \left(2 \times 10^9\,\frac{\text{cycles}}{\text{second}}\right) \times \rho_{\text{WM}} = \frac{2 \times 10^9 \rho_{\text{WM}}}{n}\text{FLOPS}.$$

For an average of $\rho_{\text{WM}} = 2$ floating point operations per word, with 10% and 90% cache-hit cases, the bounds on performance are 44.3 MFLOPS and 330 MFLOPS, respectively.

Modeling the speed of access to memory is quite complex on modern high-performance computers. Figure 1.2 indicates the performance of a hypothetical application, depicting a decrease in performance as a problem increases in size and migrates into ever slower memory systems [6] [5]. Eventually the problem size reaches a point where it can not ever be completed for lack of memory.

Such degradation would, e.g., result for an algorithm that has a fixed and sufficiently small work/memory ratio ρ_{WM}, so that peak performance cannot be achieved for data not resident in cache. In this case, Figure 1.2 represents a plot of the bandwidth μ of the various memory systems, in view of Theorem 1.3.4. It is typical for a computer's various memory systems to be progressively slower, larger, and cheaper per word of memory. See Exercise 1.7 for a specific example of this behavior for the summation problem (1.3.2).

For computers having a performance profile as indicated in Figure 1.2, algorithms with a larger work/memory ratio ρ_{WM} will perform better than ones with smaller ones. It is sometimes possible to choose algorithms that produce equivalent answers but have vastly different work/memory ratios.

1.3.3 Asymptotic analysis

In much of our analysis of algorithms and performance we will be interested in the order of the growth of a function excluding the details of multiplicative constants and lower order terms. When we look at the growth of $f(n)$ in this way, we are considering the *asymptotic* growth in the limit of large n.

For our purposes we will use the $\mathcal{O}$-notation as defined below to describe an asymptotic upper bound of a function.

Definition 1.3.7. For a function $f(n)$ the **asymptotic upper bound** $\mathcal{O}(g(n))$ implies that there exists a constant c_1, satisfying $0 < c_1 < \infty$, and an integer $n_0 \geq 0$ such that $f(n) \leq c_1 g(n)$ for all $n \geq n_0$.

Example 1.3.8. To show that the upper bound of function $f(n) = an^2 + bn$ is $\mathcal{O}(n^2)$ we seek c_1 so that the inequality

$$an^2 + bn \leq c_1 n^2$$

holds for large n. Provided that $c_1 > a$, this does hold for any $n \geq b/(c_1 - a)$.

It is important to understand that the asymptotic upper bound, say, $\mathcal{O}(n^2)$ for some performance metric, does not say the performance is $\mathcal{O}(n^2)$. Rather it does say that the worst case running time for any n is $\mathcal{O}(n^2)$. For example, *bubblesort* (Figure 15.1) can sort an already sorted list with an operation count cn, although bubblesort has a worst-case asymptotic upper bound of $\mathcal{O}(n^2)$.

Example 1.3.9. In Example 1.3.3 we found the work/memory ratio for computing A in (1.3.2) to be $\rho_{\text{WM}} = (N-1)/(N+1)$, and we concluded $\rho_{\text{WM}} \approx 1$. Now let us compare $(N-1)/(N+1)$ to one:

$$\begin{aligned}\frac{N-1}{N+1} - 1 &= \frac{N-1-(N+1)}{N+1} \\ &= \frac{-2}{N+1} = \mathcal{O}(N^{-1}).\end{aligned}$$

Thus we can say more precisely that $\rho_{\text{WM}} = 1 + \mathcal{O}(\frac{1}{N})$.

Example 1.3.10. In some instances asymptotic analysis can be misleading. A common source of confusion arises using the notation without taking into account the constant factors. Suppose we have two algorithms to solve the same problem. Algorithm F has running time $f(n) = an^2$, and algorithm G has running time $g(n) = bn$. By solving the inequality $an^2 < bn$ we find that $g(n) > f(n)$ for $n < \frac{b}{a}$. Therefore, for $n < \frac{b}{a}$, algorithm F is the better choice even though $f(n) = \mathcal{O}(n^2)$ and $g(n) = \mathcal{O}(n)$.

1.4 WHY PARALLEL?

Several factors spurred the development of parallel supercomputers. Many of these factors can be categorized as follows:

- physical limitations, e.g., the speed of light;
- economic factors (economies of scale);
- scalability (matching the computer to the problem size);
- architectural improvements (reflecting the increasing role of memory compared to processing power).

We will discuss examples of all of these, although our list is meant to be simply illustrative, not exhaustive.

1.4.1 Physical limits

At the most elementary level, physical limitations such as the speed of light[3] (see Figure 1.5) make it difficult to construct large computers that operate

[3]The speed of light imposes a physical limit on signal propagation times across computer circuitry. This physical constant is approximately 3×10^{10} cm/sec in a vacuum, an upper limit on the speed of electromagnetic propagation in various physical media, such as copper wire. Grace Murray Hopper (1906–1992) was an early pioneer in computing who was famous for handing out a nanosecond's worth of copper wire to students and admonishing them not to waste nanoseconds in their codes.

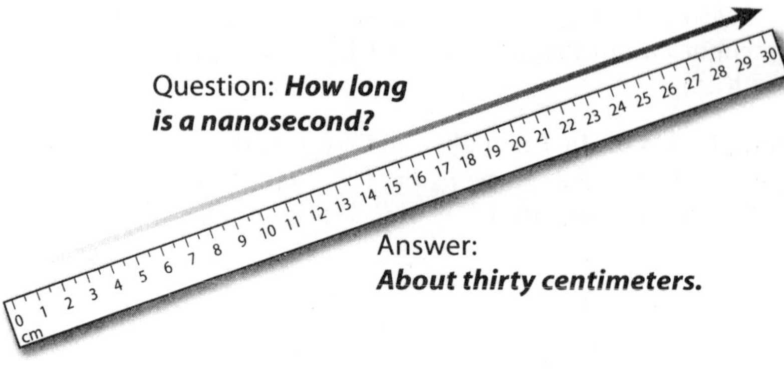

Figure 1.5 Light travels about one foot (in a vacuum) in a nanosecond.

with a clock speed on the order of a nanosecond or less. In this time, light travels only a foot or so in a vacuum (electrical signals are even slower in copper wire). This forces tolerances to be very precise in order to guarantee synchronization of even the simplest operations such as reading a word of data from memory, while demanding increasingly compact packaging of components.

Historically, processor speeds have increased exponentially, with a doubling time of something less than two years. In the last two decades, this has been exemplified by the rapid increase in performance of microprocessors. For example, Figure 1.6 depicts this increase for the Intel "86" family of computer chips which powered the personal computer revolution. Here, a fifteen-year period has led to a performance increase at the processor level by a factor of more than one hundred.

Due in part to speed-of-light limitations on the rate of data movement and lagging performance of memory subsystems, the increase in performance of vector supercomputers has been much less dramatic in the last three decades (see also Figure 1.6) than the increases in processor cycle speeds. Similarly, the performance increase of a uniprocessor workstation does not directly track processor cycle speed increases due in part to more slowly increasing memory performance with an increasing differential between processor speed and memory access time. The problem, however, has been more complex in vector processing systems due to the characteristically large memories and faster processing units.

1.4.2 Economic factors and scaling

It has always cost more to produce high-end computers than "commodity" single-processor workstations. Figure 1.7 shows this behavior with the family of workstations provided by Digital based on the SPECint92 perfor-

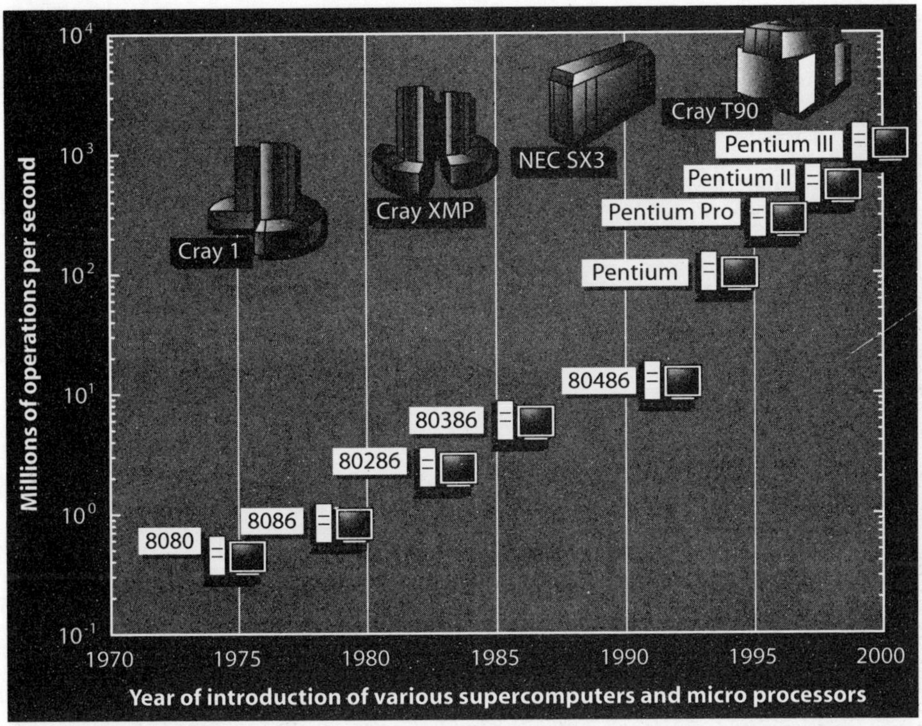

Figure 1.6 Performance of various "supercomputers" and the Intel "86" family of computer chips.

mance[4] for the DEC "alpha" workstations. It is clearly more cost effective to buy three of the lowest performance workstations than one of the higher-performance ones, in terms of the aggregate performance available. It is natural to consider combining several less powerful processors to form a single, more cost-effective computer. Of course, in doing so there may be additional costs related to providing space, electricity, sufficiently fast communications, and other factors that complicate the price/performance equation. However, the economies of scale due to using many commodity computers will frequently compensate for this.

A significant topic of this book will be how to partition a large calculation into component parts which can then be performed by a collection of individual computers with minimal interaction. If this can be done, one extra benefit is that the individual calculations done by each of the computers are smaller, e.g., in terms of the size of the data set or the number of operations performed. Figure 1.2 indicates how performance can decrease as the problem size increases due to migration of data into ever slower memory systems. In this case, a problem which can be decomposed into smaller parts can potentially run with greater than linear speedup (see Definition 2.2.1)

[4]The System Performance Evaluation Cooperative (SPEC) is a nonprofit organization founded by computer vendors in 1988 with the goal to provide realistic, standardized performance tests.

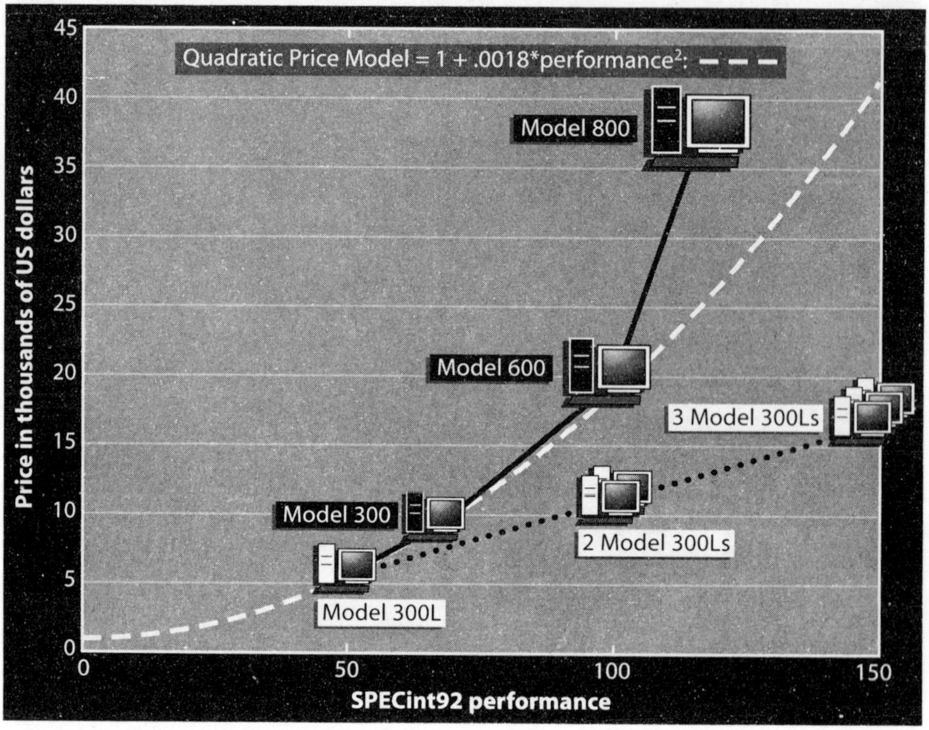

Figure 1.7 The cost of a particular computer architecture grows quadratically as a function of the performance of the computer. Plotted is the price of four Digital "alpha" workstation models (the circles on the graph) as a function of their SPECint92 performance. A quadratic curve has been fitted to the data to clarify its nonlinear behavior. Data were drawn from the 19 October 1993 *Wall Street Journal.* The dotted line indicates the price/performance associated with buying multiple machines of the cheapest model.

since the problem size for each individual computer is decreasing as the number of processors is increased. As indicated following Definition 1.3.2, the ratio of the amount of work done to the amount of memory that must be accessed is a critical factor determining performance. In any case, the ability to match the size of a parallel computer to a given problem (many processors for big problems, few for small ones) provides a way to "right size" the computer resources to ensure better resource utilization.

1.4.3 Memory

A recent but perhaps overarching reason for the success of parallel computers is that they allow the aggregate bandwidth between the processor(s) and memory to be made much larger at minimal expense. With a conventional pathway to memory, such as a bus (see Section 3.1.1), there are significant limits to how fast information can be moved between the processor and main memory. As one might expect, the cost of such a pathway also increases greater than linearly with the bandwidth achieved. A parallel computer allows one to have many pathways (as many as the number of processors or more) and thereby to keep a balance between processing power and memory bandwidth at reasonable cost.

1.4.4 Parallel conclusions

In summary, parallel computers provide the following advantages which we have emphasized:

- they postpone the limitations of the speed of light that hampered the design and manufacture of conventional supercomputers;
- they allow cheaper components to be used to achieve comparable levels of aggregate performance;
- they allow problem sizes to be subdivided and thereby achieve a better match between algorithm and appropriate system components, such as cache and RAM, leading to better system performance;
- they allow aggregate bandwidth to memory to be increased together with the processing power at reasonable cost.

1.5 TWO SIMPLE EXAMPLES

For the sake of orientation, we give two extended but simple examples which exhibit key features of parallel computing without requiring much mathematical background. This will give us some basic examples to work with as we develop ideas in the first few chapters. They illustrate the concepts introduced so far in Definition 1.3.1 and Definition 1.3.2, and they introduce some additional key concepts, presented also in a series of definitions.

1.5.1 Simple sums

We begin with the summation problem (1.3.2):

$$A = \sum_{i=1}^{N} a_i.$$

This sort of operation is often called a *reduction*; it *reduces* the vector $(a_1, \ldots, a_N)$ to the scalar A. The formal definition of a reduction will be given in Chapter 6.

Assume for simplicity that N is an integer multiple, k, of P: $N = k \cdot P$. Then we can divide the reduction operation into P partial sums:

$$A_j = \sum_{i=(j-1)k+1}^{jk} a_i \qquad (1.5.1)$$

for $j = 1, \ldots, P$. Then

$$A = \sum_{i=1}^{P} A_i. \tag{1.5.2}$$

Leaving aside the last step (1.5.2), we have managed to create P parallel *tasks* (1.5.1) each having $k = N/P$ additions to do on $k = N/P$ data points.

Definition 1.5.1. A **task** is a part of a computation that can be thought of independently from other parts. We think of a task as something that can be computed by a separate **procedure**, such as a `subroutine` in Fortran, a `function` in C, or a `method` in Java.

Recall that the work/memory ratio (Definition 1.3.2) for these computations is 1 (for k sufficiently large); that is, there is only one floating point operation to be done for each data point a_i. The ratio $k = N/P$ is often called the *granularity* of the parallel tasks.

Definition 1.5.2. The **granularity** of a set of parallel tasks is the amount of work (of the smallest task) that can be done independently of any other computation.

The basic job of parallelizing scientific computation is to discover, create, or otherwise expose independent calculations that can be done in parallel with minimal communication. When no communication is required, we give these a special name.

Definition 1.5.3. Tasks that can be done independently of any other computation, without any communication required among them, are called **trivially parallel** or **embarrassingly parallel.**[5]

The tasks in (1.5.1) are trivially parallel. However, the final step of summing the A_i's in (1.5.2) requires some form of cooperation, either communication of data or synchronization, among the P processors that computed them. We postpone detailed discussion of algorithms for forming this sum until Chapter 6, but simple algorithms will be given as examples in the sequel.

There are very few exceptions to the rule that any scientific program consists of loops, typically many. The computation of the sum (1.3.2) will

[5]Parallel computing for scientific and engineering applications remains a difficult undertaking. The act of parallelizing an application can involve Herculean efforts, or a sizable piece of a graduate student's career. Yet, there are some applications without data dependences (Chapter 4) along a richly parallel dimension, whereby the applicationists may avoid dramatic efforts in parallelization. The cliché *embarrassingly parallel* pokes fun at the good fortune of having readily available parallelism, permitting routine methods. Jay Boris, computational fluid dynamicist speaking at the 1997 DOD High-Performance Computing Modernization meeting, however, summed up the practical side of the matter: "I am not *embarrassed* about the [trivial] parallelism in my application, I am happy about it!"

be programmed typically in a *loop*, e.g., a `DO` loop in Fortran or a `for` loop in C. The concept of *iteration space* is useful to understand how to deal with parallelism in loops.

Definition 1.5.4. The **iteration space** of a given set of (possibly nested) loops is a subset of the Cartesian product of the integers consisting of the set of all possible values of loop indices. The dimension of the Cartesian product is the number of nested loops (it is one if there is only one loop). When the exact set of loop indices is not known without running the code, the iteration space is taken to be the smallest set known to contain all of the loop indices.

The iteration space for a single loop implementing (1.3.2) is simply the integers from 1 to N. The parallel algorithm embodied in (1.5.1) and (1.5.2) corresponds to dividing this set into P contiguous segments, which we call a *decomposition* of the iteration space:

Definition 1.5.5. An **iteration space decomposition** consists of a collection of disjoint subsets of the iteration space whose union is all of the iteration space.

The algorithm (1.3.2) has been parallelized using an approach referred to as *data parallelism.*

Definition 1.5.6. The concept of **data parallelism** refers to parallelizing a composite operation on a large data set in which the same (or similar) individual operations are carried out on each data item.

The data-parallel operation in (1.3.2) is summation. The key point is the homogeneity of the overall task, which allows it to be divided in arbitrary ways through multiple instances in execution of the same procedure where each instance operates on a portion of the iteration space. This kind of parallelism is very similar to the type of *loop* parallelism we will study in Section 4.2.

1.5.2 Load balancing

Figure 1.8 depicts graphically the iteration space for the summation problem (1.3.2) parallelized using the decomposition in (1.5.1). One requirement for a decomposition (which we have satisfied in the one depicted in Figure 1.8) is that the work to be done by each processor be *balanced* among all the processors. If the work is not distributed equally, then one processor may end up taking longer than the others. Since we are doing a cooperative project, the entire job cannot be finished until the slowest subtask is finished. We formalize the notion of balancing the work, or *load*, in the following definition.

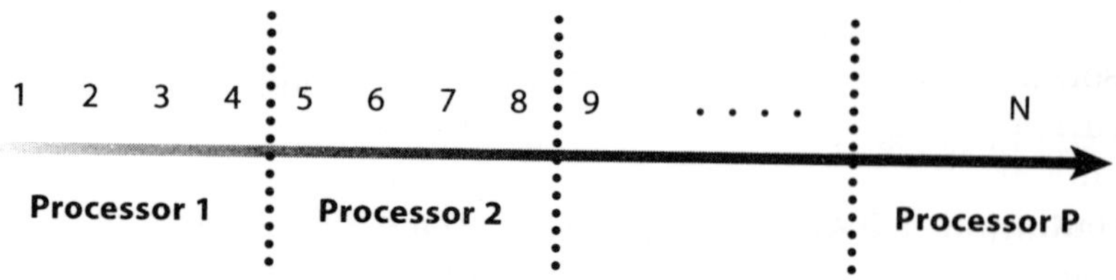

Figure 1.8 The iteration space for the summation problem with a simple decomposition indicated by dotted lines for a granularity of $k = 4$.

Definition 1.5.7. Suppose that a set of parallel tasks (indexed by $i = 1, \ldots, P$) execute in an amount of time t_i. Define the average execution time

$$\text{ave}\{t_i \,:\, 1 \le i \le P\} := \frac{1}{P} \sum_{1 \le i \le P} t_i. \tag{1.5.3}$$

The **load balance** β of this set of parallel tasks is

$$\beta := \frac{\text{ave}\{t_i \,:\, 1 \le i \le P\}}{\max\{t_i \,:\, 1 \le i \le P\}}. \tag{1.5.4}$$

A set of tasks is said to be **load balanced** if β is close to one.

The amount the load balance β differs from the ideal case $\beta = 1$ measures the relative difference between the longest task and the average task, measured in terms of run time. That is,

$$1 - \beta = \frac{\max\{t_i \,:\, 1 \le i \le P\} - \text{ave}\{t_i \,:\, 1 \le i \le P\}}{\max\{t_i \,:\, 1 \le i \le P\}}. \tag{1.5.5}$$

A set of tasks is said to be load balanced if this difference is negligible. Note that we have compared the *average* time with the maximum time, not the minimum time. The relevance of this will become clearer below and in Section 2.3.3.

We have also defined load balance in terms of time of execution instead of amount of computational work to be done. This is because the performance (Definition 1.3.1) need not be the same for different tasks, and the cost of the computation is proportional to the time it takes, not to how many floating point operations get done. Of course, we will often try to achieve load balance by balancing the amount of work to be done, since we can frequently predict this in advance, whereas we rarely know the exact execution time in advance.

Example 1.5.8. Load balancing in the summation problem is effected by assigning the same number k of summands to each processor (cf. (1.5.1)). For perfect load balance, this requires that $N = Pk$. If N is not divisible by P, then this will not be possible. For the sake of argument, suppose that $N = k(P-1) + 1$. One way to distribute the work is to let the first $P - 1$

processors sum k elements, with the last processor doing nothing. The time of execution is then proportional to k. For definiteness, suppose that the time units are chosen so that the constant of proportionality is one. Thus the execution time for process i is $t_i = k$ for $i = 1, \ldots, P-1$ and $t_P = 0$, and the minimum time is zero. We can increase the minimum time by decreasing the load of other processors, but unless we can reduce them all there will be no reduction in total (parallel) run time. Therefore the minimum time plays very little role in determining the run time.

Our goal, then, is to create embarrassingly parallel sections of code (cf. (1.5.1)) with the largest possible granularity and the smallest possible amount of nonlocal memory references (often by communication) at the points where the independent results have to be merged (cf. (1.5.2)). Moreover, we must keep the load balanced among the different processors. Of course, it may not be possible to increase granularity and decrease communication simultaneously, and increasing the granularity often is equivalent to decreasing the parallelism, as in the summation problem parallelized via (1.5.1) and (1.5.2). Also, as the granularity gets smaller, the load balancing problem often becomes more difficult. For all of these reasons, the optimization problem for parallel computing can be quite complex and will likely entail significant compromise.

1.5.3 Prime number sieve

The prime number sieve[6] provides an interesting example with a varying amount of parallelism. Recall that a prime number is an integer having no divisors other than itself and one. (An integer j is a divisor of another integer p if p/j is exactly an integer.)

The sieve works as follows. For a given integer k, suppose we have recorded the set $S(k)$ of prime numbers less than k (for example, $S(16) = \{2, 3, 5, 7, 11, 13\}$). Then we can check the primality of integers n less than k^2 by testing to see whether there are any divisors of n in $S(k)$ (if $n = j \cdot i < k^2$ then either i or j has to be less than k). So an algorithm for computing all primes is as follows.

Suppose $S(k)$ is known. Test the integers, n, in the range $k \leq n < k^2$ for divisors and if any primes are found, add them to $S(k^2)$. Note that each of these tests can be done independently of the others by a separate processor as long as it has access to all of $S(k)$. If done in parallel, the contributions to $S(k^2)$ have to be merged. Then set $k \leftarrow k^2$ and continue.

A pseudo-code for this algorithm is written as follows. It is a nested

[6] The sieve of Eratosthenes (276–196 B.C.) is a a close cousin of the method we describe here. In addition to work in various areas of mathematics, Eratosthenes is also credited with a very accurate measurement of the diameter of the earth, and he was the third director of the famous library of Alexandria, which is thought to have contained hundreds of thousands of papyrus and vellum scrolls.

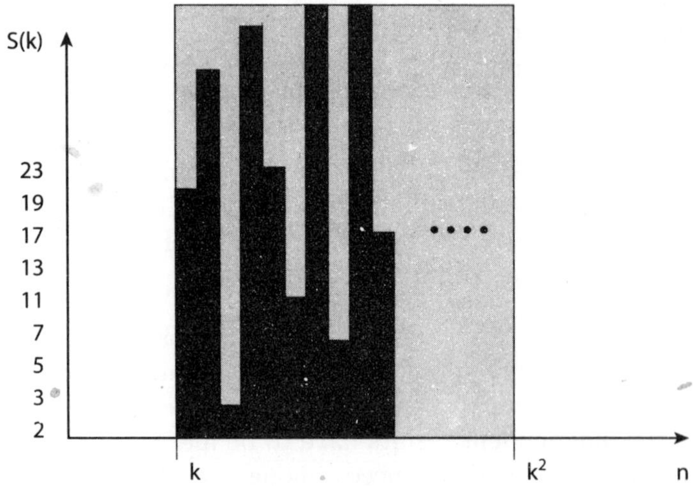

Figure 1.9 The iteration space for the prime number sieve. The n-axis has been modified to eliminate even numbers, numbers divisible by three, and so forth. The darkly shaded areas correspond to the actual values of n and π for which computation occurs, and the lightly shaded region is the maximum possible set of n and π values.

loop, three deep, but we omit the outermost loop which increments k.

```
loop on n = k, k+1, ..., k^2 - 1
    loop on π ∈ S(k)
        see if π divides n integrally
            if it does, exit the π loop since n is not prime
    end loop on π
    if loop completes for all π ∈ S(k), add n to S(k^2)
end loop on n
```

As written, this code will waste a great deal of time finding even values of n, so making the stride equal to two in the loop on n, and starting with k odd, will eliminate a substantial amount of unnecessary work. Further, we will assume that n divisible by three and five and perhaps more small primes are eliminated by adjusting the loop indices appropriately (see Exercise 1.9).

Note that the innermost operation of dividing π by n can be done independently of all others. Thus the loops can be parallelized in a number of ways. We could divide the "n" loop into P different parts, or we could divide the "π" loop into P different parts, or we could have a more complex organization. Recall the concept of iteration space in Definition 1.5.4. Figure 1.9 depicts graphically the iteration space for the prime number sieve. In this case, the iteration space is a subspace (shown in dark shading) of the Cartesian product (shown in light shading) of intervals $[k, k^2 - 1]$ and the set $S(k)$. The reason it is not all of the Cartesian product is that in

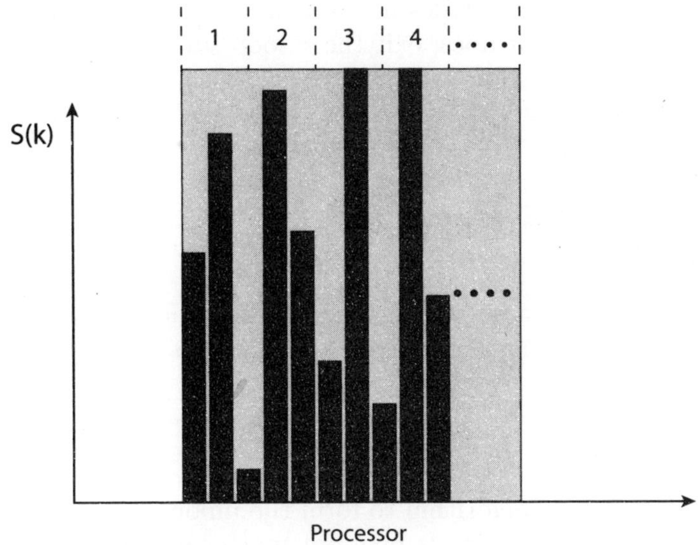

Figure 1.10 Parallelizing the prime number sieve with respect to the n loop using a strip decomposition.

executing the loops in the order indicated, the π index may not traverse all of its potential range (when a divisor is found). Note that in this case the precise iteration space is not known in advance but is determined as part of the computation.

The iteration space does not indicate *whether* loops are parallel or not. This can be only determined by studying the *dependences* in loops (see Chapter 4). However, for loops that are known to be trivially parallel, as in the sieve problem, different ways of parallelizing loops correspond to different geometric decompositions (Definition 1.5.5) of the iteration space. There are a variety of standard decompositions that are useful in parallelizing loops.

Definition 1.5.9. A **strip decomposition** or **slab decomposition** corresponds to a subdivision of only one of the dimensions, usually into segments of (about) equal length and consisting of contiguous elements in the iteration space. This corresponds to subdividing only one of the loops in a nested set of loops.

For example, Figure 1.10 shows a division of the "n" loop in the prime number sieve into P different strips. The corresponding pseudo-code looks like

$b := (k^2 - k)/P$
for each processor $p = 1, \ldots, P$
    loop on $n = k + (p-1)b, \ldots, k + p \cdot b$
        loop on $\pi \in S(k)$

```
            see if π divides n integrally
                if it does, exit the π loop since n is not prime
        end loop on π
        if loop completes for all π ∈ S(k), add n to S_p(k²)
    end loop on n
end loop on p
combine different S_p(k²) into S(k²)
```

Note that the variable p plays the role of a unique processor identifier. $S_p(k^2)$ is the set of primes found by the p-th processor, and

$$S(k^2) = \bigcup_{p=1}^{P} S_p(k^2). \tag{1.5.6}$$

We did not describe an algorithm to form the union. This requires merging the separate sets into one set. It may not matter whether the primes come in any order, or one might decide smaller divisors are more likely and that it is more efficient to start checking with smaller primes first. In that case, the separate sets needed to be merged in sorted order. Parallel algorithms for sorting and merging will be discussed in Section 15.2.2.

Each processor will do different work (starting with the n loop) because p takes on different values. In this way, a *single program* executed by different processors can evaluate a portion of the iteration space described by the n and π loops, each processor producing different results even though the code is the same.

Definition 1.5.10. The **single program** parallel approach involves having only one program which will execute differently on different processors. The differences can occur through either implicit mechanisms such as compiler directives or explicit constructs such as references to the processor number executing the code. This approach is known as **SPMD (single program, multiple data).**[7]

In the sieve example, the differences in execution on different processors all originate in the different values of the "processor I.D." reflected in the value of p. The ability to use a single code to do parallel work greatly simplifies the task of writing parallel programs. This will be discussed more formally in Section 5.5. An alternate parallelization of the sieve is given in the following.

---

[7]Convention is that SPMD programs are written in per-process name spaces, in contrast to data parallel programs, which are written in a global name space. We will occasionally use the term *data parallel* loosely to include SPMD programs. Strictly speaking, HPF is a data parallel approach whereas **P**fortran is an SPMD approach. These topics are discussed further in Chapters 5, 8 and 9.

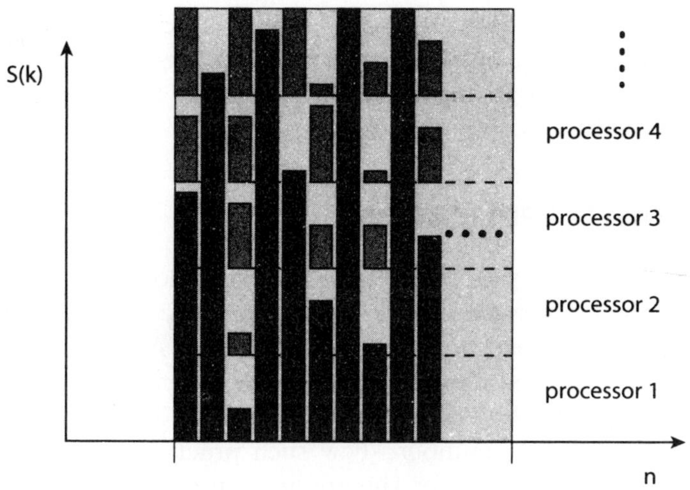

Figure 1.11 Parallelizing the prime number sieve with respect to the π loop using a strip decomposition.

Example 1.5.11. Dividing the π loop among processors as shown in Figure 1.11 corresponds to having each processor use only a restricted set of primes in its tests, but test all of the $n \in [k, k^2 - 1]$. In this case, some n will be divided by a larger set of primes π, involving more arithmetic work. The additional dark areas in Figure 1.11 indicate hypothetical extra work each processor would have to do (none of the integers in the dark area is a divisor, so the loop will not terminate until all in that area have been tested). Even if there is more arithmetic work done overall, it does not necessarily mean that the execution time is longer on a given parallel computer.

At the end, each processor has a set of candidate primes (numbers not divisible by its subset of primes), and the intersection of these must be formed to determine the actual set of primes. We postpone the discussion of parallel algorithms for forming set intersections until Chapter 6, Section 6.4.5.

The prime number sieve displays a number of interesting features. First of all, the amount of parallelism increases as k increases. Second, various parallelization strategies can be used, leading to quite different parallel algorithms for solving the same problem. Third, the amount of information that needs to be communicated (the merging of contributions to $S(k^2)$) cannot be predicted in advance. Finally, the load balance (Definition 1.5.7) is also unpredictable since the primality test may fail (when a divisor is found) after just a few tries, or it may succeed (the worst case: all potential divisors in $S(k)$ have to be tested). We leave the problem of load balancing the prime number sieve to the exercises (see Exercises 1.8 and 1.12).

The iteration space for the complete algorithm is of course three-dimensional. However, there is an essential *dependence* (see Chapter 4) between the k iterations (which go k^2, k^4, k^8, $\ldots$, k^{2^i}, $\ldots$) since we do not know S for one iteration until all previous iterations have been completed. This dependence makes it impossible to parallelize the outermost (k) loop in a straightforward way.

1.6 MESH-BASED APPLICATIONS

We now give some examples of the type of applications that will be considered as one of the main topics of this book. We start with *ordinary differential equations* and standard types of discretizations. An ordinary differential equation (o.d.e.) provides a model in which the rate of change of a quantity is related to that quantity by an explicit function. The o.d.e. is solved for a function, rather than a number. Few such practical equations admit an explicit solution, making way for the application of numerical solutions.

Ordinary differential equations and their numerical solution will give us some more challenging examples to study and will also introduce more fundamental concepts. We will necessarily draw upon some ideas from elementary numerical analysis, but we will introduce the necessary notation and background as we go.[8]

1.6.1 Initial value problems

Let us begin with an ordinary differential equation

$$\frac{du}{dt} = f(t, u) \tag{1.6.1}$$

with an initial condition provided at $t = 0$:

$$u(0) = u_0$$

for some given data value u_0. Under suitable smoothness conditions on f, this equation has a unique solution, u, which exists for some time interval $0 \leq t \leq T$.

We may be able to solve this analytically in terms of expressions that are familiar to us. For example, if

$$f(t, u) = f(u) := -u^2, \tag{1.6.2}$$

then

$$u(t) = \frac{1}{t + 1/u_0} \tag{1.6.3}$$

is the solution (see Figure 1.12).

[8]The differential calculus is credited to Sir Isaac Newton (1642–1727) and Gottfried Wilhelm von Leibniz (1646–1716). The controversy about priority regarding this development has been discussed in recent popular literature [137]. Newton's discoveries in physics and celestial mechanics culminated in the theory of universal gravitation, which will appear in Chapter 13.

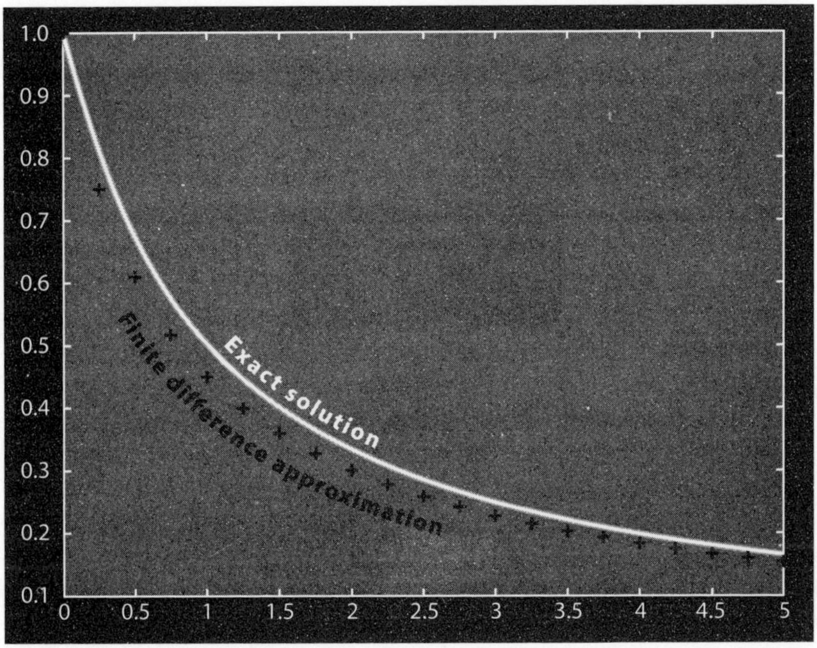

Figure 1.12 Solution of the ordinary differential equation $\frac{du}{dt} = -u^2$ and the finite difference approximation using the explicit Euler discretization.

More likely, we will not be able to recognize a solution as a combination of known functions. However, we may be primarily interested in only numerical values of u at specified points in time, or we may just want a graph of u that indicates its general behavior.

A *discretization* scheme can be used to generate approximations to the values of u at a discrete set of points. For example, let $\Delta t > 0$ be a fixed parameter, and use the definition of derivative to make the *finite difference approximation*

$$\frac{du}{dt}(t) \approx \frac{u(t + \Delta t) - u(t)}{\Delta t}. \tag{1.6.4}$$

Inserting this approximation into equation (1.6.1) we find

$$\frac{u(t + \Delta t) - u(t)}{\Delta t} \approx f(t, u(t)). \tag{1.6.5}$$

Define a sequence of time values $t_n := n\Delta t$, and using (1.6.5), a corresponding sequence of values u_n via the *explicit Euler method*

$$u_{n+1} = u_n + \Delta t f(t_n, u_n). \tag{1.6.6}$$

Here, u_n is intended to be an approximation to $u(t_n)$. Under suitable smoothness conditions on f, one can show that

$$|u_n - u(t_n)| \leq C\Delta t \quad \forall n \leq T/\Delta t, \tag{1.6.7}$$

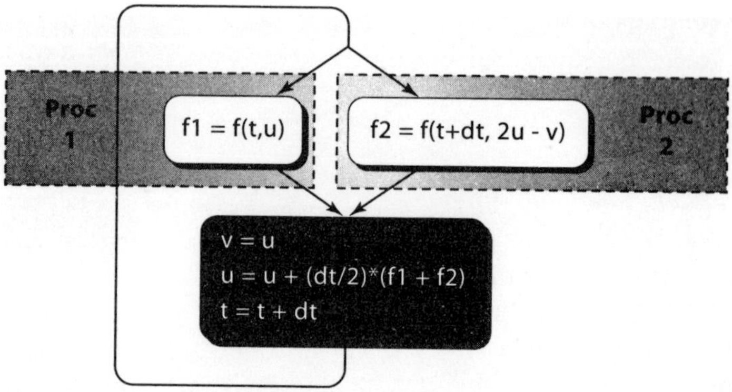

Figure 1.13 Flow chart for trapezoidal rule algorithm displaying independent tasks for $P = 2$ processors. Processor 1 computes the function `f1`, and processor 2 computes the function `f2`.

where C is a constant depending only on f and T. Figure 1.12 shows u_n for $0 \leq n \leq 20$ for $\Delta t = 0.25$ and f as defined in (1.6.2).

It is not at all necessary to have a fixed *time step* Δt. The approximation (1.6.4) allows one to define

$$u_{n+1} = u_n + (t_{n+1} - t_n) f(t_n, u_n). \tag{1.6.8}$$

for arbitrary sequences $0 = t_0 < t_1 < \cdots < t_n$.

Note that u_n depends on all u_i for $i < n$ and there is no simple way to remove these dependences. One approach to creating parallelism is to switch to a more complex difference method, with the side benefit of having a higher order of convergence. Consider

$$u_{n+1} = u_n + \frac{t_{n+1} - t_n}{2} \left(f(t_n, u_n) + f(t_{n+1}, 2u_n - u_{n-1}) \right). \tag{1.6.9}$$

Here $2u_n - u_{n-1}$ is a second order approximation to u_{n+1}, so (1.6.9) corresponds to a variant of the trapezoidal rule [27]. If the function f is expensive to calculate, then it can be useful to compute $f(t_n, u_n)$ and $f(t_{n+1}, 2u_n - u_{n-1})$ on separate processors. The resulting scheme can potentially use larger time steps since (Exercise 1.17)

$$|u_n - u(t_n)| \leq C \max_i (t_i - t_{i-1})^2 \quad \forall t_n \leq T. \tag{1.6.10}$$

The basic loop implementing (1.6.9) can be parallelized using an approach referred to as *task* or *procedural* parallelism.

Definition 1.6.1. An algorithm can be parallelized using **task parallelism** or **procedural parallelism** when there are independent parts that can be executed as separate procedures (Definition 1.5.1) without the need for communication between them.

The independent parts of an algorithm in task (procedural) parallelism are trivially (embarrassingly) parallel in the terminology of Definition 1.5.3.

Using task or procedural parallelism to parallelize (1.6.9) is depicted in Figure 1.13. The two dotted boxes indicate the parts of the algorithm that can be done in parallel, namely, the function evaluations $f(\cdot,\cdot)$ with different arguments. Here we make the fundamental assumption that there are no *side effects* (see page 99) associated with evaluating $f(\cdot,\cdot)$. In many cases, this step can be a large part of the computation (see Exercises 8.7 and 10.3 for a contrived example).

In the case that the function f in (1.6.1) is an affine function independent of t (i.e., $f(t,x) = a + bx$), then difference methods such as (1.6.9) become a **linear recursion**. Solving such a system is equivalent to solving a banded triangular linear system of equations, something discussed at length in Chapter 12.

1.6.2 Boundary value problems

Ordinary differential equations of higher order can have more than one data value specified. An important special case of this occurs when data are given at different points which form the end points for the interval of interest for the solution. These points are then the *boundary* points, and the data are known as the *boundary values.* In such a case, the independent variable often connotes something distinct from "time," so we will switch to calling the variable x instead of t.

Consider the simple second order ordinary differential equation

$$-\frac{d^2u}{dx^2} = f(x) \tag{1.6.11}$$

together with specified boundary values

$$u(0) = a, \quad u(1) = b \tag{1.6.12}$$

for some given data values a and b.

Using an approximation such as (1.6.4) twice we obtain a system of equations

$$-u_{n-1} + 2u_n - u_{n+1} = (\Delta x)^2 f(x_n). \tag{1.6.13}$$

Here we take $x_n = n\Delta x$ with $\Delta x = 1/(N+1)$ for some integer N. Equation (1.6.13), for $n = 1, \ldots, N$, forms a system of equations for $u_1, \ldots, u_N$, where we interpret $u_0 := a$ and $u_{N+1} := b$ where they occur in (1.6.13) (see Exercise 1.14).

A more general set of equations can be derived, analogous to (1.6.8), on an arbitrary *mesh* $0 = x_0 < x_1 < \cdots < x_n < \cdots < x_{N+1} = 1$. These equations are of the form

$$-\frac{2}{x_{n+1} - x_{n-1}} \left(\frac{u_{n+1} - u_n}{x_{n+1} - x_n} - \frac{u_n - u_{n-1}}{x_n - x_{n-1}} \right) = f(x_n). \tag{1.6.14}$$

These equations can be simplified somewhat by collecting terms, introducing notation for the local mesh size, e.g.,

$$h_n := x_n - x_{n-1}, \tag{1.6.15}$$

and scaling the equations by the factor $\frac{h_{n+1}+h_n}{2}$ in the form

$$\begin{aligned} \frac{h_{n+1}+h_n}{2} f(x_n) &= -\frac{u_{n+1}-u_n}{h_{n+1}} + \frac{u_n - u_{n-1}}{h_n} \\ &= \left(\frac{1}{h_{n+1}} + \frac{1}{h_n}\right) u_n - \frac{1}{h_{n+1}} u_{n+1} - \frac{1}{h_n} u_{n-1}. \end{aligned} \tag{1.6.16}$$

This represents a symmetric, tridiagonal matrix, and it can be shown to be positive definite. In particular, the i-th row of the matrix has entries

$$a_{i,i-1} = \frac{-1}{h_i}, \qquad a_{i,i} = \frac{1}{h_i} + \frac{1}{h_{i+1}}, \qquad a_{i,i+1} - \frac{-1}{h_{i+1}} \tag{1.6.17}$$

for $1 < i < N$. See Exercise 1.15 regarding the remaining two equations.

The set of equations (1.6.16) (together with the two equations from Exercise 1.15) can be written succinctly in matrix form as

$$\mathbf{AU} = \mathbf{F}, \tag{1.6.18}$$

where $\mathbf{A}$ is the matrix with entries $(a_{i,j})$, $\mathbf{F}$ is the vector whose i-th entry is $f(x_i)$, and $\mathbf{U}$ is the vector whose i-th entry is u_i.

Gaussian elimination is a "direct" (non-iterative) method for solving the system (1.6.16) which will be discussed at length in Chapter 12. For the moment, we will turn to a discussion of iterative methods whose parallelizations are easier to describe.

1.6.3 Iterative equation solvers

The solution of the system (1.6.16) can be done by a variety of iterative methods. We will consider several techniques, such as stationary methods, conjugate gradients, and multigrid. One of the simplest is the Jacobi[9] iteration. Equation (1.6.16) can be rewritten in "fixed point" form as

$$\left(\frac{1}{h_{n+1}} + \frac{1}{h_n}\right) u_n = \frac{1}{h_{n+1}} u_{n+1} + \frac{1}{h_n} u_{n-1} + \frac{h_{n+1}+h_n}{2} f(x_n). \tag{1.6.19}$$

Rescaling each equation yields

$$u_n = \frac{h_n}{h_{n+1}+h_n} u_{n+1} + \frac{h_{n+1}}{h_{n+1}+h_n} u_{n-1} + \frac{h_n h_{n+1}}{2} f(x_n). \tag{1.6.20}$$

[9]Carl Jacobi (1804–1851) is widely known for the determinant appearing in the formula for changing variables in integration, but he was also a pioneer in computational techniques and in studying first-order systems of partial differential equations.

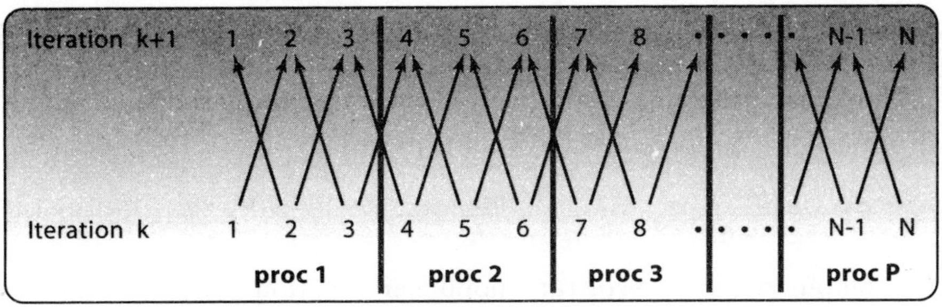

Figure 1.14 Data dependence in the Jacobi iteration.

This suggests an iterative method known variously as "fixed point" iteration or Jacobi's method:

$$u_n^{k+1} = \frac{h_n}{h_{n+1}+h_n} u_{n+1}^k + \frac{h_{n+1}}{h_{n+1}+h_n} u_{n-1}^k + \frac{h_n h_{n+1}}{2} f(x_n). \qquad (1.6.21)$$

When (1.6.21) converges (it does for arbitrary initial vectors (u_n^0), e.g., $u_n^0 = 0$ for all n), then the limit naturally must solve (1.6.20) and equivalently (1.6.16).

The algorithm (1.6.21) can be parallelized using *data parallelism* as defined in Definition 1.5.6. The data-parallel operation in (1.6.21) can be represented as multiplying a matrix times the vector (u_n^k), followed by a vector addition. Operations on vectors are typical data-parallel operations. They are parallelized simply by dividing the index space for the index n for the various vectors. This is depicted in Figure 1.14. Here, several indices are assigned to a given processor, p, say the interval $n_p \le n < n_{p+1}$. Then processor p computes (1.6.21) for these n. To do so, it must know the values u_n^k for $n_p - 1 \le n \le n_{p+1}$ (we ignore for the moment the very ends of the index set, and assume some meaning is attached to $n = 0$ and $n = N+1$).

In order to repeat the calculation (to perform the *iteration*), the values $u_{n_p-1}^k$ and $u_{n_{p+1}}^k$ will have to be obtained from neighboring processors as shown in Figure 1.14. The arrows indicate *dependences* (see Definition 4.1.3) from one iteration to the next.

There is no natural task parallelism as in Figure 1.13 since everything depends on something. On the other hand, there is data parallelism in the sense that the single operation of updating (u_n) acts on a large amount of data in parallel. Subdividing this single operation creates independent tasks, although communication between them is generated as a byproduct. However, the specific tasks are arbitrary, depending on the choice of subdivision of the index set, as opposed to being naturally part of the algorithm as in Section 1.6.1.

Data parallelism can be found in solving an ordinary differential equation (1.6.1) when the unknown $\mathbf{u}$ denotes a vector of substantial size. In such a case, the computation of the vector quantity $\mathbf{f}(t, \mathbf{u})$ can often involve opportunities for data parallelism. An example of this type can be found in Section 2.6.

Nonlinear problems can be solved by iterative methods as simply as linear ones. For example, the fixed-point iteration

$$u_n^{k+1} = \frac{h_n}{h_{n+1}+h_n}u_{n+1}^k + \frac{h_{n+1}}{h_{n+1}+h_n}u_{n-1}^k + \frac{h_n h_{n+1}}{2}f(x_n, u_n^k) \quad (1.6.22)$$

can be computed for an arbitrary nonlinear function $f(x,u)$. This corresponds to solving a finite difference equation for the boundary value problem

$$\begin{aligned} -\frac{du^2}{dx^2} &= f(x,u), \\ u(0) = a, &\quad u(1) = b. \end{aligned} \quad (1.6.23)$$

1.7 PARALLEL PERSPECTIVES

It is useful to understand the role of parallelism as a potential tool in problem solving. Parallelization is not a game unto itself, to be pursued in a vacuum. Rather it is a tool that can be effective in appropriate situations. If it does not provide significant performance gains, it may not be of interest. Here we give a brief example of how parallelization might play a role in a larger context, and we also review its historical role in computing.

1.7.1 Other options

Solving technical problems can be done in a variety of ways. We have described in Figure 1.15 a number of options that can occur. First, it is not necessary to do computation at all. Some paths in the tree refer to using analytical or experimental methods. The beginning point is not a sequential code, although often this is the case.

A good example of a problem of this type is **drug discovery**, the endeavor of finding new pharmaceuticals to fight disease. One popular approach involves combing the rain forests of the equatorial regions for exotic plants and testing them for efficacy. Another involves primarily laboratory work with test-tubes of chemicals. Another uses the computer to postulate and analyze new compounds at the molecular level. In creating any one pharmaceutical, all three of these approaches might be brought to bear in combination at various stages, so the real problem graph will not be a tree but something with more complex interactions.

Even when the computational option has been chosen for some reason, there still remain a variety of choices one can make at different stages. There are different models which provide the same level of accuracy for a given physical phenomenon, so it may be useful to choose different models for different purposes. Any given model will typically have different ways to

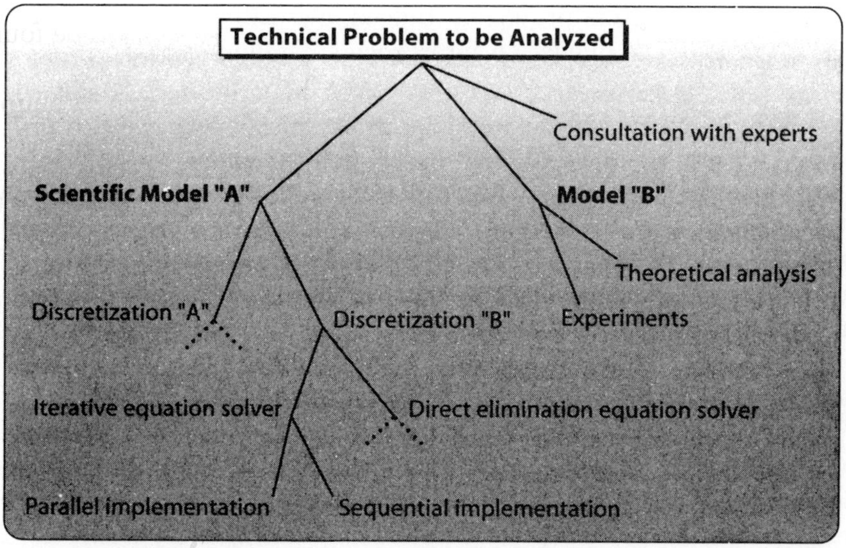

Figure 1.15 The "problem tree" for scientific problem solving. There are many options to try to achieve the same goal.

discretize it, and any discretization will have multiple ways to solve the resulting discrete equations.

It is always allowed to climb higher in the tree to find better path to the solution using new technology, such as parallel computation. Any given physical model, or discretization, or equation solver may lead to a difficult parallel computation. However, an equivalent result may be obtained more efficiently using a parallel computer by using a different model or discretization or equation solution strategy. This alternative approach should always be kept in mind when trying to utilize a parallel computer to solve a problem.

1.7.2 Parallelism in computing history

Parallelism has a long history in the development of computer systems. One early example is the representation of natural numbers as a collection of bits and the corresponding development of hardware that could work on such pairs of collections to do arithmetic. Such arithmetic units are in effect parallel computers. This type of parallelism is in use in microprocessors which now permeate everyday life, not only in pocket calculators, but in the "smart" electronics in automobiles, microwave ovens, and other home appliances.

Operating systems provided early impetus to parallel (or concurrent) programming and many of the early concepts in parallel programming languages [78, 46] were developed in this context. Much of the early work in synchronization using semaphores, guards, and critical sections had its roots in operating system problems. Indeed, a steadfast component of Unix kernels is the message queue, an interprocess communication primitive not unlike its parallel scientific counterpart, the MPI library. Unlike operating systems, however, the scientific program parallelism we are primarily concerned with is the data parallel model defined above.

I/O devices have always functioned at a slower rate than the processors to which they are connected. The use of a separate processor (or just a separate process) to handle I/O is an example of parallel processing. These methods were employed as early as the 1950s in the Univac 1, the first computer to overlap program execution with some I/O [83].[10] Early operating systems for personal computers were able to allow printers to queue data and allow control of the computer to return to the user.

Vector processor architectures introduced in the 1960s developed numerous innovations in addressing the problem of getting data to processors on time. Methods included memory interleaving to increase memory-to-processor bandwidth, overlap of computation with memory accesses (called prefetching), and out-of-order execution to improve reuse and tolerate memory delays such as with the Tomasulo algorithm developed for the IBM 360/91 [140]. Recent counterparts of the Tomasulo algorithm and CDC 6000/7000 series scoreboard [83] appear in the out-of-order instruction execution for the Intel Xeon and P4 processor lines [85]. With the benefits of these earlier developments, contemporary microprocessors execute multiple instructions simultaneously using pipelined functional units (Section 3.4).

It is natural that early vector processing methods have come full circle into today's modern commodity pipelined and multi-threaded processors. After all, computer performance depends fundamentally on having data available to the CPU with minimum delay. The methods of data reuse and tolerating memory access times appear in various guises in both architecture and software design. We will see that in order to get good performance on even a single processor of this type, it is necessary to understand basic parallel computing.

In Section 3.1.2, the notion of a memory *cache* will be discussed. As will be seen in Figure 3.6, this involves a type of parallel processing in the memory system. Moreover, one of the key issues in parallel computing is the communication that must be done between different processes. With current workstations, there are already several levels of cache, and the movement of data among them is a prime consideration in achieving good performance. Thus the issues we are studying with regard to parallelism in the large have

[10]The Univac 1, the Universal Automatic Computer, was the first commercial computer and successor to the ENIAC, the Electronic Numerical Integrator and Computer, a 30-ton computer developed at the University of Pennsylvania during World War II. Delivered to the Census Bureau in 1951, the Univac 1 weighed approximately 8 tons and could perform about 1,000 calculations per second. The first commercial sale by the Eckert-Mauchly Computer Corporation of Philadelphia was followed shortly by Remington-Rand's purchase of Eckert-Mauchly. A statistical model run on the Univac 1 and informed by early election returns predicted correctly Dwight Eisenhower's victory in the 1952 presidential election.

an important correspondence with different types of parallelism in single processors, in terms of both instruction parallelism and data movement to and from cache.

For a more detailed history of parallelism, we refer to [80] and [81]. For an intriguing look at an early proposal, see [113].

1.8 EXERCISES

Exercise 1.1. Beyond "mega" (10^6) and "giga" (10^9) are "tera" (10^{12}), "peta" (10^{15}) and "exa" (10^{18}). Determine the correct time unit (millisecond, microsecond, nanosecond, picosecond, femtosecond, ...) that it takes a single computer to do a floating point operation if it is does (1) one megaflop per second, (2) one gigaflop per second, (3) one teraflop per second, and (4) one petaflop per second.

Exercise 1.2. What is the maximum number of floating point operations possible in Example 1.3.6 for a 99% cache-hit rate and for a 1% hit rate? Assume that $\rho_{\text{WM}} = 2$.

Exercise 1.3. What is the ratio ρ_{WM} of the number of floating point operations to the number of data values that have to be obtained from memory, or written to memory, in the computation of the product of two square matrices $\mathbf{A} = (a_{ij})$ and $\mathbf{B}$ which is defined by

$$(\mathbf{AB})_{ij} := \sum_{k=1}^{n} a_{ik}b_{kj} \quad \text{for } i, j = 1, \ldots, n \tag{1.8.1}$$

as a function of n? (Assume that both A and B must be obtained from memory and the product is written back to memory. However, the denominator should just be the volume of the data, not the number of memory references that might occur in particular algorithm. For example, the term b_{11} occurs n times in (1.8.1) but should be counted only once.)

Exercise 1.4. What is the ratio of the number of floating point operations per processor to the number of data values that have to be obtained by the individual processors from other processors in the parallelization of (1.6.21) using P processors?

Exercise 1.5. Write a program to compute a summation as in (1.3.2). Test the program by computing π by the summation (1.3.1), i.e., with $a_i = (-1)^{i+1}/(2i-1)$. Determine the performance on a single processor as a function of N. A model for expected time performance t_N for computing the summation is $t_N = a + bN$. Use your timing data to estimate the parameters a and b. What are the critical values of t and N below which the timing is uncertain (see page 6) for each part? Report what computer and what timer you are using, and what its time resolution is purported to be. (Hint: plotting the observed time T_N as a function of N should, if $T_N \approx t_N$, give points lying nearly on a line with slope b; the asymptote of this line to $N = 0$ gives an estimate of a. Then plotting $(T_N - a)/N$ as a function of N should be nearly constant. Often when nearing the resolution of the timer, the data will become erratic, giving a measure of where the limit is.)

Exercise 1.6. Write a program to compute a summation as in (1.3.2). Test the program by computing π by the summation (1.3.1), i.e., with $a_i = (-1)^{i+1}/(2i-1)$. Determine the performance on a single processor as a function of N for both the computation of the a_i's and the sum (i.e., give separate performance estimates for the two parts of the computation). Determine the relationship (if any) between these times for different values of N and explain why you think this is reasonable. Report what computer and what timer you are using, and what its time resolution is purported to be.

Exercise 1.7. Write a program to compute a summation as in (1.3.2). Test the program by computing π by the summation (1.3.1). Determine the performance on a single processor as a function of N and compare this with the diagram in Figure 1.2. To do so, you need to compute $a_i = (-1)^{i+1}/(2i-1)$ separately and store it in an array. Just time the computation of the sum, not the computation of a_i. It may be necessary to repeat this k times to get an accurate timing, in such a way that $k \cdot N$ remains roughly constant as N increases. Be sure to divide by k to get the time for one sum. Try to find a virtual memory (e.g. Unix) machine with a small amount of memory so that you can do a computation involving paging to disk. Plot the results of your timings as in Figure 1.2 by plotting N/T_N as a function of N. (Explain why this gives a measure of performance for this calculation, and explain what the units are.) Choose values of N on a logarithmic scale, e.g., $n = 2^i$ for $i = 1, 2, \ldots, I$ for a suitable value of I. Make sure that your code is compiled with an optimization level to give maximum performance. Explain what computer and what timer you are using, and what its time resolution is purported to be.

Exercise 1.8. In the prime number sieve, determine the number, P, of parallel tasks that can be done for a given k when parallelizing by subdividing the n loop. Describe a way to achieve a load balanced algorithm for P processors (with P fixed and k sufficiently large). How much communication will be involved in your approach?

Exercise 1.9. Modify the loop on n in the prime number sieve to eliminate considering n divisible by 2, 3, and 5. How would you do this for more small primes?

Exercise 1.10. Consider the Jacobi iteration depicted in Figure 1.14. Describe a strategy for load balancing this parallel algorithm.

Exercise 1.11. Other decompositions of a loop can be made besides the ones shown in Figures 1.8, 1.10, and 1.11. The **cyclic decomposition** or **modulo decomposition** refers to distributing the n-th loop index to processor number n (mod P). Note that this assumes that the processors are numbered from 0 to $P-1$ as is done in many systems, since this is the range of values in "modulo" arithmetic. Make a copy of the iteration space in Figure 1.8 and indicate the processor allocation for a cyclic decomposition of the n loop using $P=3$ processors (numbered 0, 1, 2).

Exercise 1.12. Make a copy of the iteration space in Figure 1.9 and indicate the processor allocation for a cyclic decomposition (see Exercise 1.11) of the n loop using $P=3$ processors (numbered 0, 1, 2).

Exercise 1.13. The **block decomposition** is a generalization of the strip decomposition shown in Figures 1.10 and 1.11. It corresponds to dividing the iteration space into blocks, in this case distributing both the n-th loop index and the π-loop index. Make a copy of the iteration space in Figure 1.9 and indicate the processor allocation for a block decomposition using $P=4$ processors, where both the n-th loop and the π-loop are divided equally.

Exercise 1.14. Complete the definition of the matrix in (1.6.13) by making the indicated substitutions for u_0 and u_{N+1}. Show that matrix is symmetric.

Exercise 1.15. Complete the definition of the matrix (cf. (1.6.17)) in (1.6.14) by making the indicated substitutions for u_0 and u_{N+1}. Show that matrix is symmetric.

Exercise 1.16. Prove that the modified trapezoidal rule (1.6.9) is stable [27].

Exercise 1.17. Prove that the modified trapezoidal rule (1.6.9) satisfies (1.6.10). (Hint: use Exercise 1.16.)

Exercise 1.18. Show that matrix (1.6.17) has no negative eigenvalues. (Hint: use Gerschgorin's theorem [139].)

Exercise 1.19. Show that (1.6.21) converges. (Hint: use Gerschgorin's Theorem [139].)

Chapter Two
Parallel Performance

> I will pay \$100 to the first person to demonstrate a speedup of at least 200 on a general purpose, MIMD computer used for scientific computing—*E-mail challenge from Alan Karp, November 1985*

Parallel performance is more complex than sequential performance in many ways: first and foremost, it is more difficult to achieve good parallel performance, but it is also more difficult to predict and even to measure. This is due largely to the fact that essentially independent computers are cooperating on a single task. With simple (low performance) sequential processors, it has been possible to predict sequential performance based on a textual analysis of code or a mathematical description of an algorithm, by counting the number of basic operations. With parallel computation, other factors become critical, such as synchronization (Section 5.4.1), load balance (Definition 1.5.7), and communication costs. We begin by defining basic parallel performance and discussing how to measure it.

There are significant limits to utilizing parallel computers efficiently. Perhaps the most well known *caveat* is Amdahl's Law. This is a statement about the potential *speedup* achievable with a number of parallel processors. Based on the notion of speedup, one can define a notion of *parallel efficiency*.

The basic notion of speedup as addressed in Amdahl's Law relates primarily to problems of fixed size. In many cases, one deals with problems of varying size, characterized by some parameter usually related to the size of the data set. In this case, it may be appropriate to use large computers only for large problems. We have seen in Figure 1.7 that smaller computers often provide a better price/performance ratio, so this is a prudent use of resources. The notion of *scalability* relates to whether a given algorithm or code can be used efficiently on a range of problem sizes when using an appropriately chosen number of processors.

The discussion of all of these concepts will be the focus of this chapter.

2.1 SUMMATION EXAMPLE

To provide an example, we return to the simple parallel summation algorithm given in (1.5.1) and (1.5.2). For the sake of simplicity, we consider a collection of individual workstations or personal computers connected by some broadcast medium like Ethernet. From the discussion following Definition 1.3.1, we can assert that the time of execution for (1.5.1) on each processor separately should be proportional to N/P, assuming that N is divisible by P. The constant of proportionality will depend on properties of the individual processors and their own memory systems (which we assume are large enough to hold the required data). For the sake of simplicity, we will normalize so that our unit of time is such that this constant of proportionality is one. Thus the time of execution of (1.5.1) is exactly N/P.

The communication time is more complicated to estimate, depending on the nature of the communication medium that is connecting the individual processors and the algorithm used to compute (1.5.2). For example, if the communication is done on a single broadcast network, i.e., something like Ethernet connecting several workstations, then all of the communication would be in conflict. Every time a message is sent, everyone must listen to it even though it may not be for them. Let us assume we have such a system: that the algorithm to compute (1.5.2) is for each processor in turn to broadcast its value A_i and have every processor compute (1.5.2) separately. This would mean that the amount of time to complete the communication would be proportional to P, since there is one piece of data per processor to transfer. The constant of proportionality γ can be interpreted as the number of floating point additions that can be done in the time it takes to send one word. Then our time estimate for the total time is

$$T_P = \frac{N}{P} + (\gamma + 1)P, \tag{2.1.1}$$

including the time to sum the A_i's locally. In Figure 2.1, we plot the execution time as a function of the number of processors used with $\gamma = 9$ and $N = 10,000$. Note that (2.1.1) implies that T_P will eventually start to *increase* for P sufficiently large.

We will now use this simple example to illustrate several more complex measures of parallel performance.

2.2 PERFORMANCE MEASURES

The main objective in using a parallel computer is to get a simulation to finish faster than it would on one processor. Figure 2.1 depicts the hypothetical execution time of a parallel program to compute the sum indicated in (1.5.1) and (1.5.2). It plots the execution time as a function of the number of processors used. This sort of plot is very forgiving; it gives the illusion of positive achievement as long as it decreases. We may be happy as long as the time of execution is decreasing as a function of the number of processors used, but a more critical way to evaluate the behavior of our parallelization is to consider the *speedup* that has been achieved.

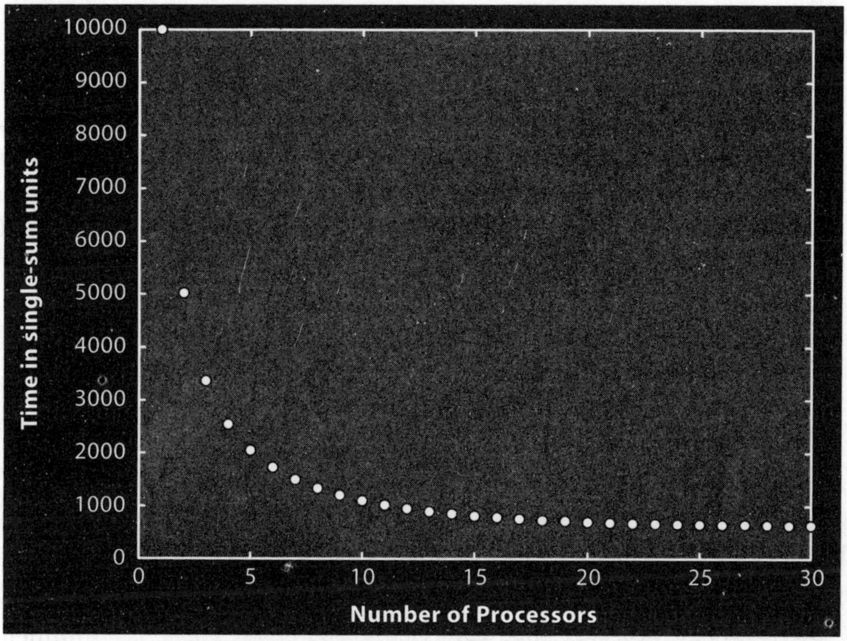

Figure 2.1 Hypothetical execution time for the summation problem (in arbitrary time units) as a function of the number of processors used with $\gamma = 9$ and $N = 10,000$.

2.2.1 Speedup

The notion of "speedup" measures parallel performance in comparison to sequential performance.

Definition 2.2.1. The **speedup**, S_P, using P processors is defined to be the ratio of the sequential and parallel execution times,

$$S_P = \frac{T_1}{T_P}. \tag{2.2.1}$$

More precisely, T_1 should be the time of execution of the best available sequential solution of the problem, and T_P should be the time of execution of the parallel solution of the problem on P processors.

If we recall (cf. Figure 1.2) that "performance" is inversely proportional to time, then we see that speedup S_P is simply the ratio of parallel performance c/T_P divided by sequential performance c/T_1 (here c is any constant of proportionality we might use to define "performance" in terms of inverse time, but taking the ratio eliminates it). Ideally, S_P should be a number close to P, that is, using P processors should make the calculation P times faster. We refer to the case $S_P \approx P$ as **linear speedup** or **perfect speedup**. In the very fortunate case that $S_P > P$ we call it **super-linear speedup**, or perhaps more grammatically correctly, **supra-linear speedup**. In practice [14], S_P can sometimes exceed P due to the effective improvement of individual processor performance due to decreasing local data size, as depicted in Figure 1.2.

Example 2.2.2. The speedup corresponding to the execution times in the model (2.1.1) can be computed as follows. First, we recognize that we should take $T_1 = N$ to be consistent with (2.1.1): there is no communication in the sequential case. It is often less confusing to compute $S_P^{-1} = \frac{T_P}{T_1}$ first:

$$S_P^{-1} = \frac{1}{P} + (\gamma+1)\frac{P}{N} = \frac{1}{P}\left(1 + (\gamma+1)\frac{P^2}{N}\right) \tag{2.2.2}$$

so that

$$S_P = P\left(1 + \frac{(\gamma+1)P^2}{N}\right)^{-1} \tag{2.2.3}$$

This is plotted in Figure 2.2 for $\gamma = 9$ and $N = 10^5$, together with the "ideal" speedup curve $S_P = P$. Note that the comparison in this case is quite simple, since (2.2.3) differs from the ideal case exactly by the multiplicative factor $\left(1 + (\gamma+1)P^2/N\right)^{-1}$. Since this factor is $\mathcal{O}(P^{-2})$, the speedup will eventually start to *decrease* (see Exercise 2.2).

Consider the parallel performance for $N = 10^7$ and $\gamma = 9$. The formula (2.2.3) becomes

$$(S_P)^{-1} = \frac{1}{P} + 10^{-6}P$$

and a bit of calculus (or a graph) shows that its minimum occurs when $P = 10^3$. Thus the maximum possible speedup is 500, and it occurs for $P = 10^3$.

Figure 2.2 shows that speedup is a more demanding view of performance as it emphasizes the deviation from the ideal linear speedup indicated by the straight line of slope one in the plot. In Figure 2.1, we saw something bad (execution time) decreasing as a function of the number of processors, so that gave us a positive feeling. But now we see something good (speedup) beginning to flag, so we begin to be more skeptical.

Often, S_P will be significantly less than P, and there is no guarantee that it will be greater than one! (If $S_P < 1$, it should be called "slowdown" not speedup.) S_P will not increase indefinitely in all cases. More likely, as in (2.1.1), it will reach a maximum and then decrease. Since S_P is inversely proportional to the execution time T_P, the maximum of S_P will occur at the minimum of T_P.

In some cases, it may not be possible to run a problem on one just processor due to memory or time constraints. In this case, we may want instead to define speedup with respect to the smallest number P' of processors for which the problem will run. Define

$$S_P^{P'} = \frac{T_{P'}}{T_P} \tag{2.2.4}$$

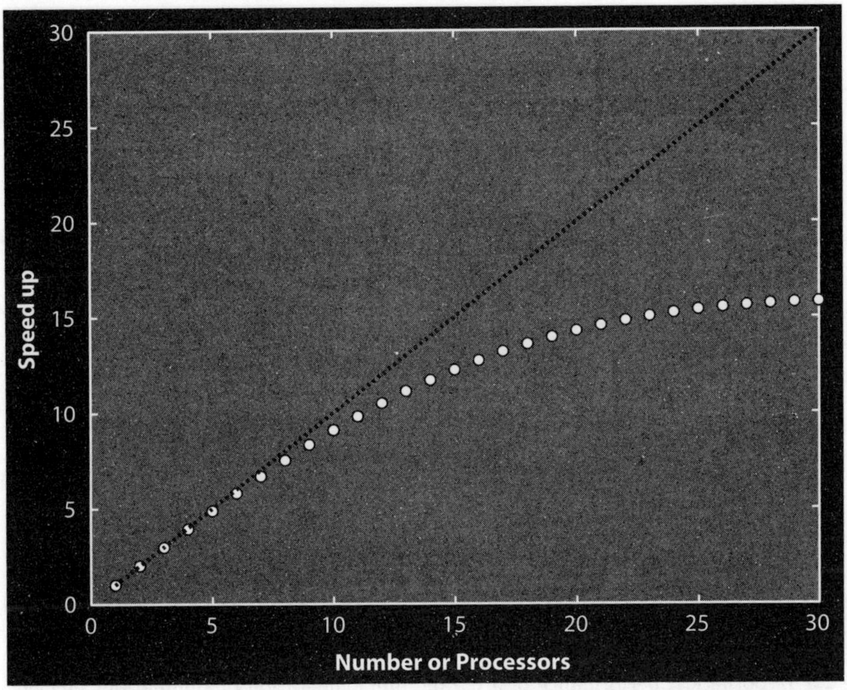

Figure 2.2 Hypothetical performance of a parallel implementation of summation: speedup as a function of the number of processors used with $\gamma = 9$ and $N = 10,000$.

to be the corresponding **relative speedup** in this case for $P \geq P'$. We expect $S_P^{P'} \approx P/P'$ in the ideal case.

2.2.2 Parallel efficiency

The most demanding view we can take of performance data is to compare the actual speedup with our notion of ideal speedup, obtaining a measure of *efficiency*.

Definition 2.2.3. The **parallel efficiency**, E_P, using P processors is defined to be the ratio of the speedup and P, that is

$$E_P := \frac{S_P}{P} = \frac{T_1}{PT_P}, \tag{2.2.5}$$

where T_1 is again the time of execution of the best sequential solution of the problem, and T_P is the time of execution of the parallel solution of the problem on P processors.

Example 2.2.4. The efficiency plot corresponding to the execution times in the model (2.1.1) can be computed by dividing the speedup (2.2.3) by P:

$$E_P = \left(1 + (\gamma + 1)P^2/N\right)^{-1}. \tag{2.2.6}$$

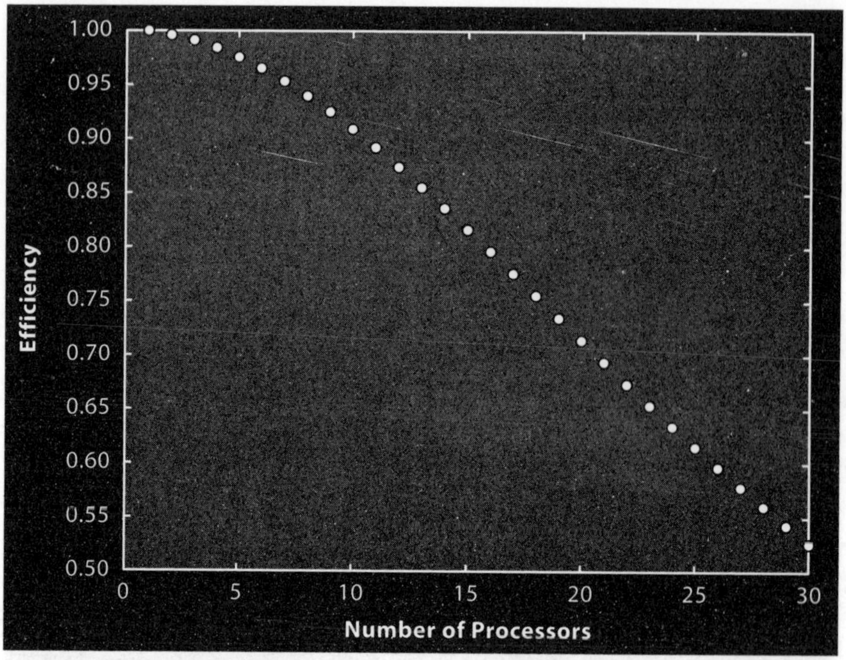

Figure 2.3 Hypothetical performance of a parallel implementation of summation: efficiency as a function of the number of processors used with $\gamma = 9$ and $N = 10,000$.

The parallel efficiency (2.2.6) is depicted in Figure 2.3 for for some particular values of γ and N. Since the efficiency is $\mathcal{O}(P^{-2})$, the efficiency will eventually go to zero (see Exercise 2.3).

Consider the parallel performance for $N = 10^7$ and $\gamma = 9$. The efficiency for $P = 1000$ (where maximal speed up occurs) is one-half (50%).

Comparing Figure 2.3 with the previous ones changes our perception of performance. Now something good (efficiency) is really going down, and maybe now we are not so pleased. However, the parallel efficiency of a code is critical to the economic viability of using it on a given number of processors. The efficiency provides a measure of the relative utilization of the resources of a parallel computer, as follows.

Note that the execution time T_P on P processors can be related to the sequential execution time using the parallel efficiency:

$$T_P = \frac{1}{E_P}\frac{T_1}{P}. \tag{2.2.7}$$

Suppose we are the owners of a parallel computer and are selling time on it to customers. If we could find P independent jobs that each execute in time T, this would provide more income than to run a job which takes time $T_1 = PT$ sequentially and runs on P processors with low parallel efficiency. The latter would take longer than T to run but might be hard to charge accordingly. The parallel job will tie up the computer longer by a factor $1/E_P$ and complete essentially the same computational job as when it is executed sequentially.

From the point of view of resource utilization, one might never want to run a code in parallel. However, there is often a balance between the need to maximize resource utilization and the need to minimize execution time to improve the productivity of the computer user. In the happy case that speedup is actually greater than P, then the parallel efficiency will be greater than 1. This simply means that it is most efficient to solve the problem in parallel.

When it is not possible to run a problem on one just processor, we can define a **relative efficiency** corresponding to the relative speedup (2.2.4) with respect to the smallest number P' of processors for which the problem will run as follows:

$$E_P^{P'} := \frac{P'}{P} S_P^{P'} \tag{2.2.8}$$

for $P \geq P'$.

We can interpret E_P as a measure of efficiency in another way as follows. A computational problem can be solved (sequentially) in T_1 time by doing a certain amount M of computation. This of course includes many things: floating point operations, memory references, I/O, and so forth. But for the sake of argument, let us think only of floating point operations. If the computation is broken into P parts, each consisting of m_i floating point operations, and any sort of need for communication is ignored, then there is still only the same amount of total computation being done:

$$M = \sum_{i=1}^{P} m_i. \tag{2.2.9}$$

If the amounts of computation are all the same, so that all $m_i = M/P$, then the computation itself can be done in time T_1/P for each piece, again ignoring performance variation among processors, communication, and *dependences* (see Chapter 4), i.e., the fact that some computations cannot be started before others are finished. This would correspond to an efficiency of one. Any deviation from this, due to communication or lack of load balance (i.e., not all the m_i's being the same) or dependences, must be viewed as a lack of efficiency in the parallel code.

Example 2.2.5. Let us be more quantitative about how parallel efficiency affects the cost of a computation. Suppose that you have to pay the same rate ρ for time for each processor used, without regard for problem size or total number of processors used. This is a very simple charging algorithm, but it will simplify our argument. The cost of using one processor to do a job is $C_1 = \rho T_1$, whereas the cost C_P of using P processors is

$$C_P = \rho T_P P = \frac{\rho T_1}{E_P} = \frac{C_1}{E_P}. \tag{2.2.10}$$

Thus the cost of using P processors is related to the sequential cost by a simple factor of $1/E_P$. A more realistic measure of the cost of using a parallel computer would be to compare it with the cost on an independent sequential computer as outlined in Exercise 2.4.

2.3 LIMITS TO PERFORMANCE

There are many things that can limit parallel performance: an essentially sequential section of code, dependences (Chapter 4), lack of load balance, and required communication. Here we present some key results that quantify some of these effects. Although there may be remedies to many of these, the resulting code complexity may be the ultimate limit to improving performance.

2.3.1 Amdahl's Law

Suppose that a particular code takes time T_1 to execute on one processor and that there is a **sequential fraction** f of this code that cannot be (or has not been) parallelized (for whatever reason). For example, Figure 1.13 depicts a problem with one part split into two essentially similar parallel computations followed by a sequential part (`v=u`, etc.). The sequential fraction for the code in Figure 1.13 will depend on the time required to evaluate the function `f(t,u)`, but it will always be there (see Exercise 2.5).

Amdahl's Law[1] assumes that, no matter how many processors P are used, the sequential part of the code will require at least fT_1 time to complete. The remainder of the code, by assumption, takes $(1-f)T_1$ time to execute on one processor. Amdahl's Law assumes that this part of the code will require at least $(1-f)T_1/P$ time to execute on P processors. Combining these two time estimates, we conclude that the time, T_P, to execute this code using P processors must be bounded below by the sum of the sequential fraction fT_1 of the execution time and the remaining fraction $(1-f)T_1$ divided by P:

$$T_P \geq fT_1 + \frac{(1-f)T_1}{P}. \tag{2.3.1}$$

[1]Gene Myron Amdahl (1922–) developed his first computer, the Wisconsin Integrally Synchronized Computer, as a graduate student at the University of Wisconsin. With a Ph.D. in theoretical physics, he began his career with IBM in 1952, becoming the chief engineer of the IBM 704, eventually leading to the IBM 7030, based on new transistor technology. In 1970 Amdahl left IBM and formed his own company where he designed and built the first computer clones, known then as "plug-to-plug compatibles." Amdahl returned to IBM and also started three other companies of varying success. Amdahl's Law put forth in [7] sparked heated debate in the scientific community about the potential of massively parallel computing.

Combining (2.3.1) and (2.2.1), we obtain **Amdahl's Law**:

$$S_P \leq \frac{1}{f + (1-f)/P}. \tag{2.3.2}$$

Even if we had an infinite number of processors, we would find that the speedup could not exceed the bound

$$S_P \leq \frac{1}{f}. \tag{2.3.3}$$

This weaker statement is also sometimes referred to as Amdahl's Law. It says that the ratio of the parallel and sequential execution times cannot be less than the sequential fraction of the code:

$$\frac{T_P}{T_1} \geq f. \tag{2.3.4}$$

Other factors can limit parallel performance in addition to the sequential fraction of a code. This is why inequalities are used in (2.3.1) and (2.3.2).

Example 2.3.1. Suppose a particular algorithm spends 1% of its time doing something that is sequential, i.e., cannot be (or has not been) parallelized. This means that $f = 0.01$ in Amdahl's Law. In particular, (2.3.3) implies that the speedup can never exceed one hundred. Suppose the other 99% has been parallelized perfectly. Then (2.3.2) implies that the speedup with ninety-nine ($P = 99$) processors could at most be fifty ($S_{99} \leq 50$).

Amdahl's Law implies that the parallel efficiency (Definition 2.2.3) is bounded by

$$E_P \leq \frac{1}{1 + (P-1)f}. \tag{2.3.5}$$

When the quantity $(P-1)f$ is small, expanding the quotient in (2.3.5) implies that E_P decreases like

$$E_P \approx 1 - (P-1)f. \tag{2.3.6}$$

Thus f can be interpreted as the slope of the efficiency curve, E_P, as a function of P, near the point $P = 1$.

2.3.2 Induced communication

Here we give one example of a "sequential fraction" that occurs frequently in parallel computation. In all the examples we have seen, there is some communication that must go on between processors that would not occur (or be simpler) in the sequential case. Thus we may assume that communication will add some additional overhead, as a general rule. This will arise in a variety of ways (through message latency, network or bus contention, or network bandwidth limitations) depending on particular architectural details of the computer, but it will almost always appear in some guise when $P > 1$.

We can model this as follows. We suppose that

$$T_P = T_{\text{comp}} + T_{\text{comm}}, \tag{2.3.7}$$

where T_{comp} is the computation time and T_{comm} is the communication time. Then, following the basic assumption of Amdahl's Law, we suppose that

$$T_1 \leq PT_{\text{comp}} \tag{2.3.8}$$

since $T_1 > PT_{\text{comp}}$ would imply that doing the P parallel tasks in a time-shared mode on a sequential computer would be a better strategy for computation than the standard sequential approach. This might be the case in unusual situations, but generally we would not expect it. Recalling the definition of speedup, we see that

$$\begin{aligned} S_P^{-1} &= \frac{T_{\text{comp}} + T_{\text{comm}}}{T_1} \\ &\geq \frac{T_{\text{comp}} + T_{\text{comm}}}{PT_{\text{comp}}} \\ &= \frac{1}{P}\left(1 + \frac{T_{\text{comm}}}{T_{\text{comp}}}\right). \end{aligned} \tag{2.3.9}$$

Simply inverting (2.3.10) gives the upper bound

$$S_P \leq P\left(1 + \frac{T_{\text{comm}}}{T_{\text{comp}}}\right)^{-1}, \tag{2.3.10}$$

which says that the speedup will be limited by the ratio of communication time to computation time. For example, if the ratio of communication time to computation time is one, the speedup can be at most $P/2$. The efficiency similarly satisfies

$$E_P \leq \left(1 + \frac{T_{\text{comm}}}{T_{\text{comp}}}\right)^{-1}, \tag{2.3.11}$$

which implies that the ratio of communication time to computation time has to stay bounded for scalable computation.

2.3.3 Load balance and efficiency

In the derivation of Amdahl's Law we assumed the best case for estimating parallel performance, namely, that the parallel work could be perfectly divided into P parts. This is the case of perfect *load balance* (Definition 1.5.7), where *load* refers to a measure of the amount of work done by each individual processor.

Recall that the definition of load balance (Definition 1.5.7) is stated in terms of the times t_i for each processor to do its part of the calculation. The calculation is load balanced when all the t_i's are approximately the same. The parallel execution time can be defined simply in terms of the t_i's as follows:

$$T_P = \max\{t_i \ : \ 1 \le i \le P\}. \tag{2.3.12}$$

It is reasonable to assume that

$$T_1 \le \sum_{1 \le i \le P} t_i. \tag{2.3.13}$$

If not, then the parallel execution could provide a faster sequential execution by executing each separate part in sequence. Applying the definition of efficiency (Definition 2.2.3) and (2.3.12) and (2.3.13), we find

$$E_P = \frac{T_1}{PT_P} \le \frac{\sum_{1 \le i \le P} t_i}{P \max\{t_i \ : \ 1 \le i \le P\}} = \frac{\text{ave}\{t_i \ : \ 1 \le i \le P\}}{\max\{t_i \ : \ 1 \le i \le P\}}, \tag{2.3.14}$$

where we recall the definition (1.5.3) of ave $\{t_i \ : \ 1 \le i \le P\}$. Thus the ratio of the average time on each processor to the maximum time on each processor, which we used as the definition of load balance (Definition 1.5.7), gives an upper bound on the efficiency of a calculation. We state this important result as the following theorem.

Theorem 2.3.2. Let t_i denote the time for the i-th processor to do its part of the calculation. Suppose that (2.3.13) holds. Then the efficiency of the calculation can never exceed the load balance:

$$E_P \le \beta := \frac{\text{ave}\{t_i \ : \ 1 \le i \le P\}}{\max\{t_i \ : \ 1 \le i \le P\}}, \tag{2.3.15}$$

where the numerator was defined in (1.5.3) and β denotes the load balance (Definition 1.5.7).

2.3.4 Combination of effects

It is permissible to combine the bounds (2.3.5) (Amdahl's Law for parallel efficiency) and (2.3.15). The latter applies to trivially parallel tasks where the sequential fraction f is zero. The parallel speedup and efficiency of two successive tasks can be estimated as follows from the corresponding speedup and efficiency of the separate tasks. Suppose that $T^a_\cdot$ and $T^b_\cdot$ denote the times of execution of the two separate tasks, labeled a and b respectively. Thus T^a_1 denotes the sequential time of task a, T^b_P denotes the parallel time of task b, and so forth. It is reasonable to assume that the sequential time T^{a+b}_1 of the combined tasks $a+b$ is the sum of the sequential times of the separate parts T^a_1 and T^b_1:

$$T^{a+b}_1 = T^a_1 + T^b_1. \tag{2.3.16}$$

On the other hand, it would be prudent only to assume that the parallel time T^{a+b}_P of the combined tasks $a+b$ is not less than the sum of the parallel times of the separate parts:

$$T_P^{a+b} \geq T_P^a + T_P^b \tag{2.3.17}$$

as there could be additional contributions to parallel execution time due to communication or synchronization. Then one can show by simple algebra (Exercise 2.9) that the corresponding speedup S_P^{a+b} of the combined tasks satisfies

$$S_P^{a+b} \leq \left(\frac{\lambda}{S_P^a} + \frac{1-\lambda}{S_P^b}\right)^{-1}, \tag{2.3.18}$$

where

$$\lambda := \frac{T_1^a}{T_1^a + T_1^b}. \tag{2.3.19}$$

Since efficiency is just speedup divided by P, we similarly have

$$E_P^{a+b} \leq \left(\frac{\lambda}{E_P^a} + \frac{1-\lambda}{E_P^b}\right)^{-1}. \tag{2.3.20}$$

2.3.5 Lack of synchronization

Another factor which limits parallel performance is lack of synchronization. This lack can be caused by bad load balance, but it can also appear more fundamentally. Some parts of a parallel computation cannot be initiated until other parts are completed. This may be viewed as a type of *dependence*, a subject studied extensively in Chapter 4. Some processors may be forced to sit idle waiting for others to complete required tasks. In this time, no useful computation is done. This means that the "parallel" computation time will not be the sequential time divided by P even if there is no sequential fraction to the code and the communication volume is minimal. A frequent cause of idleness is a lack of load balance (Section 2.3.3) in one part of the computation which is followed by some communication.

Note that the assumptions here do not take into account the fact that the individual processor performance may *increase* as depicted in Figure 1.2. This can and does allow speedup to exceed the theoretical linear limit in practical calculations [14]. Amdahl's Law assumes uniform processor behavior, which is a reasonable approximation. However, individual processor performance is becoming increasingly data-dependent, so caution should be exercised in using the model.

2.4 SCALABILITY

When parallel computers were first becoming available commercially, there was significant concern that there might be some absolute limit to speedup that could be achieved with real problems. In one case, a challenge was issued by e-mail (partially reproduced in Figure 2.4) that offered a monetary prize for anyone achieving a speedup of two hundred. This was accomplished in [63], but it was also pointed out that the standard notion of speedup needed to be modified to include data size. Later, a more substantial amount of money was offered in a more complex challenge, and the resulting Bell[2] Prizes have been awarded each year since 1988 [88].

Suppose a problem can be characterized by a data size N. The characteristics of a parallel code may vary significantly as N is varied, even more than for a sequential computation as depicted in Figure 1.2. For very large data sizes, some small effects (such as a sequential section) may become insignificant relative to the overall computation time. The notion of *scalability* reflects this [63]. For example, the parallelization of the summation problem in (1.5.1) and (1.5.2) has been modeled for a broadcast medium to have an execution time proportional to $N/P+(\gamma+1)P$ (see (2.1.1)). Choosing P as a function of N can yield arbitrarily large speedup in apparent contradiction to Amdahl's Law.

Example 2.4.1. In Example 2.2.4, we determined that

$$E_P = \left(1+(\gamma+1)\frac{P^2}{N}\right)^{-1}. \tag{2.4.1}$$

For fixed N, this implies that the efficiency goes to zero as P goes to infinity. But if we choose P as a function of N as N increases, we can obtain an efficiency that does not go to zero, as it would for the case of a fixed N. For example, suppose P and N are related by the equation $P=\sqrt{N}$. Then the efficiency is constant: $E_P=(1+(\gamma+1))^{-1}$.

2.4.1 Data-dependent performance measures

As a preliminary step in the discussion of scalability, we introduce the notions of data-dependent speedup and data-dependent parallel efficiency as a function of both the number of processors P and the data size N.

Definition 2.4.2. The **data-dependent speedup** $S_{P,N}$ using P processors for a problem with data size N is defined to be the ratio of the sequential and parallel execution times

$$S_{P,N} = \frac{T_{1,N}}{T_{P,N}}, \tag{2.4.2}$$

where $T_{1,N}$ is the time of execution of the best sequential solution of the problem with data size N for and $T_{P,N}$ is the time of execution of the

[2]Gordon Bell (1934–) spent 23 years at Digital Equipment Corporation where he was the architect of various mini-computers and time-sharing environments and led the development of DEC's VAX and the VAX Computing Environment. Bell has been involved in the design of products at Digital, Encore, Ardent, and many of other companies.

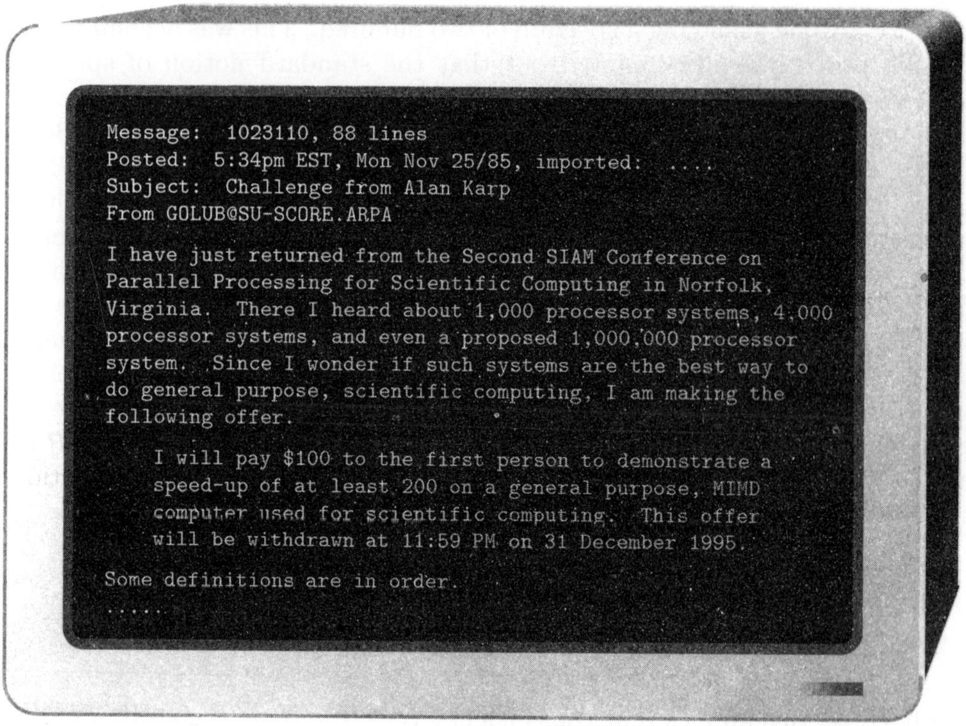

Figure 2.4 E-mail sent by Alan Karp via "NA-net" to initiate a discussion leading to a prize for achieving a speedup of two hundred on three practical algorithms.

parallel solution of the problem with data size N on P processors. The **data-dependent parallel efficiency** $E_{P,N}$ using P processors is defined to be the ratio of the data-dependent speedup and P:

$$E_{P,N} = \frac{S_{P,N}}{P} = \frac{T_{1,N}}{PT_{P,N}}. \tag{2.4.3}$$

With these notions in hand, we can define scalability.

Definition 2.4.3. An algorithm is said to be **scalable** if there is a **minimal efficiency** $\epsilon > 0$ such that, given any problem size N, there is a number of processors $P(N)$, which tends to infinity when N tends to infinity, such that the efficiency $E_{P(N),N}$ remains bounded below by ϵ, that is,

$$E_{P(N),N} \geq \epsilon > 0 \tag{2.4.4}$$

as N is made arbitrarily large.

The number of processors $P(N)$ chosen for a given data size N has not been specified in this definition, except that it should increase to infinity as N increases. Practically, one often has a precise choice of $P(N)$ for which one asks whether or not (2.4.4) holds, such as the memory constrained case

(2.4.15) described subsequently. This leads to a more restrictive notion of scalability than we have presented in Definition 2.4.3.

Example 2.4.4. Scaled performance gives a measure of the speedup and efficiency where the number of processors is a function of the problem size. In this example we analyze the scaled speedup of the summation problem in (1.5.1) and (1.5.2). Suppose the execution time is as discussed in Section 2.1, namely,

$$T_{P,N} = \frac{N}{P} + (\gamma + 1)P, \tag{2.4.5}$$

which results in a speedup

$$S_{P,N} = \frac{T_1}{T_{P,N}} = \frac{N}{\frac{N}{P} + (\gamma+1)P} = P\frac{1}{1 + (\gamma+1)\frac{P^2}{N}}. \tag{2.4.6}$$

Now suppose we choose the number of processors to be a function of the number of data such that

$$P(N) = \sqrt{N}, \tag{2.4.7}$$

where $P(N)$ is an integer ($N = 4, 9, 16, 25, \ldots$). The corresponding speedup is

$$S_{P(N),N} = k\ N^{1/2} = k\ P \tag{2.4.8}$$

with the constant $k = \frac{1}{2+\gamma}$. From (2.4.8) we see that $S_{P(N),N}$ is linear with respect to P, provided that N grows accordingly (e.g., as in (2.4.7)).

In Example 2.4.4, the efficiency turned out to be a fixed value, namely, $E_{P(N),N} = k = \frac{1}{2+\gamma}$. We arrived at that result by fixing the number of processors relative to the number of data with $P(N) = \sqrt{N}$. In the next example we consider a varying efficiency as $P(N)$ varies.

Example 2.4.5. We now show that the efficiency of the summation problem outlined in Example 2.4.4 is bounded according to Definition 2.4.3. We again suppose the speedup given in (2.4.6). Definition 2.4.3 requires that $P(N)$ can be chosen so that the corresponding efficiency is bounded from below by ϵ, for some positive ϵ (less than one). The efficiency is

$$E_{P(N),N} = \frac{S_{P(N),N}}{P(N)} = \left(1 + (\gamma+1)\frac{P(N)^2}{N}\right)^{-1}. \tag{2.4.9}$$

We apply the efficiency constraint as an inequality where $E_{P(N),N} \geq \epsilon$ and rearrange, resulting in

$$P(N) \leq \sqrt{k\,N}, \tag{2.4.10}$$

where $k = (\frac{1}{\epsilon} - 1)/(\gamma + 1)$.

The inequality (2.4.10) bounds a family of functions $P_i(N)$, for which the summation problem is scalable. These functions reside beneath the dashed curve in the sketch, with three such curves illustrated. Note that the constant k shifts the dashed curve. Any of these are acceptable choices for $P(N)$ as long as $P(N) \to \infty$ and stays below the dashed curve.

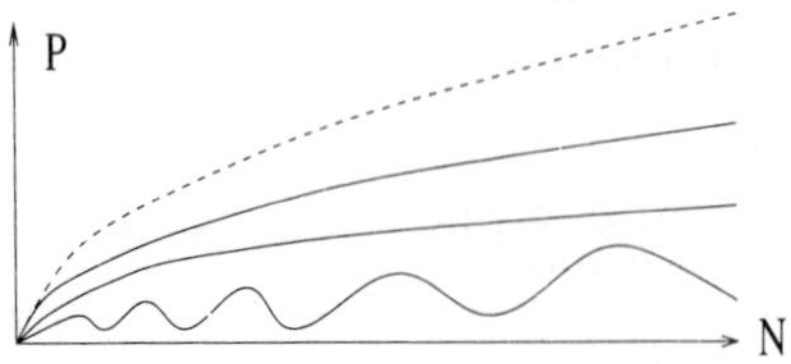

The notion of *scalability* seems at first glance to contradict Amdahl's Law, which said that if there is any sequential fraction $f > 0$ of a code then its efficiency must necessarily decrease to zero as P goes to infinity according to (2.3.5). The new ingredient that resolves the dilemma is that for a scalable code, the sequential fraction f_N itself decreases to zero as N goes to infinity. In particular, the sequential fraction f_N of a scalable algorithm must satisfy the bound (in view of (2.3.2))

$$f_N \leq \frac{C}{P(N)} \tag{2.4.11}$$

for some constant C. We will see that this holds in many cases.

2.4.2 Memory limits on performance

The memory $M(N, P)$ required to implement an algorithm with P processors and data size N may exceed the physical limits of a particular machine. Here $M(N, P)$ denotes the amount of memory required *per processor*; the total system memory required is thus P times this, i.e., $P \cdot M(N, P)$.

For a sequential problem, it would be natural to assume that

$$M(N, 1) \leq c_0 + c_1 N$$

for constants c_0 and c_1, since N measures the data size. (It may therefore be reasonable to take $c_1 = 1$ and even $c_0 = 0$, but we leave these choices flexible for the moment.)

However, for the parallel case, it is not so easy to say how the local memory size $M(N, P)$ should depend on N (and P). It may be possible to divide the memory requirements evenly among all processors, leading to $M(N, P) \leq c_0' + c_1' N/P$ for possibly different constants c_0' and c_1'. On the other hand, codes with such an ideal memory behavior may have less than ideal performance. It is common to find trade-offs between having more memory and faster execution on the one hand and less memory but slower execution on the other. For this reason it is natural to introduce a more restrictive notion of scalability which includes memory constraints as well as efficiency constraints.

Definition 2.4.6. An algorithm is said to be **scalable with respect to memory** if, given any problem size N, there is a number of processors $P(N)$, which tends to infinity when N tends to infinity, such that the efficiency $E_{P(N),N}$ remains bounded below by a positive constant as in (2.4.4), and furthermore

$$M(N, P(N)) \leq M_{\text{MAX}} \tag{2.4.12}$$

as N is made arbitrarily large, where M_{MAX} is some fixed constant.

Again, the number of processors $P(N)$ chosen for a given data size N has not been specified in this definition, except that it should increase indefinitely as N increases. We now consider one natural choice of $P(N)$ which would lead to a more restrictive notion of scalability than we have presented in Definition 2.4.6.

Example 2.4.7. We now consider the memory scalability of the summation problem in (1.5.1) and (1.5.2). With the speedup given in (2.4.6), is the summation problem scalable with respect to memory?

To be memory scalable by Definition 2.4.6 two constraints must be satisfied. The efficiency, $E_{P(N),N}$ must be bounded below by a positive constant; the region beneath the dashed function in Example 2.4.5 satisfies this constraint (see (2.4.10)). In addition, the memory usage $M_{N,P(N)} = \frac{N}{P(N)}$ is subject to the constraint

$$\frac{N}{P(N)} \leq M_0. \tag{2.4.13}$$

Therefore, $P(N)$ must be bounded above and below according to

$$\frac{1}{M_0} N \leq P(N) \leq \sqrt{k\,N}, \tag{2.4.14}$$

where $k = (\frac{1}{\epsilon} - 1)/(\gamma + 1)$.

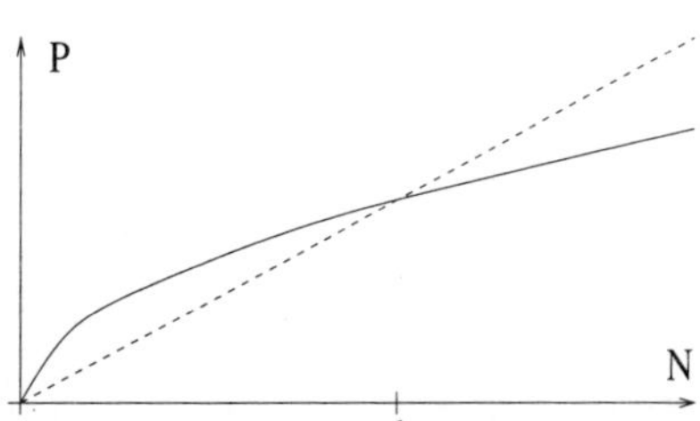

In the sketch, $P(N)$ must reside in the region bounded above by the solid curve satisfying the efficiency criterion and bounded below by the dashed curve satisfying the memory constraint criterion. These criteria can be satisfied in the region $a \leq N \leq b$; however, for $N > b$, the bounding functions have crossed, so that the constraints cannot be satisfied. We can approach this another way by rewriting (2.4.14) as $\sqrt{N} \leq kM_0$. Clearly this inequality cannot hold for arbitrary N since M_0, ϵ, and γ are constants. Thus we cannot have scalability with respect to memory.

The phrase **memory constrained scaling** refers to the performance of an algorithm for a particular amount of memory per processor, independent of N and P. This corresponds to choosing $P(N)$ such that

$$P(N) = \min\{P \; : \; M(N,P) \leq M_{\text{MAX}}\}, \tag{2.4.15}$$

where M_{MAX} is any constant (not necessarily the same as in Definition 2.4.6). Here we are making the simplifying assumption that $M(N,P)$ is always a decreasing function of P for any given N.

Even if a code is scalable with respect to memory, it may not be scalable for a particular computer if the constant M_{MAX} in (2.4.12) is too large for the computer to support. If we take M_{MAX} to be the maximum allowable for a given computer, we can then ask what the efficiency is for $P(N)$ defined by (2.4.15). If it is bounded below, then of course the code is scalable with respect to memory.

2.4.3 Other definitions of scalability

Although the definitions of scalability with respect to memory are theoretically clear, they are difficult to verify in practice, at least on certain kinds of parallel processors (e.g., distributed memory computers which have memory fixed at each processor). One might require a single processor with a very large amount of memory to do the sequential computation to determine $T_{1,N}$. Other definitions of scalability are possible. One variant of scalability, *scaled efficiency*, considers the scalability and efficiency with machine resources (memory and processors) as a function of the problem size.

Scaled efficiency has been used to study the multigrid iterative method for solving a partial differential equation [130]. The work estimate (and actual execution time) for this algorithm scales linearly with the data size N, i.e.,

$$T_{1,N} = cN. \tag{2.4.16}$$

For ideal performance, we would then expect

$$T_{P,N} = \frac{cN}{P}, \tag{2.4.17}$$

at least for N sufficiently large with respect to P.

Suppose we are interested in the efficiency of multigrid in the case that we use the same amount of memory on each processor, independent of the number of processors (cf. the memory constrained case considered previously). Let n denote this amount; the total data size is $N = nP$. Then $T_{P,nP}$ is the time we would measure for P processors. To compute the efficiency, we would need to know the time $T_{1,nP}$ which we could not run unless there were a particular processor with nP words of memory. However, (2.4.16) implies that

$$T_{1,nP} = PT_{1,n}. \tag{2.4.18}$$

Comparing (2.4.3), we see that

$$\widehat{E}_{P,n} := \frac{T_{1,n}}{T_{P,nP}} \tag{2.4.19}$$

provides an estimate of efficiency $E_{P,n}$ in which the amount of memory per processor is held fixed. This is a type of memory constrained scaling, but of course it is not a general definition. For algorithms whose time of execution is not linear in the data size, a more complex formula would be appropriate. See Exercise 2.11 for another example.

2.4.4 Theoretical lower bounds

We will demonstrate that scalable algorithms exist for many problems. One might reasonably ask if there is a simple way to determine whether a particular problem has a scalable solution. We do not address that question here, but there is some related work of interest. To begin with, let us recast what it means for an algorithm to be scalable for a given problem. We can think of this as an upper bound on the execution time of the form

$$T_{P,N} \leq C\frac{T_{1,N}}{P}, \tag{2.4.20}$$

where C^{-1} is the lower bound on the efficiency $E_{P,N}$. Here, $P = P(N)$ is the particular function in the definition of scalability, which must tend to infinity as N tends to infinity.

Certain classes of computational problems have been identified [58] based on the rate of growth of $T_{1,N}$ as a function of N. The "polynomial class" **P** is defined as the class of problems for which

$$T_{1,N} \leq CN^{\alpha} \tag{2.4.21}$$

for some finite constants C and α. That is, the problem is in **P** if the time required to compute it (serially) is at most a polynomial in the problem size. There are many important computations which are exponential in the problem size, but the rate of growth of difficulty in solving them as a function of N typically puts a severe restriction on the problem size that can be solved at any given time. So it is reasonable for the moment to restrict our attention to problems that fall into the class **P**.

Various classes of computational problems which can be solved efficiently in parallel have been defined. For example, **NC** [58] is the class of problems in **P** for which

$$T_{P,N} \leq C(\log N)^{\beta} \tag{2.4.22}$$

for $P = P(N) \leq CN^{\gamma}$, for some finite constants C, β, and γ . Analogous to (2.3.8), we can assume that

$$T_{1,N} \leq PT_{P,N} \,. \tag{2.4.23}$$

Since we have a problem in **P**, let us assume that $T_{1,N} \approx CN^\alpha$ for simplicity, and that $P(N) \approx N^\gamma$. Then (2.4.23) would imply that $\gamma \geq \alpha$. However, if $\gamma > \alpha$ we do not have a scalable algorithm. Even if $\gamma = \alpha$, we would have a scalable algorithm only if $T_{P,N} \leq C$ (i.e., $\beta = 0$) for all N. Thus membership in **NC** does not imply scalability, and it is easy to see that scalability alone does not imply membership in **NC**. Our example with $T_{1,N} \approx CN^\alpha$ will be scalable with $T_{P,N}$ growing like N^ρ for some $\rho < \alpha$ and $P(N) = cN^{\alpha-\rho}$. Therefore the class of scalable algorithms and **NC** have no simple relationship.

Both the concept of scalability and classes like **NC** are simply ways of taking limits in the two-dimensional space spanned by the entire array of possible time values $T_{P,N}$ for all N and P. Ideally in choosing a particular P to use for a given N, you would (and will in many cases discussed here) have a formula for (an estimate of) $T_{P,N}$. But limiting notions like scalability and **NC** are useful to guide the choice of algorithms. They represent two different ways to look at limits in the full space of values $T_{P,N}$. The class **NC** emphasizes time-critical calculations (such as the computer system which runs a jet aircraft), whereas scalability emphasizes resource-critical calculations. The literature on time-critical models is quite extensive [58]; we will emphasize resource-critical issues here.

One might ask whether a problem can be shown *not* to be in a class like **NC**. Indeed, one might ask whether **NC**=**P**. Recall that **NC** was defined as a subclass of **P**, so the question is simply whether everything in **P** satisfies (2.4.22) automatically or not. For example, could a **lower bound** on performance of the form

$$T_{P,N} \geq cN^\epsilon \tag{2.4.24}$$

be proved for a problem in **P** for $\epsilon > 0$? This requires a precise model (see Section 2.5.2) of parallel computation, but interesting results of the form (2.4.24) have been obtained [58, 112] which suggest that there may be problems in **P** which are not in **NC**. This would mean that they are essentially sequential in the sense that they have no highly efficient parallel version satisfying (2.4.22).

2.5 PARALLEL PERFORMANCE ANALYSIS

Performance analysis helps to determine whether a code, or parts of a code, are performing as we expect them to. The quantities being measured can be time, memory, or other resources. Performance analysis is the art of determining exactly how much of a critical resource (e.g., time) a particular part of a system consumes (e.g., the time it takes to complete its task). Although the utilization of other resources (memory, network links, and so forth) is also very important, we will be particularly interested in the time different parts of a code take to execute. Due to the computer uncertainty principle (Exercise 1.5) this is not a trivial task. The most obvious difficulty is that the act of timing itself requires some time to complete. So there is a certain level of granularity below which accurate timings may be impossible.

In the case of parallel codes, this difficulty is compounded by the fact that different events may not be synchronized. Moreover, the clocks on separate processors may run at slightly different speeds; time itself should be thought of as a parallel quantity. Therefore, timing separate processors may yield odd results. When in doubt, a good rule of thumb is to synchronize around timing sections. Of course, this adds further timing overhead.

2.5.1 Performance prediction graph

To analyze the temporal performance of each separate component of a parallelized code, we introduce a (logarithmic) **performance prediction graph**. For a code (section) that is perfectly parallelized, its time of execution will be

$$T_P = \frac{T_1}{P}.$$

In this ideal case

$$\log(T_P) = c - \log P$$

is a *linear* function of $\log P$. If we let $x = \log P$ and $y = \log(T_P)$, then we get a linear plot of slope -1.

The use of a logarithmic scale also allows effects to be represented that are on vastly different time scales. Figure 13.6 in Section 13.6.3 depicts real data on different components of the computation and communication in a parallelized version of the GROMOS code [62]. Although real performance analysis is done on real timing data, we can use our model of Section 2.1 to illustrate the concepts. In Figure 2.5, we present a hypothetical performance analysis of the summation problem (in arbitrary time units) as a function of the number of processors used with $\gamma = 9$ and $N = 10,000$. Here we break the components of the model estimate (2.1.1) into the computational part N/P and the communication time $(\gamma+1)P$. We see that when the (increasing) communication approaches the computational time, the usefulness of increasing the number of processors P begins to end.

The performance prediction graph allows total parallel performance to be broken into component parts. Parts that are decreasing are good; parts that are increasing are bad. The actual times for individual parts like communication or computation in Figure 2.5 can be compared with models (e.g., formulas we use to estimate execution time) to determine whether or not expected performance is being achieved. Moreover, one can use this information to decide when it is useful to modify sections of code. For a number of processors less than a certain critical threshold, even a component whose time is increasing will not matter. In Figure 2.5, communication is continually increasing as a function of the number of processors utilized.

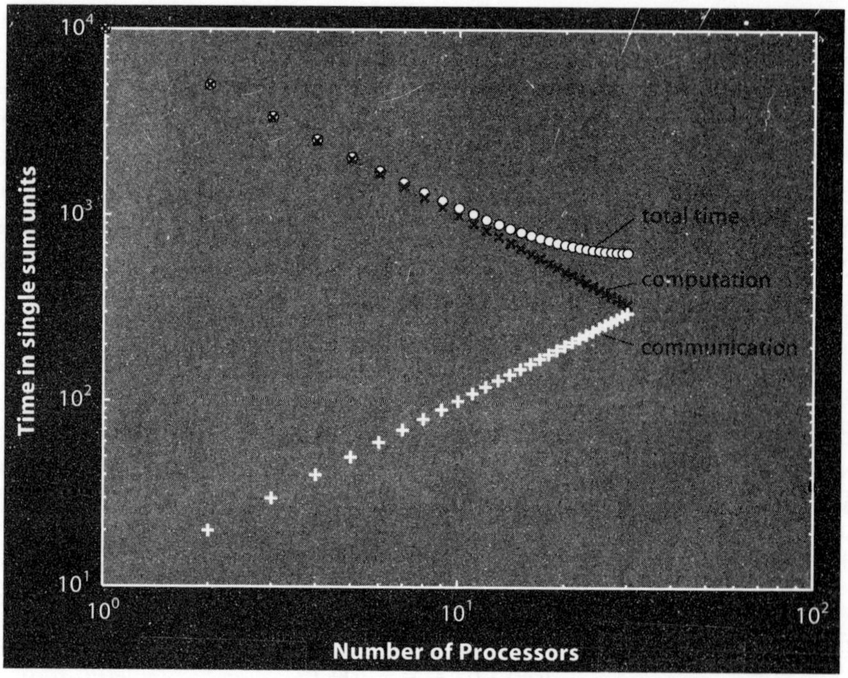

Figure 2.5 Performance prediction graph: performance analysis of the summation problem (in arbitrary time units) as a function of the number of processors used with $\gamma = 9$ and $N = 10,000$.

Once this time reaches the (decreasing) computation time, diminishing returns follow in the overall execution time. However, the graph shows clearly that well below such a critical number of processors (about 32 in Figure 2.5), the effect of communication is minimal.

The main benefit of the performance prediction graph is to allow substantiation of a model for total parallel performance. In (2.1.1) we have an estimate of the performance of a hypothetical implementation of a parallel summation. Actually, we should think of (2.1.1) as a model of execution for the summation problem in (1.5.1) and (1.5.2). Although we have not presented real data for this, Figure 2.5 depicts some hypothetical performance data following this model. If one has such data which fit a model to a high degree of accuracy, then there is a certain level of confidence in being able to extrapolate behavior on similar systems with an even larger number of processors. It is important in presenting such data to include any discrepancies between the individual components measured and the overall execution time. This could be due to a number of sources, but the key is to identify all significant ones, include them in the model, and ensure that anything remaining is quite small. In using the performance prediction graph to extrapolate behavior to a larger number of processors, one is making the tacit assumption that this quantity does not grow unexpectedly fast as a function of the number of processors.

2.5.2 Theoretical models

There are models of computation which reflect key properties of physical computers for the purpose of analyzing computation abstractly. The **random access machine** (RAM) is a popular model of a sequential computer, and there are many variants of this for parallel computation [58, 117]. We will take a slightly different approach in that we will attempt to model the behavior of real machines for a limited class of operations in a given algorithm, based on a detailed description of computer architecture presented in Chapter 3. This will provide estimates of performance that can be used to compare with measured performance using a performance prediction graph as discussed in Section 2.5.1, and it may provide rigorous upper bounds on performance. However, we will not be able to present lower bounds in a general context, since a small change in architecture may lead to a dramatic difference in performance. An example of this will be given in Section 6.6.2.

Statements about scalability of a given algorithm of course depend on the particular parallel architecture on which the algorithm is implemented. One critical variable is the time required to do communication, and in Section 2.6 we show how this can affect scalability in one example. In general, the reader should keep in mind that scalability is context-dependent. Every effort will be made to make that context clear, but the reader should remain alert to this issue.

2.6 PARALLEL PAYOFF

Having raised so many concerns about parallelism, it is reasonable to ask if it is a good idea at all. Fortunately it is for a very large number of applications, and we describe one here in some detail.

Many time-dependent phenomena in physical simulations have similar characteristics which are reflected in the important problem of heat conduction. First appreciated by the mathematician Fourier as a critical issue in the manufacture of artillery barrels, the conduction of heat remains a central issue for human existence in domains as diverse as home heating, beer manufacturing, and organ transplantation.

The "heat equation" describes the diffusion of thermal energy in a medium. In its simplest form, it may be written

$$\begin{aligned} \frac{\partial u}{\partial t}(x,t) - \frac{\partial^2 u}{\partial x^2}(x,t) = 0 \quad \forall x \in [0,1],\ t>0, \\ u(0,t) = g_0(t), \quad u(1,t) = g_1(t) \quad \forall t > 0, \end{aligned} \tag{2.6.1}$$

where $u(x,t)$ denotes the temperature of the medium at any given point x and time t.

The model (2.6.1) can describe quite complex phenomena. For example, consider the problem of predicting the temperature in a slab of material which is cyclically heated and cooled on each side of the slab. This corresponds to (2.6.1) with $g_0(t) := \sin(t)$ and $g_1(t) := \cos(t)$, with the x variable representing the position across the width of the slab. We are assuming that the slab is infinite in extent (or at least very large) in the other two directions, and that the temperature is held at the same value at all points on each face of the slab. In this case, the temperature will only be a function of x and t. One can easily see in this case that the solution is

$$u(x,t) = \sin(\tfrac{1}{2}\pi x + t), \tag{2.6.2}$$

but a numerical technique would be needed for general boundary data g_i. We now discuss such techniques.

2.6.1 Explicit Euler Time Discretization

The simplest time discretization method for the heat equation uses the forward (or explicit) Euler difference method. This is the method used in Section 1.6.1; see especially (1.6.6) and following. With a uniform time step $\Delta t = t^{k+1} - t^k$, it takes the form

$$\begin{aligned} u^{k+1}(x) = u^k(x) + \Delta t \frac{\partial^2 u^k}{\partial x^2}(x) \quad \forall x \in [0,1], \quad \forall k \geq 0, \\ u^0(x) = u_0(x) \quad \forall x \in [0,1], \\ u^k(0) = g_0(k\Delta t) \quad \text{and} \quad u^k(1) = g_1(k\Delta t) \quad \forall k > 0, \end{aligned} \tag{2.6.3}$$

where $u^k(x)$ denotes an approximation to $u(x, k\Delta t)$.

Applying the finite difference approximation (1.6.13) to (2.6.3) yields a simple algorithm. In the case of a regular mesh, $x_n = nh$ for $n = 0, \ldots, N$, the result is

$$\begin{aligned} u_n^{k+1} = u_n^k - \frac{\Delta t}{h^2}\left(2u_n^k - u_{n-1}^k - u_{n+1}^k\right) \quad \forall 0 < n < N, \\ u_0^k = g_0(k\Delta t) \quad \text{and} \quad u_N^k = g_1(k\Delta t) \end{aligned} \tag{2.6.4}$$

for all $k > 0$, where $h = 1/N = x_{n+1} - x_n$ is a uniform spatial discretization size. Here u_n^k is an approximation to $u(nh, k\Delta t)$, and the process is started with $u_n^0 = u^0(x_n)$ for all n.

The difficulty with this simple algorithm is that it is *unstable* unless $\Delta t/h^2$ is sufficiently small [86]. However, it is also reasonable to take Δt proportional to h^2 to balance the temporal and spatial accuracy, and this resolves the stability problem for a suitable constant of proportionality.

The algorithm in (2.6.4) is almost identical to (1.6.21), and it can be parallelized in the same way. In more realistic problems, the spatial variable x is multidimensional, but the basic properties of the algorithm remain the same.

2.6.2 Performance model

The performance of the parallelization of (2.6.4), or equivalently (1.6.21), can be easily estimated. At each time step, there are $4N$ operations to be done. For more complicated physical models, say with varying conductivity in the slab, the amount of work would still be proportional to N, so let us from now on assume that the number of operations being done at each time step is αN for some constant α.

Ignoring the communication needed in the parallelization depicted in Figure 1.14, the computational work can be divided equally into P parts on P processors, provided N is divisible by P as we now assume. Thus the computational time would be proportional to $\alpha N/P$. Let us assume that the constant of proportionality is the inverse of the number F of floating point operations that can be done in a given time unit (compare Definition 1.3.1). Therefore our time estimate for the computational work is

$$\frac{\alpha N}{PF}. \tag{2.6.5}$$

In particular, we can assume that this is a good prediction of the sequential time T_1 (for one time step) if we set $P = 1$:

$$T_1 = \frac{\alpha N}{F}. \tag{2.6.6}$$

The time required for communication is more complicated to estimate, depending on the nature of the communication medium that is connecting the individual processors. We will consider two simple cases without going into the details of how they might be implemented. Such issues will be discussed in Chapter 3.

2.6.3 Broadcast network

Suppose the communication is done on a single broadcast network, i.e., something like Ethernet connecting several workstations, as discussed in Section 2.1. This would mean that the amount of time to complete the communication would be proportional to βP, where β is related to the amount of data per processor to transfer. This might be a simple factor of the number (two in our simple example), or it might be a more complex function, such as the affine expression (3.3.4). Let us assume that the constant of proportionality is the inverse of the number W of floating point words that can be transmitted in a given time. Then our time estimate for the communication phase is

$$\frac{\beta P}{W}. \tag{2.6.7}$$

The total time is then

$$T_P = \frac{\alpha N}{PF} + \frac{\beta P}{W}. \tag{2.6.8}$$

The ratio of the sequential and parallel times in this case will be

$$\frac{T_P}{T_1} = \frac{1}{P} + \frac{\beta PF}{\alpha NW} = \frac{1}{P} + \frac{\gamma P}{\delta N}, \tag{2.6.9}$$

where

$$\gamma := F/W \tag{2.6.10}$$

can be interpreted as the number of floating point operations that can be done in the amount of time it takes to communicate one word (cf. (2.1.1)). In commercial systems today, this ratio can be quite high, from one hundred to one thousand. The ratio

$$\delta := \alpha/\beta \tag{2.6.11}$$

compares the amount of computation done in the spatial differencing to the number of words per data transfer. This ratio tends to be somewhat independent of the type of difference formula used [130].

The speedup is the inverse of the expression in (2.6.9),

$$S_{P,N} = P\Big/\left(1 + \frac{\gamma P^2}{\delta N}\right). \tag{2.6.12}$$

The corresponding efficiency will thus be

$$E_{P,N} = \left(1 + \frac{\gamma P^2}{\delta N}\right)^{-1}, \tag{2.6.13}$$

where γ is defined in (2.6.10). In this case, scalability would be achieved with $P = c\sqrt{N}$ for any positive constant c. The memory requirement $M(N,P)$ for each processor, however, would then satisfy

$$M(N,P) \geq N/P = \sqrt{N}/c, \tag{2.6.14}$$

and so this algorithm would not be scalable with respect to memory on a system with a single broadcast network. The efficiency would remain constant at $\left(1 + \frac{1}{2}\gamma c^2\right)^{-1}$ independent of N until the physical memory limit was reached, though. On the other hand, the memory constrained case ($N/P = C$) leads to an efficiency that decreases rapidly,

$$E_{(P=N/C),N} = \left(1 + \frac{\gamma N}{\delta C^2}\right)^{-1}, \tag{2.6.15}$$

as N increases.

2.6.4 Ring network

The performance analysis is quite different for a parallel computer system having a more sophisticated communication system. Many commercial systems today have at the minimum a *ring* topology embedded in the communication network. This means that each processor can communicate with two neighbors on either side independently of the communications between other pairs of neighbors (see Section 3.3). In this case, our time estimate for the communication phase is

$$\frac{\beta}{W} \tag{2.6.16}$$

yielding a total time given by

$$T_P = \frac{\alpha N}{PF} + \frac{\beta}{W}. \tag{2.6.17}$$

The ratio of the sequential and parallel times in this case will be

$$\frac{T_P}{T_1} = \frac{1}{P} + \frac{\beta F}{\alpha N W} = \frac{1}{P} + \frac{\gamma}{\delta N}, \tag{2.6.18}$$

where γ is defined in (2.6.10).

The speedup is the inverse of this expression,

$$S_{P,N} = P\left(1 + \frac{\gamma P}{\delta N}\right)^{-1}, \tag{2.6.19}$$

and the corresponding efficiency will thus be

$$E_{P,N} = \left(1 + \frac{\gamma P}{\delta N}\right)^{-1}. \tag{2.6.20}$$

Now scalability can be achieved by taking $P = cN$ for any constant $c > 0$. In this case, the memory requirement for each processor is only $N/P = 1/c$ words, and so this algorithm is scalable with respect to memory on a system having at least an embedded ring topology in the communication network (see Figure 3.10). The efficiency in this case is constant at $\left(1 + \frac{1}{2}c\gamma\right)^{-1}$ independent of N. This efficiency will be high when $c << \gamma^{-1}$.

2.6.5 Multidimensional problems

The generalization of (2.6.1) to problems with multidimensional spatial variables $x = (x_1, \ldots, x_d)$ introduces few mathematical complications, but it does present a further complexity with regard to parallelism. The system of equations corresponding to (2.6.4) with d spatial variables requires a fancier numbering system for spatial mesh points, but the general format is the same: the set of indices for the unknowns u forms a d-dimensional lattice. In general this could have N_i points in the i-th dimension. Using the notation $\mathcal{L}_k$ for the integers $0, \ldots, k$, we could write this space as the Cartesian product

$$\mathcal{L}_1 \times \mathcal{L}_2 \times \cdots \times \mathcal{L}_d \tag{2.6.21}$$

This is also the iteration space for the basic loop to implement the simple update in (2.6.4). We now have several options for decomposing this iteration space.

The slab decomposition is the simplest: we choose one dimension and divide that into P parts, leaving the other dimensions undivided. Suppose this is the k-th dimension. That is, we define a decomposition of $\mathcal{L}_k$ in the usual way into P parts

$$\mathcal{L}_k = \bigcup_{j=1,\ldots,P} \mathcal{L}_k^j \tag{2.6.22}$$

and decompose the iteration space (2.6.21) into pieces

$$\mathcal{L}_1 \times \mathcal{L}_2 \times \cdots \times \mathcal{L}_{k-1} \times \mathcal{L}_k^j \times \mathcal{L}_{k+1} \times \cdots \times \mathcal{L}_d \quad \forall j = 1, \ldots, P. \tag{2.6.23}$$

The block decomposition (cf. Exercise 1.13) is more complex. Due to the notational complexity, we consider only the case $d = 2$. Again, we make use of the basic decomposition of one dimension in (2.6.22) and define a *block* decomposition via the pieces

$$\mathcal{L}_1^i \times \mathcal{L}_2^j \quad \forall i, j = 1, \ldots, \sqrt{P}. \tag{2.6.24}$$

The advantage of the decomposition (2.6.24) is that it can have a smaller **surface-to-volume** ratio. This approximates the ratio of communication to computation in this type of algorithm. The amount of work done in the loop corresponding to (2.6.4) is proportional to the volume of data in each decomposition piece, and the communication is proportional to the size of the boundary, or surface. Thus the ratio of the surface to the volume gives an estimate of the ratio of communication to computation, something we would like to keep small. Note that the surface-to-volume ratio is better for a block decomposition only when P is sufficiently large (see Exercise 2.14).

2.7 REAL WORLD PARALLELISM

Many activities in the real world, both exotic and mundane, exhibit a kind of parallelism that is instructive for understanding computational parallelism. We will describe some randomly chosen examples in order to stimulate the imagination and encourage examination of everyday experience for further understanding of the problems and opportunities that parallelism presents.

A typing pool is an excellent example of parallelism. Although now largely replaced by the advent of personal computers, a typing pool was common in large organizations for the purpose of rendering handwritten documents into typewritten form. It consisted of a large number of humans seated at typewriters with a single manager at the door to distribute material to be typed. Documents were presented to the typing pools and assigned by the manager to the next available typist. This sort of workload distribution is an essential tool to achieve load balance in certain kinds of parallel computation.

On the other hand, the "master and slaves" approach to management introduces an obvious "bottleneck" (see Section 3.2), which limits overall throughput. All documents must be previewed by the manager before they can go to a typist. If they are small documents (e.g., short letters) this overhead can be substantial. It is hard to imagine a typing pool with a thousand typists and a single manager.

The building of the pyramids in Egypt and Mexico represent feats of human accomplishment that would be difficult to duplicate today even using machines. These were done using relatively weak individuals working in parallel to achieve a common goal. This image provides good inspiration for the idea of **massive parallelism**, in which a very large number of low-cost processors are used to solve large problems. The first teraflops computer (see Exercise 1.1) was built by Intel using over nine thousand Pentium Pro processors like those used in personal computers.

It was surely essential that the pyramid workers were carefully coordinated to ensure correct outcomes, and undoubtedly failure to follow the prescribed program led to injury and loss of life. Correctness of parallel programs is a significant issue that will be addressed subsequently (see Chapter 5, especially Section 5.1.1). The concept of a deterministic (see Chapter 5, especially Definition 5.1.4) result should be considered in this dangerous context.

The problem of scalability (Section 2.4) can be understood by observing contemporary behavior. The "sitting problem" solved on Saturdays in the fall of the year on college campuses consists of having someone sit in every seat of a large football stadium. This is done in parallel by tens of thousands of individual agents in an amount of time that is hard to quantify precisely, but is certainly on the order of half an hour. (It is hard to imagine the stadium filling up in just a few minutes, but conversely it does not take hours for people to find their seats.) This problem was reputedly solved sequentially at a large midwestern university in approximately two days (48 hours), in an effort to achieve some notoriety in a world record book. This would correspond to a speedup (Definition 2.2.1) of almost one hundred, but far short of the speedup one might expect with the 107,501 agents that biweekly find seats in that stadium. It is clear that there are bottlenecks (see Section 3.2), called portals in stadiums, that limit the overall speedup in the sitting problem.

Human experience can help to understand the potential extent of applicability of the single program (SPMD) programming model (Definition 1.5.10). Many religions are directed from a single text that is read by millions who derive rules for living in part as a result. Similarly, democratic governments provide simple rules for behavior that are interpreted by millions of individuals. In both types of human groups, extensive individual activity is regulated by a single document that is relatively short compared with a full description of the possible set of actions that could be taken by such large groups. Thus it is conceivable that the single program model could be used effectively for millions of processors cooperating to solve a single task.

2.8 STARTING SPMD PROGRAMMING

We illustrate SPMD programming with the summation problem (1.3.2) using the specific language constructs of Chapter 8. Assume that $N = k \cdot P$ and that we divide the reduction operation into P partial sums as in (1.5.1) that get combined via (1.5.2).

```
MYPEE = myProc
NOTOT = nProc
GRANLR = ENN / NOTOT
S = 0
do I = MYPEE*GRANLR+1, (MYPEE+1)*GRANLR, 2
   S = S + 1.0/(2*I-1)
   S = S - 1.0/(2*I+1)
enddo
SG = + {S}
end
```

Program 2.1 Code using ℙfortran to implement the parallel algorithm in (1.5.2) and (1.5.1).

The last executable statement (before the `end` statement) of Program 2.1 uses a reduction operation (Chapter 6) from ℙfortran (Chapter 8) which has the following interpretation. Since we are doing SPMD programming, every process executes the same code in parallel (independently) until the last line. At that point, there are multiple copies of the variable `S`, one for each process(or); this is a *set* of values, and the curly braces around the `S` on the right-hand side are meant to evoke this. The + in front of the set says to sum up all the numbers in this set. Thus, the last line of Program 2.1 implements (1.5.2). Of course, the preceding lines implement (1.5.1). In addition to the reduction operation, there are two more lines that are parallel-code specific. The definition `MYPEE = myProc` uses a ℙfortran reserved variable `nProc` that evaluates to different values on different processors, in fact, it *is* the process(or) number. Without this, all of the computations on different processors would be identical. The definition `NOTOT = nProc` uses the ℙfortran reserved variable `nProc` that evaluates to the number of processors executing the code.

The same algorithm can be implemented using the message passing library MPI with just a few more incantations, as shown in Program 2.2. MPI requires explicit initialization and termination commands, but there is a one-to-one mapping with most of the other steps. MPI will be discussed at more length in Sections 7.1 and 7.2.1.

2.9 EXERCISES

Exercise 2.1. If a particular algorithm spends 10% of its time doing something that is sequential, i.e., cannot be (or has not been) parallelized,

```
      MPI_Init(ierror)
      MPI_Comm_Rank(MPI_COMM_WORLD, MYPEE, ierror)
      MPI_Comm_Size(MPI_COMM_WORLD, NOTOT, ierror)
      GRANLR = ENN / NOTOT
      S = 0
      do I = MYPEE*GRANLR+1, (MYPEE+1)*GRANLR, 2
         S = S + 1.0/(2*I-1)
         S = S - 1.0/(2*I+1)
      enddo
      MPI_AllReduce(S,SG,1,MPI_REAL,MPI_SUM,
     *              MPI_COMM_WORLD,ierror)
      MPI_Finalize(ierror)
      end
```

Program 2.2 Code using MPI to implement the parallel algorithm in (1.5.2) and (1.5.1).

what is the greatest speedup possible according to Amdahl's Law? If the other 90% has been parallelized perfectly, what will the speedup be with nine (9) processors?

Exercise 2.2. Consider the parallel performance indicated in (2.1.1), and the corresponding speedup formula (2.2.3) as a function of N, P, and γ. Determine the maximum possible speedup (and the value of P where it occurs) for $N = 10^5$ and $\gamma = 9$.

Exercise 2.3. Consider the parallel performance indicated in (2.1.1), and the corresponding parallel efficiency formula (2.2.6) as a function of N, P, and γ. Determine the value of P where the parallel efficiency goes below 10% for $N = 10^5$ and $\gamma = 9$.

Exercise 2.4. Suppose that the cost of using one particular sequential processor to do a job is $C = \rho_s T$ for a computation of time T (i.e., ρ_s is the cost per unit time), whereas the cost C_P of using P processors from a parallel computer is $C_P = \rho_p T_P P$. Determine a general formula for the relationship between the costs of using the sequential processor and the parallel processor (cf. (2.2.10)).

Exercise 2.5. Consider the algorithm depicted in Figure 1.13. Suppose that the time required to evaluate the function `f(t,u)` is three times the cost of a standard floating point operation (assume that addition and multiplication take the same amount of time, and that `dt/2` in Figure 1.13 has been precomputed). Determine the sequential fraction of the code in Figure 1.13. Compute the corresponding speedup and parallel efficiency for $P = 2$.

Exercise 2.6. Consider the algorithm depicted in (1.5.1) for the summation problem. Suppose that $N = k(P-1)+1$ as in Section 1.5.1, but also that $k = P+1$, so that N is also divisible by P. One way to distribute the work is to let the first $P-1$ processors sum k elements, with the last processor doing nothing as discussed in Section 1.5.1, but show that we can also distribute $k-1$ elements to P processors in this case. Determine the total run time for (1.5.1) in both cases and determine their ratio. Determine the load balance for the first case and compare it with the ratio of run times of the two different cases. What is the load balance for the second case? What is the role of $t_{\min} = \min_i t_i$ in these two cases?

Exercise 2.7. Suppose the parallelization of the summation problem in (1.5.1) and (1.5.2) has an execution time proportional to $N/P+(\gamma+1)P$ (see (2.1.1)). Let $\epsilon > 0$ be arbitrary. Show that $P(N)$ can be chosen so that the corresponding scaled efficiency is greater than $1-\epsilon$. Give the best (largest) $P(N)$ that you can.

Exercise 2.8. Consider the parallelization of the summation problem in (1.5.1) and (1.5.2). Suppose (1.5.2) requires only an amount of time proportional to $\log_2 P$ instead of P, leading to an overall execution time proportional to $N/P + \gamma \log_2 P$. Determine the corresponding formulas for the speedup and efficiency in this case. Is this new algorithm scalable (Definition 2.4.3)? Is this new algorithm scalable with respect to memory (Definition 2.4.6)? Give a performance prediction graph of the model data analogous to Figure 2.5.

Exercise 2.9. Verify the bound on the speedup (2.3.18) under the assumptions (2.3.16) and (2.3.17).

Exercise 2.10. Verify the bound (2.4.11) on the sequential fraction f_N of a scalable algorithm.

Exercise 2.11. Gaussian elimination for a system of n equations in n unknowns requires $c_1 n^3$ time to complete sequentially and has $N = n^2$ data. Determine a formula involving $T_{1,N}$ and $T_{P,P\cdot N}$ to define a scaled efficiency similar to (2.4.19) for multigrid. (Hint: the formula corresponding to (2.4.16) is $T_{1,N} = cN^{3/2}$.)

Exercise 2.12. Give performance prediction graphs of the models presented in (2.6.8) and (2.6.17) with the parameters $\alpha = 4$, $\beta = 2$, $F = 10^8$, and $W = 10^6$, for $N = 10^4$ and $N = 10^6$.

Exercise 2.13. Implement the code in Section 2.8 and test it for for $N = 10^5$ and $N = 10^7$. Give performance prediction graphs of the results for up to sixteen processors.

Exercise 2.14. Consider the surface-to-volume ratio (Section 2.6.5) for the (uniform) slab and block decompositions of two-dimensional lattices $\mathcal{L}_N \times \mathcal{L}_N$, where $N = 2^K$ for K large. For the values of $P = p^2$ ($P = 1, 4, 9, 16, \ldots$) for which these two decompositions can be easily compared, is the surface-to-volume ratio more favorable for one decomposition or the other, or the same? Make the simplifying assumptions that the algorithm being employed is the same in both cases and does all computation before doing any communication and that the decompositions are uniform (i.e., each volume is the same, to balance the load). Explain why having the volumes the same is the optimal strategy to minimize execution time.

Exercise 2.15. Write a program to compute a summation via the parallel algorithm in (1.5.2) and (1.5.1) in **P**fortran (see Program 2.1). Test the program by computing π by the summation (1.3.1). Determine the performance on P processors as a function of N and P. Plot the performance, execution time, speedup, and efficiency as a function of P. For details, see Exercise 1.7.

Exercise 2.16. Write a program to compute a summation via the parallel algorithm in (1.5.2) and (1.5.1) using MPI (see Program 2.2). Test the program by computing π by the summation (1.3.1). Determine the performance on P processors as a function of N and P. Plot the performance, execution time, speedup, and efficiency as a function of P. For details, see Exercise 1.7.

Exercise 2.17. Write a program to compute primes using the sieve algorithm in Section 1.5.3 using MPI, **P**C, or **P**fortran. Do this for one value of k and print the primes $< k^2$ each processor finds as it finds them. Test it with $k = 31$.

Chapter Three
Computer Architecture

> What else do you expect from the country that invented rock and roll?—*Chevrolet Camero advertisement, May 1994*

In this chapter, we explore some basic concepts regarding computer architecture. The main objective is to provide a quantitative basis for modeling the performance of various (parallel) computers. Fortunately, there is a well-developed language for describing the various components, and relations between them, in a computer system. We will begin with a brief introduction to this language and illustrate it by using it to describe basic (sequential) computer concepts. Then we will use the notation to describe more advanced sequential computer concepts as well as parallel computers.

3.1 PMS NOTATION

We utilize the "PMS" notation [134] to describe key components of a computer system. The letters stand for

- Processor
  - a device that performs mathematical operations on data
- Memory
  - a device that stores data and can make it available to other devices
- Switch
  - a device that allows data to be transferred between other devices.

In a PMS diagram, the P's, M's, and S's are connected by "wires" indicated simply by lines. In the simplest case, there would be only one wire coming to a P or an M, with S's allowing multiple wires to be joined. The full model contains other letters (e.g., "K" for "control") but we will only use these three elements in our descriptions.

A PMS diagram allows essential features of a computer design to become apparent while masking inessential details. As such, it is a *model* of

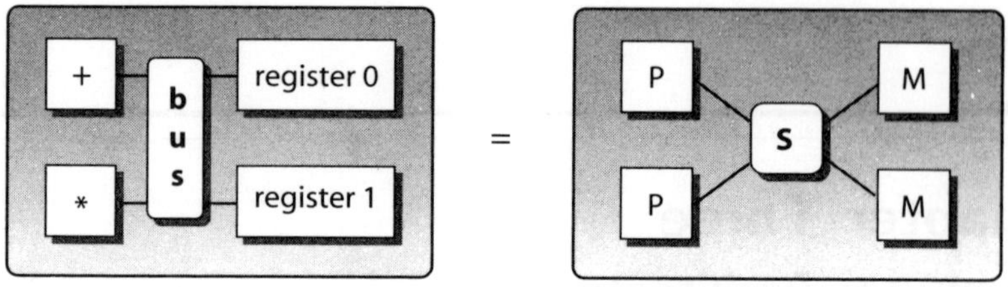

Figure 3.1 The PMS notation for a hypothetical cpu with only two registers and two functional units connected by a switch.

a computer, not a full representation. The PMS notation can be used at several levels in modeling a computer system. It can be used at a high level to describe the major components of the system, but it can also be used at a lower level to describe the functioning of different components.

We illustrate the use of PMS diagrams by introducing some basic concepts for sequential processor designs.

3.1.1 Diagram of a sequential CPU

The basic functioning of a **central processing unit** (cpu) can be explained using a PMS diagram. In Figure 3.1, we see that inside a prototypical cpu is some memory called "registers" and some devices (processors) that can perform arithmetic operations. These are connected by a switch, indicated only by the letter S on the right-hand side in Figure 3.1 and showing the logical connections. For example, it shows that the registers and memory are connected not directly but through the switch. Thus the speed of the switch is critical to the performance of the overall cpu, not just the speed of the individual components that perform arithmetic (often called **functional units**). This is of course only a toy cpu, since it has no possibility to do input or output. It is not even clear from this how a sequence of operations could be introduced, but our objective was not to give the PMS diagram for a complete cpu. Rather, the intent is to show how it might be done. Later, the cpu will appear just as a P or processor in higher level diagrams of large systems.

A typical implementation of a switch in a cpu is a **bus** as depicted in Figure 3.2. To explain how a bus works, we have introduced some cartoon elements to show how data move from point to point on the bus. A bus can be thought of as a transit device that moves around in a prescribed route, stopping at prescribed locations (a processor, memory, the floppy disk drive, and so forth) to take on passengers (data) or to deposit same.

Two of the main "sequential" computer designs can be easily be described and contrasted: the basic "von Neumann" architecture can be represented as shown in Figure 3.3; another architecture, the "Harvard" architecture is depicted in Figure 3.4. The latter is remarkably similar to Babbage's

Figure 3.2 Cartoon illustration of how a computer "bus" moves data from one component on the bus to another.

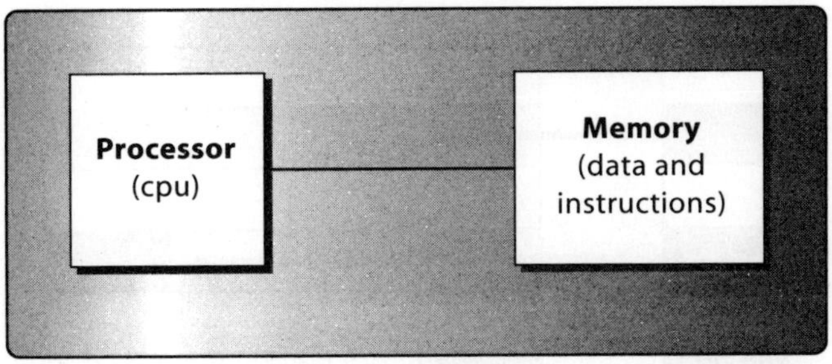

Figure 3.3 The PMS notation for the "von Neumann" architecture.

"analytical engine" [55]. It is also perhaps worth noting that von Neumann[1] advocated the architecture in Figure 3.3 while at Princeton.

What we see by contrasting the von Neumann and Harvard architectures is a major difference in design philosophy. In the Harvard architecture, there are two types of memory, one for data and one for instructions. In the von Neumann architecture, these are fused into one memory. Instructions form in some sense just a different kind of data. This architecture dominated computer design for some time; however it is quite common now to find segregated memory systems, especially at the level of the *cache* (see Section 3.1.2 and [138]).

These simple diagrams do not indicate a switch, but in practice the direct connections between memory and processor would in fact go through a switch, just as in the diagram of a simple cpu in Figure 3.1. Even a personal computer (PC) includes a bus which connects the processor, memory, and peripherals. The PMS diagram of a basic PC is left as Exercise 3.1.

3.1.2 Diagram of a cache system

Another feature now found in many PC's as well as more powerful computers is a **cache**. This is simply an additional memory (usually using faster

[1] John von Neumann (1903–1957) was one of the original six Professors of Mathematics at the Institute for Advanced Studies, appointed in 1933. His extensive and diverse contributions to computing and mathematics have been memorialized by awards that bear his name given by two different societies, SIAM and IEEE.

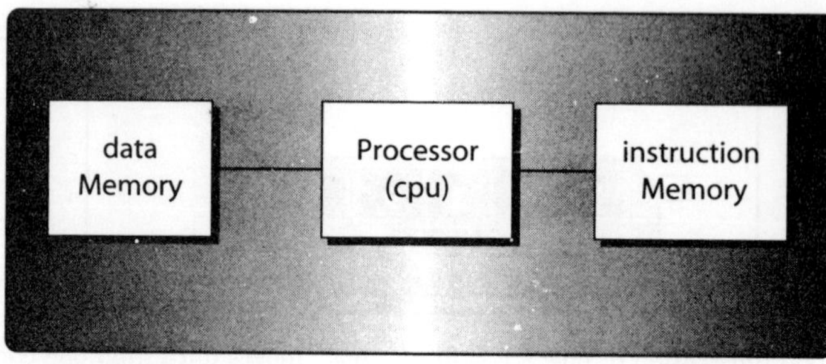

Figure 3.4 The PMS notation for the "Harvard" architecture.

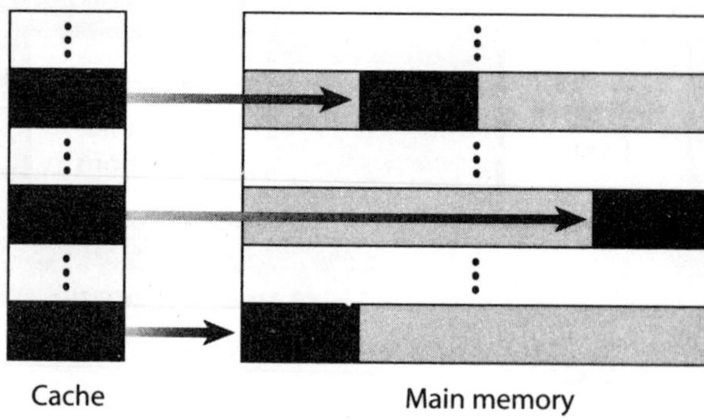

Figure 3.5 Depiction of a possible mapping between a cache and main memory. The lightly shaded areas in main memory depict regions that a given cache block could "mirror," whereas the dark areas depict the current locations being held by the cache. In some caches, temporary inconsistencies may be allowed between the cache value and the corresponding memory location.

but more expensive technology) that is designed to allow faster access by the processor [138]. A cache is not an independent memory space for the processor; rather, it is only a partial "mirror" of the main memory. There are numerous ways this is done in practice, but in general the idea is to have a many-to-one mapping of main memory to the cache, as shown in Figure 3.5. Many-to-many mappings are also used, but we avoid this complication in this discussion.

When a **memory reference** occurs (that is, when the processor attempts to read or write the contents of a memory location), a device called the "memory management unit" (MMU) decides whether this location is held in cache or not. If it is, this value is returned rather quickly for a read, but if not then the corresponding value in main memory is loaded into the appropriate cache location as well as being sent to the processor. When the latter occurs, it is called a **cache fault**. When a write to memory occurs, a similar determination is made as to whether this location is represented in the cache. If it is, then the value in cache is updated. Moreover, something must be done to deal with the fact that the cache value is more recent than the value in main memory. We do not intend to survey the different

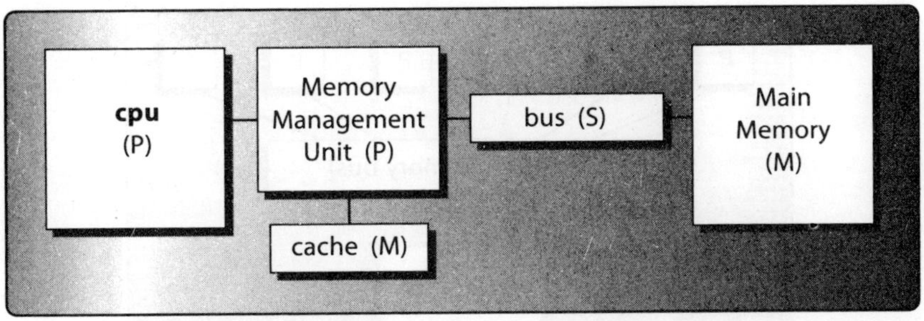

Figure 3.6 The PMS notation for a basic processor with a cache and memory management logic.

techniques for dealing with this here. Similarly, we do not consider in detail what happens on a write when the location is not in cache. But suffice it to say that one can assume that the location is brought into cache on a write and the new value is at least placed at that time in the corresponding cache location.

Strictly speaking, the MMU is another processor (a "P" in the notation) that handles memory requests from the main processor and has the cache as its own separate memory, as shown in Figure 3.6. A key point about a cache is that the contents are frequently destroyed by a memory reference. Since multiple locations in main memory map onto a given cache location, this is a necessary evil.

Another significant point is that caches are often loaded with chunks of contiguous data (an entire **cache line** or block) whenever there is a cache fault. This is done to increase performance, since it is often faster to load several contiguous memory locations at one time than to load them individually, due to the design of current memory chips and other factors. Loading several nearby memory locations at one time is motivated by the assumption of **locality of reference**, namely, that if one memory location is read now, then other nearby memory locations will likely be read soon. Thus, loading a cache line is presumed to be fetching useful data in advance.

3.2 SHARED MEMORY MULTIPROCESSOR

We now use the PMS notation to describe parallel computer architectures. One of the two principal types of parallel computer architectures is the **shared memory multiprocessor**, which was the first parallel system that was a major commercial success. Modern mainframe computers are of this type, and essentially all workstation vendors have offered shared memory multiprocessor versions of their advanced workstations. It is common to find commodity multiprocessor PC's in use, and the shared memory multiprocessor appears as single processing unit in other more complex systems. Thus it is a natural entry point for discussing parallel computer architectures.

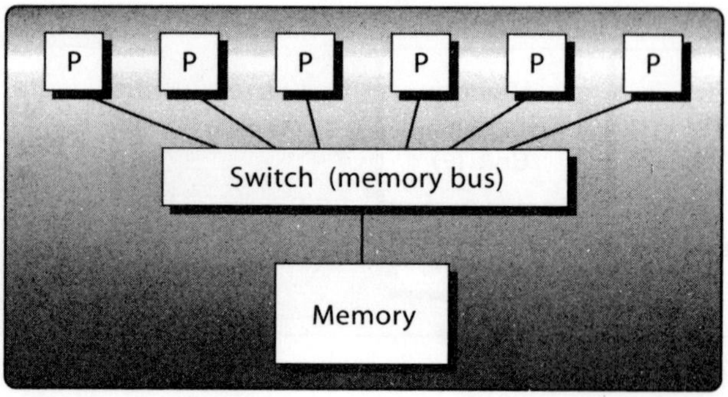

Figure 3.7 The PMS notation for the a basic shared memory multiprocessor architecture.

3.2.1 Basic shared memory architecture

The PMS diagram for a basic shared memory multiprocessor is depicted in Figure 3.7. Shown are n processors connected to a common memory via a bus. If we think of the memory as made up of separate units (say, one for each processor as would occur in the COMA architecture, Section 3.2.3), then the picture looks a bit like the social architecture of a **dance hall**, a common name for this computer architecture. We see from Figure 3.7 that the memory bus, which is the switch in this design, can be a **bottleneck** since all memory references must flow through it. The following definition makes this notion more precise.

Definition 3.2.1. We say there is **contention** for a switch (or more precisely for the link between the switch and memory) if there are two or more processors trying to read from or write to memory. More generally, we can define contention for any device as occurring when two or more agents attempt to use it simultaneously.

Performance estimates can be given based on this simple model once we know basic quantitative information about the performance of individual parts. Let us assume that each processor can do F binary operations operations per unit of time. Let us assume that generically these would require two loads from memory and a store to memory at the completion of the operation. If there is no memory at all in each processor, then every operation would presumably involve three memory references. If the bus can transfer a maximum of W words of data per unit of time, then the full potential of the shared memory architecture would be realized only if $W \geq 3PF$, where P is the number of processors. This means that there would be a limit in efficiency unless

$$P \leq \frac{W}{3F}. \tag{3.2.1}$$

We can quantify the effect of the bottleneck by estimating the time for execution of a hypothetical computation for large P. Once the bus is saturated, so that W words per time unit are being transmitted, then at most $W/3$ operations can be executed per time unit, no matter how many processors there are. So the parallel time T_P to do a total of N of such operations cannot be less than $3N/W$. We pause to record this observation as the following slightly more general result.

Theorem 3.2.2. Assume that an arithmetic computation requires ℓ memory references (loads from memory or stores to memory), and that the bus can transfer a maximum of W words of data per unit of time. Then the parallel time T_P to do a total of N such computations on a basic shared memory multiprocessor cannot be less than $\ell N/W$ times the time to do one of them, regardless of the number of processors P.

On a single processor, suppose we can do F binary operations per time unit (assume the bus is fast enough to allow this rate). So the sequential time to do a total of N of such operations would be $T_1 = N/F$. Therefore the speedup with P processors must be bounded by

$$S_P \le \frac{W}{3F} \tag{3.2.2}$$

no matter how large P becomes. In general, we have the following result.

Theorem 3.2.3. Assume that an arithmetic computation requires ℓ memory references (loads from memory or stores to memory), that F of them can be done per unit of time, and that the bus can transfer a maximum of W words of data per unit of time. Then the parallel speedup S_P to do a total of N such computations on a basic shared memory multiprocessor is limited by

$$S_P \le \frac{W}{\ell F} \tag{3.2.3}$$

regardless of the number of processors P.

The bounds given above can be stated in terms of the work/memory ratio ρ_{WM} defined in Definition 1.3.2 (see Exercise 3.4). Note that the ratio W/F measures the number of words transferred per binary operation.

3.2.2 Adding a local cache

Typical numbers for commodity microprocessors today would have F measured in billions of instructions per second, whereas a bus able to transmit billions of words of data per second is rare. So a typical value for W/F could be significantly less than one. (See Exercise 3.3 for an example.) Thus real systems often interpose a local memory (e.g., a cache, Section 3.1.2) as shown in Figure 3.8. This completely changes the performance assessment made previously, since it could be the case that substantial computations are done

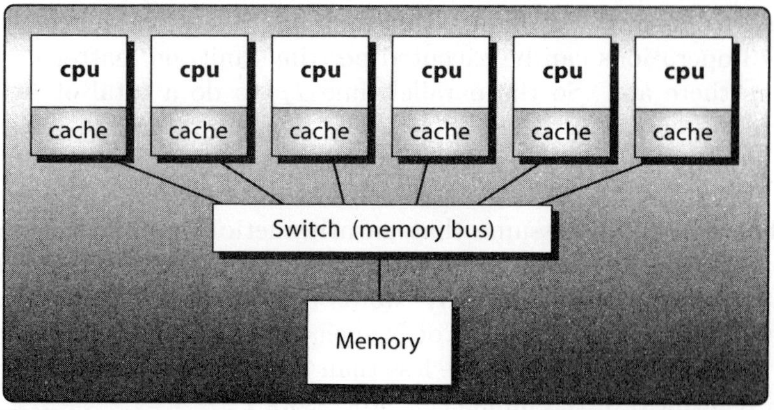

Figure 3.8 The PMS notation for the a shared memory multiprocessor with a local cache for each processor.

only on data residing completely in cache, with little traffic over the bus. As a general rule, algorithms with a larger ρ_{WM} will favor such machines.

Although this architecture is more difficult to model at an abstract level, we will see that assessments can be made for particular algorithms. Moreover, this architecture has proved to be a huge commercial success. Almost all of the workstation-class computers sold today have a parallel version with an architecture essentially of this type. Even PC's have evolved to incorporate such a multiprocessor design. These are often referred to as **symmetric multiprocessors** (SMP) reflecting the fact that all of the processors have the same role. This is meant to be in contrast to a "master-slave" relationship among processors. Symmetry is also a feature of many distributed memory parallel computers (see Section 3.3), so it is not a distinguishing feature. The SMP acronym of course also could stand for "shared memory multiprocessor" which would be a better characterization.

Another characteristic feature of the SMP architecture is uniformity (or symmetry) of memory access patterns. This does not mean that memory access *times* will be uniform, but the pathways to memory are all the same, independent of processor number or other identifier.

The introduction of a local cache at each processor increases the potential performance of the overall multiprocessor, but it also complicates the design substantially. The major problem is ensuring **cache coherence**, that is, the agreement of cache values which are mirroring the same values in shared memory. *Coherence* addresses the issue of *what* memory is updated, whereas *consistency* addresses *when* a memory location is updated. It is well beyond the scope of the book to explain the various techniques used to ensure the correctness of cache values, but suffice it to say that all of the designs are done to ensure that the multiple caches behave as if there were no cache at all, except, hopefully, that everything works faster in the typical case. The interested reader is referred to [53, 101].

The SGI Origin series, a type of distributed-shared memory computer, provide hardware support for coherent access of a global address space utilizing all memory. However, not all parallel computers implement coherent memories. The Cray T3 series of massively parallel computers include hardware support to view all of memory in a global address space (i.e., including memory at other processors), but there is no restriction on the access.

3.2.3 Cache-only architectures

If a little is good, more might be better. In fact, if there is enough cache, it may be possible to minimize the global memory. The **cache-only memory architecture** (**COMA**) was developed [90, 101, 135] to carry this concept to the extreme. As the name implies, all of the memory is cache in this system. Kendall Square Research, Inc. (KSR) termed its particular COMA design **Allcache** to emphasize this. (See Chapter 10 for more information on KSR.)

The COMA is a shared memory computer with typically a large local cache (the KSR-1 computer [90] had 32 megabytes of local cache for each processor). However, the main memory consists simply of the memory in the other processors' caches (see Figure 3.17). Any reference to data not in the local cache of a given processor results in a cache miss, together with a cache replacement in the local cache. As one might imagine, the difficult part of this architecture is to ensure cache coherence (page 78); the benefit is a shared memory computer with essentially the largest possible local cache.

3.3 DISTRIBUTED MEMORY MULTICOMPUTER

Bandwidth limitations render a single bus multiprocessor impractical for large P. Such machines have rarely exceeded thirty-odd processors. That, in addition to the limited bandwidth of a single memory module, or even a bank of interleaved memory, motivates the **distributed memory multicomputer**. These are called **massively parallel processor** (**MPP**) systems when P is sufficiently large, say a thousand or more. Since it is never clear what "massive" means, we can also take MPP to mean **moderately parallel processor**. Roughly speaking, the range $32 < P < 1000$ might characterize this range. Million-processor machines have been announced (such as the IBM Blue Gene machine [3]), so the letter M can be taken to mean all of these things.

We note the distinction between *multiprocessor* and *multicomputer* in the definitions of shared memory and distributed memory architectures, respectively. The latter is intended to evoke the impression of a collection of computers, that is, a collection of complete computer systems. The term multiprocessor highlights the fact that the processors in a shared memory multiprocessor are "multi" but the memory is not.

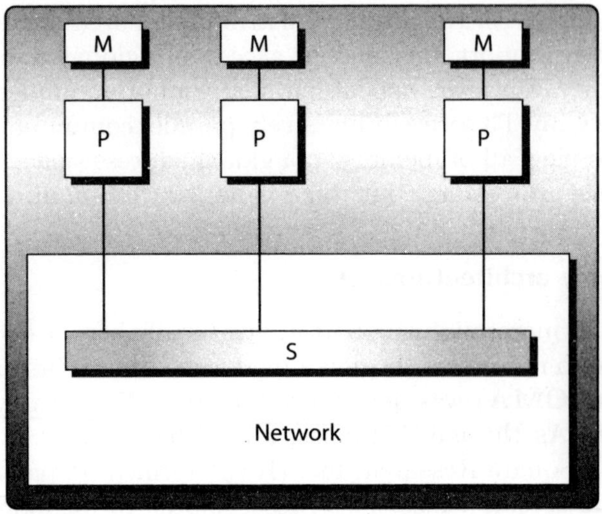

Figure 3.9 A distributed memory multicomputer with nodes (consisting of processor memory pairs) connected to the network without a separate communication system (store-and-forward approach).

The individual computers in a distributed memory multicomputer are often called **nodes**. The nodes in a distributed memory multicomputer are made of, at a minimum, a processor (cpu) and some memory. They may also have disks connected via SCSI buses, individual Ethernet connections, individual serial lines, graphics output devices, and so forth (anything a single computer might have).

3.3.1 The network

The nodes in a distributed memory multicomputer are connected via a **network** of wires which is easily described using graphs. A network can be based on any graph: the edges are the communications links and the vertices are the nodes. The physical connections may be made in a variety of ways, but we may refer to the processors being connected when we really mean that the nodes are connected (the connections may not go directly to the processor). That is, we may refer loosely to the nodes as a processor even though we do not mean that the memory in the node has disappeared. The general configuration is as in Figure 3.9 in which the network is left unspecified.

The network "topologies" which have been proposed or even implemented are as diverse as graph theory itself. One of the most basic is a ring (Figure 3.10), both because of the simplicity of implementation and because efficient algorithms exist for rings to do collective operations (see Chapter 6). In general, the network will cause **nonuniform memory access** (**NUMA**) patterns.

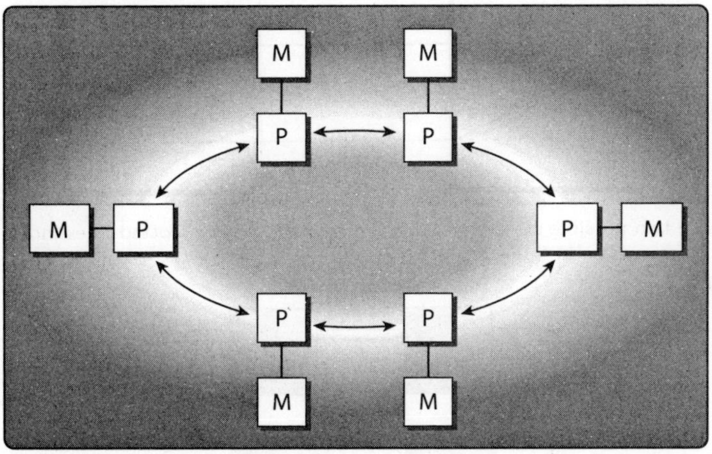

Figure 3.10 A distributed memory multicomputer with six processors connected by a network with a ring topology.

Two- and three-dimensional meshes are natural extensions of rings and are used in current commercial parallel systems. The two-dimensional mesh requires four connections per processor, while the three-dimensional mesh requires six connections per processor. The edges of meshes are often connected via wrap-around links at the boundaries of the mesh, forming the higher-dimensional analog of a ring. The nodes at the boundary of the mesh are connected so that the network can be viewed as a graph on a three-dimensional torus. The three-dimensional case is called a three-dimensional torus, by analogy.

Several commercial computers have been built with a mesh topology. The two-dimensional mesh appeared in an early system proposed by Ametek, and it was later adopted by Intel in the Delta prototype machine and then later in the commercial follow-on, the Paragon. These meshes incorporate a wrap-around and thus should be referred to as a torus mesh. The Cray T3D uses a three-dimensional mesh. It is also a (three-dimensional) torus, hence the "T" in the name T3D.

Many other graphs have been proposed, and some of them have found their way into MPP systems. These include trees, fat trees [100], and hypercubes (see Section 3.3.2). Such graphs (or networks) will also be discussed in Chapter 6 in the context of of algorithms for collective, or aggregate, operations.

Another network of current interest is based on using a **cross-bar switch**. The resulting graph can be thought of as the complete graph on P nodes, i.e., all of the nodes are directly connected. However, the connections in this case cannot be accurately represented by a static graph. More precisely, a cross-bar switch can be defined as a switch which can implement simultaneous (contention-free) communications between processors i

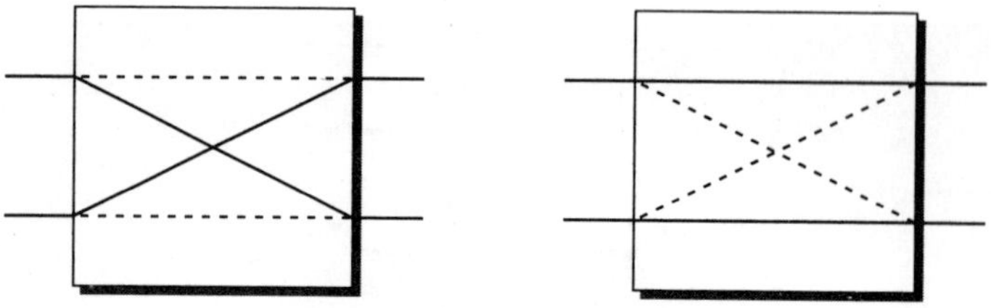

Figure 3.11 The two possible states for a 2×2 cross-bar switch. Dotted lines indicate paths not in use, and solid lines indicate connections being used.

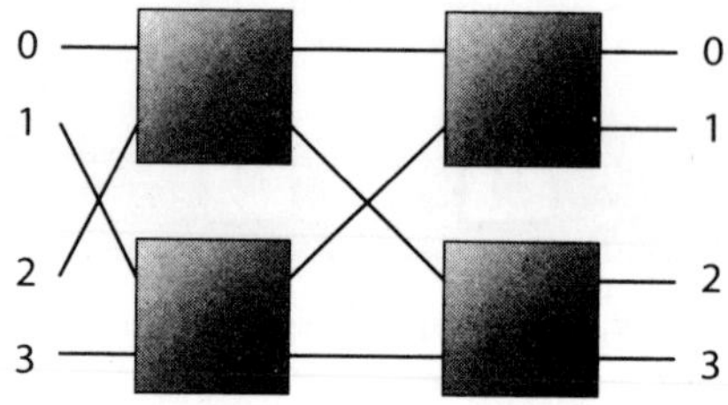

Figure 3.12 A 4×4 two-stage interconnect switch using four 2×2 cross-bar switches (the grey boxes) as basic building blocks.

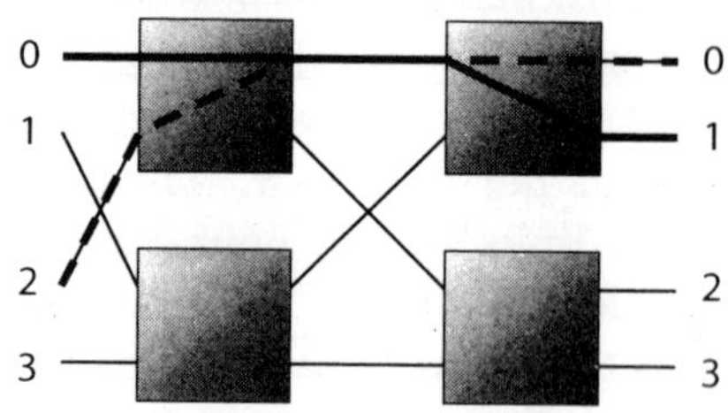

Figure 3.13 Contention in a 4×4 two-stage interconnect switch between messages from 2 to 0 (dark dashed line) and from 0 to 1 (dark solid line) which would have to use the same communication wire at the top (where the dark solid and dashed lines coincide).

and $\sigma(i)$ for all processor numbers i, where σ denotes an arbitrary **permutation**. (A permutation σ of $\{1, \ldots, P\}$ is a one-to-one mapping of this set onto itself. In particular, if $\sigma(i) = \sigma(j)$ then $i = j$.) Any of the P nodes can be effectively directly connected to any other node at any given time, but the set of simultaneous connections is at most P. For a 2×2 cross-bar switch, there are only two states for the switch, as indicated in Figure 3.11.

A similar type of switch effectively allows arbitrary connections via the use of a **multistage interconnect**. The basic building block of a multistage interconnect is a cross-bar switch, a 2×2 cross-bar switch in the simplest case. In a typical multistage interconnect, at most P paths can be in use and conflicts can reduce this number substantially. In particular, not all permutations communicate without contention simultaneously. Figure 3.12 shows a 4×4 multistage interconnect with two stages based on 2×2 cross-bar switches. Figure 3.13 indicates contention between two message routes that is typical in a 4×4 multistage interconnect.

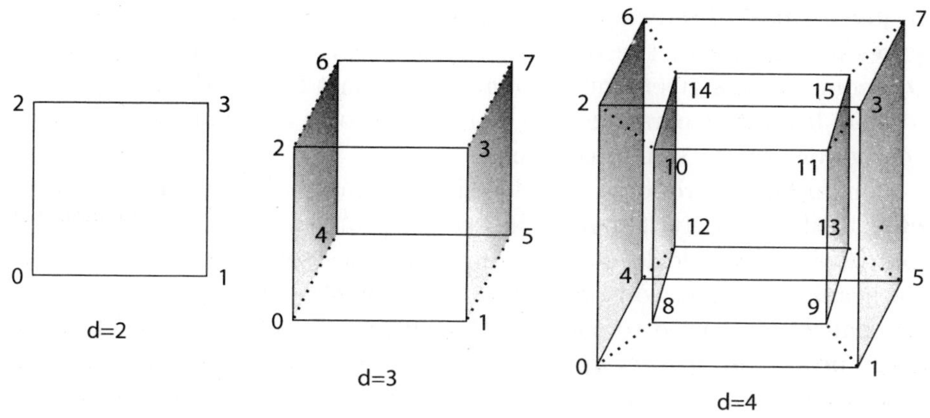

Figure 3.14 Hypercubes of dimension $d = 2, 3, 4$ constructed inductively. Dotted lines indicate links joining matching nodes from two identical copies of the lower-dimensional hypercube.

Cross-bar switches are utilized on both the IBM SP2 machine and the NEC research prototype Cenju-3 machine [93]. Their networks consists of a multistage interconnect switch using 4×4 cross-bar switches. Thus it takes only three stages to connect 64 processors, instead of the six stages that would be required using 2×2 cross-bar switches. Using larger cross-bar switches as the basic building blocks not only allows fewer stages, but it also decreases the number of communications with contention (see Exercise 3.15).

3.3.2 Hypercubes

A popular network among distributed memory machines for many years has been the **hypercube.**[2] Here the graph in question is made of the edges of a d-dimensional hypercube of unit size, with the processors naturally numbered according to the vertices of the hypercube. The vertices are at points $(i_1, \ldots, i_d)$, where each i_j takes the value zero or one. This can be viewed as the binary representation of an integer p in the range $0 \leq p \leq 2^d - 1$, that is, $p = \sum_{j=1}^{d} i_j 2^{j-1}$, whose binary representation is of course $i_d i_{d-1} \cdots i_2 i_1$. Thus a d-dimensional hypercube-connected distributed memory computer has 2^d processors. One can easily construct a hypercube as shown in Figure 3.14 by induction from the next lower dimension. Simply take two copies and connect the matching nodes.

In a hypercube, there are d connections per processor. This design allows the bandwidth to scale up as the size of the processor increases, but it also imposes some limitations. First, as processors are added the number of connections at each processor must increase. Practically this puts physical constraints on the size of the largest hypercube computer one can build

[2]nCUBE Corporation, founded in 1983, was one of the first commercial enterprises to make hypercube-connected parallel computers.

with given (fixed) hardware. Second, to increase the size of the computer requires a doubling of the budget. While many fund raisers will tell you that if someone has given you x dollars in the past then you can hope to get $2x$ dollars from that person in the future, this logic may not be appropriate for designing and/or selling computers.

One network proposed to solve the first problem is **cube-connected cycles**. Unfortunately it makes the second problem worse. The basic idea is to make building blocks out of a ring of d processors, each having at least three available connections with two used for the ring connections. The third connection is used to connect 2^d such rings in a hypercube. Thus one has $d2^d$ processors in this approach. The first Connection Machine [138] used a variant of this network in which the ring is replaced by a mesh.

Hypercubes have one feature not available with some other networks, in particular rings and meshes. Appropriate sub-cubes of a hypercube are themselves hypercubes of the appropriate dimension. Sub-meshes of a toroidal mesh can never retain the toroidal topology, so algorithms using this feature can have different behavior for sub-meshes.

Another useful feature of hypercubes is that many other networks can be embedded in them. By a **graph embedding** we mean a one-to-one mapping of the vertices of one graph into another (i.e., no vertex is mapped to another vertex more than once) in which each edge is mapped to an edge (hence neighboring vertices get mapped to neighboring vertices).

It is possible to embed a ring in a hypercube using what is known as a **Gray code**. Such codes are not unique, but are defined by the property of being **minimal switching codes** in their binary representation. That is, a Gray code is a sequence of integers $g_0, g_1, \ldots$ having the property that the binary representation of g_i and g_{i+1} differ by at most one bit for all i. They were created initially to minimize the energy expended in switching relays from one state to another.

The natural representation of a hypercube has a similar property. That is, if the number of a node has binary representation $i_d i_{d-1} \ldots i_2 i_1$, where the j-th coordinate of the vertex is i_j, then the neighbors of any node differ by at most one bit. In particular, they differ precisely in the coordinate direction corresponding to the edge between them. Therefore, any embedding of a ring *onto* a hypercube naturally defines a Gray code. Similarly, a Gray code provides an embedding of a ring of 2^d nodes into a d-dimensional hypercube.

Theorem 3.3.1. For any $d \geq 1$, there is a Gray code

$$0 = g_0, g_1, \ldots, g_{P-1} = 2^{d-1}, \tag{3.3.1}$$

where $P = 2^d$ and $0 \leq g_i < 2^d$ for all $i = 0, 1, \ldots, P-1$.

The proof is simple induction. The result is evident for $d = 1$ and the induction step uses the definition

$$g_{P-1+i} = g_{P-i} + 2^d. \tag{3.3.2}$$

The sequence defined by (3.3.2) is known as the **binary reflected Gray code** since it traverses the paired $(i-1)$-dimensional hypercubes in a reflected order while traversing dimension i (see Figure 3.14). It is easy to visualize the property of single-bit switching:

$$\begin{array}{l} 0\ldots0000,\ 0\ldots0001,\ 0\ldots0011,\ 0\ldots0010, \\ 0\ldots0110,\ 0\ldots0111,\ 0\ldots0101,\ 0\ldots0100,\ \ldots \end{array} \tag{3.3.3}$$

Toroidal meshes can be embedded into hypercubes by viewing them as Cartesian products of rings. That is, a $2^j \times 2^k$ mesh naturally embeds into a $(j+k)$-dimensional hypercube, using a pair of Gray codes, one for each coordinate. Similarly, a three-dimensional toroidal mesh of size $2^i \times 2^j \times 2^k$ naturally embeds into a $(i+j+k)$-dimensional hypercube.

3.3.3 Data exchange

The cost of exchanging data in a distributed memory multicomputer can be approximated by the model

$$\lambda + \mu * m, \tag{3.3.4}$$

where m is the number of words being sent, λ is the "latency" corresponding to the cost of sending a **null message**, i.e. a message of no length, and μ is the incremental time required to send an additional word in a message. This model does not account for contention in the network that can occur when simultaneous communications are attempted that involve intersecting links in the network.

The necessity of latency can be seen from the physical mail system, in which we use envelopes to surround messages. The envelope usually contains little important information and is discarded once the message arrives. The weight of the envelope can easily exceed the weight of the paper carrying the message.

There are at least two distinct types of message systems. In the "store and forward" approach, each message is stored temporarily by each processor in the path from the sender to the receiver (see Figure 3.9). This makes the message passing system simple to implement, as each processor deals with messages in a uniform way. However, it adds to the latency and makes λ and μ depend strongly on the length of the path. Although utilized in first-generation hypercube-connected multiprocessors [75], this approach has been abandoned in favor of the "direct-connect" scheme, which effectively employs special processors to handle messaging (Figure 3.15). This is similar to the routing of the long-distance phone system. Once a connection is established, whose route could vary from call to call even for the same pair of phone numbers, the particular routing is held fixed for the duration of the

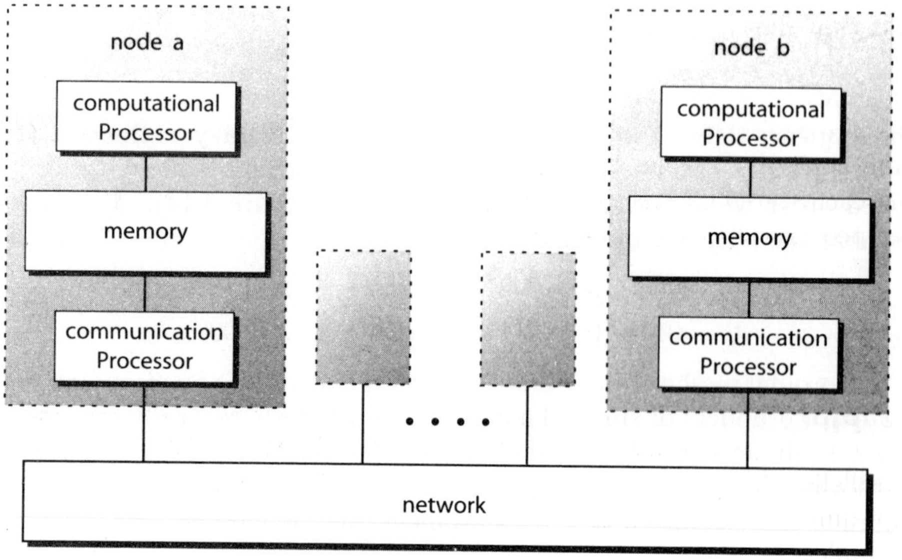

Figure 3.15 A distributed memory multicomputer with processors connected to the network with a separate communication system (direct-connect approach).

call. In the "direct-connect" message passing system, a similar connection is established, and then data move rapidly in an amount of time that is essentially independent of the distance between source and destination. To implement this requires a separate processor and buffer memory to handle the message system.

3.3.4 NOW what?

Since one basic motivation for distributed memory parallel computers came from the cost-effectiveness of workstation technology, it is natural to consider a **network of workstations (NOW)** as a parallel computer. The first such networks were connected by broadcast media such as Ethernet,[3] with relatively low bandwidth. However, the speed and complexity of the network have increased rapidly recently. For example, Myrinet is a commercial network and switch for connecting standard workstations at speeds that approach the fastest bus speeds of such machines. Architecturally, a NOW is not different from a distributed memory machine that comes all in one box, provided the network topology (or the switch) is the same.

[3]The word Ethernet derives from *luminiferous ether*, a hypothetical substance (proposed by Aristotle to exist throughout the universe) through which electromagnetic waves were to travel. The existence of this kind of ether was challenged in experiments at the end of the nineteenth century carried out by Albert Michelson (1852–1931) in the Ryerson Physical Laboratory which was constructed with channels running throughout the building to support such experiments [110]. The building is now home to the Computer Science Department at the University of Chicago, and these channels are used to run Ethernet cables.

3.3.5 Hybrid parallel architectures

It is natural when there are two competing designs to try to unify them to capture the best of both. The BBN Butterfly [95, 138] was such a combination of shared memory and distributed memory concepts. More recently, the cache-only memory architecture, or COMA (see Section 3.2.3) was developed [90, 101, 135] to provide a shared memory machine which could scale to very large numbers of processors (see Figure 3.17). How we characterize these machines is less important than our ability to predict their performance by using appropriate models.

3.4 PIPELINE AND VECTOR PROCESSORS

Parallelism in supercomputers is not a new concept. One can trace this concept quite far back, but we will consider in detail only two of the more recent examples of this. The technique of **pipelining** was used extensively in the Control Data Corporation (CDC) 6000-series (and later) machines, which provided at the time a distinctly higher level of floating point computation. The later Cray Research Corporation computers utilized vector processors to increase the level again.

A **pipelined processor** is one in which the functional units which execute basic (e.g., arithmetic) instructions are broken into smaller subatomic parts which can execute simultaneously [138]. It is analogous to an assembly line in a factory. The operands proceed down a "pipe" which has separate compartments. Once the first subtask is completed the information is transferred to the next compartment, and the first compartment is now free to be used for a different set of operands. As a result of this design, the speed of operation can be limited only by the time it takes for the longest subtask to complete. In principle, a new operation can be initiated with this frequency, even though previous ones are still in the "pipeline." On the other hand, this also means that it may take several cycles for an operation to complete. Later operations which depend on the result may have to be postponed (through the insertion of `no-ops`). Thus a greater potential speed is traded for an increased complexity. The type of dependence that can cause pipelined computations to perform less than optimally is quite similar to the type of dependence we saw in Chapter 1.

Example 3.4.1. A hypothetical example of a five-stage pipeline is indicated in Figure 3.16. Floating point numbers are stored in a normalized format, with a fractional part and an exponent. One step is required to convert these to a common base with the same exponent. Then the resulting numbers can be easily added in a subsequent stage. But the result then needs to be re-normalized, and some truncation or rounding done, before the result can be stored as a floating point number. The load and store operations appear as seperate steps for illustration, but they might be in-

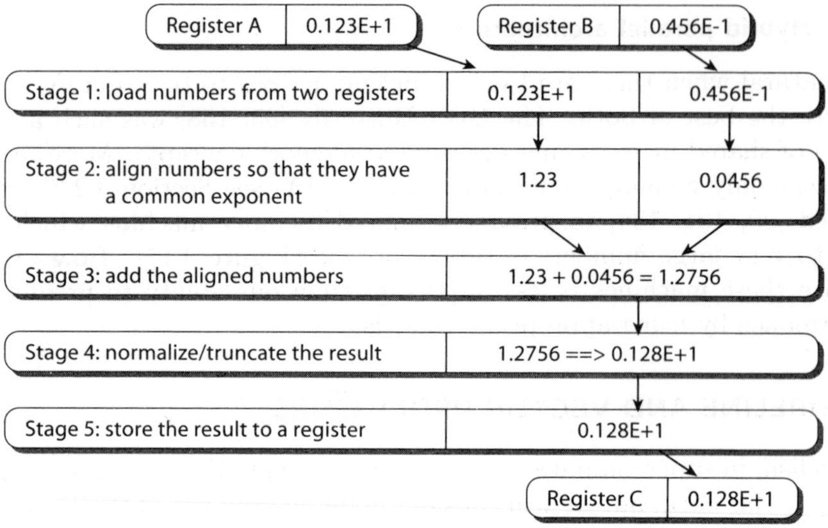

Figure 3.16 A simple model of a computational pipeline with five stages.

corporated into other steps in a real floating point addition unit. However, it might be possible to divide the internal operations of alignment, addition, and normalization into further substages to have an even deeper pipeline.

The original pipelined processors (in the CDC 6000 series computers) would initiate at most one floating point operation per cycle. However, if there are multiple functional (e.g., floating point) units (which the CDC 6000 series had), it is conceivable to have all of them initiating instructions at each cycle. Such a design has emerged with the new moniker **super-scalar**. Currently, the fastest microprocessors use this type of architecture.

The immediate successor to the original pipelined machines were **vector processors** which utilize pipelines as the main architecture but make additional restrictions on the sequencing of the functional units, based on the assumption that "vector" operations will be done. In a pipelined system, at each cycle a different floating point or logical operation could be initiated [138]. By restricting to more limited vector operations, greater performance was achieved, albeit on more restricted types of calculations.

In a super-scalar design, arbitrary sets of operations can be initiated at each clock cycle. This extra flexibility has made this design the architecture of choice for the current generation of computer chips being used in everything from high-end PC's to workstations to the individual processors in the nodes of MPP systems.

It is not our intention to include complete descriptions and analyses of pipelined, super-scalar, and vector processors, but rather to note that they can be viewed as parallel processors. A pipelined processor can be working on multiple operations in any one cycle. A super-scalar processor can fur-

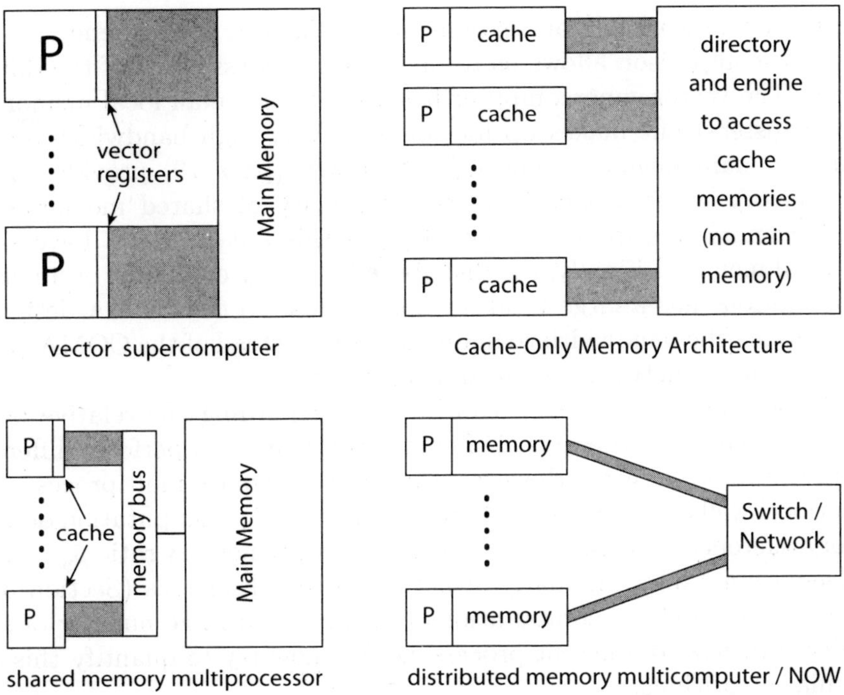

Figure 3.17 Comparison of various architectures. The shaded areas indicate the bandwidth to memory. Wider paths indicate faster speeds.

ther initiate work on multiple operations in any one cycle, while continuing to work on many more. A vector processor can appear to apply a single operation to multiple data values (e.g., add two vectors) simultaneously. The granularity of parallelism in these architectures is quite fine, often referred to as instruction-level parallelism. But the essential workings of these architectures can be analyzed in a way that is similar to the more coarse-grained type of parallelism we are considering at length here. Software support for linear-algebra kernels for vector, pipelined, and super-scalar architectures is provided by the **Basic Linear Algebra Subroutines** [97, 104]

3.5 COMPARISON OF PARALLEL ARCHITECTURES

Figure 3.17 depicts quantitative and qualitative aspects of four different commercial designs. The shaded areas depict the pathway from processors (including local memories, e.g., caches) to main memory. The width of the pathway is intended to indicate relative bandwidths in the various designs. It is roughly proportional to the logarithm of the bandwidth, but no attempt has been made to make this exact. The length of the pathway also indicates to some extent the latencies for these various designs. The vector supercomputer has a relatively low latency, where as the distributed memory computer or network of workstations has a relatively high latency.

This comparison allows us to make broad assessments of the different designs. The vector supercomputer has a relatively small local memory (its vector registers) but makes up for this in a very high bandwidth and low latency to main memory. The COMA design (page 79) provides a large local memory without sacrificing the simplicity of shared memory. The shared memory multiprocessor also retains this but does not have a very large local memory. Finally, the distributed memory computer or a network of workstations has a large local memory similar to the COMA design but cannot match the bandwidth to main memory. Instead of the COMA engine, one simply has a network to transmit messages.

No absolute comparisons can be made regarding the relative performance of the different designs. Different algorithms will perform differently on different architectures. However, the shared memory multiprocessor will not perform well on problems with limited amounts of computation done per memory reference, that is, ones for which the work/memory ratio ρ_{WM} is small (see Definition 1.3.2). Similarly, a network of workstations (Section 3.3.4) cannot perform well on computations that involve a large number of small memory transfers to different processors. We now try to quantify this with particular algorithms.

3.5.1 Summation

We can assess the behavior of different designs quantitatively by considering some basic algorithms. To begin with, consider the **norm** evaluation

$$\sum_{i=1}^{n} x_i^2 \tag{3.5.1}$$

which occurs frequently in scientific computation. This has the same form as the summation problem studied in Section 1.5.1. Here there are n memory references (to the array quantities x_i for $i = 1, \ldots, n$) and $2n$ floating point operations. This algorithm has therefore a constant work/memory ratio ρ_{WM} (defined in Definition 1.3.2); see Exercise 3.12.

If an individual processor can do F floating point operations per time unit and W words per time unit can be transmitted from memory, then the norm requires at least the maximum of n/W and $2n/F$ time units to be completed. Memory references and computation can frequently be interleaved, so the maximum of these could easily be the execution time. The ratio of the two times, communication time to computation time, is $F/2W$ for computing a norm. Note that the ratio F/W has units of *floating point operations* per *memory reference* and may be thought of as the number of floating point operations that can be done in the time it takes to store to, or retrieve from, memory one word of data. If W/F is too large, the computer will not be efficient at computing a norm because processors will be idle waiting for data. Similar linear algebraic calculations such as a dot product (Exercise 3.13) can be analyzed similarly.

In the basic shared memory computer with P processors each computing norms, the computation time stays the same, since each norm can be done independently of the others, but the communication time becomes P times larger, namely Pn/W, if all of the x_i's are different for each processor. This is because they all must pass through the same memory path, whose bandwidth is fixed. The ratio of communication time to computation time, is $PF/2W$ for computing P norms on a basic shared memory computer. Since this increases with P, this algorithm does not *scale* well for this architecture. The addition of a cache at each processor can help, but only if the x_i's are already in cache.

3.5.2 Matrix multiplication

Other algorithms have different relationships between data access patterns and computational requirements. Matrix multiplication is an example where the computation naturally exceeds the communication by an amount that grows with the size of the computation. The basic computation for $C = AB$ for square matrices $A = (a_{ij})$ and $B = (b_{ij})$ is

$$c_{ij} = \sum_{k=1}^{n} a_{ik} b_{kj} \tag{3.5.2}$$

and therefore involves $2n$ (or $2n-1$, see Exercise 3.14) floating point operations. Since this must be done n^2 times, the total computational work is, say, $2n^3$ floating point operations. On the other hand, only $3n^2$ memory references are involved, n^2 each to bring A and B from memory, respectively, and another n^2 to store the result, C. The work/memory ratio ρ_{WM} (Definition 1.3.2) for this algorithm grows linearly with matrix dimension n (see Exercise 1.3).

The ratio of communication time to computation time is $3F/2Wn$ for computing one matrix multiplication, and $3PF/2Wn$ for computing P matrix multiplications independently on a basic shared memory computer. In this case, we see that there is a chance for scalability: $P = \epsilon n$ processors could be efficiently computing matrix multiplications independently on a basic shared memory computer, as long as the ratio $\epsilon F/W$ is small enough.

These considerations are similar for distributed memory computers. Suppose we consider the case $P = 2$ and a norm calculation. Let us suppose we divide the work and the array x_i in half and give one-half to each processor. One processor will compute $s_1 = \sum_{i=1}^{n/2} x_i^2$ and the other will compute $s_2 = \sum_{i=n/2+1}^{n} x_i^2$. The two processors will then have to communicate in some way so that $\sum_{i=1}^{n} x_i^2 = s_1 + s_2$ can be determined. This latter step will take at least λ units of time, whereas the partial sums require only n/F units of time. The ratio of communication time to computation time

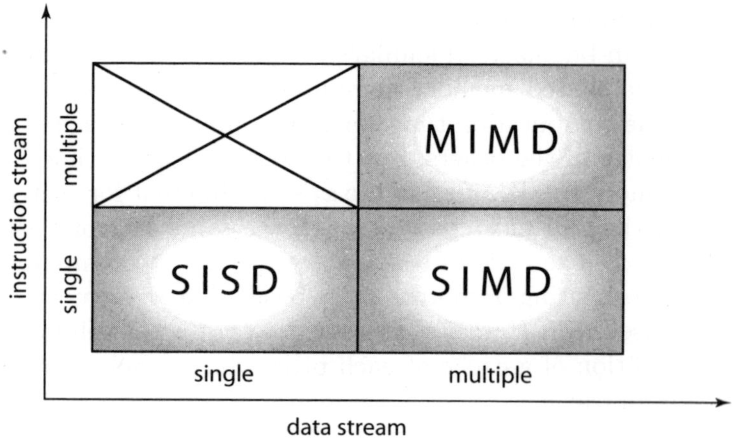

Figure 3.18 Flynn's taxonomy provides a computational model which differentiates computer architectures based on the flow of information.

is $\lambda F/n$. This is indeed favorable since it becomes small as n increases, but note also that it is inefficient if n is less than λF. The latter number (whose units are "floating point operations" without any time units) measures the number of floating point operations that can be done while waiting for a null message to complete. In some cases, this could be thousands of floating point operations.

3.6 TAXONOMIES

A **taxonomy** is a model based on a discrete set of characteristics, such as color, gender, or atomic weight. Since the model variables are discrete, a taxonomy puts items in neat "pigeonholes" even if they don't quite fit. Like any model, it provides a condensation of information that is often useful in comparing different things.

Perhaps the most famous taxonomy of parallel computing is due to Flynn (see Figure 3.18). It is based only on the logical flow of information (instructions and data) in a computer, with only two values for flow type: single and multiple. The **instruction stream** refers to the progression of instructions that are being carried out in a computer. If there are several being done at once, this instruction stream is called multiple. If there is a unique instruction at each instant, it is called single. Similarly, the **data stream** is the progression of data values being brought from memory into the cpu. If several are being brought in simultaneously, the data stream is multiple; otherwise it is said to be single. The conventional von Neumann or Harvard architecture computers (Section 3.1.1) both have a single instruction stream and a single data stream. Such a system is called **SISD** in Flynn's taxonomy. Note that this taxonomy does not distinguish the architectural differences between the von Neumann and Harvard architectures.

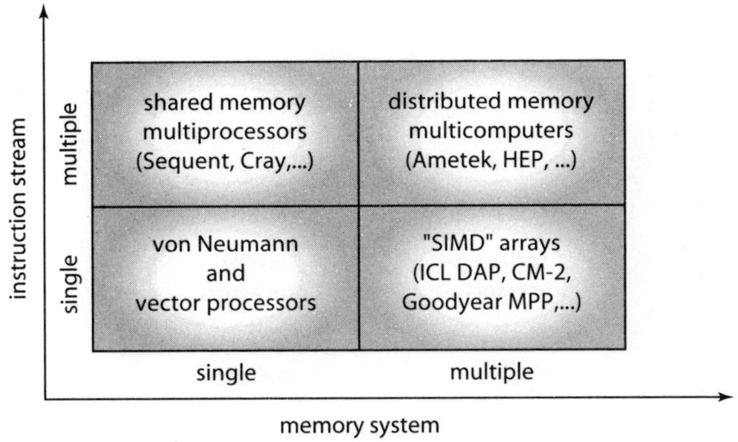

Figure 3.19 Another taxonomy provides a computational model which differentiates different computer based on the physical memory system used instead of the flow of data.

A parallel computer almost by definition should have multiple pieces of data being used at each instant. However, it is possible to have either a single or multiple instructions at any instant. The former is referred to as a single instruction stream, multiple data stream (**SIMD**) computer, while the latter is referred to as a multiple instruction stream, multiple data stream (**MIMD**) computer. Doing the same operation to different pieces of data can certainly lead to interesting results, but in Flynn's taxonomy the concept of an MISD computer is not allowed. It theoretically could exist, and it is curious to contemplate a computer performing multiple operations on a single data stream. However, there are no examples of such a computer that we are aware of, and the MISD computer apparently has not been missed so far.

Other taxonomies (models) could be constructed based on different variables, such as those depicted in Figure 3.19. Here we have substituted the data flow variable for a variable which differentiates computers based on the physical characteristics of the memory system. One can imagine this arising by rotating in three-dimensional space, keeping the vertical axis (instruction stream) fixed. With the data stream axis pointing out of the page, new information (the memory system) is exposed. Shared memory and distributed memory processors appear to move apart, whereas vector processors merge with sequential processors, leaving massively parallel SIMD computers in a separate box.

Another taxonomy can be constructed, as depicted in Figure 3.20, based on the physical characteristics of the processors and memory system. Thus there are at least four dimensions of data that could be of interest in describing different architectures.

All of these models have limitations in that they fail to capture all of the important characteristics of some machines. For example, some ma-

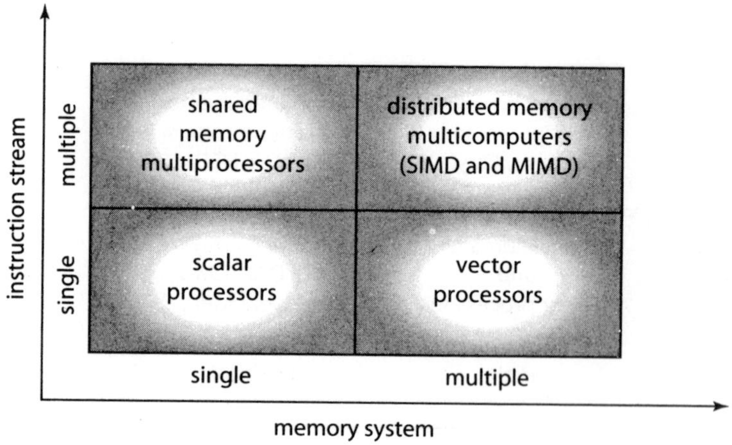

Figure 3.20 Another taxonomy provides a computational model which differentiates different computer based on both the physical memory system and the processor system used instead of the flow of information.

chines can be viewed as both shared and distributed memory machines (KSR, BBN Butterfly, DASH).

3.7 CURRENT TRENDS

It is dangerous in a book to discuss the future, and it dates a book to discuss current events. However, several trends can be seen at the moment that will continue to affect high-performance computing in the future. We will mention some of them here in the hope that the pointers to more up-to-date information may be useful.

On the chip level, one trend that is expected to continue is the exploitation of instruction-level parallelism. This is being done by having deeper pipelines (Example 3.4.1 and Figure 3.16) and more functional units executing simultaneously. Another trend is multiple levels of memory. This is happening even on the chip level. Due to the increasing density of transistors on chips, and the increasing speed at which they operate, it is beginning to take several cycles to access memory even on the cpu chip. Therefore, the number of levels of cache can be expected to grow rather than decline. Both of these trends have significant implications for the development of algorithms, whether sequential or parallel. These trends mean that cpu speed is increasing much faster than memory access speed (and I/O speed).

One significant success in parallel computing architectures is the pervasiveness of small shared memory processors today. These are now routinely constructed on a single board. Such systems are even available as commodity PC boards. As a result, parallel systems are being constructed which involve a network of such boards. Thus they represent a distributed memory architecture globally, with subsets of processors which have hardware support for shared memory. For example, it is possible to construct low cost networks of PC's which have this topology. This complicates the programming methodology substantially, since it mixes two major types of architecture in a nonhomogeneous way. However, one can expect this trend to continue, toward larger numbers of processors per board and with multiple processors per chip [3].

3.8 EXERCISES

Exercise 3.1. Draw and explain the PMS diagram of a personal computer with only a cpu, RAM, and floppy disk, connected via a bus.

Exercise 3.2. Multiple memory banks are a way to increase the transfer rate of memory systems. They are designed to ameliorate the fact that standard DRAM memory chips take multiple cycles to complete a memory reference. Give a PMS diagram of a single processor with a memory system comprised of multiple memory banks. (Hint: reverse the roles of P and M in the basic shared memory multiprocessor architecture in Figure 3.7.)

Exercise 3.3. The Silicon Graphics "Power Challenge" was a machine with 36 processors each having a peak floating point rating of 300 megaflops, but only 1.28 gigabytes per second bus bandwidth. Assuming 8 bytes per word, how many operations must be done by each processor (working within its local cache) per data transfer on the bus in order for the maximum rating of 10.8 gigaflops to be achieved? (Assume the bus use is distributed uniformly among the processors.)

Exercise 3.4. Derive the bounds presented in Section 3.2.1 in terms of the work/memory ratio ρ_{WM} defined in Definition 1.3.2. That is, prove a general result giving an upper bound on the number of processors that can efficiently use the bus in terms of ρ_{WM} for that algorithm. Then apply this result to the hypothetical binary operation considered in Section 3.2.1.

Exercise 3.5. Draw two-dimensional and three-dimensional versions of a "cube-connected cycles" graph. How many processors are required in these cases? How many processors are required in the four-dimensional case?

Exercise 3.6. Derive the formula for the number of processors P as a function of the dimension d for a d-dimensional "cube-connected cycles" graph.

Exercise 3.7. Derive the Gray code for the integers zero through fifteen defined by Lemma 3.3.1. (Hint: just use the formula (3.3.2).)

Exercise 3.8. Draw the Gray code for the integers zero through fifteen defined by Lemma 3.3.1 on a copy of Figure 3.14. (Hint: first do Exercise 3.7.)

Exercise 3.9. Prove that a ring of size $j \cdot k$ can be embedded in a $j \times k$ toroidal mesh. (Hint: define a numbering scheme for a mesh based on Cartesian coordinates.)

Exercise 3.10. The total memory bandwidth of a distributed memory machine depends on the ratio of the number of edges to the number of vertices in the graph representation of the network. For example, this ratio is one for a ring. Determine this ratio for a two-dimensional toroidal mesh and for a three-dimensional toroidal mesh. (Hint: consider the number of edges emanating from each vertex, and then account for redundancies.)

Exercise 3.11. Determine the ratio of the number of edges to the number of vertices in the graph representation of for a hypercube network of dimension d. (Hint: see Exercise 3.10.)

Exercise 3.12. Determine the work/memory ratio ρ_{WM} (defined in Definition 1.3.2) for the norm evaluation algorithm described in Section 3.5.1.

Exercise 3.13. The *dot product* of two vectors $(x_i : 1, \ldots, n)$ and $(y_i : 1, \ldots, n)$ is a simple variant of a norm evaluation: $\sum_{i=1}^{n} x_i y_i$. Determine the work/memory ratio ρ_{WM} (defined in Definition 1.3.2) for the evaluation of a dot product.

Exercise 3.14. Just how many arithmetic operations are required to compute each sum in (3.5.2)? Show that there are two different ways: one takes $2n$ FLOPs and the other one less. (Hint: the difference is in the initialization of the summation loop.)

Exercise 3.15. Show that there are fewer communication patterns with contention in a 4×4 cross-bar switch than in a 2-stage multistage interconnect switch using 2×2 cross-bar switches. (Hint: any permutation is available with the former, and only certain permutations can be done with the latter.)

Exercise 3.16. Determine the number of permutations in Figure 3.12 which result in contention (cf. Figure 3.13). Which ones are in contention? How many are contention-free?

Exercise 3.17. Prove that a $2^i \times 2^j$ mesh can be embedded in a d-dimensional hypercube if $i + j \leq d$.

Exercise 3.18. Prove that a $2^i \times 2^j \times 2^k$ mesh can be embedded in a d-dimensional hypercube if $i + j + k \leq d$.

Exercise 3.19. Prove that a complete binary tree of depth $d-1$ (which has $2^d - 1$ nodes) can **not** be embedded in a d-dimensional hypercube if $d \geq 3$. (Hint: consider the parity of the binary representation of the nodes of the hypercube. In going from one level to another in the tree, show that the parity must change. Count the number of nodes of one parity and prove that a hypercube must have the same number of even and odd parity nodes.)

Exercise 3.20. A cross-bar switch can be used as a basic building block for many networks. Show how one can implement a network similar to a four-dimensional cube-connected cycles network, with $P = 64$, using sixteen 4×4 cross-bar switches.

Exercise 3.21. An Ethernet "hub" is a device that merges network connections via its "ports." An 8-port hub can be used much like a 4×4 cross-bar switch as a basic building block for many networks. Show how one can implement a network similar to a four-dimensional cube-connected cycles network, with $P = 64$, using sixteen 8-port hubs.

Exercise 3.22. Suppose d is an integer, $d \geq 2$. What is the minimum number of 4×4 cross-bar switches required to connect $P = 2^d$ processors? Give the best bound you can, as a function of d for $2 \leq d \leq 8$. What about for general $d \geq 8$? (Hint: there must be at least one connection to the network from each processor; see Exercise 3.20.)

Chapter Four
Dependences

I wish I didn't know now what I didn't know then—
from the song "Against the Wind" by Bob Seger

Dependences between different program parts are the major obstacle to achieving high performance on modern computer architectures. There are different sources of dependences in computer programs. In "imperative" programming languages like Fortran and C, dependences are indicated by

- flow of data (through memory), hence *data dependences*, and
- flow of control (through the program), hence *control dependences.*

We will limit discussion to data dependences in this chapter. See [4] for more information on dependence analysis.

Our goal is to comprehend techniques for identifying dependences in codes and determining whether they can be easily remedied. Such techniques can guide restructuring of codes to remove dependences, or determine when such changes are not possible. This will include some basic techniques that are used automatically by compilers, so it will provide the basis for assessment of what is reasonable to expect from "automatic parallelizers" currently. Such techniques play a crucial role in the parallel programming language HPF (Chapter 9).

We will see that there are significant limitations to what can be surmised based on the text of the code alone. Dependences can be hidden in subroutine or function evaluations as a result of modification to variables as **side effects** of the subroutine or function call, that is, some modification of memory that occurs as a result of invoking the routine, independent of assignments based on the returned values. With **interprocedural analysis**, the techniques described in this chapter can be extended to cover such situations, by considering the larger context of the meaning of subprograms in a given code.

Knowledge of the underlying algorithms allows further opportunities for optimization that cannot currently be done by compilers. Some language constructs, such as `!HPF$Independent` in HPF (Chapter 9), permit the programmer to assert a lack of dependences in a section of code. Such assertions can be crucial to obtain efficiency, but they also can lead to errors if they are not valid. We will see here how one can prove that assertions like these are valid in some cases where it would be difficult for a compiler to do so.

4.1 DATA DEPENDENCES

Dependences force order among computations. Consider the two fragments of code shown in Program 4.1. The last two statements in the left column can be interchanged without changing the resulting values of `x` or `y`. However, the last two statements in the right column cannot be interchanged without changing the resulting value of `y`. In either case, the assignment to the variable `z` (the first line of code in both columns) must come first. The requirement to maintain execution order results since the variables used in one line *depend* on the assigned values in another line. Our purpose here is to formalize the definitions of such dependences.

```
z = 3.14159          z = 3.14159
x = z + 3            z = z + 3
y = z + 6            y = z + 6
```

Program 4.1 Two code fragments displaying dependences.

We will refer to the operations corresponding to a fragment of code such as in Program 4.1 as a *computation*. We will then define the dependence of one computation on another. We will be interested in *well-formed* code fragments, by which we mean that they are contiguous parts of the program text that can be parsed and executed on their own. The fragments above are both well-formed Fortran statements. Were each line followed by a semicolon, they would both be well-formed statements in C or C++. However, a fragment such as

```
x+y+z
```

would not be considered well-formed in any of these languages, since there is no assignment involved. Similarly, a code fragment which entered a subprogram, but did not return from it, would not be well-formed.

Definition 4.1.1. A **computation** is a set of operations carried out by a well-formed sequence of instructions in a code and executed by a machine.

We leave the notions of *operation, instructions, code,* and *machine* informal, although they can be made quite formal and precise. The reader can imagine the operations carried out as specified in a typical Fortran, C, or C++ code compiled for an actual computing machine like a favorite workstation. We assume that our "machine" has memory locations which store the variables described in the codes we will consider. Among other things, a computation C reads data from, and writes data to, memory locations.

Definition 4.1.2. The **read set** $\mathcal{R}(C)$ of a computation C is the set of memory locations from which data are read during this computation. The **write set** $\mathcal{W}(C)$ of a computation C is the set of memory locations to which data are written during this computation. The **access set** $\mathcal{A}(C)$ is defined to be $\mathcal{R}(C)\bigcup\mathcal{W}(C)$.

Sometimes the read set $\mathcal{R}(C)$ is called the `Use` or `In` set, and the write set $\mathcal{W}(C)$ is called the `Def` or `Out` set.

Definition 4.1.3. Suppose that C and D are computations in a code. There is a **(direct) data dependence** between C and D if one of the following **Bernstein's conditions** [21] hold:

$$\mathcal{W}(C)\bigcap\mathcal{R}(D) \neq \emptyset, \text{ or} \tag{4.1.1}$$

$$\mathcal{R}(C)\bigcap\mathcal{W}(D) \neq \emptyset, \text{ or} \tag{4.1.2}$$

$$\mathcal{W}(C)\bigcap\mathcal{W}(D) \neq \emptyset. \tag{4.1.3}$$

We are considering codes in languages which have a specified order of computation. In Fortran, C, or C++, the order of computation is specified (in part) by the order of the lines of code in various files, together with rules for special instructions such as branches, e.g., `goto` in Fortran. This order induces a partial order, which we denote by $\uparrow$, on the set of computations that a code can specify. In particular, we say that the computation C **occurs before** the computation D, and write $C\uparrow D$, if all of the lines of C precede all of the lines of D (with no overlap) in the standard order of execution.

Note that the order of C and D in Definition 4.1.3 does not affect whether we declare a data dependence between them. That is, if there is a data dependence for $C\uparrow D$, then there is also a dependence for $D\uparrow C$. However, the specific dependences (4.1.1) and (4.1.2) do depend on the order. If (4.1.1) holds for $C\uparrow D$, then (4.1.2) holds for $D\uparrow C$, and vice versa. The condition (4.1.3) is independent of order. It is important to distinguish between the different types of dependences in some cases, and so special names are given for the different subcases, as follows.

Suppose that the computation C occurs before the computation D. If (4.1.1) holds, then we say there is a **true dependence**, **flow dependence**, or **forward dependence** (all equivalent terminology) from C to D.

Example 4.1.4. Consider the fragment of code in the left-hand side of Program 4.1. Let C denote the second line and D denote the third line. Then $\mathcal{W}(C) = \{\mathtt{x}\}$ and $\mathcal{R}(D) = \{\mathtt{z}\}$. Thus $\mathcal{W}(C)\bigcap\mathcal{R}(D) = \emptyset$, and there is no forward dependence from C to D. But in the code fragment in the right column there is a forward dependence. Again, let C denote the second line and D denote the third line. Then $\mathcal{W}(C) = \{\mathtt{z}\}$ and $\mathcal{R}(D) = \{\mathtt{z}\}$. Thus $\mathcal{W}(C)\bigcap\mathcal{R}(D) = \{\mathtt{z}\}$ is not empty.

If (4.1.2) holds, then we say there is an **anti-dependence** or a **backward dependence** between C and D. There is no backward dependence in either column in Program 4.1 (Exercise 4.1). If (4.1.3) holds, then we say there is an **output dependence** between C and D. There is no output dependence in either column in Program 4.1 (Exercise 4.1).

A useful tool to simplify the examination of possible dependences is the following result.

Lemma 4.1.5. If a variable x does not appear in the write set of either computation C or D, then it cannot contribute to a dependence between C and D.

The proof of this result is immediate, since the hypothesis means that x cannot appear in any of the three intersections (4.1.1), (4.1.2), or (4.1.3) because all three involve at least one write set.

When there is any dependence between computations, we cannot execute them in parallel, since the result will depend on the exact order of computation. We will therefore be most interested in proving that there are *not* dependences between computations in many cases. However, proving that there *are* dependences between computations can be useful too: it can halt a futile effort to parallelize code before it starts.

Dependences between separated blocks of code may be difficult to trace, since what is written in the first block may be read in between and then used to modify something that will be read by the second block. Thus we can only be sure of knowing complete dependences in consecutive computations. Our main interest ultimately will be in loops where dependences in the entire loop body (between different iterations of the loop) are considered. The main reason for studying dependences is the following, which we state without proof.

Theorem 4.1.6. If two consecutive computations C and D have no data dependences, then they can be computed independently (in parallel) without changing the result of the overall computation.

There is one more bit of formalism we need to introduce to minimize possible confusion. In the fragments at the beginning of the section, all of the variables appearing there are initialized in that fragment itself. However, it would be awkward (and in fact not useful) to limit our definition of *computations* to such situations. In fact, dependences can be different depending on different *executions* of the code. For example, the dependences in the code Program 4.2 can only be determined once the data `i` and `j` are read in. Different executions of the code could clearly lead to different values for `i` and `j`. For this reason, we will add a subscript to a particular computation S to indicate the particular execution of it, e.g., S_e, where the subscript e denotes the particular execution.

```
read i,j
x(i)=y(j)
y(i)=x(j)
```

Program 4.2 Code with potential dependences based on I/O.

The index for the "execution" could also be thought of as the *environment* of S [116] [121]. From now on, we implicitly assume that there is a particular environment or execution associated with each computation that defines any uninitialized variables in the text defining that computation. However, the only significant use of this concept we will make is to indicate the execution of a particular text of code in different iterations of a loop. In this case, we will use the loop indices as subscript to indicate this concept.

4.2 LOOP-CARRIED DATA DEPENDENCES

One especially important form of parallelism is **loop-level parallelism**, in which each loop iteration (or group of iterations) is executed in parallel. The primary consideration for studying dependences here is that they inhibit parallelism. However, dependences in loops lead to inefficiencies even on current scalar processors, such as those with long pipelines (Section 3.4). Thus it is very important to know whether there are dependences between computations in different loop iterations. Such dependences are called *loop-carried data dependences.* We begin the discussion with an example to clarify the issues.

Consider the computation of a norm (3.5.1). As observed there, this has a form similar to the summation problem studied in Section 1.5.1. However, it has twice as much computation per memory reference, and it is quite a common subtask in scientific computation. In Fortran this might be written as shown in Program 4.3. In a pipelined processor, we see that it will be difficult to achieve very high performance because we need to complete one iteration of the loop before we can start the next: we must wait for the new value of sum to be computed. We will see that this is caused by a loop-carried data dependence.

```
sum = x(1)*x(1)
do  I = 2,N
   sum = sum + x(I)*x(I)
enddo
```

Program 4.3 Simple code for norm evaluation.

One way to break the dependence is to reorder the summation, e.g., by adding the odd- and even-subscripted array elements separately. This could be written in Fortran as shown in Program 4.4. This **loop splitting** [84] can dramatically change the performance; cf. Figure 4.1.

```
sum1 = x(1)*x(1)
sum2 = x(2)*x(2)
do i = 2, n/2
  sum1 = sum1 + x(2*i-1)*x(2*i-1)
  sum2 = sum2 + x(2*i)*x(2*i)
enddo
sum = sum1 + sum2
```

Program 4.4 Code with a split loop for norm evaluation.

The number of splittings in Program 4.4 is defined to be one, whereas Program 4.3 is the case of zero splittings. Any number of splittings k can be done via the code shown in Program 4.5. Figure 4.1 depicts the performance of Program 4.5 for the evaluation of a norm (3.5.1) for vectors of length $n = 16,000$ on popular workstations made by Sun, Digital, IBM, and H-P, as well as for the Cray C90 [84]. The key point is the distinct increase in performance of the workstations as the number of splittings is increased, at least to eight or so.

```
do j = 1,k
  summ(j) = x(j)*x(j)
enddo
do i = 2,N/k
  do j = 1,k
    summ(j) = summ(j) + x(k*(i-1)+j)*x(k*(i-1)+j)
  enddo
enddo
sum = 0.0
do j = 1,k
  sum = sum + summ(j)
enddo
```

Program 4.5 Code for norm evaluation with arbitrary number of loop splittings. Note that this is a cyclic decomposition of the summation problem.

It is worth noting that loop splitting is not a universal panacea, since it severely degrades the performance on the Cray C90 (and also on the H-P system for large numbers of splittings). However, we will see that this type of re-ordering of loops plays a significant role in achieving parallelism both at the instruction level as depicted in Figure 4.1 and at a more coarse-grained level. We can describe loop splitting in the terminology of parallelism as a cyclic (or modulo) decomposition of (3.5.1) (see Definition 1.5.5).

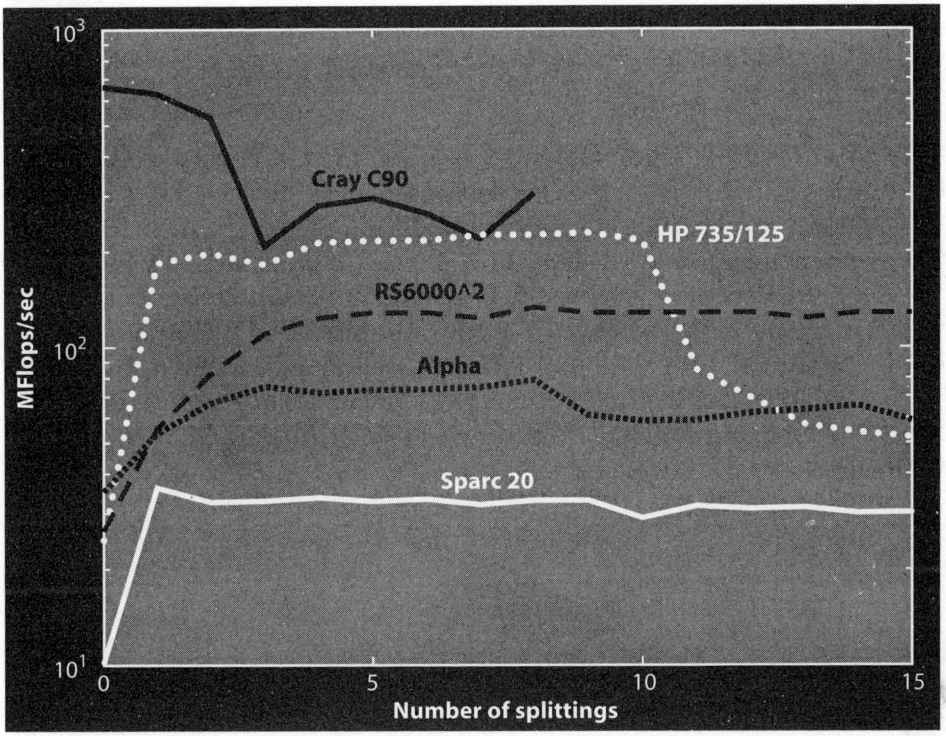

Figure 4.1 Performance of norm evaluation for vectors of length $n = 16,000$ on various computers as a function of the number of loop splittings.

4.2.1 Some definitions

We now turn to a detailed study of dependences in loops so that we can formalize what loop splitting does as well as prepare for the study of more complex loops. Loop-carried data dependences between program parts are an important special case of what we have considered so far in Definition 4.1.3. Let us now restrict attention to loops which are *definite* (having explicit loop bounds) and written in *normalized form.*

Definition 4.2.1. A loop is in **normalized form** if its index increases from zero to its limit by one.

Any loop can be converted into normalized form by an affine change of index variables. For example, the loop

```
do  I = 11,31,3
  A(I)=B(2*I)
enddo
```

is normalized by writing $\mathtt{I} = 11 + 3\mathtt{J}$, yielding the normalized loop

```
do  J = 0,6
  A(11+3*J)=B(2*(11+3*J))
enddo
```

That is, all "strides" are eliminated by the obvious change of loop index, and loops with decreasing index are reversed. See Exercise 4.2.

The set of loop indices for normalized *nested* loops are **multi-indices** – n-tuples of non-negative integers, $I := (i_1, i_2, \ldots, i_n)$, where n is the number of loops. In Program 4.5 the `DO 2` and `DO 3` loops are a nested pair of loops ($n = 2$). By convention, i_1 is the loop index for the outermost loop, and so on with i_n being the loop index for the innermost loop. We use the symbol $\vec{0}$ to denote the n-tuple consisting of n zeros. There is a natural total order "<" on multi-indices, *lexicographical order*, that is, the order used in dictionaries.

Definition 4.2.2. The **lexicographical order** for all n-tuples of integers is defined by

$$(i_1, i_2, \ldots, i_n) < (j_1, j_2, \ldots, j_n)$$

whenever $i_k < j_k$ for some $k \leq n$, with $i_\ell = j_\ell$ for all $\ell < k$ if $k > 1$.

We can then write $I \leq J$ if either $I < J$ or $I = J$, and similarly we write $J > I$ if $I < J$.

The standard order of evaluation of nested normalized loops in Fortran, C, C++, and other languages provides the same total order on the set of loop indices (i.e., on multi-indices) as the lexicographical order $<$ defined in Definition 4.2.2. Indeed, the loop execution for index I *comes before* the loop execution for index J if and only if $I < J$. See Exercise 4.24 for another possible loop ordering.

If S a computation that is enclosed in at least $n \geq 1$ definite loops with main index variables $l_1, l_2, \ldots, l_n$, then S_I denotes the execution of S for which

$$(l_1, l_2, \ldots, l_n) = (i_1, i_2, \ldots, i_n) =: I.$$

Definition 4.2.3. There is a **loop-carried data dependence** between parts S and T of a program if there are loop index vectors (i.e., multi-indices) I and J, with $I < J$, such that there is a data dependence between S_I and T_J.

A loop-carried dependence can be described more precisely as forward (4.1.1), backward (4.1.2), or output (4.1.3), depending on which of the Bernstein's conditions hold. Note that we do not assume that the parts S and T are disjoint or in any particular order. The ordering required following Definition 4.1.3 is enforced by the assumption $I < J$. In view of this, $S_I \uparrow T_J$ in Definition 4.2.3.

Example 4.2.4. Program 4.3 has a forward dependence in the line with Fortran identifier "1" since `sum` is in both the write set and the read set of this line. To complete the verification of the definition, it is sufficient to pick any `I` less than any `J` in the loop bounds. The split code in Program 4.5 still has loop-carried dependences in the "`DO 3 i`" loop, but there are no loop-carried dependences in the "`DO 2 j`" loop. The latter fact explains why modern super-scalar architectures (and their compilers) are able to achieve such high performance, by exploiting the parallelism there.

4.2.2 Distance vectors

We now introduce the notions of distance vectors and carriers for loop-carried dependences. The difference $J - I$ of two multi-indices I and J is defined to be the n-tuple whose k-th entry is $j_k - i_k$ for all $k = 1, \dots, n$. However, it is not in general a multi-index. Whenever $I < J$, the difference $H = J - I$ will have entries

$$h_\ell = 0 \quad \text{for all} \quad \ell < k \quad \text{for some} \quad k, \tag{4.2.1}$$

and the first nonzero element h_k will be positive. However, subsequent entries could have either sign. Symbolically, we can write the typical difference as

$$I < J \implies J - I = (0, \dots, 0, +, \pm, \dots, \pm). \tag{4.2.2}$$

Such n-tuples have a special role so we give them a special name.

Definition 4.2.5. An n-tuple I of integers is **lexicographically positive** if the first nonzero entry is positive, i.e., $i_k > 0$ and

$$i_\ell = 0 \quad \text{for all} \quad \ell < k,$$

if $k > 1$. The index k is called the **carrier index** of I.

An n-tuple I of integers is lexicographically positive if and only if $I > \vec{0}$, where $\vec{0}$ denotes the n-tuple consisting of n zeros (see Exercise 4.8).

Definition 4.2.6. Suppose $I := (i_1, i_2, \dots, i_n)$ and $J := (j_1, j_2, \dots, j_n)$ are multi-indices with $I < J$. If there is a dependence between $S_{(i_1, i_2, \dots, i_n)}$ and $T_{(j_1, j_2, \dots, j_n)}$, then

$$J - I := (j_1 - i_1, j_2 - i_2, \dots, j_n - i_n) \tag{4.2.3}$$

is called a **distance vector** for that dependence.

Example 4.2.7. In the loop in Program 4.3 for the norm evaluation (3.5.1) the set of distance vectors consists of all positive integers. In the nested loop pair in Program 4.5, the set of distance vectors consists of all multi-indices of the form (i, j), where i is a positive integer. In particular, there is no dependence distance vector of the form $(0, j)$ for any j.

As noted in (4.2.1) or (4.2.2), the difference of lexicographically ordered multi-indices is lexicographically positive. The position of the (positive) first nonzero, i.e., the carrier index, is important for distance vectors, so we give it a special name.

Definition 4.2.8. The loop corresponding to the first (from the left) nonzero element of a dependence distance vector is called the **carrier** of that dependence.

The carrier of a dependence corresponds to the carrier index (Definition 4.2.5) of the dependence distance vector.

Example 4.2.9. If we rewrite the nested loop pair in Program 4.5, as shown in Program 4.6, then the set of distance vectors consists of all multi-indices of the form $(0, j)$, where j is a positive integer. Thus the second index is the carrier of these dependences. We can execute each of the `i` loop instances independently (in parallel). Note that Program 4.6 represents a block decomposition of Program 4.3.

```
do i = 1, N/k
  summ(i) = x(k*(i-1)+1)*x(k*(i-1)+1)
  do j = 2,k
    summ(i) = summ(i) + x(k*(i-1)+j)*x(k*(i-1)+j)
  enddo
enddo
sum = 0.0
do j = 1,k
  sum = sum + summ(j)
enddo
```

Program 4.6 Code for norm evaluation with block decomposition.

Again, we state without proof the main theorem about dependence distance vectors.

Theorem 4.2.10. Let D denote the set of all dependence distance vectors for the entire loop body for a given loop nest L. Suppose that all $d \in D$ have carrier indices greater than j. Then the outermost j loops in L can be executed in parallel.

4.2.3 Privatization of variables

An important notion regarding loop-carried dependences is the privatization of variables. It may happen that some loop-carried dependences can be removed if some variables are declared **private** or **local** to the loop. This is equivalent in some sense to adding an extra array index to the variable to make it different for each iteration of the loop. The simple code in Program 4.7 gives an example of a dependence caused by the use of the temporary variable `temp`.

```
do i=1,100
  temp = i
  a(i) = 1.0/temp
enddo
```

Program 4.7 Simple code with a dependence caused by the use of a temporary variable.

There is a dependence between the second and third lines, and more importantly, a loop-carried dependence for the entire loop body. However, it is clear that these are not essential dependences. If we write this as in Program 4.8 there is no longer a dependence. The addition of a line of the form

```
C*private temp
```

to the code in Program 4.7 is intended to produce the equivalent result as if we had explicitly made `temp` a different variable for each index as is done in Program 4.8.

```
do i=1,100
  temp(i) = i
  a(i) = 1.0/temp(i)
enddo
```

Program 4.8 Simple code with a dependence caused by the use of a temporary variable.

Privatizing a variable in a loop is therefore a very simple concept. However, it is clear that not all variables can be made private without destroying the correctness of the loop. The following simple results regard correct privatization of variables.

If a variable `v` is not in the write set of any of the statements in a loop, then it cannot cause a loop-carried dependence due to Lemma 4.1.5. Thus when discussing privatization of variables, we are only concerned with ones which do appear in some write set (that is, in an assignment). If such a variable `v` is in the write set of some statement, but it is only in the read set in the first executed statement in the loop in which it occurs, then it cannot be safely privatized. This is because the first read in the `i`-th iteration will be referring to the value set in the (`i`−1)-st iteration. Note that the first statement in which a variable occurs may not be the first executed statement, since it may be preceded by a conditional branch.

We do not attempt here a statement of a complete theorem regarding the possibility of privatization, but suffice it to say that it is not possible to get necessary and sufficient conditions based on static code analysis alone. Consider the code shown in Program 4.9. Let us assume that `parity` is a user-supplied function that (correctly) computes whether a number is even or odd, and returns 0 or 1 accordingly. Then we can prove that `temp` will always be initialized before its use in the statement labeled "1" but a compiler would have to assume that there might be cases when `parity` is neither 0 nor 1, so that "1" becomes the first executed statement in which `temp` occurs.

```
do i = 1, 100
  if ( parity(i) .EQ. 1)
    temp = i
  endif
  if ( parity(i) .EQ. 0)
    temp = 0
  endif
  a(i) = temp
enddo
```

Program 4.9 Simple code with apparent difficulty for automatic privatization.

To indicate that a variable is to be considered private to each loop iteration, we will use a notation such as

```
C*private  temp
```

which can be read as a comment (in Fortran) if not being interpreted as a privatization command. Many compilers for shared memory multiprocessors recognize *directives* such as this. We take it to mean that `temp` is private regardless of correctness.

4.3 DEPENDENCE EXAMPLES

We now review some of the numerical examples introduced in Chapter 1 and consider dependences related to such codes. In this section, we consider mainly ones in which "privatization" (Section 4.2.3) of temporaries can remove dependences.

The symmetric, tridiagonal matrix for a two-point boundary-value problem on a general mesh (1.6.14) of mesh size h_i = `h(i)` is initialized by the code shown in Program 4.10. Here `diag` is an array holding the diagonal terms $a_{i,i}$ in (1.6.14), and `offdiag` is an array holding the off-diagonal terms $a_{i,i+1}$. We assume the array `h(i)` has been previously computed. Due to symmetry of the matrix only one off-diagonal array is necessary. Since each array element on the left-hand side of the assignments (denoted by the "=" sign) depends only on data previously computed, each element can be computed independently of all others (see Exercise 4.3).

```
do i=1,n
  diag(i) = (1.0/h(i)) + (1.0/h(i+1))
  offdiag(i) =    - (1.0/h(i+1))
enddo
```

Program 4.10 Simple code for initialization of finite difference matrix.

Modern compilers would tend to avoid duplication of the "divide" operation in this code. But suppose we used the "old ways" of writing Fortran? The simplest type of dependence arises due to the use of temporary variables. Suppose that the code were written as shown in Program 4.11. Now there is a loop-carried dependence (see Exercise 4.4) because the temporary variables `dxo` and `dxi` will be overwritten by different loop iterations. Declaring `dxo` and `dxi` to be `private` will remove the loop-carried dependences in the code while preserving its correctness (see Exercise 4.5).

```
do i = 1,n
  dxo=1.0/h(i)
  dxi=1.0/h(i+1)
  diag(i) = dxo + dxi
  offdiag(i) =    - dxi
enddo
```

Program 4.11 Complex code for initialization of finite difference matrix.

The loop-carried dependences are more complicated if instead we write the code as in Program 4.12. Here we compute `1.0/h(i)` only once and shift old values to `dxo`. Now, declaring `dxo` and `dxi` `private` will produce incorrect code, although it will remove the dependences.

```
dxi=1.0/h(1)
do I = 1,n
  dxo = dxi
  dxi=1.0/h(I+1)
  diag(I) = dxo + dxi
  offdiag(I) =    - dxi
enddo
```

Program 4.12 More complex code for initialization of finite difference matrix.

These dependences can be removed correctly by expanding the loop by hand. We subdivide the iteration into `P` parts and initialize each one separately as shown in Program 4.13. This code computes the same set of values, although it requires $P-1$ additional divisions. If `dxo` and `dxi` are declared `private` in the outer loop then there are no loop-carried dependences in the "`for IP`" loop, and the code is correct (see Exercise 4.7). Program 4.13 represents a block decomposition (see Definition 1.5.5) of Program 4.12. For $P = 1$, Program 4.13 and Program 4.12 are identical.

```
do IP=0,P-1
  dxi=1.0/h(IP*(n/P)+1)
  do i=IP*(n/P)+1, IP*(n/P) + n/P
    dxo = dxi
    dxi=1.0/h(i+1)
    diag(i) = dxo + dxi
    offdiag(i) =   - dxi
  enddo
enddo
```

Program 4.13 Explicitly parallel code for initialization of finite difference matrix.

4.4 TESTING FOR LOOP-CARRIED DEPENDENCES

Potential loop-carried dependences can be caused by the use of indirection arrays. Suppose `l1, l2, ..., ln` are loop indices, and we have a code containing the following statement:

```
(S)     A(F(l1,l2, ... ,ln)) = ... A(G(l1,l2, ... ,ln)) ...
```

There is a loop-carried dependence between `S` and itself if and only if

$$F(i_1, i_2, ..., i_n) = G(j_1, j_2, ..., j_n) \tag{4.4.1}$$

for some values of the loop indices $i_1, i_2, ..., i_n$ and $j_1, j_2, ..., j_n$ which are within loop bounds. Such equations are called **dependence equations**.

There are no dependences possible involving `(S)` if (4.4.1) can be shown to have no solutions for the given array expressions. Solutions to (4.4.1) must satisfy loop bounds and be integers. Such discrete equations with inequality-constraints can be solved a priori if F and G are simple enough. However, in general the solution set of such equations is difficult to analyze. Many dependence tests are based on the following theorem [61]:

Theorem 4.4.1. Let a, b, and n be integers. The linear (Diophantine) equation $ax+by = n$ has an integer solution pair x, y if and only if $\gcd(a, b)|n$, where $\gcd(a, b)$ denotes the greatest common divisor of a and b.

Consider the simple code shown in Program 4.14. Suppose, for example, that

$$F(l) = a_0 + a_1 l \text{ and } G(l) = b_0 + b_1 l. \tag{4.4.2}$$

Then there is a pair i, j satisfying $F(i) = G(j)$ if and only if

$$a_1 i - b_1 j = b_0 - a_0, \tag{4.4.3}$$

which is true by Theorem 4.4.1 if and only if

$$\gcd(a_1, b_1) | b_0 - a_0. \tag{4.4.4}$$

The **GCD test** determines that there is no dependence if $\gcd(a_1, b_1)$ does *not* divide $b_0 - a_0$. We summarize this as Theorem 4.4.2.

```
      do l = 1,n
(S)     A(F(l)) = somefun( A(G(l)) )
      enddo
```

Program 4.14 Simple code with potential loop-carried dependences.

Theorem 4.4.2. Suppose F and G are given by (4.4.2). Then the code (S) in Program 4.14 does not have a loop-carried dependence if $\gcd(a_1, b_1)$ does **not** divide $b_0 - a_0$.

As an example, consider the simple code in Program 4.15. We can never have

$$2k = 2\ell + 3$$

for any integers k and ℓ since this would imply that two divides three. Thus the GCD test allows us to conclude that there are no dependences possible in Program 4.15.

```
do l = 1,n
  A(2*l) = A(2*l+3) + 1
enddo
```

Program 4.15 Simple code with no dependences: GCD test.

The GCD test is for unconstrained equality, that is, it does not include the effects of loop bounds, and so it is only a sufficient test to preclude dependences, not a necessary condition. That is, we can have $\gcd(a_1, b_1) | b_0 - a_0$ but still have no solutions satisfying the loop bounds.

The GCD test can be overly pessimistic regarding potential dependencies since it ignores loop bounds. A diametrically opposed dependence test is based on checking *only* the loop bounds, ignoring whether or not the solutions are integers. If

$$F(x) - G(y) = 0 \tag{4.4.5}$$

has a solution for x and y in a suitable region R, then

$$\min_{x,y \in R} (F(x) - G(y)) \le 0 \le \max_{x,y \in R} (F(x) - G(y)). \tag{4.4.6}$$

If F and G are as in (4.4.2) and the region R is given by

$$1 \le x < n \qquad 1 < y \le n \qquad x < y, \tag{4.4.7}$$

we can compute the minimum and maximum (see Exercise 4.11)

$$\begin{aligned} \max_R(F(x) - G(y)) &= a_0 + a_1 - b_0 - 2b_1 + (n-2)(a_1^+ - b_1)^+, \\ \min_R(F(x) - G(y)) &= a_0 + a_1 - b_0 - 2b_1 + (n-2)(a_1^- - b_1)^-, \end{aligned} \tag{4.4.8}$$

where $t^+ = t$ if $t \geq 0$ and is zero otherwise and $t^- = t$ if $t \leq 0$ and is zero otherwise.

Combining (4.4.6) and (4.4.8) leads to **Banerjee's inequality**

$$(n-2)(a_1^- - b_1)^- \leq b_0 + 2b_1 - a_0 - a_1 \leq (n-2)(a_1^+ - b_1)^+. \tag{4.4.9}$$

Banerjee's dependence test determines whether (4.4.9) holds. If it does not, there can be no dependence. We summarize this as Theorem 4.4.3.

Theorem 4.4.3. The code (S) in Program 4.14, where F and G are given by (4.4.2), does not have a loop-carried dependence if (4.4.9) does not hold.

The general problem of determining whether (4.4.1) has integer solutions falls in the mathematical realm of number theory. See [144] for results that generalize both Theorem 4.4.2 and Theorem 4.4.3 by combining a characterization of solutions of (linear) Diophantine equations together with inequalities coming from loop bounds. Exercise 4.23 gives an example involving a quadratic Diophantine equation in which one can prove a dependence by exhibiting a simple solution to a well-known quadratic equation. The question of deriving an algorithm for solving nonlinear Diophantine equations is Hilbert's Tenth Problem[1] [107], which is in general unsolvable. See Exercise 4.23 for an exotic application of number theory to the study of dependences.

4.5 LOOP TRANSFORMATIONS

Recall (Definition 1.5.4) that the *iteration space* (or iteration *set*) of a group of nested loops is the set of index tuples which satisfy the loop bounds. Each point represents the actions of the body of the loop corresponding to the coordinates of the point. When the loops are normalized (Definition 4.2.1), as we now assume, the points of the iteration space are multi-indices. The iteration space of any double loop of the form in Program 4.16 is

$$\left\{(i,j) \in Z^2 \ : \ 1 \leq i \leq j \leq 10\right\}.$$

[1]At the beginning of the twentieth century, David Hilbert (1862–1943) proposed a list of 23 problems that continue to inspire mathematical research. Hilbert's work in integral equations stimulated the field of functional analysis, where the Hilbert space, an infinite-dimensional analog of Euclidean space, plays a central role.

```
do I = 1 , 10
  do J = I , 10
    ...
  enddo
enddo
```

Program 4.16 Some loop bounds to define an iteration space.

Points of iteration sets can serve as points of a **dependence graph** if we only care about the loop body as whole. That is, each point in the graph corresponds to the entire loop body for a given tuple of loop indices. This is a coarse view of possible dependences, but in many cases it is sufficient. We can indicate the loop-carried dependences by drawing any distance vectors (Definition 4.2.6) from each iteration multi-index to its corresponding iteration multi-index where the dependence occurs. For example, consider the code shown in Program 4.17. Figure 4.2 shows the corresponding dependence graph for the case $\mathtt{m} = \mathtt{n} = 10$, cf. Exercise 4.12. It is interesting to note that there are only two distance vectors in each case, $\binom{1}{0}$ and $\binom{0}{1}$. This is typical for loops with very regular structure. Unfortunately, each distance vector has a different carrier index, so no parallelism is available directly (see Theorem 4.5.3).

```
do i = 1, m
  do j = 1, n
    A(i, j) = A(i   , j-1) + 1
    B(i, j) = B(i-1, j   ) + 1
  enddo
enddo
```

Program 4.17 Simple code with loop-carried dependences.

Because the iteration space may be viewed as a vector space, we can apply linear transformations [139] to iteration sets. Applying the transformation $\left(\begin{smallmatrix}1 & 0\\ 1 & 1\end{smallmatrix}\right)$, to the loop indices above we get new indices $\mathtt{ii}$ and $\mathtt{jj}$ defined by

$$\begin{pmatrix}\mathtt{jj}\\ \mathtt{ii}\end{pmatrix} = \begin{pmatrix}1 & 0\\ 1 & 1\end{pmatrix}\begin{pmatrix}\mathtt{i}\\ \mathtt{j}\end{pmatrix} = \begin{pmatrix}\mathtt{i}\\ \mathtt{i}+\mathtt{j}\end{pmatrix}.$$

We can write the original loop indices in terms of the new ones:

$$\begin{pmatrix}\mathtt{i}\\ \mathtt{j}\end{pmatrix} = \begin{pmatrix}1 & 0\\ -1 & 1\end{pmatrix}\begin{pmatrix}\mathtt{jj}\\ \mathtt{ii}\end{pmatrix} = \begin{pmatrix}\mathtt{jj}\\ \mathtt{ii}-\mathtt{jj}\end{pmatrix}$$

using the matrix $\left(\begin{smallmatrix}1 & 0\\ -1 & 1\end{smallmatrix}\right)$ which is the inverse of $\left(\begin{smallmatrix}1 & 0\\ 1 & 1\end{smallmatrix}\right)$. In terms of the new loop indices, the loop becomes as shown in Program 4.18. The dependence graph for the transformed loop is depicted in Figure 4.3.

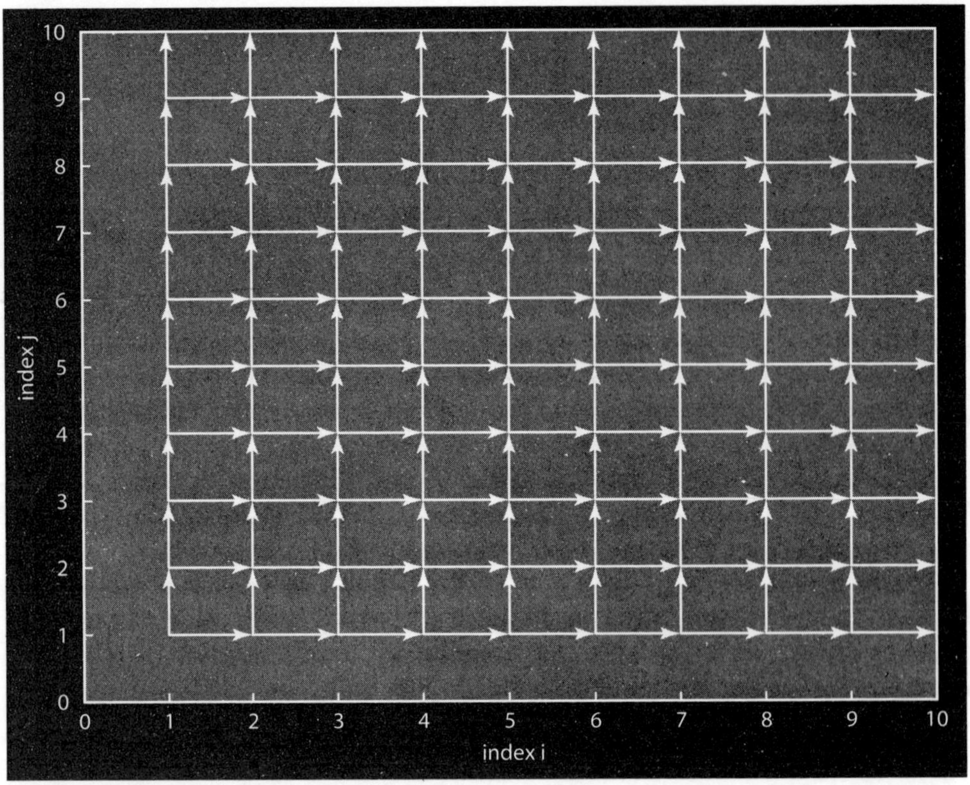

Figure 4.2 Dependence graph for the double loop in Program 4.17 with ten iterations in each loop.

```
do jj = 1,m
  do ii = 1 + jj, n + jj
    A(jj, ii-jj) = A(jj , ii-jj-1) + 1
    B(jj, ii-jj) = B(jj-1, ii-jj ) + 1
  enddo
enddo
```

Program 4.18 Transformed code with loop-carried dependences.

Observe that the *dependence distance vectors for the transformed loop are transformed by the matrix* $\left(\begin{smallmatrix}1 & 1\\ 1 & 0\end{smallmatrix}\right)$. That is, the dependence distance vectors in Figure 4.3 are

$$\begin{pmatrix}1\\1\end{pmatrix} = \begin{pmatrix}1 & 0\\1 & 1\end{pmatrix}\begin{pmatrix}1\\0\end{pmatrix} \quad \text{and} \quad \begin{pmatrix}0\\1\end{pmatrix} = \begin{pmatrix}1 & 0\\1 & 1\end{pmatrix}\begin{pmatrix}0\\1\end{pmatrix}, \tag{4.5.1}$$

where we have written the dependence distance vectors as column vectors. The first of these distance vectors is easier to identify if we write the second line of the loop as

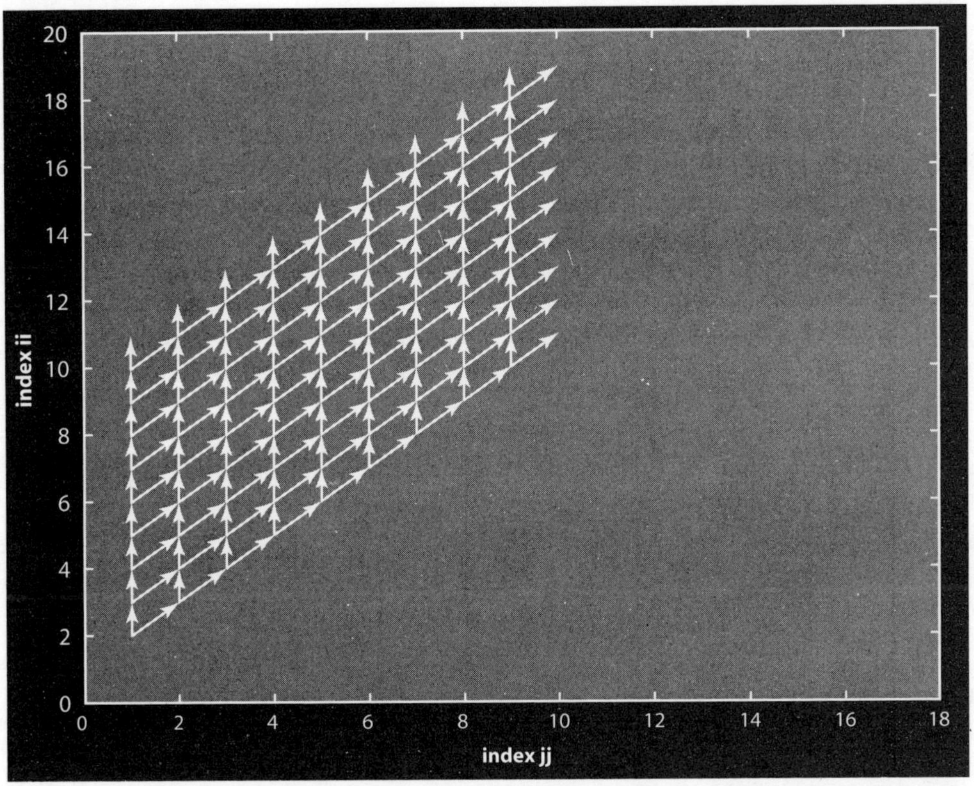

Figure 4.3 Dependence graph for a transformed double loop with ten iterations in each loop.

```
B( jj, ii-jj ) = B( jj-1, (ii-1) - (jj-1) ) + 1 .
```

If we want the transformed loop to be normalized, we must require loop transformation matrices to have inverses with integer entries. Otherwise the resulting loop indices would take on non-integer values (see Exercise 4.13). Such matrices are sometimes called **unimodular**. We recall the following result on unimodular matrices (see Exercise 4.20):

Theorem 4.5.1. An integer matrix T has an integer inverse if and only if $|\det(T)| = 1$.

It is simple to describe the unimodular matrices for standard loop transformations. For example, interchanging the loops in a nested pair of loops is achieved by multiplying by the matrix

$$\begin{pmatrix} 0 & 1 \\ 1 & 0 \end{pmatrix}. \tag{4.5.2}$$

Applying this matrix to the transformed loop above results in the same thing as doing one transformation using the **matrix product** of the two matrices:

$$\begin{pmatrix} 0 & 1 \\ 1 & 0 \end{pmatrix} \begin{pmatrix} 1 & 0 \\ 1 & 1 \end{pmatrix} = \begin{pmatrix} 1 & 1 \\ 1 & 0 \end{pmatrix}. \tag{4.5.3}$$

The resulting distance vectors would be $\binom{1}{1}$ and $\binom{1}{0}$, and the corresponding dependence graph would just be the reflection of Figure 4.3 with respect to the diagonal `ii=jj`. The resulting transformed code appears in Program 4.19. It now becomes apparent (Exercise 4.14) that the inner loop can be executed in parallel as it has no loop-carried dependences. This can also be determined from the reflected version of Figure 4.3. All distance vectors point away from the lines of constant `ii` (with `jj` varying). Moreover, the inner loop is not a carrier for either dependence distance vector (see Theorem 4.5.3).

```
do ii = 2 , m + n
  do jj = max{1, ii-n}, min{ii-1, m}
    A(jj, ii-jj) = A(jj , (ii-1)- jj ) + 1
    B(jj, ii-jj) = B(jj-1, (ii-1)-(jj-1)) + 1
  enddo
enddo
```

Program 4.19 Another transformation of the code in Program 4.17 which eliminates loop-carried dependences in the inner loop.

4.5.1 Distance vector calculus

We now give the general rules for transformation of loops and the corresponding transformation of dependence distance vectors. We have already seen many of these in the example above.

If a loop nest with set of dependence distance vectors D is transformed by a linear transformation T, then the set of dependence distance vectors for the transformed loop nest is

$$TD = \{Td \, : \, d \in D\}. \tag{4.5.4}$$

In our example in Program 4.17, we started with a loop having distances vectors

$$D = \left\{ \begin{pmatrix} 0 \\ 1 \end{pmatrix}, \begin{pmatrix} 1 \\ 0 \end{pmatrix} \right\}.$$

Using the final transformation (4.5.3) in the previous section, $T = \left(\begin{smallmatrix} 1 & 1 \\ 1 & 0 \end{smallmatrix}\right)$, (4.5.4) becomes

$$TD = \left\{ \begin{pmatrix} 1 \\ 1 \end{pmatrix}, \begin{pmatrix} 1 \\ 0 \end{pmatrix} \right\},$$

with code as shown in Program 4.19.

Repeating successive transformations T and then U can be achieved with one transformation using the matrix product UT, as seen in (4.5.3).

Fortunately, the product of unimodular matrices is again a unimodular matrix (see Exercise 4.21).

Not all unimodular transformations will lead to correct code. For example, $\begin{pmatrix} -1 & 0 \\ 0 & -1 \end{pmatrix}$ is unimodular (it is its own inverse as well) and corresponds to an index reversal in both loops. Reversing the order of the loop indices in Program 4.17 will not yield the same result. The following tells us when transformations are allowed. We omit its proof.

Theorem 4.5.2. A linear loop transformation produces correct code if and only if every dependence distance vector of the original (normalized) loop is transformed into an integer vector that is lexicographically positive (Definition 4.2.5).

A principal use of linear loop transformations is to yield parallel code. The following theorem (whose proof we also omit) tells us when this is possible.

Theorem 4.5.3. In a loop nest with index vector $I = (i_1, i_2, \cdots, i_n)$ and dependence distance vector set D, we can run the k-th loop, from the outermost (with index i_k), in parallel if and only if the k-th loop is not the carrier of any dependence.

The condition of Theorem 4.5.3 is satisfied if and only if for every $d \in D$, k is not the carrier index (see Definition 4.2.5) for d. This is true if, for all $d \in D$, either $d_j > 0$ for some $j < k$ or $d_k = 0$.

In our example, we had three sets of distance vectors:

$$D_1 = \left\{ \begin{pmatrix} 0 \\ 1 \end{pmatrix}, \begin{pmatrix} 1 \\ 0 \end{pmatrix} \right\}, \quad D_2 = \left\{ \begin{pmatrix} 1 \\ 1 \end{pmatrix}, \begin{pmatrix} 0 \\ 1 \end{pmatrix} \right\}, \quad D_3 = \left\{ \begin{pmatrix} 1 \\ 1 \end{pmatrix}, \begin{pmatrix} 1 \\ 0 \end{pmatrix} \right\}. \tag{4.5.5}$$

For the first two sets (D_1 and D_2), there are carriers in both loops. The carrier index for $\binom{1}{0}$ is one, the carrier index for $\binom{0}{1}$ is two, and the carrier index for $\binom{1}{1}$ is again one. In the last one (D_3), there is no carrier in the second (inner) loop; the carrier index for both distance vectors is one.

4.5.2 Transforming loop bounds

Computing transformed loop bounds is straightforward. It is similar to using Fubini's theorem in multiple integrals where you must interchange the order of variables and figure out how to write the domain in the new coordinates. There are two approaches, a geometric one and an algebraic one.

In the geometric approach, we use the fact that the loop transformation is based on a linear transformation on the iteration space. For example, such transformations map parallelograms to parallelograms. If our initial iteration set is a parallelogram, we can compute the image parallelogram by computing the vertices. (The linear transformation maps vertices to vertices and edges to edges.) In the example transformed by (4.5.3), the vertices are $(1,1)$, $(1,10)$, $(10,1)$, and $(10,10)$, and they are mapped to $(2,1)$, $(11,1)$, $(11,10)$, and $(20,10)$. From such a geometric picture, one can then deduce the corresponding loop limits. However, it is often useful to take advantage of at least some parts of the algebraic approach.

The algebraic approach works with the inequalities that are implicit in the loop bounds. One follows the recipe:

- find inequalities describing original iteration set,
- find maxima and minima of original indices,
- substitute new indices for the original ones to get new maxima, minima, and inequalities, and
- from outermost new index to innermost new index, calculate loop bounds.

Example 4.5.4. In the example transformed by (4.5.3), start with

$$1 \le i \le 10 \quad \text{and} \quad 1 \le j \le 10, \tag{4.5.6}$$

which means that

$$i_{\text{min}} = 1,\ i_{\text{max}} = 10,\ j_{\text{min}} = 1, \text{ and } j_{\text{max}} = 10.$$

Substituting the definition of `i` and `j` in terms of `ii` and `jj` in (4.5.6) yields

$$1 \le jj \le 10 \quad 1 \le ii - jj \le 10$$

and correspondingly

$$ii_{\text{min}} = 2, \quad ii_{\text{max}} = 20, \quad jj_{\text{min}} = 1, \quad \text{and} \quad jj_{\text{max}} = 10.$$

So ii must run from 2 to 20, and jj must be bounded below by both

$$ii - 10 \quad \text{and} \quad 1$$

and bounded above by both

$$ii - 1 \quad \text{and} \quad 10.$$

4.6 DEPENDENCE EXAMPLES CONTINUED

In a time-stepping scheme (e.g., (1.6.6) or (1.6.8)) for an ordinary differential equation (1.6.1), one cannot parallelize so easily. Consider the code in Program 4.20 for the explicit Euler method (1.6.8) in the special case that f is independent of t. We cannot parallelize Program 4.20 in a simple way because the computation of the `I`-th iteration requires the previous iteration. The simplest alternative is to use a different time-stepping scheme algorithm as described in Section 1.6.1 (see (1.6.9)). In the special case f

is linear and independent of t, we will see that there are alternative parallelizations in Section 12.2. Finally, in Section 14.5 we consider a way to apply the techniques of Section 12.2 to the case of nonlinear f.

```
oldsol = somethin
do i = 1,n
  soln(i) = oldsol + h(i)*f(oldsol)
  oldsol = soln(i)
enddo
```

Program 4.20 Simple code for an ordinary differential equation where `H(I)` is the mesh size of the `I`-th interval.

4.6.1 Jacobi and Gauss-Seidel iterations

The Jacobi iteration for solving the discretization (1.6.14) of the two-point boundary-value problem given in (1.6.11) and (1.6.12) can be described via the code in Program 4.21 using the arrays defined in Section 4.3. Neither loop in Program 4.21 has any loop-carried dependence; they are perfectly parallel. However, the Gauss-Seidel variant is

- much more efficient,
- easier to program,
- (but unfortunately) essentially sequential.

```
do i = 1,n
  snew(i)=(f(i)-soln(i+1)*offdiag(i)
*                 -soln(i-1)*offdiag(i-1))/diag(i)
enddo
do i = 1,n
  soln(i) = snew(i)
enddo
```

Program 4.21 Code for a single step of Jacobi iteration for a two-point boundary value problem for an ordinary differential equation.

The Gauss-Seidel iteration for solving the two-point boundary-value problem is coded as in Program 4.22 for the basic step. This has a loop-carried dependence, and thus the loop on `I` cannot be computed in parallel. Here, `SOLN(I-1)` is a value just computed, thus is a "new" value, whereas `SOLN(I+1)` is the value from the previous iteration, an "old" value. As in the ODE case, the computation of the `I`-th iteration requires all of the previous iterations.

```
      do i = 1,n
         soln(i)=(f(i)-soln(i+1)*offdiag(i)
     *                -soln(i-1)*offdiag(i-1))/diag(i)
      enddo
```

Program 4.22 Code for a single step of Gauss-Seidel iteration for a two-point boundary value problem for an ordinary differential equation.

4.6.2 Pipelining

Because the matrix is tightly banded, a "pipelining" approach can be used to achieve some parallelism for the Gauss-Seidel iteration. Suppose the overall iteration is Program 4.23. Note we have changed the iteration limits slightly as well as explicitly including the outer iteration. The distance vectors for Program 4.23 are $\binom{x}{-1}$ (for any positive integer x up to `somelimit`) and $\binom{0}{1}$. Since there is a carrier in both loops, we cannot execute it in parallel. However, the loop transformation `I = II - 2*KK`, where `II` and `KK` are the new loop variables (we take `KK=K`), changes the code in Program 4.23 to the form shown in Program 4.24. It is easy to see that there are no dependences in the inner loop in Program 4.24.

```
      do k = 0,somelimit
         do i = 0,n
          soln(i)=(F(i)-soln(i+1)*offdiag(i)
     *                -soln(i-1)*offdiag(i-1))/diag(i)
         enddo
      enddo
```

Program 4.23 Code for Gauss-Seidel iteration with outer iteration included.

The loop bounds also must be transformed. Using the geometric approach from Section 4.5.2, we see that the new iteration set is a parallelogram with vertices at `(0,0)`, `(0,N)`, `(somelimit,2*somelimit)` and `(somelimit,2*somelimit+N)`. Thus `KK` ranges from zero to `somelimit` and `II` ranges within the parallelogram. The limits on `II` can be determined from the algebraic approach in Section 4.5.2 as follows. Let i' denote the numerical values of `II`, let k' denote the numerical values of `KK`, and let s denote `somelimit`. We have

$$0 \leq i' - 2k' \leq N \quad \text{and} \quad 0 \leq k' \leq s.$$

These inequalities are equivalent to

$$i' \geq 2k' \geq i' - N \quad \text{and} \quad 0 \leq i' \leq N + 2s.$$

Combining we find

$$\max\{0, \tfrac{1}{2}(i' - N)\} \leq k' \leq \min\{s, \tfrac{1}{2}i'\}$$

which provides the limits for the KK loop in Program 4.24.

```
      do II = 0, 2*somelimit + N
        do KK = max(0,(II-N)/2), min(somelimit,II/2)
          soln(II-2*KK) = (F(II-2*KK)
     *           - soln(II-2*KK+1)*offdiag(II-2*KK)
     *           - soln(II-2*KK-1)*offdiag(II-2*KK-1)
     *                    )/diag(II-2*KK)
        enddo
      enddo
```

Program 4.24 Transformed code for Gauss-Seidel iteration with explicit outer iteration.

The transformed code in Program 4.24 is referred to as a *pipelined* version of Program 4.23 because we start the computation of later iterations of the original K index as soon as the information required is available. Otherwise said, computed information is "piped" into the later iterations as needed. There are at least two drawbacks to this approach. A small one is that the amount of parallelism (the size of the KK loop) is variable; however, this only leads to a load balancing problem (see Definition 1.5.7). A more serious problem is the fact that `somelimit` is often determined adaptively by some termination criterion on the vector SOLN. However, the limit can be determined adaptively at the expense of doing a few extra calculations (for incomplete iterations beyond the termination point).

4.7 EXERCISES

Exercise 4.1. Consider the two code fragments in Program 4.1:

```
        z = 3.14159          z = 3.14159
C:      x = z + 3            z = z + 3
D:      y = z + 6            y = z + 6
```

Prove that there is no backward dependence (4.1.2) and no output dependence (4.1.3) between C and D, where C denotes the second line and D the third, in the codes in either column. (Hint: see Example 4.1.4.)

Exercise 4.2. Consider the loops

```
      do 1 I=3,9,2
  1   A(I) = B(I+1)
      do 1 I=9,2,-1
  1   B(I) = C(I+1)
```

Write these in normalized form (see Definition 4.2.1).

Exercise 4.3. Prove that there are no loop-carried dependences in the code in Program 4.10.

Exercise 4.4. Determine all of the loop-carried dependences in the code in Program 4.11. Give all of the details of your derivation (i.e., give a complete proof).

Exercise 4.5. Suppose that `DXO` and `DXI` are declared local in the `for I` loop in Program 4.11. Prove there are no loop-carried dependences in the resulting code. (Hint: write the code with loop indices added to `DXO` and `DXI` and study the resulting dependences.)

Exercise 4.6. Prove that the codes in Program 4.12 and Program 4.13 produce exactly the same values for the arrays `DIAG` and `OFFDIAG`. (Hint: use induction to show both codes are equivalent to Program 4.10.)

Exercise 4.7. Suppose that `DXO` and `DXI` are declared local in the `for IP` loop in Program 4.13. Prove there are no loop-carried dependences in the resulting code, and that the code is correct. (Hint: write the code with loop indices added to `DXO` and `DXI` and study the resulting dependences.)

Exercise 4.8. Prove that an n-tuple I of integers is lexicographically positive if and only if $I > \vec{0}$, where $\vec{0}$ denotes the n-tuple consisting of n zeros.

Exercise 4.9. Prove that any n-tuple I of integers is either lexicographically positive, lexicographically negative (i.e., $I < \vec{0}$), or $\vec{0}$. Prove that $-I$ is lexicographically positive if I is lexicographically negative. (Hint: characterize what it means to be lexicographically negative; cf. Definition 4.2.5.)

Exercise 4.10. Use the GCD test Theorem 4.4.2 to determine whether there are any possible dependences in the code

```
do l = 1,n
  A(9*l) = A(6*l+2) + 1
enddo
```

Exercise 4.11. Prove the equalities in (4.4.8). (Hint: the max/min of a linear function occur at the vertices, which are $(1,2), (n-1,n), (1,n)$ in this case. The set of values to consider is thus $a_0 - b_0 + a_1 - 2b_1 + (n-2)\{0, a_1 - b_1, -b_1\}$. Prove that $\min\{0, a+b, b\} = (a^- + b)^-$ and $\max\{0, a+b, b\} = (a^+ + b)^+$.)

Exercise 4.12. Prove that Figure 4.2 correctly depicts the distance vectors for the indicated loops, namely, $\binom{1}{0}$ and $\binom{0}{1}$.

Exercise 4.13. Prove that a necessary condition for the transformed loop to be normalized is that the inverse matrix for the transformation have integer entries. (Hint: normalized loop indices get incremented by a unit vector at each step. The transforms of this vector correspond to a way of incrementing the transformed loop indices. Write the original loop indices in terms of the transformed loop indices times the inverse matrix. Since the transformed loop indices are normalized, show that a fractional inverse matrix would lead to fractional loop indices in the original variables.)

Exercise 4.14. Prove there are no loop-carried dependences in the inner loop in Program 4.19.

Exercise 4.15. Determine the distance vectors for Program 4.20.

Exercise 4.16. Find the read and write sets of $\mathtt{S}_{(i,j)}$ for each index pair (i, j) of the following loop nest:

```
          do i = 1 , m
            do j = 2 , n-2
S:             a(j+1) = .33 * (a(j) + a(j+1) + a(j+2))
            enddo
          enddo
```

Find the dependence distance vectors of the loop nest in `S` and draw its dependence graph. Which loop is the carrier of the dependences? Can either the `i` or the `j` loop be run in parallel? Why?

Exercise 4.17. Find a linear loop transformation for the loop in Exercise 4.16 so that the innermost loop of the transformed loop nest does not carry a dependence (and so can be run in parallel) and draw the dependence graph of the resulting loop nest.

Exercise 4.18. Apply the transformation you found in Exercise 4.17 to the loop nest in Exercise 4.16.

Exercise 4.19. Write a small program to verify that the transformed loop (with $m = 3, n = 20$ and $a(0 : 20) = 1$ initially) leaves the same result in a as the original loop nest in Exercise 4.16.

Exercise 4.20. Prove Theorem 4.5.1. (Hint: use a formula for the inverse matrix to show that the inverse of an integer matrix with determinant one must be integer. Then write $I = TT^{-1}$ and use the fact that $1 = \det T \det T^{-1}$. Note that the determinant of an integer matrix must be an integer.)

Exercise 4.21. Prove that the set of unimodular matrices is closed with respect to multiplication. (Hint: use the fact that $\det UT = \det U \det T$ and Exercise 4.20.)

Exercise 4.22. Prove there are loop-carried dependences in the code Program 4.25 for MAX sufficiently large.

```
      DO 1  I = 1, MAX
        DO 1  J = 1, MAX
          DO 1  K = 1, MAX
1              A(K**2)  = 1/(1 + A(I**2 + J**2) )
```

Program 4.25 A code with loop-carried dependences.

Exercise 4.23. Prove there are no loop carried dependences in the code Program 4.26 for any value of MAX. (Hint: use Fermat's Last Theorem.)

```
      DO 1  I = 1, MAX
        DO 1  J = 1, MAX
          DO 1  K = 1, MAX
            DO 1  N = 3, MAX
1              A(K**N)  = 1/(1 + A(I**N + J**N) )
```

Program 4.26 A code with no loop-carried dependences.

Exercise 4.24. There is another natural partial order "$\preceq$" on multi-indices, which is defined by $(i_1, i_2, \cdots, i_n) \preceq (j_1, j_2, \cdots, j_n)$ whenever $i_k \leq j_k$ for all $k = 1, \ldots, n$. Whenever $I \preceq J$, the difference $J - I$ is the multi-index whose k-th entry is $j_k - i_k$. Determine an execution order so that the loop execution for index I comes before the loop execution for index J if and only if $I \prec J$.

Exercise 4.25. In the case of n nested loops with exactly n distance vectors, one can try to determine a transformation to put all of the carriers in the first loop as follows. Let D be the matrix whose columns are the distance vectors. Suppose that D is unimodular. We seek a transformation T such that $U = TD$ consists of column vectors all of which have carrier index equal to one, so that the transformed loops have dependences carried only in the outermost loop. Determine a matrix U with this property, and prove that the resulting matrix T exists (give some formula). Give conditions under which this defines a unimodular matrix T. Give an example for $n = 2$.

Exercise 4.26. Extend the GCD and Banerjee dependence tests to nested loops. (Hint: the algebra must be extended to n dimensions.)

Chapter Five
Parallel Languages

In the beginning, there was the word—*from John 1.1*

We have seen that the aim of parallel computing is to partition a computation into subcomputations that can be executed in parallel. In the spirit of a subcomputation being a unit of work, we use the generic term *task* for them. Parallel programming languages provide some degree of expression of the coordination among tasks, which by our definition can execute in parallel. These languages come in various forms from the ordinary to elaborate. A plain parallel application without specialized support written in C using Unix system calls could begin with a single process that forks a number of copies of itself with different arguments passed to the forked instances. The forked processes could use standard system resources such as message queues, semaphores, sockets, or even files to share data and coordinate. Alternatively, a special compiler can attempt to transform a sequential program into a parallel program. Commonly, however, a parallel program is written in a high-level language with parallel constructs that produce code that works together with parallel runtime libraries. The added parallel constructs can be part of the language, executable compiler directives, non-executable directives, or library calls such as those to a message passing system.

With the wide variety of parallel programming languages, the notion of a task takes many forms. What it has in common among parallel languages is that by definition a task can be executed in parallel. One difference is what can be executed in parallel. A task can be as simple as a single instruction scheduled to execute on one of many processors of an SIMD architecture, or as complex as a Unix process executing a complex mathematical model time-sharing 32 processors of a shared memory computer. An abstract object in an object-oriented parallel programming language can comprise a task. In this case the implementation of the task may not be known by the programmer. What should be known by programmers (or they will likely encounter problems) is the behavior of the task. In object-oriented parallel program models, an object can execute in parallel with other objects, it can have state by way of private variables, and it may share other variables. The object-oriented parallel object may be implemented as a single process, as a single thread, or as a function call within a thread where the thread is shared by many objects. A central point is that a parallel language provides constructs to coordinate tasks that can run in parallel, and these tasks may exchange values and share memory. In this book we often refer to tasks as processes or threads since that is a common way to implement them, but it is not the only way. We may even refer to a task as a processor, slipping into language that emerged around early parallel computing systems where a task was often a single process running on a dedicated processor. In all cases the term should be clear from the context. This variation in terminology exemplifies the variety of models that have been developed.

High-level languages like Fortran and C allow programs to be ported to different computers and operating systems by compiling into a machine's native assembly language. High-level languages also provide expressibility, resulting in programs that are easier to write and manage. Similarly, parallel programming languages have been developed with constructs to express data distribution, data ownership, data communication, and so on. The mix of the constructs depends on the language. Programs written in sequential languages can be transformed by automatic parallelizing compilers [144] (also see Section 5.7). However, typical sequential code often obscures opportunities for parallelism, so some sort of code rewriting at the application level is often essential.

In this chapter we will look at fundamental issues that a programmer with a parallel language commonly addresses to produce efficient programs. Such issues are the same as those an automatic parallelizing compiler must confront, but a parallel language lets the programmer assert solutions to hard compiler problems that would not be computationally tractable (such as the number-theoretic questions arising in dependence analysis described at the end of Section 4.4).

Here we present a general framework to understand the characteristics that such languages must possess. There is no standard notation like the PMS diagram (Chapter 3) for describing languages at a high level of abstraction. We attempt to construct a rough taxonomy, but it is much less precise than for architectures. We will describe several critical issues regarding languages. Of these, the memory model will be seen to be of central importance. We will then describe how various parallel programming languages deal with these. Our objective is to survey the main ideas (but not to provide full details) for a selection of contemporary languages.

Behind any programming language is a programming model which the programming must work within. All programming models discussed here will be SPMD (single program, multiple data) (see Definition 1.5.10). That is, one program is written with multiple instances of it executed. This greatly simplifies the programming since one works with a single sequential-looking source code. We saw in the prime number sieve example (Section 1.5.3) that the SPMD model can be used to do significant computations. This model will be discussed further in Section 5.5 on page 145.

Languages have both syntax (how you say something) and semantics (what you actually mean). Syntax is the form, and semantics the content, of the expression of programs in a language. It is difficult to separate form and content in any type of human expression [132], and it is no different in programming. We will begin by talking about semantics abstractly, but ultimately one must deal with the syntax to appreciate the full impact of a programming paradigm.

5.1 CRITICAL FACTORS

Several actions must occur in parallel programs, independently of how they are expressed. These include

- data distribution among processes,
- work distribution among processes,
- data exchange among processes, and
- synchronization of different processes.

Different parallel programming models deal with these in different ways. Moreover, how they are dealt with can affect the correctness and the efficiency of a parallel code. In the SPMD model, work distribution usually amounts to iteration distribution; we use these terms interchangeably.

We will focus on how the characteristically parallel operations are addressed in programming languages we study. This discussion will serve to define and amplify the issues. In addition, other characteristics of parallel languages play an important role. We focus on a representative group and describe two of them at length in subsequent sections. By considering all of the aspects of parallel languages discussed here, we approximate a taxonomy by differentiating languages according to how they approach these features.

One additional feature we consider is the **control structure** of the language with respect to how to assign a program's subcomputations to processes. We discuss this at length in Section 5.2.2. The choice of **memory model** in a parallel programming language also has a significant impact on how efficient it will be for a given set of applications. The memory model determines how process memory is presented and accessed in the programming language. We discuss memory models at length in Section 5.3.

A critical issue for understanding the behavior of the SPMD approach is whether variables are replicated or not. That is, do the variable names in the code represent distinct values in different processors or do they represent a single address space? We will consider programming models in which both of these two possibilities occur. This is an example of a fundamental difference in memory model. In the program model this is often called local (or distributed) memory versus shared (or global) memory.

A language's synchronization model can significantly affect what a correct program looks like, the implementation of the language, and the efficiency of the implementation. We describe synchronization issues in the models covered in this chapter, and in Chapter 8 we consider a specialized synchronization. But first let us address some aspects of correctness which are particular to parallel programs.

5.1.1 Correctness of parallel codes

The **correctness** of any program refers to whether or not it computes reliably what it purports to compute. This is difficult to prove even for a sequential code, and it is beyond the scope of this book to address this issue in a formal way.[1] However, even starting with a sequential code that is correct for some set of input still leaves a great deal to be done to assure correctness of a parallelized version. Central problems that can affect the correctness of results of parallel computing include issues described in the following definitions.

Definition 5.1.1. A parallel program is **sequentially consistent** if:

i) its execution appears as some interleaving of the sequential execution of the parallel processes, and

ii) the execution order in each process appears to have occurred in the order specified in the source program.

It might seem sufficient to demand sequential consistency for a parallel program to be correct, but there are many ways in which a parallel program can fail to perform the way its sequential counterpart would. Here we discuss three main ways in deadlock, livelock, and race conditions. In Chapter 9 we discuss a parallel language which supports sequential consistency.

Definition 5.1.2. Two processes are said to **deadlock** if one process is waiting for the other process to do something it will never do.

Deadlock is like gridlock in rush hour traffic. For example, suppose one process is waiting to receive something from the process on its right before sending something to the process on its left. If this condition holds for all nodes in a ring (see Figure 3.10), nothing will ever happen. It is often useful to distinguish between different forms of deadlock. Gridlock involves a cycle of dependences, but there are other situations in parallel computing which are more like sitting at a red light which will never turn green due to some system failure. The term **livelock** is used for the situation when one process is waiting for another to do something which the second process is

[1] In general it is undecidable to prove that a given program is correct.

not programmed to do, at least for a particular set of operating conditions (e.g., for a certain set of inputs). Livelock has many of the characteristics of deadlock, and it may lead ultimately to deadlock, but distinction can be useful to make.

Definition 5.1.3. A **race condition** occurs when the order of arrival of different processes at a given program point affects subsequent behavior of a parallel computation.

Differences in rates of progress between different processors can cause processes to arrive in different orders at any given point in a program. The result of a race condition could be as simple as a small change in results of an arithmetic computation (due to a change in the order of the computation). Or it could result in more dramatic outcomes, such as deadlock. We give an example of a race condition in Program 5.2 and show in Section 5.4.1 how it can be avoided using *semaphores*.

One result of race conditions is that the results of computation are not predictable: the same inputs can lead to different outputs at different times of the day, with different loads on the parallel computing engine, or even with temperature gradients in the machine room. Such variation can be troublesome for many reasons, so it is useful to draw a distinction between computations where such variation can occur and ones where it does not.

Definition 5.1.4. A computation is said to be **deterministic** if the results cannot vary from run to run provided all input data are the same. A computation is said to be **nondeterministic** if the results **can** vary from run to run even though all input data are the same.

Nondeterminism is like gambling in that the results are not predictable in detail. This may explain why some people are not opposed to nondeterministic computations, since gambling is such a popular pastime and source of revenue for state governments. However, as in gambling, you are virtually certain to lose over the long haul with nondeterministic programs. The authors admit a strong prejudice against nondeterministic parallel programs.

There are various causes for determinism to be lacking in a parallel computation. One is due to variable orders of computation in sensitive numerical computations. For example, in the summation problem in (1.3.1), one can get different answers depending on the grouping of the terms. For example, suppose two processes collaborate to compute the sum, with one processor doing the positive terms and the other the negative terms. Since each of the partial sums is divergent, the result for a large number of terms could be quite different from what would be obtained with another grouping of terms. If these groupings are determined arbitrarily in some way, then the final result will be nondeterministic. A race condition will allow such nondeterminism.

Determinism and sequential consistency are very closely related, but not exactly the same concept. You could have a nondeterministic sequential code and a sequentially consistent parallel companion code, which would therefore also be nondeterministic. A sequentially consistent parallel version of a deterministic sequential code will of course be deterministic. However, we will often suggest deterministic parallel solutions to problems which are not sequentially consistent with any given sequential code. A particularly good example of this is Chapter 12, which presents several different parallel algorithms for solving a banded linear system.

From now on, we will assume that parallel computations should be, to the best of our ability, done in a deterministic way, at least if we are intending to do a computation that can be done deterministically. This restriction does not preclude simulating stochastic (or random) behavior; it is possible to do such simulations in a deterministic way [69]. We will describe different programming languages that assure this will be the case, and we will describe ways to avoid nondeterminism in the ones that do not.

5.1.2 Efficiency of parallel codes

Once the correct answer is obtained from a parallel program implementation, one's interest turns to how quickly it executes. In almost all cases, the most critical factor leading to improved performance is the minimization of data movement between the memory of different processes. This arises whether or not one is using a distributed memory model or a shared memory model. In either case, memory that is not local to a given processor extends the uniprocessor memory hierarchy presented in Section 1.3.2. Memory-hierarchy concepts of spatial and temporal locality have analogies with respect to interprocess memory accesses.

In distributed memory, interprocess access is achieved by sending messages, much as one sends a letter in an envelope. It is critical for efficiency in message passing between process memories, which may or may not be on the same computer, to minimize the number and size of messages.

For shared memory, it might seem easy to access "nonlocal" memory, but it requires coordination using synchronization operations. With messages, processes avoid synchronizing the access to values in memory locations. Instead, a consumer of some value from another process waits until a copy of it arrives in a message from the producer. When the message arrives it can be used regardless of what the producer is doing. This is possible because the message captures some state of the producer, that is, the message captures the memory content at some previous time in the producer's history. In shared memory, processes synchronize around memory to ensure they have a certified copy as is provided by the message. This poses one tradeoff in synchronization overhead versus message passing overhead. It also shows that different programming styles can be more or less suitable depending on the algorithm.

One advantage of messages is that they permit the producer to continue ahead of the consumer, reusing the memory location from which the consumer has yet to utilize values. In fact, many instances of values (in messages) from that same memory location can be queued, awaiting use by the consumer. These messages must be labeled in some way so that the message with the value of a variable from, say, iteration i can be distinguished from a value of the same variable at iteration $i + 1$. While the producer can go about its business ahead of the consumer, so too can the consumer do useful work while waiting for messages from the producer provided it has enough information to do so. When this production and consumption of messages is done in clever ways, one can overlap the delivery of message with other computation, thereby masking message passing latency. That is, rather than waiting for a message to make its transit, the involved processes can be performing useful work. This can lead to quite efficient programs. One disadvantage of messages over shared memory is that organizing the exchange of data between processes can be an arduous task for the programmer. Yet synchronization over shared memory can be complex as well. In the end, the preferred method, from efficiency and programming viewpoints, depends on the algorithm, language model, runtime system, operating system, and computer architecture.

5.1.3 Practical matters

Using a parallel programming language effectively requires some attention to details about the language model. We have seen that the memory model critically determines the style of the program; in conjunction with the algorithm it is also central to the efficiency. The memory model has a tight interplay with the algorithm. For example, a shared memory model may be more suitable for a data decomposition that must be determined dynamically throughout program execution.

Similarly, task unit allocation is a feature of the language model. Tasks can be allocated implicitly or explicitly by the language. Implicit allocation is performed by the compiler and runtime system, whereas explicit allocation requires some statement at execution time or by the programmer. Some systems may require the number of processes to be declared along with the compilation for optimization purposes. Some models use a fixed number of tasks, whereas others allow the number of active tasks to shrink and grow during the computation. In some language models the number of tasks is available as a reserved variable, where in others this detail is hidden from the programmer. The algorithm requirements can determine the suitability of the language model.

The input and output model of a language is another variable. Historically input and output was often left by the wayside, in part because it is a hard problem for compilers and runtime systems. Consequently, I/O support in parallel applications is sketchy. Language models can view files and operations differently. Some I/O models are sequential: each process sees its own file descriptor space along with the corresponding files. Others might permit simultaneous access to files, providing atomic operations on the file, or not. We will discuss various programming models without discussing I/O issues. In some cases, one can find that the same programming model is implemented on two different machines with two different I/O models.

5.2 COMMAND AND CONTROL

The way parallelism is expressed and controlled in different parallel languages is quite varied. In this section, we discuss some ways this is done in some contemporary parallel languages.

5.2.1 Explicitness in parallelism

We can characterize different languages according to the explicitness or implicitness with which they deal with parallelism. *Implicit* languages attempt to achieve parallelism without any explicit parallel constructs. Rather they attempt to restrict the programming style so that programs exhibit the maximum possible parallelism, and this is then exploited by the compiler. Applicative or constraint languages [46] are examples of this. Automatically parallelized sequential languages also fall into this category, but conventional languages do not appear to be good candidates for automatic parallelization.

Data partitioning annotations, as in HPF (Chapter 9), and control partitioning annotations (Chapter 10) follow the middle of the road with respect to *explicitness*. They introduce compiler directives that indicate work and data distribution, but complete details are left to the compiler. An HPF-conforming program is sequentially consistent (see Definition 5.1.1), although control-partitioning annotations (Chapter 10) are not guaranteed to produce correct results. These annotations can be thought of as a "DO it anyway" loop parallelization strategy, whereas the former is a "DO it if you can" approach.

Explicit parallel languages provide the most control, but at the expense of requiring more detailed knowledge of the algorithm and a more detailed description of the parallelization strategy. Explicitly parallel subcomputations (threads, processes) can be specified. A suitable model of memory is required to allow different subcomputations to exchange data. Examples are the IPlanguages (Chapter 8) and the Linda languages [52].

5.2.2 Control structures

The distribution of work must be controlled in some way. As in any system involving independent members, one can choose different approaches. One key variable is the granularity (Definition 1.5.2) of the control mechanisms. In human systems (e.g., business, government, education, the military, religion) one is familiar with management systems that vary from "micromanagement" at one extreme to loosely organized systems at the other (see Section 2.7).

It is useful to consider human systems in trying to assess how to organize parallel computations, as human systems have been functioning for millennia and have achieved quantifiable goals. Several of these were discussed in Section 2.7. Others have additional implications for parallel languages, which we now describe briefly.

Most religious groups are very loosely organized, with a central text used for guidance but interpreted by the individual members independently. Other human systems (government, the military, and large corporations) typically have some sort of hierarchical organization which is used to coordinate activities. Educational systems can vary in structure. Many universities are only loosely controlled, with curricula determined by individual professors. Typical K-12 systems in large cities are more rigidly controlled by a hierarchical structure.

From these examples, we see that various types of control mechanisms can be used effectively in different contexts. We now examine how different programming models can vary in the way independent computations are controlled.

Synchronous models are ones that are rigidly controlled; similar, if not identical, computations occur on each processor simultaneously, or at least do not proceed at an arbitrary rate. Examples include vector models (e.g., Fortran 90) and other "data parallel" models such as HPF and C* [74]. Such a control structure is often associated with SIMD machines, and indeed many SIMD machines have come equipped with compilers for "synchronous" control languages. The data parallel model provides a single name space, in contrast to the SPMD model, where each process has an explicit and separate name space at the program model level, even though the same source code is used.

Asynchronous models are ones that where processes coordinate less tightly than in, say, the data parallel model. Arbitrary processes (or threads) can be initiated, merged, or terminated, but during execution processes proceed independently.

Definition 5.2.1. A **process** is an instance of a program in execution. Operationally, a process is an operating system entity with a state that includes data, instructions, register contents, an address space, program counter, and various data structures. A process executes tasks (Definition 1.5.1), can request and hold system resources, and can change the state of other processes.

Most operating systems are structured as a collection of processes.

For example, Unix uses many "daemon" processes to do various tasks such as schedule processes for execution, manage login sessions, and send and receive e-mail from the network. A **thread** is similar in spirit to a process, but is intended to be more "lightweight," since it requires less overhead to represent and invoke than a process and, moreover, typically shares the address space of some process with other threads.

Asynchronous models provide flexibility but require vigilance by way of explicit programmer intervention in order to maintain correctness. The primary examples include shared memory programming models based on the standards effort PCF [98] and thread libraries (e.g., Posix threads) now available on most workstations.

The middle of the road with respect to **synchronicity** is open to interpretation and depends largely on the granularity at which one is focusing. However, HPF (Chapter 9) and the **IP** models (Chapter 8) can be viewed in this middle ground, as can the "tiling" constructs (Chapter 10) in shared memory programming systems. These languages have natural synchronization points but in typical usage would allow a large amount of computation to be done asynchronously. We will examine these programming languages in detail.

5.3 MEMORY MODELS

The two main categories of memory models are "shared" and "distributed." They differ conceptually in ways that are analogous to the architectural models of shared memory and distributed memory systems. However, there is no essential restriction to compiling a distributed memory program on a shared memory computer, or vice versa.

5.3.1 Shared memory

Shared memory is the model closest to what is used in sequential programming. In parallel programming, it implies equal access to memory by all subcomputations. The memory-access *time* may not be uniform, but the linguistic manner in which it is addressed is identical. If the control structure is asynchronous, then there is a need for synchronization mechanisms to assure that correct usage of shared memory occurs (cf. Exercise 5.15). A key point is that a memory reference by a process, to all of memory in the parallel computer, is a part of the language. These language constructs can be translated to a memory reference (i.e., a *load* or a *store*) on a shared memory architecture in an obvious and straightforward way.

5.3.2 Distributed memory

Distributed memory implies there is no direct access to memory by different subcomputations. In order to interact, data must be exchanged in some way, typically via *message passing* (Section 5.5). Message passing is similar to ordinary physical mail or to e-mail. One puts information inside a wrapper, which includes information about who it is from and instructions about where to send it, and then deposits it in some receptacle for delivery. This system is largely mysterious to most people, and indeed mail sometimes gets lost in it. You may not realize there is a wrapper when you send e-mail, but it is certainly evident when it arrives. The "header" information frequently exceeds the message by a large factor. This points out the key shortcoming of message passing, which correlates with the large latency of communication associated with distributed memory architectures discussed in Section 3.3.

5.3.3 Compare and contrast

To continue the analogy of message passing with physical mail or e-mail, by comparison, the ability to make a direct reference to memory in a shared memory language is more like sending a FAX. The latter is convenient, and often cheaper and faster: a one-page letter can be sent at night by FAX anywhere within the United States for less than the cost of a first-class postage stamp. On the other hand, many people have found it prudent to add a "wrapper" for FAXes, giving the sort of destination, origination, and message size information that are involved in a message passing system (Section 5.5). This helps to avoid lost or garbled messages, for which the basic FAX concept provides no protection.

By considering our conventional forms of communication, ordinary mail, e-mail, and FAX, we see some natural trade-offs that are relevant in assessing the differences between shared memory languages and architectures and distributed memory languages and architectures. For large missives, it does not much matter that a wrapper has been added. An exabyte of data (10^{18} bytes) could be sent around the world in a few weeks on 8mm tapes via one ship (see Exercise 5.2). But FAXing this amount of information via a single FAX machine would take millions of years at current modem speeds (see Exercise 5.4). The tapes could be sent faster by a fleet of airplanes, but the cost would be much higher.

It is for shorter messages that the overhead of message passing becomes significant. Consider the extra data that would be sent if the following exchange were made by e-mail.

Mary: Lunch?
John: Sure.
Mary: Where?
John: Don't care.
Mary: When?
John: Anytime.
Mary: OK

Our main conclusion from these analogies is that what determines efficiency of communication is different for different sizes of data exchange. For large messages, the **throughput** is most critical, where throughput is defined to be the total volume of information sent in a given amount of time. A ship carrying tapes probably has the greatest throughput of any communication system (see Exercise 5.3). However, for short messages, minimizing the overhead of a wrapper is most important.

Distributed memory parallel processing could be based on sending work instead of data. The concept of **remote procedure call** (RPC) was invented to implement this approach, and it is used in many operating systems (e.g., Unix) in an essential way. Making an RPC can also involve the transmission of data.

5.3.4 Other memory models

More recently, other memory models have emerged which have been applied in parallel computing. For example, **associative memory** is a model that is very convenient for databases and has been utilized in the Linda languages [52] for parallel computing. In associative memory, the data space is referenced by attribute rather than location. An example is the *glass slipper* in the Cinderella story. The Prince does not know her address, so he seeks Cinderella by *shoe size*, i.e., by determining whom the shoe fits. In the conventional version of the story, he searches the data space (the set of all female subjects) sequentially and happens to find Cinderella before finding some other subject with the same shoe size. Even allowing for shoe sizes with ten lengths and five widths, it would have to be either a very small kingdom or very good luck that this happened.

Associative memory may have non-unique information satisfying the attribute. In the Cinderella story, finding the wrong person would have produced the wrong ending. However, in some cases, non-unique results do not matter. If you need to contact someone at the University of Maryland whose e-mail address you can't remember, you might "grep"[2] on your file of old mail for `umd` and get lots of people to try there to see if they know the address. In other cases, it might be important to identify data in a unique way, and this can be done with associative memory through the use of a rigorous protocol followed by a careful programmer.

The Linda system [52] uses the associative memory model as an integral part of its design. Linda C and Linda Fortran have been commercial successes that have allowed parallel programs to be written that can be ported between a variety of machines. The control structure in Linda is asynchronous, with individual computational agents having a local (logically distributed) memory. Sharing of information is done through the associative memory, implemented as a "tuple" space, that is, a free-form Cartesian

[2] *grep* is the Unix command which searches its input for a pattern, i.e., gets a repetition.

product of standard data types.

Many computations in science and engineering can be accomplished with a deterministic approach. Determinism aids in debugging and assures that computations can be repeated if additional information is required that was not saved or simply not registered on previous computations. The $\mathbb{P}$ model (Chapter 8) allows a certain degree of asynchronous computation while guaranteeing determinism and providing a mechanism to detect deadlock at runtime. It does so through the use of **guarded memory**, which incorporates *labels* for memory that are private to another processor. The concept of a *guard* will be discussed in the context of synchronization techniques in Section 5.4.2. The $\mathbb{P}$ model will be developed at length in Chapter 6 and Chapter 8. Current implementations include $\mathbb{P}$C, $\mathbb{P}$fortran, and $\mathbb{P}$C++ [13].

5.4 SHARED MEMORY PROGRAMMING

Raw shared memory programming allows uniform access to all variables. While this may seem beneficial at first, multiple agents will be accessing this shared resource, so mechanisms are needed to ensure correct results. The key ingredient needed is the ability to synchronize actions by different processes. Here we describe some standard techniques to do this. These include *semaphores* and *barriers*. Synchronization is implicit in other parallel programming paradigms, such as *message passing*, which will be discussed in Section 5.5.

The simplest computer has an operating system that allows multiple processes to run simultaneously and need to be coordinated. As simple an event as printing a file requires that two different agents be able to access the file (the author and the printer). This is typical of a shared memory object. An operating system typically is written using shared memory programming and must provide appropriate synchronization to ensure correct results.

In our principal applications, we will be thinking about separate processors executing in parallel. However, each of these processors will have its own process, so we will simply think of multiple processes (the logical perspective) rather than multiple processors (the physical perspective). Indeed, there might be reason for having more than one process per processor. On the other hand, we may drift back to talk about different processors to emphasize our main objective. We hope that this slight confusion will not deter the reader.

There are various ways in which one can indicate that work is to be done in parallel (that is, independent of other processes). At the lowest level, separate processes or threads must be activated to manage the work. We will assume the existence of a **parallel do** statement which effectively indicates that each iteration in a loop should be done in parallel with (that is, independently of) all of the other iterations of the loop. More complex constructs are necessary to write an operating system, but this is sufficient as an introduction for scientific computation.

5.4.1 Synchronization via semaphores

A **semaphore** is a signal to coordinate processes, based on two operations:

- *lock* (P) and
- *unlock* (V).

The letters P and V are traditional abbreviations for the corresponding words in another language (Exercise 5.1). The terminology is that one locks and unlocks a given semaphore. Typically, one would declare a distinct semaphore for each place where coordination is needed preceding some critical section, that is, a section involving write accesses to shared data.

In our mini-language, we will assume that `Semaphore` is a type of variable to which we can apply functions `lock` and `unlock`. There are only two possible values of a `Semaphore` variable: locked and unlocked. The meaning of the `unlock` operation is simple. When a semaphore is unlocked by the authorized process, other processes are free to access and lock it. The result of a process attempting to lock a semaphore can be complex. If it is unlocked, then the process locks the semaphore, and it remains locked until that process unlocks it. In equivalent terminology, a process is said to **acquire a lock** or **acquire a semaphore** when it locks the semaphore. If another process tries to lock it before the first process unlocks it, the second (and subsequent) process(es) wait until it is unlocked. Once it is unlocked, the next process is allowed to lock the semaphore.

Physical semaphores were originally used to avoid collisions by trains. Suppose that in a particularly treacherous mountain region there is a section where the usual double set of tracks (one pair for each direction of travel) is reduced to a single pair of tracks that curves so sharply around a steep promontory that it is difficult to see (or hear) anything more than a few yards ahead. Also suppose the two points where the double tracks converge to a single track happen to be just on either side of the promontory, where a flag can be posted to indicate if one has passed into the treacherous curved section of single track. The protocol is to take the flag when entering the section, replacing it when leaving. If the flag is not there, then of course it is only prudent to assume that another train is in the treacherous curved section, possibly coming toward you, and to wait until it is returned. If the protocol is followed, everyone can use the track safely.

The flag in this description is a physical version of a logical semaphore. Taking the flag "locks" it, whereas returning it "unlocks" it. Consider the silly example in Program 5.1 in which a variable is to be incremented in parallel by multiple processes. The lock placed around the line `x = x + 1` ensures that only one process(or) will be active at a time. The `Semaphore` `s` plays the role of the flag in the train analogy above.

```
Semaphore s
parallel do i=1,n
  lock(s)
  x = x+1
  unlock(s)
end parallel do
```

Program 5.1 Pseudo-code to illustrate the use of a semaphore.

If the lock were not used in Program 5.1, there would be a chance that a process(or) would read `x` while another one was about to increment it, a classic case of a race condition (see Definition 5.1.3). Since the code `x = x + 1` involves multiple steps (read `x`, increment this value, write `x`, increment the loop counter), there is a real danger. We need to ensure that the four steps are executed in full before another process(or) reads `x`. Consider the effect of the sequence of steps shown in Program 5.2. In this case, the different contributions of the two processors are completely garbled.

```
  Processor 0                 Processor 1
  . . . . .                   . . . . .
read x                      increment value of x
increment value of x        write x
write x                     increment loop
increment loop              read x
read x                      increment value of x
increment value of x        write x
write x                     increment loop
increment loop              read x
  . . . . .                   . . . . .
```

Program 5.2 Pseudo-code to illustrate the danger of not using of a semaphore which occurs due to a race condition.

5.4.2 Critical sections

A **critical section** is a section of code in which only one subcomputation is active, such as the statement

```
x = x + 1
```

between the `lock(s)` and `unlock(s)` lines in Program 5.1. That is, only one processor will be in a critical section at one time. In the train example described in Section 5.4.1, the treacherous curved section of single track is the critical section.

The use of critical sections is clearly needed to provide correctness (page 130). However, it is obvious that adding locks will contribute overhead, and one might make an argument for taking some risk. There is a clear tradeoff between safety and efficient parallelism. We will not try to assess the risk but rather seek methods to achieve correct code (zero risk) with minimal cost.

The use of locks typically has two parts: acquiring and releasing, as in Program 5.1. In the train example, if someone fails to return the flag, the single line of track becomes forever unusable. The concept of a **guard** was introduced to simplify the pairing of acquiring and releasing. Instead, a critical section is simply *guarded* by an object that has the semantics of an acquire/release pair.

5.4.3 Barriers

A **barrier** is a point in a parallel code where all processors stop to synchronize. The semantics of a barrier are that all processors wait there until all others have arrived. Once they have all arrived, they are all released to continue in the code. The same effect could be achieved using locks that all processors interact with, but a barrier function provides this in one simple step (see Exercise 5.16).

Barriers are often useful in scientific applications. They are used to synchronize after a section of code that can be done in parallel by a number of processes. The pseudo-code in Program 5.3 presents the main idea through a hypothetical example of how they are used. The use of results in one

```
parallel do i=1,n
  "local part of computation"
  call barrier()
  "use results computed by others"
end parallel do
```

Program 5.3 Pseudo-code to illustrate the use of a barrier.

processor which were computed by others is only safe once it is certain that the others have completed computing these values.

A barrier ensures that no processor passes before all have arrived at this point. Legend has it that railroad law in one Midwestern state decreed that "if two trains meet on a single track, then neither shall proceed until the other is safely by." A barrier is something like this, but its mission is more carefully crafted to avoid the obvious deadlock this law would imply.

5.4.4 Example: summation

We begin with the problem (1.3.2) of adding elements of an array, parallelized via (1.5.1) and (1.5.2). Program 5.4 depicts an implementation of this in our simple shared memory parallel programming model. Note that there are no dependences carried by the `do k` loop.

```
real x(10000), sum, localsum(0:p-1)
Semaphore slok
N=10000
...
parallel do k = 0, P-1
  localsum(k) = 0.0
  do i = 1+k*(N/P), (k+1)*(N/P)
    localsum(k) = localsum(k) + x(i)
  enddo
end parallel do
barrier()
sum=localsum(0)
do k = 1, p-1
  lock(slok)
  sum = sum + localsum(k)
  unlock(slok)
enddo
```

Program 5.4 Parallel implementation of summation in a shared memory model.

The last loop in Program 5.4 may not be very efficient for computing

$$\sum_{k=0}^{P-1} \texttt{localsum}(k)$$

especially for large P. See Section 6.6 for more efficient algorithms.

5.5 MESSAGE PASSING

Distributed memory parallel computers require some mechanism to allow separate processors to cooperate. In the shared memory model, this is done by passing information through shared variables, and these are not available in a distributed memory model. Moreover, it may be conceptually easier to think of separate processes as having separate memory spaces to avoid overwriting data by rogue (i.e., incorrectly programmed) processes. For both of these reasons, the *message passing* model was developed.

The term **message passing** refers to a programming model loosely based on "communicating sequential processes" (**CSP**) [78] and augmented based on other language research. In CSP this communication was done via "channels" that connect separate processes which are declared statically in the code. One problem with the notion of channels was that there might need to be a lot of them to keep the communications unambiguous. They did not provide the flexibility needed to communicate with a large number of partners at distinct times with distinct intents.

In the language PLITS (for programming language in the sky) [46], the idea of using *tags* to identify messages was introduced. A **tag** is an identifier for a message that can be specified by the programmer to provide uniqueness to a given message. The tag value can be determined at run time and changed as needed during execution. This allows particular messages to be identified uniquely even if they go between the same pair of processors.

The availability of the message passing model was a key ingredient in the commercial success of the original "hypercube" distributed memory parallel computers [75]. Numerous message passing libraries have been developed over the years and made available on a large number of vendors' machines in an effort to establish some standards in the area. These include `tcgmsg` [73], `pvm` [50], and `mpi` [136].

5.5.1 Send and receive

The two key elements of the message passing model are

- send
  - a message containing data to a particular processor,
- receive
  - a message containing data from a particular processor.

The basic operations of "send" and "receive" will vary from one system to another, but they will typically be of the form

```
snd(tag, memlocat, type, procwich, size),
rcv(tag, memlocat, type, procwich, size).
```

Here `memlocat` is the memory location of the (beginning of the) message being sent or where the message being received should be put. This is assumed to be an array of length `size`, and the `type` tells how many bytes there are per array location. The variable `procwich` indicates the processor destination for the message for `snd` and the source of the message for `rcv`. Thus

```
call snd(314159, A(7), 8, 0, 100)
```

will send `A(7:106)` (which consists of 800 bytes) to processor `0`. If processor 1 has sent this message, then

```
call rcv(314159, B(1), 8, 1, 100)
```

will correctly put this information into `B(1:100)` on processor `0`.

In order for message passing to work easily, it is often useful to be able to refer to one's own processor number. This can often be accomplished via a function call, which we will refer to as `nodeid()`. Thus the code in Program 5.5 would copy `A(7:106)` to `B(1:100)` on all processors.

```
next = nodeid() + 1
call snd(314159, A(7), 8, next, 100)
prev = nodeid() - 1
call rcv(314159, B(1), 8, prev, 100)
```

Program 5.5 Message passing code using `nodeid()`.

Although not a strict part of the message passing paradigm, it is usually the case that message passing codes are SPMD (Single-Program Multiple-Data-stream); cf. Definition 1.5.10. That is, every process (or processor) executes the same code, with the only difference being that `nodeid()` evaluates to a different number for different ones. This simplifies the task of coding greatly for problems with homogeneous parallelism. All of our examples in this section are written in SPMD style. Due to the fact that the individual processors in a distributed memory machine are often called *nodes* (see page 80), an SPMD code is often called **node code**.

The code in Program 5.5 works fine if there are an infinite number of processors, but on real machines there is a limit. This limit (the total number of processors) is also often available via a function call, we we will refer to as `nnodes()`. If we change the code fragment in Program 5.5 to Program 5.6, then messages will be exchanged correctly. Note that if `nodeid() = nnodes() - 1` then `next = 0`, and correspondingly if `nodeid() = 0` then `prev = nnodes() - 1`.

```
pee = nnodes()
next = mod(nodeid() + 1,pee)
call snd(314159, A(7), 8, next, 100)
prev = mod(nodeid() - 1,pee)
call rcv(314159, B(1), 8, prev, 100)
```

Program 5.6 Message passing code using `nnodes()`.

There is some necessary magic in the exchange of messages, in that you do not need to `rcv` a message before it can be `snd`. Buffers are provided so that, if it has been sent, it will be there when you ask to `rcv` it. If it has not yet arrived, you will just wait there until it arrives.

5.5.2 Collective operations

Message passing systems are typically augmented by further operations to ease the programming burden and provide more efficient operations, such as

- broadcast
  - a message containing data to all processors
- combine
  - specified data at all processors.

The latter operation is frequently a *reduction* operation (see Chapter 6) and the resulting data may be automatically broadcast to all processors in some cases. See Section 2.8 for a simple example of syntax for a reduction operation.

Collective operations work with collections of data, distributed among different processors. These can be coded using *send* and *receive*, but there is frequently an opportunity to optimize them at a lower level, and vendors often provide such optimized routines. In the summation example in Section 5.5.4 a simple algorithm is given, but much more efficient ones will be provided later (in Section 6.6).

5.5.3 Synchronization in message passing

The message passing paradigm implicitly involves synchronization at the point that messages are successfully exchanged. The receiver of a message can be assured that the sender has passed a certain point, if the message identifiers (the tag, size, etc.) are sufficiently unique. Using this fact, synchronization mechanisms (such as a barrier, Exercise 5.10) can be created using message passing.

A form of lock can be created in message passing. The code in Program 5.7 uses the metaphor of baton passing in a relay race. Imagine a team of runners who run in some sequence chosen by their coach, with the current runner in possession of the single baton. Each runner except for the first will wait in turn for the pass of the baton, which signals a runner's turn to snap into action.

Baton passing is a way to order processes, so they can, for example, perform some activity in some order. The program segment in Program 5.7 results in the processes outputting "hello world" according to their logical ordering.

The "lock" is the baton. When one holds it, certain actions can be taken as in the train example (Section 5.4.1), where the train was then allowed to pass into a critical section of track. In Program 5.7, the holder of the baton will print out a message. Because a lock has been used, we can guarantee the order of the messages.

```
integer*4 baton
baton = 0
do i=0, nnodes()-2
  if(nodeid() .eq. i)
    print*, 'hello from', nodeid(), baton
    baton = baton + 1
    call snd(i, baton, 4, i+1, 1)
  else if(nodeid() .eq. i+1)
    call rcv(i, baton, 4, i, 1)
  endif
enddo
if (nodeid() .eq. nnodes()-1)
   print*, 'hello from', nodeid()
endif
```

Program 5.7 Message passing code to illustrate synchronization via "baton" passing.

5.5.4 Example: summation

We repeat the problem (1.3.2) of adding elements of an array, parallelized via (1.5.1) and (1.5.2). In Section 5.4.4, we presented a shared memory implementation of this in Program 5.4. Here we present this in message passing. For simplicity, we assume that each processor has a full copy of the array `x` containing the right data to be summed. Then the partial sums (1.5.1) are easily computed via the code in Program 5.8. The only difference between Program 5.8 and the sequential version is the restriction on the limits in the `do i` loop.

At the end of the computation in Program 5.8, the variable `localsum` has different values at each processor. The different values must be combined to complete the computation. The algorithm used in the shared memory case can be approximated by the code in Program 5.9.

At the end of the computation in Program 5.9, only processor number `nnodes()-1` will have the correct value stored in `sum`. This value could then be broadcast to other processors (if desired). We leave this for Exercise 5.8. See Section 6.6 for more efficient algorithms for computing what Program 5.9 does, and for algorithms for doing a broadcast when such an operation is not supported directly.

5.5.5 To pass a mess

The message passing paradigm is quite error prone. In the example in Program 5.6, if either the tag (= `314159` in the example) or the processor number did not match, the transfer would not be made. Deadlock would result. If `B` were declared `Real*4` instead of `Real*8`, information would be placed incorrectly.

The need for a tag can be seen if two messages are being sent at

```
real x(10000), sum, localsum
N=10000
...
localsum = 0.0
k = nodeid()
do i = 1+k*(N/P), (k+1)*(N/P)
   localsum = localsum + x(i)
enddo
```

Program 5.8 Message passing code to compute partial sums (1.5.1).

```
sum=localsum
do k = 1, p−1
  if(nodeid().eq.k−1) snd(k, sum, real, k, 8)
  if(nodeid().eq.k)
    call rcv(k, sum, real, k−1, 1)
    sum=sum+localsum
  endif
enddo
```

Program 5.9 Message passing code using `nodeid()`.

roughly the same time from one processor to another. (The construction of appropriate code to illustrate this is left as Exercise 5.9.) There is nothing in the message passing model that guarantees the order of arrival as a function of the order of sending, although some systems may specify restrictions on order of arrival in some cases.

There are several subroutine arguments, in paired subroutine calls, that must match exactly to effect the correct transfer of the values of one set of variables in one processor to those in another. The need to surround each data exchange with identifying information requires extra coding (e.g., the `tag` must be given a value), which increases the possibility of errors or inefficient code.

The $\mathbb{P}$ language model (Chapter 8) can be thought of as fusing "send" and "receive," into one operation, denoted by "@". This allows type checking (and even conversion) to be done by a compiler. Since much of scientific computation can be parallelized with matched pairs of "send" and "receive," we will postpone more extended discussion of the message passing paradigm until Chapter 8.

5.6 EXAMPLES AND COMMENTS

We present in Table 5.1 a simple review of the two main programming styles considered here. To illustrate the similarities and differences, we now consider the iterative method (1.6.21) from Section 1.6.2, one-dimensional

	message passing	*shared memory*
data distribution	stored separately	none
work distribution	done implicitly by SPMD	explicit `parallel do` statements
data exchange	done explicitly by messages	done implicitly by memory reference
synchronization	done implicitly by messages	done explicitly by semaphores
memory model	distributed memory	shared memory

Table 5.1 Compare and contrast message passing and shared memory programming styles.

Jacobi iteration. A sequential implementation is depicted in Program 5.11. All of the codes in this section require some additional declarations, which are given in Program 5.10; the variable `NoIters` is the number of times the Jacobi iteration is to be repeated.

```
real x(0:10001), newx(0:10001), dx2
n=10000
dx2 = (1.0/n)**2
NoIters=100000
```

Program 5.10 Declarations required for all Jacobi iteration codes.

```
do i = 1 , n
  x(i) = 1.0
enddo
x(0) = 0.0
x(n+1) = 0.0
do k = 1, NoIters
  do i = 1 , n
    newx(i) = .5 * (x(i-1) + x(i+1) - dx2 * x(i))
  enddo
  do i = 1 , n
    x(i) = newx(i)
  enddo
enddo
```

Program 5.11 Sample Jacobi iteration sequential code.

5.6.1 Jacobi iteration in shared memory

The code in Program 5.11 can be written in the shared memory model as depicted in Program 5.12, together with the declarations in Program 5.10.

Here we assume for simplicity that `n/p` is an integer. Synchronization is achieved using only a barrier (Section 5.4.3).

```
parallel do me = 0, p−1
  lo = me * (n/p) + 1
  hi = lo + (n/p) − 1
  do i = lo, hi
    x(i) = 1.0
  enddo
  if (me .eq. 0) x(0) = 0.0
  if (me .eq. p−1) x(n+1) = 0.0
  do k = 1, NoIters
    call barrier()
    do i = lo , hi
      newx(i) = .5 * (x(i−1) + x(i+1) − dx2 * x(i))
    enddo
    call barrier()
    do i = lo , hi
      x(i) = newx(i)
    enddo
  enddo
end parallel do
```

Program 5.12 Shared memory parallel implementation of Jacobi iteration.

The code in Program 5.11 introduces a parallel loop (`parallel do me`) around the sequential version, and for each value of `me` executes part of the basic sequential loops. These loops are the same as the sequential loops except that the loop limits have been modified (to `lo` and `hi`).

Note that in the line

```
newx(i) = .5 * (x(i-1) + x(i+1) - dx2 * x(i))
```

each process(or) will access values `x(lo-1)` and `x(hi+1)` that have been recently modified by another process(or). This is the implicit communication that occurs in the shared memory parallel implementation of Jacobi iteration.

5.6.2 Jacobi iteration in message passing

The code for Jacobi iteration in Program 5.11 can be parallelized in message passing, as depicted in Program 5.13, together with the declarations in Program 5.10. Again we assume for simplicity that `ln = n/p` is an integer. Synchronization is achieved through the pairing of sends and receives. Moreover, the communication that was implicit in the shared memory parallel implementation of Jacobi iteration now is quite explicit.

```
integer p, me, l, tag
me = nodeid()
p = nnodes()
tag = 0
ln = n/p
do i = 1, ln
  x(i) = 1.0
enddo
if (me .eq. 0) x(0) = 0.0
if (me .eq. p-1) x(ln+1) = 0.0
do k = 1, NoIters
  if (me - 1 .ge. 0) snd(tag, newx(1), 8, me-1, 1)
  if (me + 1 .lt. p) rcv(tag, x(ln+1), 8, l, me+1, 1)
  tag = tag + 1
  if (me + 1 .lt. p) snd(tag, newx(ln), me+1, 1)
  if (me - 1 .ge. 0) rcv(tag, x(0), l, me-1, 1)
  tag = tag + 1
  do i = 1 , ln
    newx(i) = .5 * (x(i-1) + x(i+1) - dx2 * x(i))
  enddo
  do i = 1 , ln
    x(i) = newx(i)
  enddo
enddo
```

Program 5.13 Message passing parallel implementation of Jacobi iteration.

Note that the data structures `x` and `newx` have been distributed. The local variables correspond to blocks of the original sequential or shared memory versions. The amount of memory required per processor is only $\mathcal{O}(n/p)$. The declaration for memory allocation (cf. Program 5.10) can also be correspondingly reduced. However, the work done on the respective parts is the same as in the shared memory version. Instead of having the loop bounds `lo` and `hi`, which take on different values depending on the value of `me` as in the shared memory case, the loop bounds have the same values `1` and `ln` for every processor.

5.6.3 Determinism revisited

Neither the message passing nor the shared memory paradigm is by its nature deterministic (Definition 5.1.4). In the shared memory paradigm, there is no requirement to use semaphores, so the example in Section 5.4.1 provides an example of nondeterminism in this programming style. Correspondingly, the example in Section 5.5.5 provides an example of nondeterminism in message passing. The $\mathbb{P}$ language model (Chapter 8) and HPF (Chapter 9) provide parallel programming paradigms which *are* naturally deterministic.

5.6.4 Threads versus processes

Threads are often described as "light weight" processes. That is, they are intended to be less costly to initiate than processes. But in common usage (e.g., in Unix-based operating systems) there is a substantial difference from the point of view discussed in this chapter. Both threads and processes provide ways to initiate a group of interacting parallel computations, but the memory models are different. Threads function in a shared memory world when on the same computer, whereas processes have what can be viewed as distributed memory by way of the private address space each process operates within. The process distributed memory paradigm applies whether processes are on one or on different computers.

Processes and threads can communicate by **sockets**, and, when on the same computer, with other Unix interprocess communication primitives; these include message queues and shared memory segments. The general model is that processes operate in independent address spaces, and therefore a collection of processes adhere to a distributed memory paradigm. A thread is typically a component of some process: threads created from the same process have shared memory access to the parent process's address space; threads created in different processes can interact with each other as do processes. Thus, when we talk about threads resembling a shared memory model, this applies to threads created in the same process. Another way of thinking about this is that threads are simply independent flows of control within a process, where the threads can be scheduled independently of one another by the operating system.

Sockets function somewhat like channels in CSP (Section 5.5), whereas message queues are a message passing primitive for processes on a single machine.[3] In Section 7.3, we will discuss the evolution of the process and thread concepts and terminology.

5.6.5 Mapping distributed memory to shared memory

There is a natural mapping of the distributed memory programming model to shared memory. We simply partition shared memory and assign the i-th partition to the i-th processor. Thus, any algorithm that has been programmed in a distributed memory style and be easily and automatically converted to shared memory.

The converse is not true. The random access of shared memory cannot be easily represented in distributed memory. Thus we can view that shared memory offers a broader range of possible algorithms, whereas distributed memory programming is more generally applicable.

[3] Try the command *ipcs* on a Unix computer to see a list of message queues, semaphores, and shared memory segments.

5.7 PARALLEL LANGUAGE DEVELOPMENTS

Operating system research motivated much early development in parallel constructs and languages. Concurrent Pascal was developed for this purpose by extending Pascal with monitors [77] in a shared memory model [66]. Many concurrent programming languages followed [9]. An early scientific programming language with domain decomposition constructs, OCCAM, appeared in 1985. OCCAM was developed by Inmos building on constructs from CSP (Section 5.5) to program transputer arrays [118].

The influential *cosmic cube* developed by Charles Seitz developed in 1981 set the stage for distributed memory computers such as the Intel hypercube [85]. The programming model was based on processes on nodes, executing concurrently either by running simultaneously on separate nodes, or with interleaved execution on a single node. *Cosmic cube* programs were written in high-level procedural languages such as C or Pascal, using message passing primitives managed by the kernel [131].

The message passing, SPMD program model persisted throughout the the 1990's on machines such as the nCUBE and Intel Hypercube, and the mesh-architecture Intel Paragon, through to today with networks of workstations. The success of message passing led to its standardization in MPI (Section 7.1), and popular public domain implementations [60].

The scalability limits of shared memory "dance hall" architectures (Section 3.2.1), where all shared memory is equally far from all processors, contributed to the proliferation of large-scale distributed memory computers. Some applications, however, benefited from the shared memory model and the large processing capabilities of distributed memory computers. The Global Array Toolkit [114, 115] and Treadmarks [89] provided a shared memory model on distributed memory systems including networks of workstations.

The Global Array Toolkit was motivated in part by requirements of *ab initio* codes for electronic structure calculations that included management of memory-intensive integral tables shared irregularly in a distributed memory environment [72].

Shared memory constructs were introduced into a high-level language with Co-array Fortran, an SPMD model. The co-array extends Fortran with a construct to distribute and access data on shared memory computers through memory-to-memory copies with the co-array variables in shared memory [142].

OpenMP (Chapter 10) is a thread-based shared memory model with SPMD support using a small set of compiler directives [30, 142], with the first implementation appearing in 1997.

The HPF (Chapter 9) initiative beginning in 1991 developed contemporaneously with the standardization of MPI and other runtime library developments. HPF provided compiler directives that assisted the compiler in parallelizing the data-parallel code, without altering the underlying program.

Legacy applications and arcane program structures obscuring loop dependences in addition to intrinsic irregular data accesses [146, 38] can foil attempts by the compiler to deduce dependences [34], a problem with automatic parallelization in general. Automatic parallelizing compilers confront a number of NP-hard problems including optimally determining data decompositions and distributions which enhance locality. Advances made in this area have used 0-1 programming methods in the context of HPF [45], and affine transformations in the context of CC-NUMA architectures [10], and it remains an area of research [99].

5.8 EXERCISES

Exercise 5.1. Determine a language (or languages) in which the letters "P" and "V" are abbreviations for the corresponding words *lock* and *unlock*.

Exercise 5.2. Five gigabytes can be stored on standard 8mm tapes that fit in a box that is $4 \times 2.75 \times 0.75$ inches^3. Prove that this corresponds to a density of approximately 1 terabyte/cubic foot.

Exercise 5.3. Suppose that a ship has a cargo hold with a volume corresponding to a rectangular box 40 feet wide, 27 feet deep, and 800 feet long, and suppose it can go from any one port to another in 80 days. Show that this corresponds to a throughput of approximately 1 terabit/second. (Hint: see Exercise 5.2.)

Exercise 5.4. What data rate is needed to send an exabyte of data (10^{18} bytes) in 3 million years?

Exercise 5.5. How many years does it take to send a million terabytes of data via 10-Mbit Ethernet assuming 1Mbyte/sec throughput?

Exercise 5.6. Write a program to compute the solution to the ordinary differential equation (1.6.1) using the second order method (1.6.9) in the shared memory paradigm.

Exercise 5.7. Write a program to compute the solution to the ordinary differential equation (1.6.1) using the second order method (1.6.9) in the message passing paradigm.

Exercise 5.8. The value of `sum` that is computed in the code fragment in Program 5.9 is available only at one processor. Write a code to broadcast (Section 5.5.2) a value to all the processors in message passing. (Hint: see Section 2.1.)

Exercise 5.9. Give an example in which messages may be incorrectly interpreted if tags are not used in message passing.

Exercise 5.10. Using message passing, write a barrier, that is, a subroutine that assures that no process leaves before all have arrived.

Exercise 5.11. Consider the example of baton passing in Section 5.5.3. If each processor were to print out the value of `baton` (before incrementing it) together with `nodeid()`, as shown on line 5 in Program 5.7, what would it be?

Exercise 5.12. In the example of baton passing in Section 5.5.3, is it necessary to increment the value of `baton`? Modify the code to eliminate the passing of a meaningful value, implementing a "no pass, no print" rule.

Exercise 5.13. In the example of baton passing in Section 5.5.3, is it necessary to increment the value of the tag (which is taken to be the iteration index `i`)? What would happen if we replaced the send/receive pair by

```
call snd(0, baton, 4, i+1, 1)
call rcv(0, baton, 4,  i,  1)
```

that is, would the code still execute correctly? Why or why not?

Exercise 5.14. Show how locks can be implemented using logical variables (`true` and `false`) together with suitable conditionals.

Exercise 5.15. Explain how a synchronous (Section 5.2.2), shared memory (Section 5.3.1) model could achieve determinism without explicit synchronization mechanisms (Section 5.4.1).

Exercise 5.16. Show how a barrier (Section 5.4.3) can be implemented using semaphores (Section 5.4.1).

Exercise 5.17. Are both barriers needed in Program 5.12? Why or why not?

Exercise 5.18. Is it necessary to increment `tag` twice in the `do k` loop in Program 5.13? Why or why not?

Chapter Six
Collective Operations

The totality of ourselves is a very mysterious affair—
attributed to don Juan Matus

Collective operations are operations involving a group of processors to produce a single data structure or take a particular action. These were introduced in Section 5.5.2. A barrier in shared memory computing (Section 5.4.3) is a collective action that causes a group of processors to pause until all are present. A broadcast in message passing (Section 5.5.2) sends data from one processor to the group. Collective operations require efficient algorithms since they can involve potentially a large number of processors and large amounts of data. Moreover, they provide a good first introduction to some complex parallel algorithms.

There are different algorithms suitable for collective operations on different processor architectures. However, there is a natural mapping (Section 5.6.5) from the distributed memory model to the shared memory model, so we will describe algorithms in the distributed memory case.

A *reduction* is a particular type of collective operation which takes as its input a set of values and returns a particular value. These have a general mathematical structure that will be discussed in Section 6.3.

6.1 THE @ NOTATION

There is a simple notation that we can use as a device to talk about data at different processors. It is similar to the way we do e-mail. We are known as

`someone@somewhere.what`

where `someone` is our e-mail name on the `somewhere.what` system. The latter might be a commercial system like `aol.com` or `msn.com`, or it might be a university (e.g., `uchicago.edu`) or government lab (e.g., `anl.gov`), or indeed a variety of other types of domains. In the past, the system name might have referred to a specific machine. The e-mail name might be something very common like `jack` or `jill`, but we are able to distinguish between `jack@msn.com` and `jack@anl.gov`. In many cases, this is the same as the `login` name on a particular machines or group of machines.

The e-mail naming scheme provides an analogy for naming variables at different processors. In an SPMD model, everyone has the same variable names, so we can talk about `x@p` and `x@q`, where `x` is one of the variables and `p` and `q` are different processor identifiers. Of course, the values of `x@p` and `x@q` need not be the same. For simplicity, we assume that the processors are identified by integers, numbered from zero to $P-1$, where P is the total number of processors.

Using this naming convention, we can talk about exchanging data between different processors by name, using the equal sign for assignment as usual. Thus, `x@p=y@q` means that the value of `y` at processor `q` is sent to processor `p` and stored in its variable `x`. Indeed, this type of notation has been used in a theoretical model of parallel computing [117], and it has been suggested as a practical way of describing data exchange in parallel computing [129]. Moreover, we will see in Chapter 8 that it can be used as a precise programming construct related to guarded memory (Section 5.3.4).

The statement `x@p = y@q` specifies the assignment of the value of `y` at process `q` to the variable `x` at process `p`. In message passing terms, the statement is a **fusion** of send and receive. In many applications, send/receive pairs occur naturally. We will see that many applications can be written with this simple notation.

6.2 TREE/RING ALGORITHMS

We now consider some algorithms based on simple binary trees but where the tree structure will be implemented using a ring topology. These algorithms are of two types, known respectively as *divide-and-conquer* and *recursive doubling* algorithms. These algorithms have impressive performance with relatively simple implementations, and they are naturally dual to each other. We begin with the simple problem (cf. (1.5.2)) of summing numbers across P processors. We follow that with the problem of broadcasting a number to P processors. In Section 6.5, we will consider so-called prefix algorithms. In all of these, the time required will be proportional only to $\log_2 P$. That is, at most $\log_2 P$ communication steps are required, and these are contention-free if communications are done in a ring (see Figure 3.10).

Program 6.1 defines a mapping `proc(i,j)` that effectively immerses a binary tree in a ring, as shown in Figure 6.1. By an **immersion**, we mean a mapping of the vertices of one graph to the vertices of the other such that the edges are either internal to one node or mapped to an edge. Thus neighboring vertices get mapped either to the same vertex or to neighboring vertices. In this case, `proc(i,j)` is the mapping of the tree to the ring, where we represent the vertices of the tree as a pair (i, j). The index i is the depth in the tree, with $i = 0$ corresponding to the root of the tree, and $j = 0, \ldots, 2^{i-1} - 1$ are the vertices at depth i.

In Program 6.1, the root of the tree is processor `n`, and its children in the tree are represented by the node itself and the node opposite it in the ring (halfway around). The children of these nodes are again themselves and

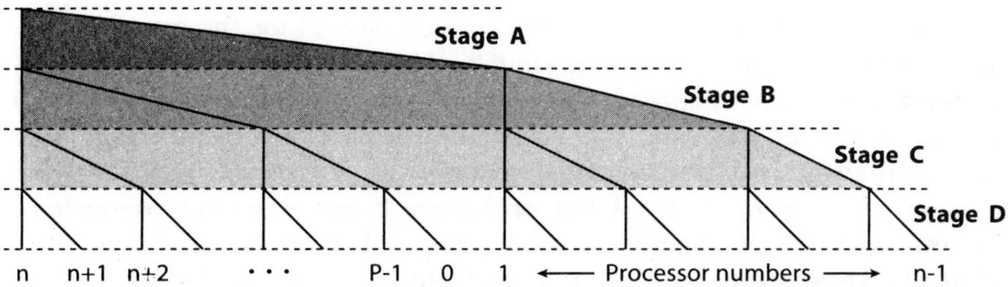

Figure 6.1 Immersion of a tree in a ring rooted at processor n. Broadcast proceeds with Stage A first, Stage B second, and so forth. Summation reverses the order of the stages. Vertical edges represent edges that are internal to the indicated processor in the ring.

```
dist=P/2
q=1
proc(0,0) = n
do i=1,d
  do j=0,q-1
    proc(i,2*j)=proc(i-1,j)
    proc(i,2*j+1)=MOD(proc(i-1,j)+dist,P)
  enddo
  q=2*q
  dist=dist/2
enddo
```

Program 6.1 Definition of mapping of a complete binary tree rooted at n into a ring of $P = 2^d$ processors.

the nodes a quarter of the way around the ring. Half of the tree edges are internal to one processor, and communications corresponding to these edges require no overhead. The other half are contention free at each stage for any network as long as point-to-point communications of a ring are available.

6.2.1 Broadcast in a ring

We will present a broadcast algorithm in Program 6.2 using a tree immersed in a ring, but first let us consider a very simple algorithm to shed some light on the question of executing a broadcast in general.

A broadcast can be accomplished using P point-to-point communications

```
x@p = y@n
```

for p= $0, \ldots, P-1$. This can be implemented via a simple loop on the processor number p (see Exercise 8.4). Thus it requires only P steps for P processors. Using the model for communication cost in Section 3.3 we see that this requires $P(\lambda+\mu)$ time. For small P, this may not be too bad, but it turns out that this can be improved dramatically.

For simplicity, suppose $P = 2^d$ (cf. Exercise 8.15 for the general case). Consider the code shown in Program 6.2. This implements a **divide-and-conquer** algorithm to spread the value of y to other processors. First, y is sent halfway around the ring. Now the roots of two (semi-)rings have y (a **semi-ring** is a network of processors $k, \ldots, \ell$, where i and $i+1$ are connected for $i = k, \ldots, \ell - 1$ but processors k and ℓ are not connected). We now *divide* our perspective to (semi-)rings of half the size and repeat the algorithm, recursively, until all processors are involved. In the last step in the broadcast algorithm above (for the iterations with i=d in Program 6.2), all the communications are to nearest neighbors.

```
mee=myProc
itd=nProc
dee=log(itd)/log(2)
do k=1,dee
   gee=itd*int(mee/itd)
   itd=itd/2
   t@(gee+itd)=t@gee
enddo
```

Program 6.2 Broadcast on a ring of $P = 2^d$ processors using $\log_2 P$ steps. All communication in this algorithm appears in a single line of code with two @ symbols.

Each of the point-to-point communications t@(gee+itd)=t@gee can be done in a ring topology without contention, that is, without interfering with other communications. Thus, each communication in the do k loop can be done simultaneously, in $\lambda + \mu$ time units. Therefore a complete broadcast requires only $(\lambda + \mu)d = (\lambda + \mu) \log_2 P$ time, a dramatic improvement. Note the similarity of the broadcast algorithm in Program 6.2 and the second phase of the parallel prefix algorithm (Section 6.5), both depicted in Figure 6.3.

In the ring broadcast algorithm, information passes through a processor's communication links many times before it is officially "received" by that processor. If it were possible for processors to do **snooping** on the communication channels, then a broadcast could be done much more quickly. (Snooping means that a processor has the ability to listen to messages passing through its communication hardware that are not necessarily intended for it.) In particular, processor n could send to processor $n-1$ going in the wrong direction and propagate information to everyone in one step, if snooping were possible. Whether a system can do snooping or not is a hardware issue: it may or may not be supported. However, it is for this reason that many commercial systems have built-in system software for doing very efficient broadcasts.

The cost of snooping may seem small, but imagine doing this in an optical network. The direct-connect state for a node in the communication system could consist of having light piped directly (without interference) to the next communication node. However, to do snooping, some of the light would need to be diverted and decoded. This might require amplification of the signal if there is not sufficient power to allow any light to be diverted. Note that the amount of energy diverted would have to grow (at least logarithmically) with the number of processors.

6.2.2 Summation in a ring

Using the immersion of a tree in a ring provides a **recursive doubling** algorithm to compute a sum rapidly on a ring. We start with nearest neighbors and do a summation of their values. Now half of the processors have the sum of two values. If we repeat this again, some of the processors will then have the sum of four values, and so forth, *doubling* the number each time, recursively. Program 6.3 indicates this algorithm, and the algorithm is depicted in Figure 6.2. All (leaf) nodes start with `sum=y`. The odd-numbered leaf nodes send `sum` to its parent, which adds this to the current `sum`. This process is continued "up" the tree until the root is reached.

```
sum=y
mee=myProc
itd=nProc
dee=log(itd)/log(2)
itd=1
do k=1,dee
    itd2=itd*2
    gee=itd2*int(mee/itd2)
    t@gee=sum@(gee+itd)
    sum=sum+t
    itd=itd2
enddo
```

Program 6.3 Algorithm to sum values from $P = 2^d$ processors using a tree immersed in a ring. All communication in this algorithm appears in a single line of code with two `@` symbols.

Note that the only communication required in this summation algorithm can be written in a single line of code in Program 6.3 with two `@` symbols. However, the values of the processor identifiers depend on the processor numbers determined by `myProc`. Indeed, these are the values that are computed by the algorithm in Program 6.1. But writing the communications in one line makes it clear that they go on independently of each other. Therefore the summation is completed in $(\lambda + \mu)\log_2 P$ time.

At the completion of Program 6.3, it will have computed the `sum` of all the `y` values from all the processors, but this value will be the complete sum only at processor `n`. The remaining processors will have some partial sum. If it is desired to have the total sum at all processors, something more

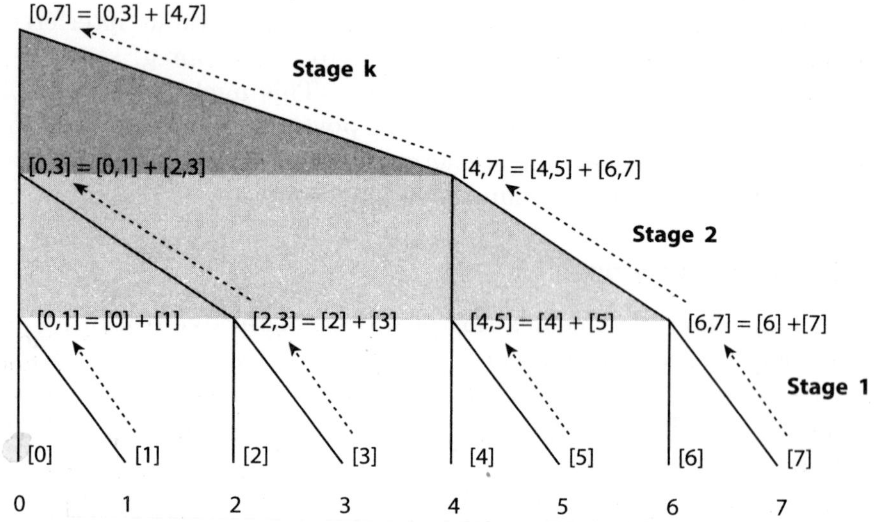

Figure 6.2 Ring algorithm to sum values from $P = 8$ processors. It also forms part 1 of the parallel prefix algorithm for $P = 8$ processors. The notation [j,i] refers to the sum `y@j+` $\cdots$ `+y@i` in the former case, and to $h_j \oplus \cdots \oplus h_i$ in the general parallel prefix case.

must be done. Let us consider how such a value might be broadcast to all processors.

6.3 REDUCTION OPERATIONS

A **reduction operation** *reduces* a *set* of data to a single datum of the same type through the repeated application of a binary operator on pairs of the data. The summation (1.5.2) is the prototypical example. However, we will see that it is useful to think of this type of operation quite generally.

A reduction operation is frequently defined such that the result will itself be distributed in the same way the operands were distributed. However, more complex distributions are possible as occur in the *parallel prefix* algorithm which appears in Section 6.5. That algorithm is similar to the simple summation problem initiated in Section 1.5.1, but it distributes partial sums to processors in a specified way.

It is common practice to restrict the notion of reduction to operations which are not dependent on the order of evaluation, that is, to operations that are associative (and possibly commutative). In mathematical terminology, we are assuming that the set of values being reduced forms a **semigroup** (called Abelian[1] if the operation is commutative) with respect to

[1] The term Abelian memorializes the short life of Niels Henrik Abel (1802-1829), who established fundamental results in algebra. The Abel Prize in Mathematics complements the Nobel prizes, which do not directly recognize mathematical research. The first recipient was Jean-Pierre Serre in 2003, the amount of the prize being 6 million Norwegian kroner.

the binary operator. Let G denote the data type to which we apply the reduction, and let $\oplus$ denote the operator.

The assumption that operations are **associative** means that the order of *evaluation* of the operations does not matter. That is, we assume that $(a \oplus b) \oplus c = a \oplus (b \oplus c)$. However, this may be only approximately true, e.g., with floating point operations. In such a case, it is reasonable to require that the operations be evaluated in a predictable and repeatable order. The order of evaluation of a reduction may depend on the particular architecture or even the number of processors. However, we describe algorithms that are deterministic in the sense that they will always be done in the same order on a given machine with a given number of nodes. In floating point calculations, this can lead to different results on different numbers of processors and different machines, but the results will be repeatable on the same machine with the same number of processors.

The result of a reduction operation can be written mathematically as

$$A = B_0 \oplus B_1 \oplus \cdots \oplus B_{P-1} \tag{6.3.1}$$

for P processors. Here, B_i is the value of B at the i-th processor, and A is the result of the operation $\oplus$ on the *set* of values $\{B_i = \texttt{B@i} \; : \; i = 1, \ldots, P-1\}$ as indicated in (6.3.1). Note that there are no parentheses in (6.3.1); we assume that $\oplus$ is associative, so the evaluation order (placing of parentheses) does not matter.

The assumption that operations are **commutative** means that the order of the *operations* does not matter. That is, it means that $a \oplus b = b \oplus a$ for any $a, b \in G$. This property does not hold for many interesting operations, so in general we do not utilize commutativity. Clearly, commutativity would allow for a richer class of algorithms, and we note when certain operations are commutative.

A critical property of a semi-group is that it has a *unit* u with the property that $u \oplus a = a$ for all a in G. The unit for the usual + operator is zero. This is critical for initializing the value that will hold the result of the reduction operation. We only require that $(G, \oplus)$ forms a semi-group since we never utilize the *group* property of always having an inverse. Many of the operations we consider do correspond to groups, and one could look for algorithms involving inverses, but these seem exotic for our purposes.

The algorithm for summation in a ring in Section 6.2.2 can be applied to a general reduction operation $\oplus$ on a semi-group (see Exercise 6.8). Examples of operators $\oplus$ abound, such as many of the operations that are built in for standard data types. The multiplication operator `*` on numeric types is an associative binary operator. Similarly, various brands of `min` and `max` are found in Fortran, C, and other languages, and these are associative when viewed as binary operators (see Exercise 6.2). Similarly, binary logical operators (`and`, `or`, etc.) are associative on logical variables (see Exercise 6.3).

In a shared memory language, a reduction may not appear as a formal operation, but rather a reduction *variable* is indicated when a loop is parallelized (see Section 10.3.4). The compiler takes care of providing the appropriate synchronization mechanisms to assure that the operation is done correctly. In some systems, a reduction may be done by a nondeterministic algorithm, so caution is advisable in using them.

6.4 REDUCTION OPERATION APPLICATIONS

The reduction of a set of distributed data by a binary operator is a common occurrence in scientific and engineering computations. Here we give some simple examples to show what kinds of structures can arise. We refer to these as user-defined reductions since they are not associated with intrinsic operations of typical programming languages.

Having a concise and intuitive notation streamlines programs, resulting in enhanced readability. Furthermore, by representing the operation in a single statement, efficient algorithms can be implemented by a single algorithm such as described in Section 6.3. These operations are then efficiently implemented in at most $\log_2 P$ steps on a variety of networks with P processors.

6.4.1 Vector algebra

Vector (or array) addition is a familiar group operation, and the vector length can be as large as memory allows. For this new data type, we define *addition* by introducing a subroutine `addvec` that adds two vectors and returns their sum, as shown in Program 6.4. Notice that the length of the vector needs to be known only at run time.

```
subroutine addvec(a,b,c,D)
dimension a(1),b(1),c(1)
do i = 1,D
  c(i) = a(i) + b(i)
enddo
return
end
```

Program 6.4 Code to add two vectors.

Program 8.13 presents an algorithm to multiply a matrix times a vector in parallel that uses a reduction associated with `addvec`. Note that the function `addvec` is clearly associative and commutative; the corresponding reduction adds all the components among all processors.

6.4.2 Matrix multiplication

The operation of matrix multiplication arises in areas as diverse as computer graphics and quantum physics. We consider matrix algebra in detail in later chapters, so we consider only the simplest of cases here. A matrix is simply a vector of vectors (or array of arrays). The smallest interesting case is the two by two matrix, for example,

$$A = \begin{pmatrix} a & b \\ c & d \end{pmatrix}, \quad B = \begin{pmatrix} e & f \\ g & h \end{pmatrix}, \tag{6.4.1}$$

and so forth, where $a, b, \ldots, h$ can be any numeric type (integers, floating point numbers, complex numbers, rational numbers, etc.) but all should be of the same type.

The matrix product is defined in various ways, and it is an important theorem that they are all equivalent, but here we just take by fiat that

$$A \otimes B = \begin{pmatrix} (a \cdot e) + (b \cdot g) & (a \cdot f) + (b \cdot h) \\ (c \cdot e) + (d \cdot g) & (c \cdot f) + (d \cdot h) \end{pmatrix}, \tag{6.4.2}$$

where $a \cdot e$, $b \cdot g$, and so forth indicate ordinary multiplication for the individual entries. Notice that we have rotated the $\oplus$ notation to $\otimes$ so that it looks more like a standard notation for multiplication.

It is well known that matrix multiplication is associative (it follows easily from one of the standard definitions of matrix multiplication, but might be tedious to verify from the definition in (6.4.2)). However, matrix multiplication is not generally commutative:

$$\begin{pmatrix} 1 & 1 \\ 0 & 1 \end{pmatrix} \otimes \begin{pmatrix} 1 & 0 \\ 1 & 1 \end{pmatrix} = \begin{pmatrix} 2 & 1 \\ 1 & 1 \end{pmatrix} \text{ but } \begin{pmatrix} 1 & 0 \\ 1 & 1 \end{pmatrix} \otimes \begin{pmatrix} 1 & 1 \\ 0 & 1 \end{pmatrix} = \begin{pmatrix} 1 & 1 \\ 1 & 2 \end{pmatrix}. \tag{6.4.3}$$

6.4.3 The `minmod` function

We now consider an unusual operator defined on a standard data type: floating point numbers. The `minmod` function arises in discretizing hyperbolic partial differential equations which typically model the transport of some continuum entity. The flux of a quantity of this entity at a point is defined by the spatial derivative of the quantity, and it is often approximated by finite differences of the quantity at neighboring points. Often "shocks" or discontinuities in the quantity can form, and this makes the derivative ill-defined; taking finite differences yields ambiguous results depending on which side of the discontinuity you are working on. Thus the flux of a quantity at a point is often characterized by the smaller of the finite differences of that quantity in some vicinity of the point, because near a shock (jump in quantity) the larger values may be unreliable. The binary function `minmod` is used to find the smaller value. It is defined as follows.

Given two input values of the same sign, `minmod` returns the value with the minimum modulus (absolute value). When there is a sign disagreement between two values, zero is returned. (This corresponds to the case of a variable that cannot decide whether it is coming or going.) We define the scalar function `minmod` as shown in Program 6.5. We leave as Exercise 6.4 to show that this is an associative operation.

```
      real function minmod(s1,s2)
      if (s1*s2 .gt. 0.0 .and. s1.lt.0.0) then
C       s1 and s2 are < 0
        minmod = AMAX1(s1,s2)
      else if (s1*s2 .gt. 0.0)      then
C       s1 and s2 are > 0
        minmod = AMIN1(s1,s2)
      else
C     If s1 and s2 are not of the same sign or one is 0
         minmod = 0.0
      endif
      return
      end
```

Program 6.5 Code to compute the `minmod` function.

6.4.4 Pivot determination

A slightly more complicated application of a reduction operation arises in Gaussian elimination (the standard algorithm for solving systems of linear equations, cf. Section 12.1.1) with row pivoting. Not only does this involve a novel operation, but the semi-group of values to which it applies is more complex. It is a Cartesian product of a discrete type (integers) and floating point numbers.

Define the space $\mathcal{X} \equiv \mathcal{Z}^+ \times \mathcal{R}^+$, where $\mathcal{Z}^+ \equiv$ *positive integers* and $\mathcal{R}^+ \equiv$ *non-negative real numbers*. This space represents the Cartesian product of *row numbers* with absolute values of *pivot entries* from the matrix. We now define a function $\mathcal{C} : \mathcal{X} \times \mathcal{X} \to \mathcal{X}$, where

$$\mathcal{C}\big((i,x),(j,y)\big) = \begin{cases} (i,x), & \text{if } x > y, \\ (j,y), & \text{if } y > x, \\ (i,x), & \text{if } i < j,\ y = x, \\ (j,y), & \text{if } j < i,\ y = x, \\ (i,x) = (j,y), & \text{if } i = j,\ y = x. \end{cases} \tag{6.4.4}$$

Thus (see Exercise 6.5), $\mathcal{C}$ is associative and commutative and can be utilized in a reduction operation. The meaning of $\mathcal{C}$ may be somewhat obscure, but it is in some ways similar to `minmod`. It is also very similar to the "arg-max" function used frequently in optimization problems. Given two (index,value) pairs, it returns the maximum value and the index that was associated with it. The extra logic in (6.4.4) has to do with making decisions in case of ties.

A Fortran implementation of $\mathcal{C}$ called `Cpivot` is given in Program 6.6. It would be an error in Gaussian elimination if the pivot function were given two values with the same index, so the code flags this error. In Gaussian elimination, (index,value) pairs come from array elements, that is, they are of the form (i, a_i). If the indices were the same then so would be the value. Note that we define a value for $\mathcal{C}(w, w)$ in the last line of (6.4.4) for completeness. The pivot function is always applied initially to the absolute value of the matrix entries.

```
subroutine Cpivot(p1,p2)
real* 8 p1(2),p2(2)
integer* 4 i,j
real* 4 v,w
v = p1(1)
i = p1(2)
w = p2(1)
j = p2(2)
if ( v .gt. w ) then
  p2(1) = p1(1)
  p2(2) = p1(2)
else if ( v .eq. w ) then
  if ( i.eq.j ) then
    print* , Error: Cpivot() has same row p1 and p2
  else if ( i .lt. j ) then
    p2(1) = p1(1)
    P2(2) = p1(2)
  endif
endif
return
end
```

Program 6.6 Code to determine the pivot between two possible choices, **p1** and **p2**, which contain an array element from row(k) and the array index k.

6.4.5 Set operations

It is often necessary to perform operations on sets. These can be represented in a variety of ways. In the prime number sieve described in Section 1.5.1, it is necessary to form the union of all the primes that are found by separate processors when the algorithm is parallelized by dividing the "n" loop. Since the order of the primes is irrelevant to the algorithm (at least as described there), we could simply use arrays of integers to represent the set. The union operation consists simply of making the array longer. We leave it as an exercise (see Exercise 6.6) to code such an operation using message passing.

When the prime number sieve algorithm is parallelized by dividing the "π" loop, it is necessary to form a set intersection in order to determine the "true" primes. A standard representation of a finite set is via a "bit" vector, that is, an array whose bit-wise values indicate set membership. More precisely, suppose we want to consider sets of integers in the range k to k^2 for some integer k. We represent subsets of $[k, k^2]$ via an array of 32-bit integers of length $(k^2 - k)/32$. If the i-th bit of the array is one, then $k + i$ is in the set. If it is zero, then it is not. With this representation, set intersection is done by a bit-wise "and" operation.

6.5 PARALLEL PREFIX ALGORITHMS

The **parallel prefix** algorithm can be used for a very general type of operation [100]. Suppose we have an operator $\oplus$ that is associative and we wish to compute all of the partial "sums" ($\oplus$'s)

$$g_i := h_i \oplus h_{i-1} \oplus \cdots \oplus h_1 \tag{6.5.1}$$

for $i = 1, \ldots, 2^d$. Moreover, suppose that we start with each datum h_i at the i-th processor, and that we want to have the results g_i distributed to the i-th processor as well.

For motivation, imagine that $h_i =$ `y@i` and $\oplus$ is just ordinary addition. The partial sums play no role in the summation problems considered so far, but they do in more complex applications such as those discussed in Section 12.2.3. Using a binary tree immersed in a ring as defined in Program 6.1 via the array `proc`, we can compute this as follows in two phases.

In the first phase, the i-th leaf node starts with $t = h_i$ and sends t to its parent. Each parent node receives t_ℓ and t_r from its left and right children, respectively, and then computes the operation $t = t_\ell \oplus t_r$ and sends t to its parent. (For a tree immersed in a ring, as defined by the mapping defined in Program 6.1, the parent of the left child is the same as the child itself.) This process is continued "up" the tree until the root is reached. This is identical to the summation algorithm depicted in Figure 6.2, except that now "+" should be interpreted more generally as the operation $\oplus$ in (6.5.1).

In the first phase, processors need to accumulate more than just a working data structure. For example, at the end of the first phase (with eight processors), processors will have data as shown in Table 6.1. Thus the number of distinct data items is $\log_2 P$ in the worst case (at processor zero).

In the second phase, the parent nodes send data back to their right children, who then use it to compute the required results. Right child nodes compute $t = t_\ell \oplus t$ and pass the result down to (right) child nodes. This process is continued "down" the tree until the leaf nodes are reached. The second phase of this algorithm is depicted in Figure 6.3. Note its similarity to the broadcast algorithm in Program 6.2.

The two phases complete in $2d = 2 \log_2 P$ steps. Note that certain terms are computed redundantly by different processors. These computations could be replaced by appropriate communications instead. For ex-

processor number	data stored
0	[0] [0,1] [0,3] [0,7]
1	[1]
2	[2] [2,3]
3	[3]
4	[4] [4,5] [4,7]
5	[5]
6	[6] [6,7]
7	[7]

Table 6.1 Data storage for parallel prefix algorithm.

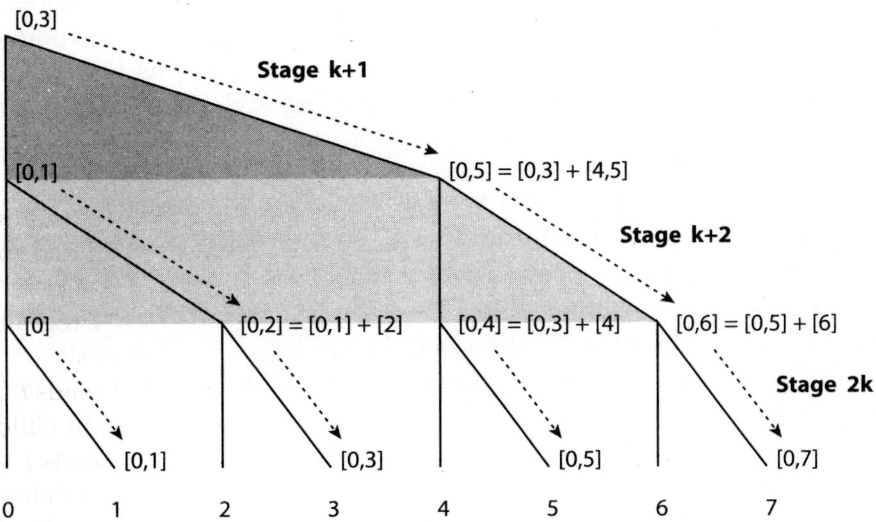

Figure 6.3 Parallel prefix algorithm for $P = 8$ processors: phase 2.

ample, processor zero has $h_3 \oplus \cdots \oplus h_0$, and this could be sent to processor three, avoiding an intermediate computation, but at the expense of increased communication. See Section 12.2.3 for an example where this might be appropriate.

6.6 PERFORMANCE OF REDUCTION OPERATIONS

We now consider the performance of different implementations of reduction operations on a distributed memory computer. There may be hardware support for a broadcast, but what we have seen is that a broadcast would require at most $(\lambda + \mu)\log_2 P$ time in any network that includes a ring with point-to-point communications that can execute independently.

The summation algorithm in Program 6.3, together with the required

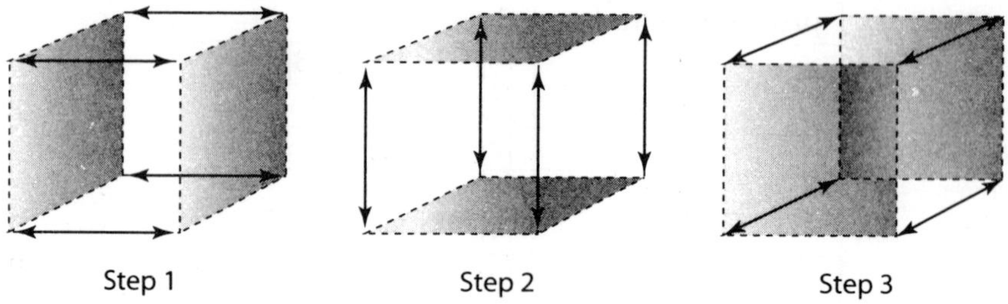

Figure 6.4 Dimensional exchange algorithm for a three-dimensional hypercube.

broadcast in Program 6.2, is completed in $2(\lambda + \mu)\log_2 P + F \log_2 P$ time, where F denotes the time required to do the operation `sum=sum+t`.

It is possible to compute a reduction faster on different networks, although the improvement may be only by a constant factor. On a hypercube, the **dimensional exchange** algorithm is quite effective, as illustrated in Figure 6.4. We present it in a message passing style in Program 6.7 to emphasize its efficiency and simplicity. Here `xor` is the logical "exclusive or" function, and `cubedim` is the dimension of the hypercube, that is, the number of processors $P = 2^{\mathtt{cubedim}}$. The algorithm is a recursive doubling algorithm, iterating over the dimensions of the hypercube. At each iteration, or "stage," exchanges are made between neighbors in that dimension, and the results are added together. After the j-th step, each node has the sum of 2^j numbers. This algorithm requires only $(\lambda+\mu)\log_2 P + F\log_2 P$ time units if the exchanges can be done simultaneously, and $2(\lambda + \mu)\log_2 P + F\log_2 P$ time units if not.

```
      pvar=1
      do 10 dim = 1, cubedim
         call snd(dim,sum,type,xor(myProc,pvar), size)
         call rcv(dim,temp,type,xor(myProc,pvar), size)
         sum=sum+temp
         pvar=pvar *2
   10 continue
```

Program 6.7 Hypercube algorithm to sum values from $P = 2^d$ processors. The loop index `dim` plays the role of "tag" for the messages.

6.6.1 Combining large things

A reduction that adds large vectors (e.g., `Y(1:100000)`) can be done by any of the reduction algorithms as above, with a time complexity of $c(\lambda + \mu N)\log_2 P + FN\log_2 P$ time units, with $N = 100000$. For N sufficiently large, the latency λ is no longer the dominant factor in this complexity estimate; rather, the throughput, measured by μ, is more important.

The optimal implementation of a particular reduction operation will depend, in general, on the size of the data being exchanged. The summation of vectors can be done more efficiently by recursively subdividing the vector and adding parts of the vector at each step when `N` is sufficiently large [49]. (However, for small `N` this approach is suboptimal [141].) The resulting complexity is only $c(\lambda \log_2 P + \mu N) + FN \log_2 P$ time units, providing an improvement in performance by a factor of $\log_2 P$ for large N. We will not give the complete algorithm for this here, but it is very close to an algorithm for concatenating vector entries, which we now describe.

Suppose the j-th processor starts with only a segment of an array `XI` defined, namely,

$$\texttt{XI}(jN/P + 1 : (j+1)N/P),$$

and we wish to combine these into one vector having all of the elements. This could be done by putting zeros in every location not in each processor's segment and using a vector sum reduction. This would again result in a time complexity of $c(\lambda + \mu N) \log_2 P + FN \log_2 P$ time units. However, in Program 6.8, we present an improved algorithm (compare this with Program 8.8). The key step is exchange with neighbors in a hypercube which doubles the size of the vector exchanged at each step, i.e., recursive doubling. This has a complexity of $c\lambda \log_2 P + \mu N + FN$ time units; note that $\log_2 P$ no longer multiplies N. The constant c is 1 if the exchanges can be done simultaneously, and 2 if not.

```
      mask = 1
      muchmo = N/P
      do idim = 1, CUBEDIM
        XI(1+XOR(myProc,mask)*muchmo :
     1    (1+XOR(myProc,mask))*muchmo)
     2    = XI(1+XOR(myProc,mask)*muchmo :
     3         (XOR(myProc,mask)+1)*muchmo )@XOR(myProc,mask)
        mask = mask*2
        muchmo = muchmo*2
      enddo
```

Program 6.8 Hypercube-based recursive doubling algorithm to concatenate vectors.

6.6.2 "Optimal" algorithms

In general, the question of the optimal algorithm for a particular architecture and a particular number of processors is an open problem. Depending on the particular hardware support available, there may be faster algorithms. For example, consider a communication system that has hardware support for

- multicast (the ability to send the same message to many destinations

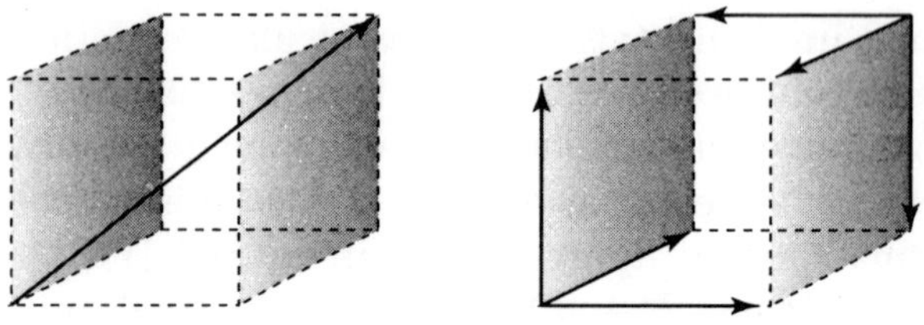

Figure 6.5 Special exchange algorithm for a three-dimensional hypercube using only two stages.

at once, in the same amount of time as a single message),

- direct-connect (see Section 3.3.3) point-to-point communications (but without snooping).

Communication paths are not allowed to cross at any given instant; i.e., the direct-connect, point-to-point communication paths must not intersect. To be more precise, consider all paths in a fixed stage and write the i-th communication path in this stage as a sequence of nodes $n_0^i \to n_1^i \to \cdots \to n_{k_i}^i$. We assume that any set of such paths has the property that

$$\bigcap_i \{n_j^i \; : \; j = 1, \ldots, k_i\} = \emptyset \tag{6.6.1}$$

and if $n_0^i = n_j^\ell$ for some i, j, ℓ then $j = 0$. That is, the only possible coincidences in nodes occur at the starting nodes for a multicast.

This type of communication network can be supported by a very simple switch at each node. For systems with such hardware, we can derive faster algorithms for basic reduction operations. For simplicity, we assume that communication times are independent of path length.

For example, suppose a three-dimensional cube network architecture supports a multicast operation to the nearest neighbors as well as point-to-point communications to all processors. Then one can do a broadcast in two stages instead of the three required by dimensional exchange, as indicated in Figure 6.5. First, make a point-to-point exchange with the processor at the opposite corner. This can be done by a variety of routes along three consecutive edges. Then have this processor and the original one use the nearest neighbor multicast operation to complete the transmission to the remaining six processors. Since this reduces the factor multiplying the latency and bandwidth from three to two, it is potentially faster.

One can generalize this type of routing of information to networks using higher-dimensional hypercubes.[2] For example, we can show how to do it in a four-dimensional hypercube, as follows. Write the four-cube as a pair of three-dimensional cubes, and multicast to the antipodal point of

[2]The following results in this section represent a collaboration with Stuart Kurtz and Janos Simon.

the three-cube having the starting point together with two antipodal points in the other cube. By inspection (see Exercise 6.16), this can be done via routes that do not have any vertices in common (other than the starting vertex). The second stage is now the same as the three-dimensional case in the two separate subcubes.

One can give simple lower bounds on the number of stages k needed to route without contention via multicast to a hypercube of dimension d. At each stage, the increase in the number of nodes that have gained information cannot be more than a factor of $d+1$. In k steps, at most $(d+1)^k$ nodes will have the required information, so to broadcast to all nodes we must have $(d+1)^k \geq 2^d$, or

$$k \geq \frac{d}{\log_2(d+1)}. \tag{6.6.2}$$

Thus for $d \geq 6$, we need at least three stages. In Exercises 6.18 and 6.20, you are asked to show that three stages are sufficient for dimensions $d = 6$ and $d = 7$, respectively. Although (6.6.2) does not suffice, Exercise 6.21 shows that three stages are also necessary for $d = 5$. We leave as exercises to work out some algorithms for some other cases as well.

6.7 DATA MOVEMENT OPERATIONS

A broadcast simply moves data from one processor to many processors. There is no mathematical (or other) operation performed on the data in the process, unlike reduction operations. There are other types of data movement that are often useful that involve collective actions.

Since the broadcast sends data from one to many, it is reasonable to consider if an inverse operation (from many to one) makes sense. A reduction is a form of this, but it involves a mathematical operation to reduce the collection of objects to a single object. This does not work if we want to collect apples and oranges. The result of a general collection process must be thought of as a set (or array) of data. Thus a **gather** operation is one in which data are sent from a group of processors to a single processor and put into an array at that processor. The inverse **scatter** operation sends an array of data from one processor to a group of processors. Detailed syntax for such operations will be presented in Section 7.2.2.

The dual operations "scatter" and "gather" have different meanings in different contexts. In vector computing (Section 3.4), they are used to compress (gather) noncontiguous data into contiguous storage so that efficient vector operations can be performed. Results may then need to be scattered to corresponding noncontiguous locations for further processing. This use of scatter-gather corresponds to a sequential paradigm, but we could think of what it might look like in a shared memory parallel context. If memory were partitioned and ownership assigned to different processors (see Section 5.6.5), then a gather might move data from the ownership areas of one collection of processors to another.

Other combinations of these concepts are possible. For example, you may want to gather a collection of data from many processors to one processor, and then broadcast this collection to a group of processors. This is possible in one step in MPI using the MPI "AllGather" routine (Section 7.2.2). An example of this appears in Program 8.5.

6.8 EXERCISES

Exercise 6.1. What are the partial sums at the various processors at the completion of the ring-summation algorithm in Program 6.3? Show this explicitly for $P = 16$. Assume that the root of the computation is processor zero for simplicity.

Exercise 6.2. Explain how the `max` and `min` functions can be viewed as binary operators and prove that they are associative. Are they commutative as well? If so, prove this; if not, give an example.

Exercise 6.3. Which logical operators (e.g., `and`, `or`, etc.) can be viewed as associative binary operators (prove that they are associative)? Are they commutative as well? If so, prove this; if not, give an example.

Exercise 6.4. Prove that the `minmod` function can be viewed as an associative binary operator. Is it commutative as well? If so, prove this; if not, give an example.

Exercise 6.5. Prove that the pivot function (6.4.4) can be viewed as an associative and commutative binary operator.

Exercise 6.6. Use message passing or the `@` notaton to perform unions of sets of integers computed on separate processors. Allow for the cardinality of the sets to be arbitrary (including zero). Apply this to the prime number sieve parallelization via the "n" loop as described in Section 1.5.1.

Exercise 6.7. Use message passing or the `@` notaton to perform intersections of sets of integers computed on separate processors. Apply this to the prime number sieve parallelization via the "π" loop as described in Section 1.5.1.

Exercise 6.8. Describe an algorithm with $\log_2 P$ steps for a general, noncommutative reduction operation $\oplus$ on a ring with $P = 2^d$ processors. Prove that it is correct. Does the order of evaluation depend on P? (Hint: see Program 6.3; keep the order right at each step.)

Exercise 6.9. Describe an algorithm using dimensional exchange as shown in Figure 6.4 for a reduction for a *noncommutative* operation $\oplus$ on a hypercube with $P = 2^d$ processors. (Hint: keep the order right at each step.)

Exercise 6.10. Describe an algorithm with $1+\log_2 P$ steps for a general reduction operation $\oplus$ on a ring for the general case with $P \neq 2^d$ processors. (Hint: embed the ring into one with $P = 2^d$ processors and apply Exercise 6.8.)

Exercise 6.11. Describe a $\log_2 P$ algorithm for a general reduction operation $\oplus$ on a mesh.

Exercise 6.12. Write an algorithm to compute the sum of vectors `A(1:N)` that recursively subdivides `A(1:N)` and sums the smaller pieces, on a hypercube network. Assume that $N = 2^k$ for some integer k and that the number of processors $P = 2^d$ for some integer $d < k$. (Hint: see Program 6.8.)

Exercise 6.13. Write an algorithm to compute the sum of vectors `A(1:N)` that recursively subdivides `A(1:N)` and sums the smaller pieces, on a ring network. Assume that $N = 2^k$ for some integer k and that the number of processors $P = 2^d$ for some integer $d < k$. (Hint: see Program 6.8.)

Exercise 6.14. Prove that the dimensional exchange algorithm, as depicted in Figure 6.4 and in Program 6.7, is correct, that is, that it computes the correct sum at all nodes. (Hint: do an induction on the dimension.)

Exercise 6.15. Consider strings Σ^* from an alphabet Σ with binary operation $a.b$ given by concatenation. Write a parallel program with a user-defined reduction to compute the following string:

```
the quick brown fox jumped over the lazy dog
```

Exercise 6.16. Show that contention-free routing can be done as described in Section 6.6.2 to all nodes in a four-dimensional hypercube in two steps. (Hint: you just need to draw a picture to show that the first step can be done without contention as claimed.)

Exercise 6.17. Show that contention-free routing can be done via multicast to all nodes in a two-dimensional subcube of a three-dimensional hypercube in one step. (Hint: you just need to route to the corner; go to the back of the cube, up and over, then back to the front.)

Exercise 6.18. Show that contention-free routing can be done via multicast to all nodes in a six-dimensional hypercube in three steps. (Hint: write the six-cube as a two-cube with four-cubes at each vertex. Use Exercise 6.17 to route to all of the vertices of the two-cube in step one. Now use the result previously derived for each four-cube.)

Exercise 6.19. Show that contention-free routing can be done via multicast to all nodes in a three-dimensional subcube of a seven-dimensional hypercube in one step. (Hint: look at Exercise 6.17.)

Exercise 6.20. Show that contention-free routing can be done in a seven-dimensional hypercube via multicast to all nodes in three steps. (Hint: write the seven-cube as a three-cube with four-cubes at each vertex. Use Exercise 6.17 to route to all of the vertices of the three-cube in step one. Now use the result previously derived for each four-cube.)

Exercise 6.21. Show that contention-free routing can **not** be done to all nodes in a five-dimensional hypercube in two steps. (Hint: show that it is not possible to cover the five-cube with six balls of radius one, where vertices are distance one away if they differ in only one dimension.)

Exercise 6.22. Show that contention-free routing can **not** be done to all nodes in a eleven-dimensional hypercube in less than four steps. (Hint: use (6.6.2).)

Exercise 6.23. Show that contention-free routing **can** be done to all nodes in a eleven-dimensional hypercube in five steps. (Hint: view the eleven-cube as a three-cube each of whose vertices is a four-cube whose vertices are four-cubes. Use Exercise 6.19 and the result for four-cubes in Section 6.6.2.)

Chapter Seven
Current Programming Standards

> The problem with standards is that they keep changing—*who said that?*

It dates a book to say anything about anything current. But it is helpful to examine current programming standards for two reasons. First it provides an easier entry point for using them to implement specific algorithms. Second it illustrates the abstract principles presented so far. We therefore give a brief introduction to two widely accepted parallel programming standards, one related to the message passing paradigm (MPI) and the other to the shared memory paradigm (Posix threads).

7.1 INTRODUCTION TO MPI

Message passing libraries have a long history. Most of the early commercial distributed memory machines had their own libraries. Although these had many key features in common, the syntax often had slight differences. These inconsistencies made porting codes between machines tedious. One early attempt to provide a common message passing interface was TCGMSG [73], developed in the Theoretical Chemistry Group (TCG) at Argonne National Laboratory. Libraries with the TCGMSG subroutine interfaces were then developed for many commercial parallel processors.

Later, the Parallel Virtual Machine (PVM) [50] message passing library was developed which allowed parallel execution not just on different parallel computers but on a collection of different architectures simultaneously. To do so requires exchanges of data in different binary formats. Most recently, the Message Passing Interface (MPI) developed as a community-wide effort to define a comprehensive message passing interface for parallel computation. The most popular message passing library currently is MPI [47]. Here we give a brief introduction for those who want to start programming with this system. For further information, consult [59, 136].

7.1.1 Message passing in MPI

As described in [59], one can think of MPI as either a large or a small system. Here we focus on MPI as a small system, both for simplicity and because the small system can be viewed as a version of the pure message passing paradigm introduced in Section 5.5. The MPI library has similar bindings for Fortran, C, and C++, so we illustrate its use just with Fortran, but we use the case-sensitive C/C++ names.

The two basic operations of send and receive (cf. Section 5.5.1) in MPI have the syntax

```
MPI_Send(memlocat, size, type, procwhich, tag,
         comunikatr)
MPI_Recv(memlocat, size, type, procwhich, tag,
         comunikatr, status)
```

where the variables `memlocat`, `size`, `type`, `procwhich`, and `tag` have the same meaning as in Section 5.5.1. The new variable `comunikatr`, which indicates the **communicator** being used, allows for the concept of user-defined (sub-)groups of processors to be utilized, as well as the notion of a "context" [59]. Here we will just assume that the communicator being used is the default one including all processors which is denoted by

```
MPI_COMM_WORLD
```

and is an MPI key word (that is, it should not be used in your code in some other way, e.g., you should not make an assignment to it). The additional variable `status` in the MPI receive command gives feedback on the message actually received, e.g., on the size of the message. The syntax of various types for messages includes

```
MPI_LOGICAL      MPI_CHARACTER      MPI_INTEGER
MPI_REAL         MPI_COMPLEX        MPI_DOUBLE_PRECISION
```

but see [59, 136] for a complete list, as well as for the C and C++ counterparts.

The number `nProc` of processors and the identity `myProc` of the processor executing the code are determined in MPI by the calls

```
MPI_COMM_RANK(MPI_COMM_WORLD, myProc, ierror)
MPI_COMM_SIZE(MPI_COMM_WORLD, nProc, ierror)
```

where the variable `ierror` just provides information on potential errors that may occur. Note that the default communicator appears as a variable as well.

At the beginning and end of an MPI code, there is a need for explicit initialization and termination, which are achieved by the calls

```
MPI_INIT(ierror)
MPI_FINALIZE(ierror)
```

respectively. An example of the baton passing code (cf. Program 5.7) written in MPI is given in Program 7.1.

```
      integer*4 baton
      MPI_INIT(ierror)
      baton = 0
      MPI_COMM_RANK(MPI_COMM_WORLD, myProc, ierror)
      MPI_COMM_SIZE(MPI_COMM_WORLD, nProc, ierror)
      do i=0, nProc-2
        if(myProc .eq. i)
          print*, 'hello from', myProc, baton
          baton = baton + 1
          call MPI_Send(baton, 1, MPI_INTEGER, i+1, i,
     *                  MPI_COMM_WORLD )
        else if(myProc .eq. i+1)
          call MPI_Recv(baton, 1, MPI_INTEGER, i, i,
     *                  MPI_COMM_WORLD, status)
        endif
      enddo
        if (myProc .eq. nProc -1)
          print*, 'hello from', myProc
        endif
      MPI_FINALIZE(ierror)
      end
```

Program 7.1 MPI code to implement baton passing.

Finally, the invocation of an executable MPI code (consult your local system regarding linking to the MPI library when compiled) is done on most machines by syntax something like

```
mpirun -np 1000 codename
```

which indicates that the executable named `codename` is to be run on 1000 processors.

7.1.2 MPI message blocking and buffering

MPI allows for the distinction between blocking and nonblocking communication. When data are sent from a given processor, there are several situations that may arise in different applications. It may be that the sending processor is free to proceed no matter when or whether the receiving processor gets the message. In this case, a **nonblocking** send is appropriate.

It might be natural to think of "send" as nonblocking, but the issue to consider is when it is safe to access the data stored in the data buffer being sent (`memlocat` in the examples in Section 7.1.1). Using a blocking send ensures correctness even if the very next line of code modifies this data (e.g., writes to `memlocat`).

There is also a subtle distinction between the standard (blocking) send discussed previously, which may wait until the message is received, and the following variants:

- a "ready" send (**Rsend**), which may not start until a matching receive is posted,
- a buffered send (**Bsend**), where the message is buffered locally, and then the sender is released,
- and a synchronous send (**Ssend**) (or **rendezvous**), in which the sender waits until the receive is completed at the receiving processor.

Further, users are given control over buffers in that they are allowed the option of providing guaranteed buffer space for messages. The blocking routines are thus

```
MPI_Send()          MPI_Bsend()          MPI_Ssend()
MPI_Rsend()         MPI_Recv()
```

It might be equally natural to think of "receive" as always blocking. But there are many uses for a less restrictive type of approach. For example, you might post the receive as soon as you are ready for the data, continue to do other computations, and only stop when you really need the data that you have asked to receive. A blocking receive forces the initial and final actions to occur simultaneously, leaving no room for intermediate work. The nonblocking routines are

```
MPI_Isend()         MPI_Ibsend()         MPI_Issend()
MPI_Irsend()        MPI_Irecv()
```

The letters after the I and before **send** indicate a "ready" send (r), a buffered send (b), and a synchronous send (s), which are related to the concepts for blocking sends just discussed. We defer to the manuals on MPI for more details about these send commands. Here we focus on the main nonblocking commands Isend and Irecv.

In using nonblocking sends and receives, what is needed is some way to tell if the actions have been completed. MPI introduces the concept of a **request** which provides a way to name a particular communication. The syntax is the same as for the standard blocking routines except for the addition of a request variable at the end, viz.,

```
MPI_Isend(memlocat, size, type, procwhich, tag,
          comunikatr, rekwest)
MPI_Irecv(memlocat, size, type, procwhich, tag,
          comunikatr, status, rekwest)
```

where the variable rekwest is the "request" handle. There are two routines to deal with requests:

```
MPI_Wait(rekwest, stadus, ierror)
MPI_Test(rekwest, flagg, stadus, ierror)
```

where the variable `rekwest` is specified in a nonblocking message as above or others (replace `I` by `Ib`, `Ir`, etc.) The `stadus` variable indicates the status of the completed message. The flag variable `flagg`, which is "true" if the message is completed and "false" otherwise, is simply a type of semaphore (Section 5.4.1). Thus the functionality of "wait" is the same as doing an "if" test on the flag using the "test" routine.

7.1.3 MPI fusions

MPI provides a way to support something similar to message fusions (Section 6.1), that is, combinations of sends and receives. The MPI command

```
MPI_Sendrecv(memlocat, size, type, procto, sendtag,
             omemlocat, osize, otype, procfrom, rcvtag,
             comunikatr, status)
```

has syntax similar to a combination of MPI "send" and "receive" commands, except now everything is combined in one line. Of course, this allows more complicated types of operations than simple fusions like `y@n= x@m`, and `Sendrecv` is a collective operation in that everyone must both send and receive at the same time. Fusions of this type are discussed in Chapter 8.

7.2 COLLECTIVE OPERATIONS IN MPI

MPI provides a broad spectrum of collective operations, including reductions, data-movement operations, and parallel prefix operations.

7.2.1 Reductions in MPI

A simple use of a reduction operation appears in Program 2.2. The two basic reduction operations in MPI have syntax like

```
MPI_Reduce(in, out, size, type, reduxwho, procwhich,
           comunikatr, ierror)
MPI_Allreduce(in, out, size, type, reduxwho,
           comunikatr, ierror)
```

where the variables `comunikatr`, `type`, and `ierror` have the same meaning as in Section 7.1. The variable `in` is the thing being reduced, which needs to be an array of length `size` and type `type`. The result of the "Reduce" reduction will be stored in `out` on the processor `procwhich`, whereas the result of the "AllReduce" reduction will be stored in `out` on all processors involved in the specified communicator.

The types of reduction possible, which are indicated by the variable `reduxwho`, include

```
MPI_SUM        MPI_MAX        MPI_MIN        MPI_PROD
MPI_LAND       MPI_BAND       MPI_MAXLOC
```

as well as others. The "MAXLOC" reduction is very similar to the action of pivot determination described in Section 6.4.4. MPI also provides a "MIN-LOC" reduction that is analogous to the "argmin" function often used in optimization (which returns a point at which the minimum occurs).

MPI provides for the parallel prefix, or **scan**, algorithm (Section 6.5) via

```
MPI_Scan(sendbuf, recvbuf, size, type, opuradur,
         comunikatr, ierror)
```

where the variables `comunikatr`, `type`, and `ierror` have the same meaning as in Section 7.1. The buffer `sendbuf` contains the thing being reduced, which needs to be an array of length `size` and type `type`. The result of the "scan" reduction using the operator `opuradur` will be stored in `recvbuf` on all processors as in the parallel prefix algorithm.

7.2.2 MPI data movement operations

MPI also includes a broadcast routine with the syntax

```
MPI_Bcast(commbuf, size, type, root, comunikatr, ierror)
```

where the variables `comunikatr`, `type`, and `ierror` have the same meaning as in Section 7.1. The buffer `commbuf` contains the thing being broadcast, which needs to be an array of length `size` and type `type`. The buffer `commbuf` is sent from processor `root` to all processors in `comunikatr` and placed in the corresponding storage location. Thus `commbuf` is both input and output for the broadcast.

Example 7.2.1. The "AllReduce" statement in Program 2.2 is equivalent to the two statements

```
MPI_Reduce(S, SG, 1, MPI_REAL, MPI_SUM, 0,
           MPI_COMM_WORLD, ierror)
MPI_Bcast(SG, 1, MPI_REAL, 0, MPI_COMM_WORLD,
          ierror)
```

MPI includes other operations that are frequently needed in practice. The dual operations "scatter" and "gather" (Section 6.7) in MPI have the specific syntax

```
MPI_Gather(memlocat, size, type, omemlocat,
           osize, otype, root, comunikatr, ierror)
MPI_Scatter(memlocat, size, type, omemlocat,
           osize, otype, root, comunikatr, ierror)
```

where the data variables are similar to the "sendreceive" command and `root` is the source (resp., destination) processor for the scatter (resp., gather); precisely, `memlocat, size, type` define the input and `omemlocat, osize, otype` define the output.

The MPI gather takes individual values and creates an array of them at one processor. It may be useful to then broadcast the result to all processors. MPI provides for this operation via

```
MPI_Allgather(memlocat, size, type, omemlocat,
              osize, otype, comunikatr, ierror)
```

Note that there is no need to specify a "root" since it is an all-to-all operation. Using the `@` notation introduced in Section 6.1, a we can describe the "AllGather" command as achieving `O(p)=M@p` for all processors `p` in `comunikatr`, where `O` is stored starting at `omemlocat` and `M` is stored starting at `memlocat`.

A more complicated all-to-all operation is

```
MPI_Alltoall(memlocat, size, type, omemlocat,
             osize, otype, comunikatr, ierror)
```

which can be described using the `@` notation. It corresponds to

```
Om(p)@q=Me(q)@p
```

for all processors `p` and `q` in `comunikatr`, where `Om` is stored starting at `omemlocat` and `Me` is stored starting at `memlocat`.

7.2.3 MPI user-defined reductions

In addition to built-in reduction types, there is a facility for user-defined reductions. The key ingredient is

```
MPI_Op_create(usrfunk, commute, opname)
```

where `usrfunk` is a user-supplied function, `commute` is a logical variable indicating whether `usrfunk` is a commutative operation or not (it is assumed to be associative), and `opname` is a handle that can be used in a reduction statement to name the type of reduction, that is, it would take the place of `reduxwho` in the examples above.

The user-supplied function (`usrfunk` in our example) must have a prescribed form, for example,

```
usrfunk(inputvec, inoutvec, lenth, whatype)
```

where `inputvec` and `inoutvec` are the input vectors, and `inoutvec` is the output vector, both of length `lenth` and type `whatype`. In Section 8.3.2, we will see a similar type of functionality with a slightly more flexible interface (allowing optional variables to define how `usrfunk` works).

7.2.4 More MPI collective operations

MPI provides a barrier (Section 5.4.3)

```
MPI_Barrier(comunikatr, ierror)
```

which acts as a barrier to all of the processes in `comunikatr`. There are also vector variants of many of the reduction commands to allow efficient reductions with arrays as inputs.

7.3 INTRODUCTION TO POSIX THREADS

The concepts of threads and processes are quite old by computing standards. In Section 5.6.4, we discussed how they differ in current usage with regard to memory model. However, the concepts emerged over time, and the names evolved as well. In early work of Dijkstra[1] [41], the concept of a "process" appeared in a shared memory context. The Unix process was later introduced with a virtual address space, thus providing a model of distributed memory. The move back to the original concept of parallel "things" working in shared memory then coined them "threads" to evoke in part their light weight.

As MPI is to the general concept of message passing, so POSIX (for Portable Operating System Interface) threads are to the general concept of shared memory programming. POSIX threads (or **pthreads** for short) provide portability for shared memory codes across different computer platforms.

7.3.1 Parallel do in pthreads

The main concept of a "parallel do" statement is incorporated in a function that creates independent threads that can each do independent work. This has the syntax

```
pthread_create( &athred, athredattribut,
                (void *)&thredfunkshun, (void *) &sumarg);
```

The action is done by the user-defined function named `thredfunkshun` in this example.

The summation problem is represented in Program 7.2 using POSIX threads in C, with several of the "include" statements omitted for readability. This code computes the partial sums in (1.5.1) in parallel using the user-defined function named `localsum`. The pthreads "create" command does the main job of setting off separate tasks, but there are several additional commands that must be invoked to prepare the way, as indicated in Program 7.2.

[1]Turing Award winner Edsger Wybe Dijkstra (1930–2002) introduced key concepts to computing, such as structured programming, synchronization, guarded commands, and semaphores. He

The performance of Program 7.2 on a 12-processor Sun Microsystems SunFire 6800 is presented in Figure 7.1. It is interesting to note the limit on scalability and the unpredictability of the performance once there are as many threads as processors.

We will not present an extensive introduction to POSIX threads beyond the one implicit in Program 7.2. However, Program 7.2 does not demonstrate any complex synchronization in pthreads, and the way synchronization is done in pthreads provides a useful review of the concepts in Section 5.4.

7.3.2 Synchronization in pthreads

There are different ways that synchronization can be done in pthreads, reflecting the different types of synchronization concepts presented in Section 5.4. We briefly describe these here.

POSIX threads provide the basic data type of semaphore, which takes the form of a type specification:

```
Semaphore shudeyego;
```

At initialization, each semaphore has the value of one, which corresponds to the "safe to proceed" value. The code fragment

```
semaphore_init( &shudeyego );
```

indicates how each individual semaphore gets initialized.

There are then two operations that can be done on semaphores. The "down" operation

```
semaphore_down( &shudeyego );
```

blocks if the semaphore `shudeyego` is less than or equal to zero (the "not safe" state). When it can go safely, it begins by decrementing the value of `shudeyego` by one. The semaphore can be returned to the "safe" state by the "up" command:

```
semaphore_up( &shudeyego );
```

A "destroy" command is also available to free the resources allocated to the semaphore.

The use of integers for semaphores in pthreads is more than a convenience. The basic notion of semaphore is extended using

```
semaphore_decrement( &shudeyego );
```

to allow for a situation where multiple "up" commands need to be issued before threads cease to be blocked.

---

was also widely known for his critique of the Fortran `go to` construct [42].

```
#include <pthread.h>
#define MAXTHREADS 1024
int nThreads;
#define MAXIZ 100000000
double locsum[MAXTHREADS];
/*** following is the code that each thread will execute ***/
void *localsum(void * arg)
{
  double lsum=0.0;
  int myProc=*(int *) arg;
  int ic;
  for (ic=0; ic<MAXIZ/nThreads; ic++) {
       lsum += 1.0/(1.0+((double)(myProc+nThreads*ic)));
       }
    locsum[myProc]=lsum;
  return arg;
}
/******** following is the main thread's code */
int main(int argc,char *argv[])
{
  int worker;
  pthread_t threads[MAXTHREADS];  /* thread name info    */
  int ids[MAXTHREADS];            /* thread argumentss */
  int *status;                    /* return status code */
  double sum=0.0;
  sscanf(*(++argv),"%d",&nThreads); /* read number of threads */
  /* create the threads */
  for (worker=0; worker<nThreads; worker++) {
    pthread_attr_t attr;
    ids[worker]=worker;
    pthread_attr_init(&attr);
    pthread_attr_setscope(&attr, PTHREAD_SCOPE_SYSTEM);
    pthread_create(&threads[worker], &attr, localsum, &ids[worker]) ;
  }
  /* collect the threads upon exit */
  for (worker=0; worker<nThreads; worker++) {
    /* wait for thread to terminate */
    pthread_join(threads[worker],(void *) &status);
  }
  /* compute the global sum from the local sums */
  for (worker=0; worker<nThreads; worker++) {
    sum+=locsum[worker];
  }
  printf("global sum for N= %d is %f\n",MAXIZ,sum);
  return(0);
}
```

Program 7.2 POSIX thread code to implement simple summation.

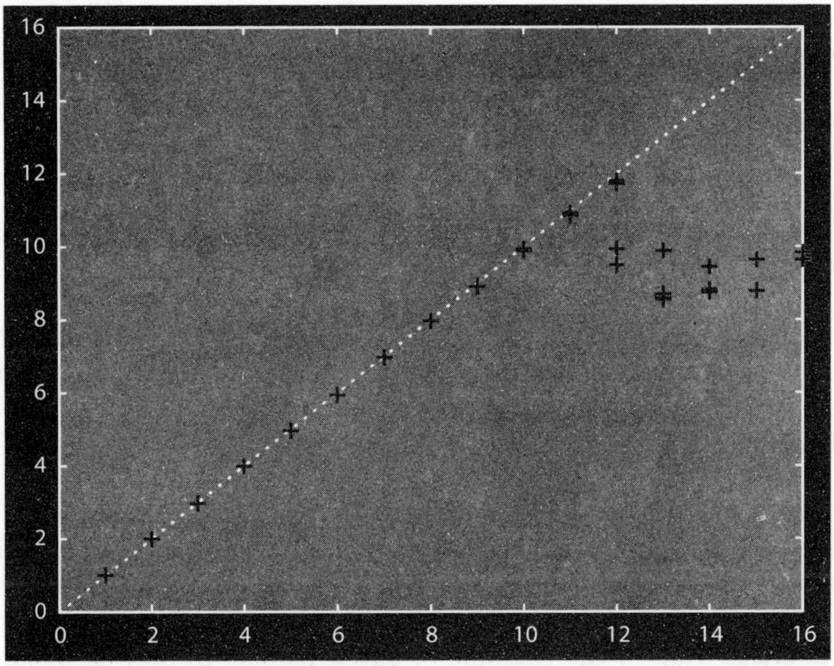

Figure 7.1 The summation problem again. Observed speedup for a number of different runs as a function of number of threads on a twelve processor machine. Notice the scatter in the data once you get to twelve or more threads.

POSIX threads also include a functionality called **mutex** (for "mutual exclusion") to guard a critical section (cf. a guarded command). A mutex has two states: locked and unlocked. When a mutex is locked by a thread, other threads attempting to lock the mutex will block. When the thread releases (or unlocks) the mutex, one of the blocked threads will acquire (lock) it and proceed.

7.4 EXERCISES

Exercise 7.1. Write a program to compute the solution to the ordinary differential equation (1.6.1) using the second order method (1.6.9) in MPI.

Exercise 7.2. Write a program to compute the solution to the ordinary differential equation (1.6.1) using the second order method (1.6.9) in pthreads.

Exercise 7.3. Write a code in MPI to broadcast (Section 5.5.2) the value of `sum` to all the processors that is, computed in the code fragment in Program 5.9. (Hint: see Section 2.1.)

Exercise 7.4. Using MPI, write a barrier, that is, a subroutine that assures that no process leaves before all have arrived.

Exercise 7.5. Program the baton passing example in Section 5.5.3 in MPI.

Exercise 7.6. Program the baton passing example in Section 5.5.3 in pthreads.

Exercise 7.7. Consider the example of baton passing in Section 5.5.3. If each processor were to print out the value of `baton` (before incrementing it) together with `nodeid()`, as shown on line 5 in Program 5.7, what would it be?

Exercise 7.8. In the example of baton passing in Section 5.5.3, is it necessary to increment the value of `baton`? Modify the code to eliminate the passing of a meaningful value, implementing a "no pass, no print" rule.

Exercise 7.9. In the example of baton passing in Section 5.5.3, is it necessary to increment the value of the tag (which is taken to be the iteration index `i`)? What would happen if we replaced the send/receive pair by

```
call snd(0, baton, 4, i+1, 1)
call rcv(0, baton, 4,  i,  1)
```

that is, would the code still execute correctly? Why or why not?

Exercise 7.10. Show how locks can be implemented using logical variables (`true` and `false`) together with suitable conditionals.

Exercise 7.11. Use MPI to perform unions of sets of integers computed on separate processors. Allow for the cardinality of the sets to be arbitrary (including zero). Apply this to the prime number sieve parallelization via the "n" loop as described in Section 1.5.1.

Exercise 7.12. Use MPI to perform intersections of sets of integers computed on separate processors. Apply this to the prime number sieve parallelization via the "π" loop as described in Section 1.5.1.

Exercise 7.13. Program in MPI an algorithm with $\log_2 P$ steps for a general, noncommutative reduction operation $\oplus$ on a ring with $P = 2^d$ processors. Test this with simple addition and with matrix multiplication and verify that it is correct. Does the order of evaluation depend on P? (Hint: see Program 6.3; keep the order right at each step.)

Exercise 7.14. Program in MPI an algorithm with $1 + \log_2 P$ steps for a general reduction operation $\oplus$ on a ring for the general case with $P \neq 2^d$ processors. (Hint: embed the ring into one with $P = 2^d$ processors and apply Exercise 7.13.)

Exercise 7.15. Program in MPI an algorithm to compute the sum of vectors `A(1:N)` that recursively subdivides `A(1:N)` and sums the smaller pieces, as on a hypercube network. Assume that $N = 2^k$ for some integer k and that the number of processors $P = 2^d$ for some integer $d < k$. (Hint: see Program 6.8.)

Chapter Eight
The ℙlanguage Model

> If the #2 pencil is the most popular, why is it still #2?—*George Carlin*

The ℙlanguages are simple extensions of Fortran (ℙfortran) and C (ℙC), cast in an SPMD model of parallel computation. The ℙlanguages are an *explicitly parallel* approach in which all variables are replicated. All processes execute the same text, with parallelism exploited by explicit partitions of data and control flow (see Section 5.5). In this chapter we will describe the basic ideas of the ℙlanguage extensions. The complete details can be found in their respective manuals [15] and [12].

The main feature of the ℙlanguages is the memory model: guarded memory [13]. This allows us to formalize the notation `x@n` introduced in Section 6.1. The main difference between message passing and the ℙlanguages is the memory model. In message passing, the names of variables at other processors are opaque to us: the messages we send and receive are just data, not variables (see Figure 8.1). In the ℙlanguages, we can refer to variables at other processors by name. The notation `i@q` means the value of the variable `i` at the processor `q`, but it should be thought of as the variable `i` *guarded* by processor `q` (see Section 5.4.2). It is the role of the guarding processor to ensure correct access.

As noted in Section 6.1, a statement such as `x@p = y@q` can be viewed as a *fusion* of a send and receive in message passing terms. Abstracting the send and receive with an operator streamlines code and reduces development time without degrading performance on message passing systems [94]. Errors in writing explicit message passing logic are reduced. The semantics require that the value assigned to `x@p` be the value of `y@q` at the point in the program text where `q` executes `y@q` and `p` executes `x@p`. The matching pair of fusion objects correspond to the producer and the consumer.

The ℙlanguages must be translated to some form of low level code for execution. However, the strategy for doing this could be different on different architectures. For example, on a distributed memory machine, it would be natural to compile into message passing. But on a shared memory machine, a different strategy is available [57]. We will not dwell on the machine-dependent features of the compilation process, but we will mention some issues.

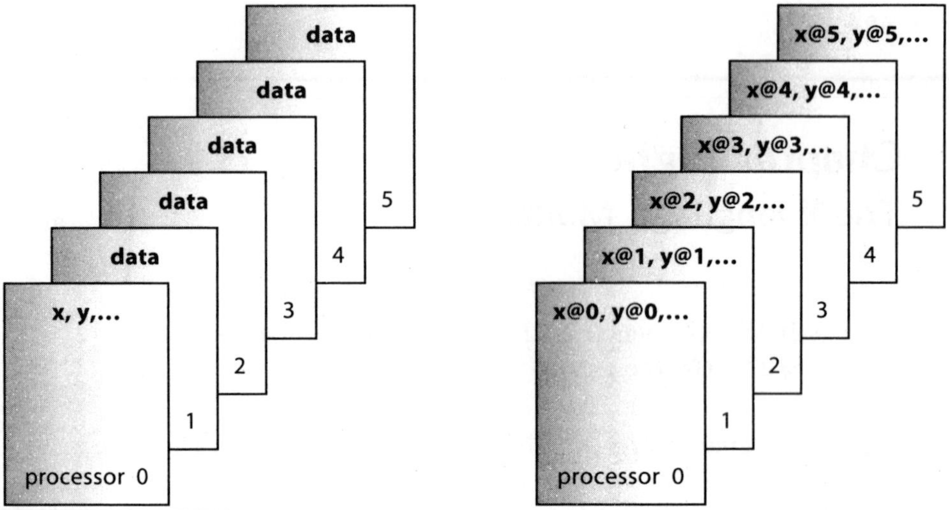

Figure 8.1 Comparison of memory models for message passing (left) and guarded memory (right), as seen from processor 0. In the former model, all that can be seen at other processors is uncharacterized data. In guarded memory, actual variables are visible.

```
do n= 0, nProc-1
  x(n) = y@n
enddo
sum=0.0
do n = 0, nProc-1
  sum = sum + x(n)
enddo
```

Program 8.1 Simple program segment to compute a sum of values.

8.1 IPLANGUAGE DETAILS

Program 8.1 gives a simple program segment to compute a sum of values as in (1.5.2), stored at each processor, say in the variable `y`. First, all processors broadcast their own value and then each sums the values independently.

In Section 6.2, we presented several more sophisticated algorithms written only with simple fusions (i.e., `@` symbols). All of these can now be viewed as examples of IPfortran codes. Let us now give more details of the languages. To begin with, we explain the variable `nProc` which appears in Program 8.1.

8.1.1 IPlanguage processor numbering

The IPlanguages define the following constants:

- `myProc` is the logical processor number of the processor executing the program,

- `nProc` is the total number of processors allocated to execute the code.

These are "reserved variables" which cannot be modified, that is, may not appear on the left-hand side of an assignment statement. Processors are logically numbered 0, ..., `nProc`−1.

As with message passing, any logic in the program involving the variable `myProc` can potentially cause different processes to be in different states, meaning that for at least one variable name in the replicated program there will be different values.

8.1.2 Fusion synchronization

A key property of fusions is *implicit* synchronization. In the statement above, `p` will not progress beyond the assignment until `q` has reached the statement. This is a *one-sided synchronization* where `p` must wait for `q` to reach the assignment, but `q` need not wait for `p`. We call this **give-and-go semantics**. It can be shown that two processes which execute the same fusion statement can synchronize on that statement and execute deterministically [13].

Some care must be taken in compiling a fusion into separate sends and receives, as there is a potential to cause deadlock. The strategy to avoid deadlock is to apply the **golden rule**: first send to processors that require data and then receive from the processor sending data to you [129]. A greedy approach in which you attempt to receive data before it is sent can result in deadlock. This will be discussed in more detail in Section 8.1.7, where the compilation of functions of `myProc` are discussed.

To determine the processes that interact through a fusion statement requires analysis of the program logic with runtime support. Data movement with unspecified consumers such as `a=b@p` and reduction operations involve some **implicit process group**. The *implicit process group* is defined by control flow, and consists of the subset of processes reaching the statement in question. In contrast, an MPI communicator (Section 7.1) provides for **explicit process groups**. Implicit process groups are formed in any SPMD execution through predicates which evaluate differently on different processors. If the communicator defined in MPI does not match thc implicit process group defined by the control flow logic, deadlock could result.

The consumed value of the i-th instance of a fusion corresponds to the fusion value at the producer process during its i-th access of the same fusion statement. In other words, there is a one-to-one correspondence between the series of fusion values (*versions*) at the *producer* and those obtained by the *consumer*. For a fusion accessed once in a program there is only one version; for a loop there can be multiple versions. In Program 8.2, the i-th version of `a@q` (which has different values in different iterations) is assigned to `b(i)@p`, corresponding to the i-th loop iteration.

It is up to the implementation to determine how versioning is enforced.

```
do i = 1, 10
   if (myProc.EQ.q) then
      a = f(i)
   endif
   b(i)@p = a@q
enddo
```

Program 8.2 Loop with repeated accesses to a single variable.

```
integer*4 baton
baton = 0
if (myProc.EQ.0)
   print*, 'hello from',myProc
   baton = baton +1
endif
do i = 1, nProc - 1
   baton@i = baton@(i-1)
   if (baton.EQ.myProc)
      print*, 'hello from',myProc
      baton = baton +1
   endif
enddo
```

Program 8.3 A Pfortran code to illustrate synchronization via "baton" passing.

Since there could be uneven progress by processes, the implementation might buffer the versioned data, or stall the producer. Buffered message passing, for example, retains versions in messages indexed by tags. The implementation could also synchronize processes at each fusion statement.

Example 8.1.1. We recall the simple code to implement a form of synchronization using the metaphor of passing a baton in a relay race; cf. Program 5.7. In the Pfortran version of this code, shown in Program 8.3, the variable `baton` is exchanged using an `@` sign in sequence between successively numbered processors. This single statement replaces two subroutine calls in the message passing version depicted in Program 5.7.

The key point is not the value of the baton, but simply that it is being passed (cf. Exercise 8.14). However, in Program 8.3, the value of `baton` is used as part of the synchronization logic. See Exercise 8.13 regarding the value of `baton` as the code progresses, and see Exercise 8.14 for a version that does not use the value of `baton` in a material way.

8.1.3 @ operator precedence and domain

The operator precedence in ℙfortran, from highest to lowest precedence, is

$$@ \qquad ** \qquad (*, /) \qquad (+, -).$$

So, for example, `a=b@p+1` is not equivalent to `a=b@(p+1)`, and `a@p+1 = b@q` is meaningless (not allowed) where `a@(p+1) = b@q` is not. The operator `@` is non-associative; therefore, `x=y@i@p` is illegal but `x=y@(i@p)` and `x=(y@i)@p` are legal.

The `@` operator is defined only on the integers `0`, ..., `nProc` $- 1$.

8.1.4 Multiple assignments not allowed

A statement such as

```
x@0 = y
```

is not allowed in the ℙlanguages. This would mean that every process(or) would send the value of `y` to processor 0 to be stored in `x`. This would correspond to multiple values being assigned to a single variable. There might be a way to define this so that its result would be predictable, but we do not see a reason for this, so we simply define it to be a programming error.

8.1.5 Local vs. global values

The technique in Program 8.1 for summing values over all processors, while not efficient, serves to illustrate an important point concerning our assumption about communication in ℙfortran. In the first loop in Program 8.1, the processor from which we receive data is a variable. However, at each step in the iteration the value of this variable is the same at each processor. Thus `n` denotes a value universally agreed upon at each iteration, a value *global* to all P processors. If the value of `n` were different in different processors, then it would be called a *local* value and a more complicated implementation would be needed to translate this into correct code.

Values are global unless they depend on the logical processor number `myProc`. The values at each processor, corresponding to some variable, can be partitioned into two classes that we call *local* and *global. Local* values are (or more accurately, *could be*) different from other corresponding values at other processors. *Global* values are known to be the same at all processors (in general, *local* and *global* can be applied to a subset Q of processors). It is useful for the programmer to be aware of the distinction as it can affect efficiency.

If values referring to processor numbers are global, we can predict the communication pattern required for the data exchange. Otherwise, for processor numbers given by local values, the communication pattern must

```
i=f()
x=y@i
```

Program 8.4 The code fragment results in communication patterns that cannot be determined by a compiler.

```
i=f()
do j=0, nProc−1
   ithere(j) = i@j
enddo
do j=0, nProc−1
   x@j = y@ithere(j)
enddo
```

Program 8.5 The code fragment changes local memory references to global references in arbitrary communication patterns.

be determined at run time. This is not difficult to do, but it requires a significant amount of overhead.

Consider the code fragment in Program 8.4. In this it is likely that i will not have the same values at all processors. An example of converting local variables to global ones is contained in Program 8.5. The set of the values `ithere` can be collected in a much more efficient way using various algorithms to be discussed subsequently.

8.1.6 Determinism and deadlock avoidance

A principal benefit of the guarded memory model is that it can easily lead to deterministic codes that do not deadlock [13]. Unfortunately, it cannot avoid *livelock*, the situation when processors attempt to communicate with other processors which are unaware of their interest in communicating. For example, a code like Program 8.6 will livelock in that processor 0 will wait for processor 1 to send it something whereas processor 1 will never execute the code containing the guard. The formation of implicit process groups (Section 8.1.2) creates situations in which certain communications do not make sense. For example, in Program 8.6 the variable `y` may not be initialized on processor `0` in Fortran.

In a certain sense, the SPMD model is broken when communication is attempted between processors that are not executing the same code branch. It is possible to track the formation of implicit process groups at runtime [57], and this would allow the detection of attempts to communicate outside of a process group. However, the general concept of SPMD programming would suggest that such communications be avoided in the first place.

```
if(myProc.eq.0)
   y=3
   x=y@1
endif
```

Program 8.6 A code fragment that results in livelock.

8.1.7 Jacobi in ℙfortran: functions of `myProc`

We now consider the iterative method (1.6.21) from Section 1.6.2, the one-dimensional Jacobi iteration depicted in Program 5.11. This can be expressed in ℙfortran as shown in Program 8.7. This code is essentially equivalent to the message passing version of Jacobi iteration shown in Program 5.13, except that the sends and receives are fused, and there is no need to increment tags in ℙfortran. See Exercise 8.11 for the two-dimensional analogue of this Jacobi iteration.

```
ln = n/nProc
x(0)@0 = 0.0
x(ln+1)@(nProc-1) = 0.0
do k = 1, NoIters
  x(0) = x(ln) @ max(myProc-1, 0)
  x(ln+1) = x(1) @ min(myProc+1, nProc-1)
  do i = 2 , ln-1
    newx(i) = .5 * (x(i-1) + x(i+1) - dx2 * x(i))
  enddo
  do i = 1 , ln
    x(i) = newx(i)
  enddo
enddo
```

Program 8.7 One-dimensional Jacobi iteration in ℙfortran.

The Jacobi iteration in Program 8.7 provides an example of the use of functions of `myProc` [129]. It is possible to determine communication patterns from functions `f(myProc)` in a way that does not require additional communication, as is required for simple local processor references (cf. Section 8.1.5 and Program 8.5). An equation must be solved to determine who requires data from whom. Each processor must send data to all nodes in the set given by

$$\mathtt{f}^{-1}(\mathtt{myProc}) := \{i = 0, \ldots, \mathtt{nProc} - 1 \ : \ \mathtt{f}(i) = \mathtt{myProc}\}\,. \tag{8.1.1}$$

This is the set of processors for whom `f` applied to their value of `myProc` evaluates to your value of `myProc`. This can be determined without any communication, and potentially at compile time. Further it may be possible to invert the relationship expressed by `f` symbolically to avoid the implicit tabulation in (8.1.1). The set of processors to whom a given processor may need to send data can include more than one processor, although it will receive data from only one processor. The strategy to avoid deadlock is to apply again the *golden rule* (see Section 8.1.2); first send to processors that require data and then receive from the processor sending data to you [129].

8.2 RANGES AND ARRAYS

Ranges are sections of an array indicated by ":" as in Matlab and Fortran90 syntax. For example, `A(2:7)` refers to six continuous array values. Ranges can be multidimensional as well, referring to rectangular sections of the corresponding multidimensional array. For example, `A(2:7,3:8)` refers to thirty-six array values. It is useful to refer to sets of variables with one notation, and ranges offer a simple notation for a commonly used set.

8.2.1 Ranges of variables

It is often necessary to exchange collections of variables among different processors, not just singletons. This is allowed in IPfortran using array syntax based on ranges. For example, if `nProc = 2**CUBEDIM` then the array `ithere` can be collected via the loop in Program 8.8. Here, `OR`, `NOT`, and `AND` are the logical "or," "not," and "and" functions, respectively (see Program 15.5 in Section 15.2.2 for an example of how these can be implemented). At each step, twice as much is exchanged with the neighbor in the `idim`-th dimension in a hypercube, so that after $\log_2$(`nProc`) steps, the entire array has been exchanged. We note that this algorithm would execute correctly on any architecture but there could be potential communication contention on ones that are not based on a hypercube network. See Exercise 8.9 for algorithms appropriate for other topologies. Ranges of variables will be discussed at more length in Section 8.2.3.

8.2.2 Ranges of processors

There are many instances in which sets of processors are useful objects. In the IPlanguages, *ranges* of processors can appear on the left-hand side of an assignment statement. For example,

```
x@(1:5) = y@0
```

means: "Assign the value of variable `y` at processor 0 to variable `x` at processors 1 through 5." On the right-hand side, the range logically returns multiple values. For expression

```
x@(i:j) = y@(r:s)
```

the range `(r:s)` will map 1:1 onto the range `(i:j)` on the left-hand side; if $j - i \neq s - r$, then the statement is not defined with unpredictable results.

```
muchmo = 1
mask = 1
mmask = nProc − 1
ipadr=myProc
do idim = 1, CUBEDIM
  notmask=NOT(mask)
  ieven=AND(ipadr,notmask)
  iodd=OR(ipadr,mask)
  ievbot=AND(mmask,ieven)
  ievtop=ievbot+muchmo−1
  iodbot=AND(mmask,iodd)
  iodtop=iodbot+muchmo−1
  ithere(iodbot:iodtop)@ieven = ithere(iodbot:iodtop)@iodd
  ithere(ievbot:ievtop)@iodd = ithere(ievbot:ievtop)@ieven
  mask = mask*2
  mmask = mmask*2
  muchmo = muchmo*2
enddo
```

Program 8.8 Program to combine a set of values using dimensional exchange with $P = 2^d$ processors (d = `CUBEDIM` in the code).

In addition to a single range or scalar processor identifier, lists of scalars and ranges are allowed, but only with a 1:1 correspondence if more than one processor is specified on the right-hand side. Some examples follow:

```
a@(i,j,k) = b@(m,n,o)
a@(1,2,3,4) = b@0
a@(k+m:n) = b@0
```

8.2.3 Arrays

In a distributed computing model where parallelism is expressed explicitly, it is essential to have some way of expressing operations on entire arrays or sections of arrays. ℙfortran supplements FORTRAN77 array notation with a subset of Fortran 90 syntax. Array names may be used in three settings to reference

i) a single scalar `A(i,j)`,

ii) a section `A(:,j)`,

iii) the entire array `A`.

In ℙfortran, any of these three references can be used in expressions where `@` is used or as actual parameters to reduction operations (Section 8.3).

ℙfortran permits arrays to be referenced in simple assignments of the type `A(m:n) = B(m:n)@p`. In the assignment `A(2:4)@q = A(1:3)@p`, if `p = q`, then `A` refers to the same array, and the subarrays, therefore, share storage. The assignment to the left-hand side is made using the values of `A(1:3)` prior to the assignment. If `A(1:4)`$\equiv (1, 2, 3, 4)$, then after the assignment `A(1:4)`$\equiv (1, 1, 2, 3)$ and not $(1, 1, 1, 1)$.

8.2.4 Performance considerations: array sections

The use of array sections may add a copy overhead to the compiled **IP**fortran program. To transmit a block of data to another processor, the communication subsystem is given an address of a data buffer, a byte count, and a destination address. The communication subsystem, expecting to find the data contiguous in memory, will either copy the data to a system buffer, or send the data to the destination processor directly from the user's address space.

Since the array section is a portion of some parent array, it may not be contiguous in memory. For sections derived from *rank*≥ 2 arrays, the array section may be copied into a buffer by the application in order to achieve contiguous storage, although this is done automatically by the **IP**fortran translator.

8.3 REDUCTION OPERATIONS IN IPfortran

Recall the concepts related to *reductions* introduced in Section 6.3. A reduction operation can be associated with either intrinsic functions or user-defined functions; we consider examples of each. The general forms of the reduction procedure invocations are

function: `out = f1{in,...}`

subroutine: `call s1{in,out,...}`

where `in` is the distributed operand. `f1` and `s1` implement some binary operation with the results assigned to the distributed variable `out`. The corresponding function and subroutine definitions are of the form

function: `"type" FUNCTION f1(in1,in2,...)`

subroutine: `SUBROUTINE s1(in1,in2,out,...)`

where `"type"` denotes the type (e.g. `REAL` or `INTEGER`) of the function `f1`, and the dots correspond to optional parameters which might be needed for some operations.

The main point to observe is that the definition of a "reducible" function or subroutine has one more input in its definition than it does when it is actually called in a reduction. With a function, the returned value is passed through the function return mechanism, whereas in using a subroutine, the parameter `out` is provided. In both cases, the parameters `in1` and `in2` are not used to return results.

The user-defined reduction operations may include optional parameters. These parameters are assumed to be global parameters (the same at all processors, see Section 8.1.5), and they are not communicated, but are included in the calling sequence as shown below. These parameters can carry type information for the parameters `in` and `out`, or can be used in generating side-effects with the reduction operation. For example,

```
CALL addvec { Ain, Aout, D }
```

illustrates the use of the optional parameter `D`. The corresponding subroutine definition is given in Program 6.4. Here `D` is the optional parameter and `Aout` is the output parameter. There can be any number of optional parameters. The input and optional parameters supplied to the function or procedure implementing a binary operator may only be used nondestructively, that is, read-only.

The reduction of a function, e.g. `out=opratr{in,param1,param2}`, requires a function with the definition

```
REAL FUNCTION opratr(in1,in2,param1,param2).
```

Functions and subroutines used along with {} are called *reducing functions* and *reducing subroutines*, respectively.

The most basic examples of reduction operations that one may reduce include the intrinsic (binary) Fortran functions: MIN, MAX, OR, AND, etc. Thus the statement

```
y = AMIN1 { x }
```

computes the minimum of all values of `x` in all processors and assigns this value to the variable `y` (at all processors). Some further simple examples of this are as follows:

```
m=max{n}
k=min{k}
krim=AND{punish}
```

IPfortran also provides the reduction operation + for adding numbers:

```
x=+{y}
```

In Section 8.3.1, the extension of the reduction operation + to vectors is also described. Other binary operators (e.g., user-defined operations) can be cast as reduction operations as we now describe.

8.3.1 Intrinsic vector-sum reduction

The accumulation of the values of the elements of an array into a target array of the same shape is a common operation worthy of an intrinsic function.

Suppose we wish to write code for the following sum:

$$\forall i, j, \quad A(i)@j = \sum_{k=1}^{p} A(i)@k. \tag{8.3.1}$$

Using **P**fortran we could of course write a code implementing (8.3.1). Alternatively, we write the more concise expression using the **P**fortran intrinsic reduction operator, $+\{\cdot\}$, namely,

```
A = + { A }
```

to sum the entire array `A`. Sub-arrays can be summed in the same way, e.g.,

```
B(7:11) = + { A(8:12) }
```

If the ranges on either side do not agree, it is an error, and no promises are made about what will happen. If no range is specified, then the entire array (as dimensioned) will be exchanged.

8.3.2 User-defined reductions

In addition to using the intrinsic binary operators and functions defined in Fortran, one may also reduce user-defined functions. Consider a user-defined reduction operation implementing a summation of a set of scalars distributed across P processors into a single scalar. By defining a function, `mysum`, as shown in Program 8.9, we can write

```
result = mysum{scalar}
```

to compute the same result as the intrinsic

```
result = +{scalar}
```

```
real*8 function mysum(in1,in2)
  mysum = in1 + in2
return
end
```

Program 8.9 Simple function to add two numbers; example of a user-defined reduction to add a collection of numbers.

Another example of a reduction is presented in Program 8.10, which accumulates the array `ithere` described in Section 8.1.3 (see Program 8.5). The subroutine `intplus` referred to in Program 8.10 is defined in Program 8.11. In Section 8.3.3, we give more extensive examples of user-defined reductions.

```
izero=0
do j=0, nProc−1
   jthere(j)=0
enddo
jthere(myProc)=i
call intplus{jthere,ithere,izero,nProc}
```

Program 8.10 Use of a reduction to add a collection of arrays.

```
subroutine intplus(ithere,jthere,kthere,istart,n)
dimension ithere(1), jthere(1), kthere(1)
if(n.le.0) stop
do j=istart,istart+n−1
   kthere(j)=ithere(j)+jthere(j)
enddo
return
end
```

Program 8.11 Subroutine to add two integer arrays with two optional parameters.

8.3.3 Reduction operation applications

Let us review the examples in Section 6.4. Recall the scalar function `minmod` as defined in Program 6.5. To compute the `minmod` of a set of values `myslope` over all processors, one simply writes `slope = minmod{myslope}`.

The subroutine in Program 6.6 defines `Cpivot` to calculate a row-pivot element in Gaussian elimination. In Program 8.12 we see how it can be used to determine the pivot among a group of processors via a reduction. Note that we could have equivalently used the statement

```
call Cpivot {pivot}
```

above, as `pivot` has been dimensioned to be of length 2.

In Section 11.4, we study parallel algorithms for matrix-vector products. Here we are mainly interested in the syntax of how such methods might be described in ℙfortran. The following approach to computing a matrix times a vector, `matvec`, uses the reducing version of `addvec`, a subroutine that adds vectors defined in Program 6.4. In the following, note that `D` is the dimension of the matrix and `N` <<`D` is the number of columns stored in each node. The index `global(i)` (i= 1,...,`N`) indicates how the columns are distributed across processors, but the details of a particular choice of such a distribution is left unspecified. One such choice is defined in the following:

```
global(j) = myProc + j*NN
```

where `NN=D/N`. The matrix is assumed to be distributed in a similar way. Program 8.13 presents the algorithm to multiply a matrix times a vector in

```
c       LOOP OVER COLUMNS OF MATRIX
        do 500 k = 1, n
c      basis: determine pivot row from local rows
          pivot(1) = B(1,k)
          pivot(2) = myProc+1
          do 20 irow = 2, m/nProc
            row = myProc + 1 + (irow-1)*nProc
            pivot2(1) = B(irow,k)
            pivot2(2) = row
            call Cpivot(pivot2,pivot)
   20     continue

c     determine pivot row globally
          call Cpivot {pivot(1:2)}
  500 continue
```

Program 8.12 Code to determine best pivot among a collection of choices.

parallel. Note that the function **addvec** is clearly associative and commutative; its global version adds all the components among all processors.

```
      subroutine matvec(res, mat, vec, D, N)
      dimension res(N), mat(D,N),vec(N), s(1024),t(N)
      do i=1, D
        s(i) = 0.0
        do j=1, N
          s(i) = s(i) + mat(i,j) * vec(j)
        enddo
      enddo
      addvec{s,t,D}
      do i=1,N
        res(i) = t(global(i))
      enddo
```

Program 8.13 Code to multiply a matrix times a vector using the subroutine **addvec** defined in Program 6.4.

8.4 INTRODUCTION TO ℙC

ℙC extends C in the same way that ℙfortran extends Fortran. We give a quick overview of the main features.

8.4.1 The operator @

ℙC defines the infix operator @ for accessing nonlocal variables in the same way as IPfortran (except for the ending semicolon ubiquitous in C). For example,

```
x = y@0;
```

means: assign the value of variable y of processor 0 to x (in every processor). This is simply a *broadcast* from processor 0 to all other processors. Similarly

```
x = y@[n+1];
```

means: assign the value of variable y of processor n+1 to x (in every processor). If the value of an expression is not in the range 0, ..., nProc-1, then assignment does not occur.

We can now give a simple example of a code to compute the sum of values contained in each processor, say in the variable y. The idea is simply for everyone to broadcast their own value, and then each processor sums the values independently. This is shown in Program 8.14; compare this with the IPfortran version in Program 8.1.

```
for(n=0; n < nProc; n++)
        x[n] = y @ n;
sum=0.0;
for(n=0; n < nProc; n++)
        sum = sum + x[n];
```

Program 8.14 Simple program in IPC to compute a sum of values.

8.4.2 Ranges of processors and arrays

IPC allows *ranges* of processors or arrays of values in the same way as IPfortran. For example,

```
x@[1:5] = y@0;
```

means: assign the value of variable y in processor 0 to variable x in processors 1 through 5. The code

```
x[0:5]@[1:5] = y[1:6] @ 0;
```

treats x[0:5] and y[1:6] as vectors and assigns the elements consecutively in processors one through five. We do the same consecutive assignment for arrays with higher dimension. For example

```
x[ni:nf][mi:mf]@[1:5] = y[ji:jf][ki:kf] @ 0;
```

has the same ultimate effect as

```
for(n=ni; n <= nf; n++)
      for(m=mi; m <= mf; m++)
            x[n][m]@[1:5] = y[ji+ni-n][ki+mi-m] @ 0;
```

but its implementation is much more efficient since block moves are utilized.

8.4.3 Functions of `myProc`

The construct

```
x = y@[(myProc+1) % nProc];
```

means: assign the value of variable `y` of processor

```
(myProc+1) % nProc
```

to `x` in `myProc`. Within the parentheses we can have any expression which mentions `myProc` *explicitly* (including functions which return integers, arithmetic operators, etc.).

8.5 REDUCTION OPERATIONS IN $\mathbb{P}$C

The syntax for reduction operations in $\mathbb{P}$C is quite similar to $\mathbb{P}$fortran. For example, the summation problem can be written succinctly as

```
sum = +{y};
```

Similarly,

```
x = max{y@[0:7]};
```

assigns to `x` in every processor the maximum of the values of `y` in processors 0 through 7, provided `x` and `y` are integers and we have defined a function called `max` as shown in Program 8.15.

```
int max(int i, int j)
{
    return( ( i > j) ? i : j );
}
```

Program 8.15 Function to compute the maximum of integer values in C.

Since C has a richer "type" structure (using `struct`'s), quite complex commutative operators can be utilized. Consider the following approach to computing a matrix times a vector (`matvec`) that uses the "globalized" version of `addvec`, a function that adds vectors. We begin by introducing a data structure for vectors:

```
typedef struct {double v[D];} VECTOR;
```

For this new data type, we define *addition* by introducing a function that adds two vectors and returns their sum in Program 8.16.

Finally, we put all this together to define matrix multiplication using the "globalized" version of `addvec` in Program 8.17. The function `addvec` is clearly associative and commutative; its global version adds all the components among all processors.

```
#define D 3
typedef struct vector {
   float v[D];
} Vector;

Vector addvec(Vector a, Vector b)
{
   Vector r;
   int i;
   for (i=0; i<D; i++) r.v[i] = a.v[i] + b.v[i];
   return(r);
}
```

Program 8.16 Function to compute the sum of vectors in C.

	message passing	ℙlanguages
data exchange	done explicitly by messages	done explicitly by fusions
synchronization	done implicitly by messages	done implicitly by fusions
memory model	distributed memory	guarded memory
deterministic	no	yes

Table 8.1 Comparison of message passing and the ℙlanguages. Omitted are work and data distribution where the two models are the same.

Note that `D` is the dimension of the matrix and `N<<D` is the number of columns stored in each node. The index `global(i)` (i= 1, . . . ,`N`) indicates how the columns are distributed to each processor, but the details of a particular choice of such a distribution are left unspecified. One such choice is defined in the following:

```
global(j) int j; { return(myProc + j*NN); }
```

where `NN=D/N`. The matrix is assumed to be distributed in a similar way. The ℙC version of `matvec` in Program 8.17 should be compared with the ℙfortran version of `matvec` in Program 8.13. Note the different implementation of `addvec` for these codes.

8.6 ℙLANGUAGES VERSUS MESSAGE PASSING

We present in Table 8.1 a simple comparison of the ℙlanguages with message passing. We omit from the table areas where they are the same, such as data and work distribution. Comparing this table with Table 5.1 provides a comparison with shared memory programming.

```
#define N 1024
#define D 3
typedef struct vector {
    float v[D];
} Vector;

void matvec(double res[N], double mat[D][N], double vec[N])
{
  int i, j, li, lj;
  Vector s;
  for(i=0; i<D; i++) {
      s.v[i] = 0.0;
      for(j=0; j<N ;j++){
        s.v[i] += (mat[i][j] * vec[j]);
      }
   }
   s = addvec{s};
   for(i=0; i<N; i++) res[i] = s.v[global(i)];
}
```

Program 8.17 Function to compute the product of a matrix times a vector in IPC.

```
sum=y
do n=1, nProc - 1
  sum = sum@MOD((myProc+1), nProc)
  sum = sum + y
enddo
```

Program 8.18 Program segment to compute a sum over all processor numbers using a logical ring communication scheme.

8.7 EXERCISES

Exercise 8.1. Implement Program 8.9 and compare this with using +{ }.

Exercise 8.2. Prove that Program 8.18 produces the same result as `sum=+{y}`.

Exercise 8.3. Write a code using IPC or IPfortran that writes to your terminal the message "hello world" from each processor. Then modify the code to write "hello world from n," where n is the processor number writing the message. Finally, modify the code to print the message "hello world from n" in increasing order in n. (Hint: see Program 8.3.)

Exercise 8.4. Write a program to broadcast from one processor to $P-1$ other processors using ℙC or ℙfortran using P point-to-point communications of the form `x@p = y@n`.

Exercise 8.5. Write a program to compute the simple sum in Section 1.5.1 using ℙC or ℙfortran. Determine the performance as a function of N and P as well as the error

$$\frac{\pi}{4}-\sum_{i=1}^{N}\frac{(-1)^{i+1}}{2i-1}$$

as a function of N. Use `x=+{x}` to sum the partial sums computed on each separate processor.

Exercise 8.6. Write a program to compute primes using the sieve algorithm in Section 1.5.3 using ℙC or ℙfortran. Do this for one value of k and print the primes $< k^2$ in **ascending order**, either by merging them on one processor or by controlling the order of printing from individual processors. Test it with $k = 31$.

Exercise 8.7. Write a program to compute the solution to the ordinary differential equation (1.6.1) using the second order method (1.6.9) in ℙC or ℙfortran. Run this on one and two processors and determine the speedup and communication time. Do 100 time steps with a $\Delta t = .01$. Let $f(x)$ be determined by the code in Program 8.19. Let a and b be typed as floating point numbers, and set $a = 2.0$ and $b = 1.0/a$. How does the two-processor speedup depend on the choice of k?

$f \leftarrow x$
for $i = 1, \ldots k$
$f \leftarrow f^a$
$f \leftarrow f^b$
endfor
$f \leftarrow -f^a$.

Program 8.19 Arbitrarily complex function for testing o.d.e. codes.

Exercise 8.8. Code Program 8.5 and test it by starting the vector `ithere` having the values generated by the code in Program 8.20. (Hint: the negative values can be useful in the debugging process.)

Exercise 8.9. Give an algorithm for concatenating `ithere` (see Program 8.8) suitable for a ring, mesh, and hypercube.

```
do j=0, nProc-1
  ithere(j) = - myProc
enddo
ithere(myProc) = myProc
```

Program 8.20 Initialization for example in Section 8.1.5.

Exercise 8.10. Implement the one-dimensional case of the Jacobi iteration in Program 8.7 in Section 8.1.7 (see (1.6.21) and Section 1.6.2) using ℙC or ℙfortran. Do a performance analysis and give a performance prediction graph for the resulting timing data.

Exercise 8.11. Do the two-dimensional case of the Jacobi iteration (Section 8.1.7, (1.6.21), and Section 1.6.2) using ℙC or ℙfortran. The original sequential code reads as in Program 8.21. Use array syntax throughout your code to transmit the border information between processors. Do a performance analysis and give a performance prediction graph for the resulting timing data.

```
real*8 newx(1000,1000), x(1000,1000), datuh(1000,1000)
integer bignum
bignum = 1000
delta_x = 1.0/float(bignum - 1)
dxsq = delta_x**2
do i=1, bignum
  x(1,i) = 0.0
  x(bignum,i) = 0.0
  x(i,1) = 0.0
  x(i,bignum) = 0.0
enddo
do i=2, bignum - 1
 do j=2, bignum - 1
  newx(i,j)=(x(i-1,j)+x(i+1,j)+x(i,j-1)+x(i,j+1)
*          -dxsq*datuh(i))*0.25
 enddo
enddo
do i=2, bignum - 1
 x(i) = newx(i)
enddo
```

Program 8.21 Implementation of two-dimensional Jacobi iteration.

Exercise 8.12. Implement in ℙC or ℙfortran the parallel prefix algorithm in Section 6.2 for the operator $\oplus$ being simply addition for real numbers. Do it in the case that the number of processors in the ring is $P = 2^d$

for $d = 2, 3, 4$. To test it, assume each processor starts with $t =$ `myProc`. Have each processor print the (partial sum) value at the end.

Exercise 8.13. What is the value of `baton` at each iteration `i` and each processor in the code Program 8.3? Write it as a matrix of values with `i` as the row index and `myProc` as the column index. Modify the IPfortran code Program 8.3 to verify your answer (by printing `baton` at each iteration at all of the processors).

Exercise 8.14. Write and test a version of the code Program 8.3 in which the value of `baton` is not incremented at all. (Hint: do Exercise 8.13 to see what the value of `baton` is in Program 8.3, then figure out how to do the logic based on the loop index `i`.)

Exercise 8.15. Modify Program 6.2 to broadcast from one processor to $P - 1$ other processors using IPC or IPfortran using at most $1 + \log P$ steps in the case that P is not a power of two. (Hint: use a binary tree of depth $1 + \log P$ and introduce phantom processors, which do nothing, for the missing processors.)

Exercise 8.16. The b-norm (originally due to Banach) of a vector $X = (x_1, \ldots, x_n)$ is defined by

$$\|X\|_b := \left(\sum_{i=1}^{n} |x_i|^b \right)^{1/b},$$

where b can be any positive real number, but usually restricted to $b \geq 1$ (otherwise it is not a "norm"). Write a function `bnorm(X,Y,b)` and show how it could be used to compute the b-norm of the distributed vector whose i-th component is `x@i` via a user-defined reduction.

Exercise 8.17. Use the technique introduced in Section 8.1.5 to convert Program 8.18 to a program involving only global values.

Chapter Nine
High Performance Fortran

Don't look back. Something might be gaining on you—*Leroy "Satchel" Paige*

High Performance Fortran (HPF) [92, 109] is an extension of Fortran which is *sequentially consistent.* It is often called a **data-parallel language** because it supports and exploits data-parallelism as a central theme. Parallelism is indicated *implicitly* by **data distribution directives** which suggest how data structures should be distributed among processors. A minor point is that the directives appear as comment statements instead of executable statements. This allows sequential code to be modified without losing the ability to compile it correctly for a sequential machine.

The decomposition of work is inferred from the data distribution by the **owner-computes rule** [28]. This rule directs computation to the processor that owns (according to the distribution directives) the data that will be assigned the result of the computation. The compiler is required to manage any data movement necessary [17] to do the computation, but this management can be done automatically in a way to ensure sequential consistency. HPF is an SPMD language in the sense that it certainly has only a single program, and it implements multiple data through its distribution directives.

HPF shares characteristics of both distributed memory and shared memory programming. It is like the latter in that the memory model is that of shared memory from the programmer's point of view (any part of memory can be referenced directly, independently of how it may be distributed by the directives). However, it is like the former in that data are explicitly distributed to different processors. One of the main features of HPF is that it can combine these seemingly contradictory characteristics and generate efficient parallel code for distributed memory machines.

There is an important duality between shared memory programming and HPF. In the former, work is explicitly distributed. Guaranteeing correctness in this case is not possible in general due to issues such as race conditions. However, distributing memory (and inferring work distribution from it) does allow sequentially consistent execution.

9.1 HPF DATA DISTRIBUTION DIRECTIVES

The concept of *ownership* is central to HPF. We say that a process *owns* an array element if that process has been assigned the array portion containing the element. We usually talk about arrays, although generally, any data structure can be distributed. It turns out, however, that the intrinsic type *array* is the foundation for many complicated data structures in Fortran codes.

HPF specifies ownership through the `DISTRIBUTE` and `ALIGN` directives and their executable counterparts, `REDISTRIBUTE` and `REALIGN`. These directives and statements are used to map data arrays onto a logical processor array. The directives appear as comments in ordinary Fortran, with a character in column 1 of the line, followed by the characters `HPF$` to indicate that the directive is for HPF (and not some other system). We use the character `C` and the exclamation point in our examples. For example, Program 9.1 illustrates how to parallelize a simple loop which assigns an integer to each element of an array, `x(128)`, where `nProc=4`. The owner-computes rule links the data distribution to a decomposition of the iteration space through the iteration variable `i`, which has been boxed in Program 9.1. We can imagine how to generate code for either shared memory or distributed memory to support this decomposition (see Exercises 9.1 and 9.2).

```
      real x(128)
CHPF$ DISTRIBUTE x(BLOCK)
      do i = 1, 128
         x(i) = ....
      enddo
```

Program 9.1 Simple loop where array access matches loop induction variable. Distributed array and corresponding loop indices are boxed.

9.1.1 Distribution specifications

An array distribution can be specified with the basic distributions `block` and `cyclic` (case does not matter). An optional argument, `m`, may be used as in `BLOCK(m)` and `CYCLIC(m)`; the default values of `m` are $\mathtt{m} = \frac{\mathtt{N}}{\mathtt{P}}$ for `BLOCK(m)` and `m=1` for `CYCLIC(m)`. Figure 9.1 (a and c) use the default value of `m` along with `N=8` and `P=4`.

Figure 9.1 illustrates several distributions for a one-dimensional array, `X(8)`, and a two-dimensional array, `X(4,8)`, where `nProc=4`. Each cell represents an array element labeled with the owner processing element, $p \in \{0, 1, 2, 3\}$. Notice that the distributions in Figure 9.1 (b) and (c) are the same, as are the distributions (a) and (d). (See Exercises 9.5 and 9.6.)

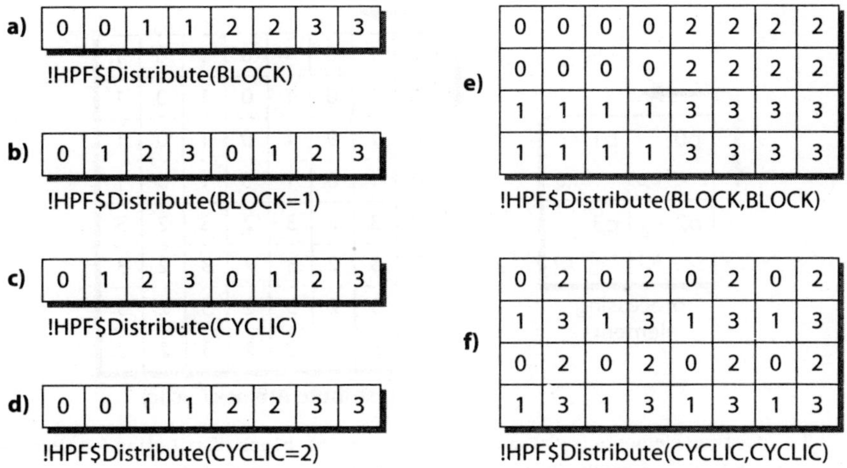

Figure 9.1 Decompositions of `X(8)` (a–d) and `X(4,8)` (e–f) for `nProc=4`.

A distinguishing feature of `block` distributions is the locality they provide. Loops often iterate through a monotonically increasing or decreasing index, so assigning contiguous blocks of memory, to which assignments will be made, tends to minimize data transfers from main memory to cache. The `cyclic` distribution can be contrary to spatial locality; however, it is useful in many scenarios for load balancing. For examples of this, consider a column or row distribution of Gaussian elimination (Section 12.1) and the pair list construction for molecular dynamics (Section 13.4.1).

`BLOCK(m)` means that for some array $\mathtt{A}(1:\mathtt{d})$, element $\mathtt{A}(\mathtt{j})$ is stored in the memory of the processing element $\lceil \frac{\mathtt{j}}{\mathtt{m}} \rceil - 1$. We use the conventions that array index spaces are one-based (that is, the index numbering starts at one) and the process coordinate systems and logical identification numbers are zero-based. Similarly, `CYCLIC(m)` means that element `j` is stored in the memory of processing element $(\lceil \frac{\mathtt{j}}{\mathtt{m}} \rceil - 1) \bmod \mathtt{p}$. Consider the two-dimensional array, `A(8,8)`, in Figure 9.2, right; the owning processing element p is given for each array element for a `(BLOCK,CYCLIC)` distribution. In general, for array element $\mathtt{X}(\mathtt{i}_1, \mathtt{i}_2, , \ldots, \mathtt{i}_k, \ldots, \mathtt{i}_n)$, of array $\mathtt{X}(\mathtt{d}_1, \mathtt{d}_2, , \ldots, \mathtt{d}_k, \ldots, \mathtt{d}_n)$, the processing element coordinate, r_k for dimension k, is $\lceil \frac{i_k}{m_k} \rceil - 1$ for a `block` distribution, and $(\lceil \frac{j}{m_k} \rceil - 1) \bmod p$ for a `cyclic` distribution. Thus, the one-based logical number

$$p = r_1 + p_2(r_2 + \cdots + p_k(r_k + \cdots + p_n r_n) \ldots).$$

In Figure 9.2 the processing element coordinate,

$$(r_1, r_2) = \left(\lceil \frac{i_k}{m_{\text{block}}} \rceil - 1, \; (\lceil \frac{j}{m_{\text{cyclic}}} \rceil - 1) \bmod p \right),$$

for $p = r_1 + p_2 r_2$, where $p_1 = p_2 = 2$, $m_{\text{block}} = 2$ and $m_{\text{cyclic}} = 1$ using the default values. We have assumed that the target processing element array

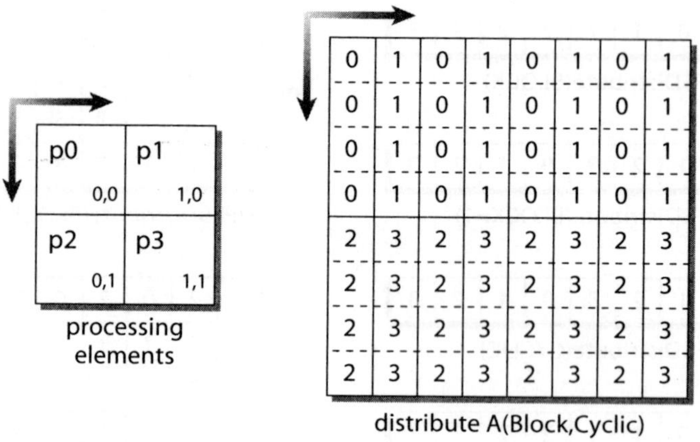

Figure 9.2 Processing elements (*pe's*) mapping for a `cyclic, block` distribution for `nProc=4`. The *pe* coordinate system, on the left, assigns two *pe's* on each two dimensions with the *pe* logical numbering given along with the *pe's* coordinates, `(i,j)`. On the right, the assigned *pe's* are shown for each element of the array `A(8,8)`. Note that the process coordinate system and process identification numbers are zero-based.

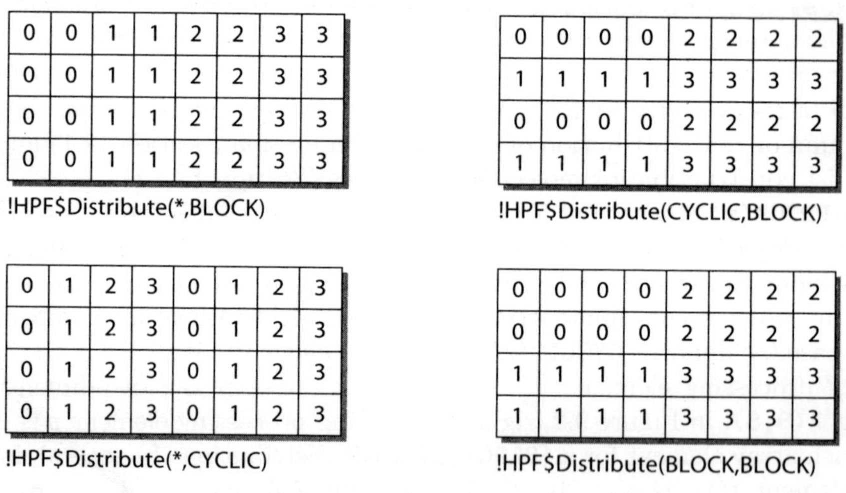

Figure 9.3 Decompositions of `X(4,8)` for `nProc=4`.

is two-dimensional, and that the four processing elements are uniformly distributed along each dimension. (The processing element array can be declared with the `ONTO` clause; see Section 9.2.2.)

In addition to distribution, an array dimension can be replicated. Replication can be thought of as compressing a dimension so all processing elements will own the full range of the array along the replicated dimension(s). The syntax for replication is the asterisk as illustrated in Figure 9.3.

9.1.2 Loop dependences

The role of the owner-computes rule is to limit the computation that must be done by a given processor. However, it may not be possible to do the resulting chunks of work in parallel. This requires standard dependence analysis (Chapter 4) to determine loop-iteration independence. Consider the program in Program 9.2. Without knowledge of the function, `f`, the compiler must serialize the loop iterations. Thus the directives in this case have no impact on the serial code. Sequential consistency demands a sequential execution.

However, if it is known that the loop iterations are independent, an assertion can be made that there are not any loop-carried dependences with the HPF directive `INDEPENDENT` (Program 9.3). `INDEPENDENT` asserts that the do-loop iterations can be executed in *any* order. If the outcome is order-dependent, e.g., if the function $f(i, x) = x(i - 1)$, then the program is incorrect. When we say that HPF is sequentially consistent, we mean that this holds only if all `INDEPENDENT` directives were indeed valid.

```
      real x(128)
CHPF$ DISTRIBUTE x(BLOCK)
      do i = 1, 128
         x(i) = f(i,x)
      enddo
```

Program 9.2 Without knowledge of the function `f`, the compiler will serialize the loop iterations of the program.

```
      real x(128)
CHPF$ DISTRIBUTE x(BLOCK)
CHPF$ INDEPENDENT
      do i = 1, 128
         x(i) = f(i,x)
      enddo
```

Program 9.3 The HPF directive `INDEPENDENT` asserts to the compiler that the do-loop iterations can be executed in any order.

9.1.3 Data alignment and locality

HPF code is written in a *global name space* resembling shared memory. In principle the programmer need not attend to the local name space node code output by the HPF compiler: the compiler produces the logic to move data between processes, assigns loop iterations to processes, and so forth. In practice, however, the data location and movement costs can affect efficiency.

Take, for example, the program in Program 9.4, where the array x is distributed as columns and the array y is distributed as rows. For a program this size, it is difficult to imagine that anyone would write such logic. However, in production codes orthogonal distributions can and do occur. Assuming that the compiler adheres to the distributions, then to satisfy the dependences in Program 9.4, each outer loop iteration will require off-process data. One can use the ALIGN directive to map the columns of x and y to the same processing element as shown in Program 9.5, thereby having the same effect as using the same distribution for x and y.

The complete HPF data mapping model is two-level. First, data objects are aligned relative to one another. Then alignees are distributed by virtue of the distribution of the objects they are aligned with. Alignment is transitive, where, if $a \preceq b \preceq c$, then $a \preceq c$ (read *a is aligned with c*). With the ALIGN directive, one can devise distribution patterns that cannot be achieved with the DISTRIBUTE directive alone. (See Exercise 9.7.)

```
      real x(100,100),y(100,100)
CHPF$ DISTRIBUTE x(*,BLOCK)
CHPF$ DISTRIBUTE y(BLOCK,*)
      do j = 1, 100
         do i = 1, 100
            x(i,j) = x(i,j) + y(i,j)
         enddo
      enddo
```

Program 9.4 The orthogonal distribution in the HPF program results in an exchange step on every outer loop iteration.

```
      real x(100,100),y(100,100)
CHPF$ DISTRIBUTE x(*,BLOCK)
CHPF$ ALIGN y(*,:) with x(:,*)
      do j = 1, 100
         do i = 1, 100
            x(i,j) = x(i,j) + y(i,j)
         enddo
      enddo
```

Program 9.5 The orthogonal distribution is avoided by specifying that columns of arrays x and y are mapped to the same processor using the ALIGN directive.

9.1.4 Subroutine Arguments

HPF provides several methods for specifying data distribution at procedure interfaces. Whatever the distribution method, HPF guarantees that on exit from a subroutine, data mappings will be the same as before entry into the subroutine; however, data can be remapped in the subroutine. We list below the three mappings for formal parameters provided by HPF.

Prescriptive prescribes a mapping for the subroutine; remapping can occur. Used in cases where some data distribution and alignment are desirable for a subroutine. The remapping can be expensive.

syntax: CHPF$ DISTRIBUTE A(*,BLOCK).

Transciptive copies the actual parameter distribution from the calling program to the formal parameter distribution so that remapping never occurs. Subroutine performance can be negatively affected in order to handle *any* incoming distribution.

syntax: CHPF$ INHERIT A

Descriptive describes the distribution of the formal parameter and asserts that no remapping will take place.

syntax: CHPF$ DISTRIBUTE *A(*,BLOCK)

9.2 OTHER MECHANISMS FOR EXPRESSING CONCURRENCY

The `DISTRIBUTE` and `ALIGN` directives say something about how data structures will be partitioned and mapped to processes. HPF provides additional directives used by the compiler in conjunction with the data distribution statements to distribute computational work.

The `INDEPENDENT` directive is one example we have already seen. HPF has several other constructs useful for expressing concurrency to the compiler. These include the `FORALL` statement Fortran 90 reductions.

9.2.1 HPF FORALL statement

The `FORALL` statement resembles the Fortran 90 array assignment. For example, the `FORALL` statement

```
FORALL(I=1:N) A(I) = A(N+1-I)
```

is equivalent to the Fortran 90 statement `A(1:N) = A(N:1)`. That being the case, we see that the `FORALL` statement is *not* a loop since the evaluation order of the right-hand side and the assignment order of the left-hand side can occur in any order with the same results. The syntax of the `FORALL` is

FORALL *(triplet*$_1$*,...,triplet*$_n$*, mask) assignment*

where $triplet_i$ has the form: *subscript* = *lower_bound* : *upper_bound* : *stride*, *mask* is optional, and *assignment* is some *lhs* = *rhs*; *assignment* is evaluated for the indices defined by the triplets and mask. The following statement zeros the array `A`:

```
FORALL(I=1:N) A(I) = 0
```

We can set to zero the array `B` by assigning this `A` to it:

```
FORALL(I=1:N,J=1:N) B(I,J) = A(I)
```

We define `C` to be the identity matrix via

```
FORALL(I=1:N,J=1:N,I==J) C(I,J) = 1.0
FORALL(I=1:N,J=1:N,I/=J) C(I,J) = 0.0
```

The `FORALL` construct is a multistatement counterpart of the `FORALL` statement [92]. The `FORALL` concept has also been adopted in the Fortran 95 standard [1].

9.2.2 Other HPF language features

HPF includes Fortran 90 intrinsic functions, including the reduction function, `SUM`, and the `MINLOC` and `MAXLOC` functions, which return the location of the minimum and maximum location in an array. In addition, HPF adds the binary, commutative bitwise operations `IALL`, `IANY`, and `IPARITY`, which correspond to the familiar bitwise operations *and*, *or*, and *exclusive or*, respectively. The intrinsic functions `NUMBER_OF_PROCESSORS` and `PROCESSORS_SHAPE` can be used to inquire about the processor configuration in effect to execute the program.

The `processors` directive provides a means to describe rectilinear processor arrays. The `template` directive can be used to create an abstract index space for aligning and distributing data structures. The executable statements, `redistribute` and `realign`, are executable counterparts to the directives `distribute` and `align`. The `PURE` attribute declares that the function or procedure it is applied to is free of side effects, except for returning a value or modifying arguments. A function evoked by a `FORALL` statement must be *pure*. The procedure attribute `EXTRINSIC` provides an "escape hatch" to non-HPF procedures. A non-HPF procedure should be declared *extrinsic*.

9.3 COMPILING HPF

A compiler could attempt to locate parallelism by analyzing FORTRAN77 code without any HPF directives whatsoever. However, purely automatic parallelization of Fortran without directions from the programmer is a difficult task [28, 143, 8]. HPF simplifies the process in several ways, making the compilation process more effective. We briefly explain two of the ways this is done.

Data-parallel algorithms (cf. Definition 1.5.6) operate by subdividing data structures among processes, with all processes applying similar numerical operations to a portion of the total data set. HPF exploits such parallelism via data distribution directives. These directives provide information that limits the scope of the optimizations that a compiler might attempt.

In addition, HPF does not just rely on compile-time analysis. There are many expressions that are opaque at compile time but become transparent at run time. For example, a simple indirection in an array reference, such as `A(I(j))`, foils dependence analysis unless `I(j)` is an explicit formula. The **inspector-executor** paradigm [22, 17] introduces an "inspector" phase in which array references such as these are disambiguated via a limited amount of computation. Based on this, dependence analysis can be done, as well as the scheduling of required communication (for distributed memory execution).

In many ways the data-parallel program is easier to write than the SPMD program. The paradigm frees the programmer from partitioning data and iterations, leaving the explicit distribution of data and work, along with interprocess data movement, for the compiler to determine. In this way, HPF is a high-level specification for more explicitly parallel SPMD programs. However, this means that the programmer has less control over the code that ultimately is executed, and there is a need to develop a programming style which will allow the compiler to infer correctly the underlying parallelism [34]. Writing such programs from the outset largely embraces good software engineering techniques (such as the structured programming approach advocated by Dijkstra [42]).

Some structural complexities are intrinsic to an algorithm. Irregular data accesses (which we can define to be any access patterns indeterminate at compile time) pose problems of their own. Nonlinear subscripts are a typical example of irregular access patterns. Irregular accesses are not uncommon in scientific applications. In one survey [133] of subscripts in six numerical packages, 47% of the one-dimensional array references and 45% of the two-dimensional array references were nonlinear (without the help of user assertions in performing dependence analysis). With user assertions, 28% of the one-dimensional array references and 15% of the two-dimensional array references remained nonlinear. Yet, many programs yield to the HPF approach, including those with irregular accesses.

9.4 HPF COMPARISONS AND REVIEW

We present in Table 9.1 a simple comparison of HPF and shared memory programming. This helps to summarize the key points of HPF. Comparing

	HPF	*shared memory*
data distribution	explicit directives	none
work distribution	inferred from data distribution	explicit `parallel do` statements
data exchange	done implicitly by compiler	done implicitly by memory reference
synchronization	done implicitly by compiler	done explicitly by semaphores
memory model	shared memory	shared memory
sequential consistency	yes	no

Table 9.1 Comparison of HPF and shared memory programming styles.

this table with Table 5.1 provides a comparison with distributed memory programming.

HPF programs are written in a global name space, i.e., a shared memory model. Processes are not referenced by name, logical or otherwise, and iteration spaces are not explicitly partitioned. HPF utilizes a data-parallel metaphor to achieve parallelism through data decomposition directives. HPF is sequentially consistent to the extent that user-declared `INDEPENDENT` loops are indeed independent.

9.5 EXERCISES

Exercise 9.1. Show how to generate code in distributed memory to implement the iteration-space decomposition determined via the owner-computes rule in Program 9.1.

Exercise 9.2. Show how to generate code in shared memory to implement the iteration-space decomposition determined via the owner-computes rule in Program 9.1.

Exercise 9.3. Write a program to compute simple sums as in section 1.5.1 in HPF. Determine the performance as a function of N and P as well as the error as a function of N.

Exercise 9.4. Write a program for solving a system of N equations using the Jacobi method (see (1.6.21) and Section 1.6.3) in HPF. Determine the performance as a function of N and P as well as the error as a function of N.

Exercise 9.5. Let `A(1:d)` be a one-dimensional array of size `d`, and consider both `CYCLIC(m)` and `BLOCK(m)` distributions of `A`. What relationship among d, m and the number of processors P will result in same data distributions with CYCLIC(m) and BLOCK(m)? (Hint: BLOCK implicitly asserts that the distribution of data to processors will not wrap around processors, whereas CYCLIC inherently involves wrap-around.)

Exercise 9.6. Given array $\mathtt{A}(d_1, d_2, \ldots, d_n)$ and processing element configuration $\mathtt{P}(p_1, p_2, \ldots, p_k, \ldots, p_n)$, then for what values of m, p, and d do

a) BLOCK(m) and CYCLIC(m) result in the same distribution? **solution**: for $mp \geq d$.

b) BLOCK and CYCLIC result in the same distribution? **solution**: for $p \geq d$.

Exercise 9.7. State in words the distribution pattern corresponding to the following ALIGN directive:

```
CHPF$ ALIGN X(I) WITH Y(2*I).
```

Can the pattern be achieved with a DISTRIBUTE directive?

Exercise 9.8. The standard Gauss-Seidel (Section 4.6.1) algorithm has dependences that preclude a conventional HPF implementation, but a hybrid Jacobi Gauss-Seidel method can be used [128]. The compound algorithm uses a Jacobi iteration across processors and the Gauss-Seidel method interior to each processor, More precisely, the equations are partitioned into P sets, $\mathcal{I}_p$, $p = 0, \ldots, P-1$, and the iteration in each processor becomes

$$\xi_i^n = \Big(\sum_{j \in \mathcal{I}_p, j \neq i} a_{ij} \xi_j^n - f_i \Big) / a_{ii} + \Big(\sum_{j \notin \mathcal{I}_p} a_{ij} \xi_j^{n-1} - f_i \Big) / a_{ii}, \quad i \in \mathcal{I}_p. \quad (9.5.1)$$

At the completion of this, all processors exchange values of ξ_j as necessary.

i) Write the *node code* for the hybrid algorithm.

ii) Is it possible to write the hybrid algorithm in HPF? If so, provide the code. If not, explain.

iii) Calculate the communication costs for the Jacobi method (see Exercise 9.4) and the hybrid method.

You may assume n is an integer multiple of P.

Exercise 9.9. Perform a sum of the array elements of a block distributed array, A, initialized as

```
FORALL(I=1:N) A(I) = I
```

in the following ways:

- Using a DO loop and a scalar sum, where $sum = sum + a(i)$.
- Using the Fortran 90 intrinsic function, SUM.

Time your results for 4, 8, and 16 processes. Explain the user time differences.

Exercise 9.10. Aligning arrays in accordance with the computation can help to reduce communication between processes. However, different computations within the same program could benefit from two different data distributions. Consider the following situation involving the two arrays `v(1:n)` and `b(1:n,1:n)`. Suppose the algorithm requires the calculation of two vectors `dot1(1:n)` and `dot2(1:n)` calculated as follows:

```
do i = 1, N
   do j = 1, N
      dot1(i) =  dot1(i) + v(j)*b(j,i)
      dot2(i) =  dot2(i) + v(j)*b(i,j)
   enddo
enddo
```

Program 9.6 calculates `dot1` without communication, and then it redistributes the data so that, for `dot2`, no communication is required (apart from the redistribution).

Now suppose instead of the redistribution, we transform the second loop in the program above as in Program 9.7.

For the following questions, assume the outer loop of the (level-2) loop nests in Program 9.6 and Program 9.7 have been distributed. This is in accordance with the owner-computes rule for Program 9.6; however, it is not for Program 9.7.

i) Find the communication cost for calculating `dot1` in Program 9.6.

ii) Find the communication costs for calculating `dot2` in Program 9.6 **without** redistributing the array `b` prior to the second loop nest for each case.

   (a) Communication takes place at the time and place it is needed (inside the inner loop).

   (b) The compiler hoists the communication out of the loop.

   Clearly state any assumptions. Communication costs should state the number of messages and the total amount of data.

iii) Consider the calculation of `dot2` in Program 9.7. What data should be communicated by the compiler, and where in the program? Keep in mind the distribution of the *calculation* of `dot2`.

iv) Calculate the communication costs for the calculation of `dot2` in Program 9.7.

Calculate communication costs as the *number of messages* and the *number of data* per processor.

```
c distribute b by columns
CHPF$ DISTRIBUTE b(*,BLOCK)
c replicate v
CHPF$ DISTRIBUTE v(*)
c distribute dot1 and dot2
CHPF$ DISTRIBUTE dot1(BLOCK)
CHPF$ DISTRIBUTE dot2(BLOCK)
c column access of b
CHPF$ INDEPENDENT
      do i = 1, n
        do j = 1, n
          dot1(i) = dot1(i) + v(j)*b(j,i)
        enddo
      enddo
c redistribute b by rows
CHPF$ REDISTRIBUTE b(BLOCK,*)
c row access of b
CHPF$ INDEPENDENT
      do i = 1, n
        do j = 1, n
          dot2(i) = dot2(i) + v(j)*b(i,j)
        enddo
      enddo
      end
```

Program 9.6 Program that calculates dot product `dot1` without communication, and then redistributes the data so that for `dot2`, so no communication is required (apart from the redistribution).

```
CHPF$ DISTRIBUTE b(*,BLOCK)
C replicate v
CHPF$ DISTRIBUTE v(*)
C replicate dot2
CHPF$ DISTRIBUTE dot2(*)
C row access of b converted to column access
CHPF$ INDEPENDENT
        do j = 1, N
          do i = 1, N
            dot2(i) = dot2(i) + v(j)*b(i,j)
          enddo
        enddo
        end
```

Program 9.7 Program that calculates dot product `dot2` by transforming the second loop instead of doing the redistribution.

Chapter Ten
Loop Tiling

> The rumors of my demise are much exaggerated—
> *Mark Twain*

We have already seen that there is at least one industrial strength implementation of the basic shared memory programming model via POSIX threads in Section 7.3. We now consider another model that allows a higher-level approach to shared memory programming. This has a relatively long history (in comparison with other parallel programming languages), which we will not describe in detail. Reference [98] is an important waypoint in this history. We will describe this approach abstractly using the term **tiling** that was used by Kendall Square Research (KSR)[1] as its primary programming model.

10.1 LOOP TILING

The concept of a tiling in mathematics refers to a repetitive decomposition of (typically, multidimensional) space using a small number of building blocks, or **tiles**. In general, the building blocks can be quite complex and lead to impressive artistic images [29, 122]. However, simpler shapes provide practical and familiar floor and wall coverings. It is this type of simple tiling that inspires our terminology here.

The phrase **loop tiling** refers to the decomposition of an iteration space, for the purpose of parallel computation, via simple subdivisions of the space of loop indices. For multiple loops, this corresponds to a regular tiling of the multidimensional iteration space. Loop tiling can be used as a program transformation by a compiler to automatically parallelize a loop [144]. It can also be used to specify a loop decomposition explicitly, providing a shared memory programming model with a high-level interface that simplifies the coding in typical decompositions (or "tilings") of the iteration space of loops. By studying its use in the latter context, we will also learn

[1]KSR (see Section 3.2.3) was founded in 1986 by Henry Burkhardt III (1945–2000), who had co-founded both Data General (where he designed the Nova computer) and Encore Computer Corp., maker of the Multimax shared memory parallel computer. KSR was investigated by the Securities and Exchange Commission for its improperly recognized revenue and was de-listed by the NASDAQ in 1994. KSR patents were bought by Sun Microsystems in the subsequent bankruptcy.

some ways it might be used implicitly in systems that attempt automatic parallelization. Since the memory model is *shared*, all that is needed (at the simplest level) is a way to divide work.

For concreteness, we focus on OpenMP [30], a standard for shared memory programming at a higher level than POSIX threads (Section 7.3). The basic construct for loop tiling in OpenMP is the `parallel do` directive. This name is far from universal; SGI systems use the construct `doacross` in a similar context (cf. [98]), whereas the KSR name was `tile`. For definiteness, we describe the syntax of OpenMP to indicate the various tiling **directives**, following the general industry convention, which appear as comment statements instead of executable statements. This way, the parallel code can still be executed on a serial processor which just treats the parallel constructs as comments. All of the OpenMP directives begin (in Fortran) with `C$omp` followed by different key words. We compare and contrast OpenMP with the syntax used by the Kendall Square Research KSR compilers, with some slight modifications. Another key contributor to the material discussed here is a standards effort that produced an earlier shared memory parallel version of Fortran [98].

10.2 WORK VS. DATA DECOMPOSITION

Parallelizing by dividing *work* is naturally dual to the approach taken by High-Performance Fortran (Chapter 9) in which *data* are decomposed. With the latter approach, a division of work is inferred from the data decomposition. The resulting efficiency of the code depends on the success in analyzing data dependences (Chapter 4). However, correctness can be assured with that approach.

In specifying a work decomposition, the disposition of work is controlled explicitly, but this may not lead to the best possible efficiency. Subdividing loops can balance the amount of computation done, but it could lead to excessive and/or imbalanced data movement (cf. Exercises 10.6 and 12.7). Moreover, now correctness cannot be assured so easily. Here, we intend the concept of loop tiling to be a **do it anyway** `parallel do` loop, meaning that the loops will be executed in parallel whether or not there are dependences, since this is the approach that has been taken in practical systems of this type. The optimum may be to combine work and data distributions in some way, as discussed in [31, 16].

10.3 TILING IN OPENMP

Tiling is achieved in OpenMP by using the `parallel do` compiler directive. OpenMP directives provide instructions to the compiler, but the directives themselves are not translated into code. In the simplest case, the `parallel do` directive implies that the loop following it is to be subdivided into as many separate threads as are available (which would be a system-dependent default value; see Section 10.3.5 regarding specification of the number of threads). The basic directive takes the form `c$omp parallel do` (see Program 10.1 for a simple example).

```
c$omp parallel do
        do i = 2 , n-1
          newx(i) = .5 * (x(i-1) + x(i+1) - dx2 * x(i))
        enddo
c$omp end parallel do
c$omp parallel do
        do i = 2 , n-1
          x(i) = newx(i)
        enddo
c$omp end parallel do
```

Program 10.1 Jacobi iteration using basic OpenMP tiling.

The `parallel do` directive must appear just before a `do` construct in Fortran, and its scope (implicitly) is the scope of the Fortran `do` construct that follows it. It is permissible to make this scope explicit by adding a

```
c$omp end parallel do
```

directive after the end of the scope of the Fortran `do` construct. Either with or without the `end parallel do` directive, the end of the scope of the `do` statement becomes an implicit barrier synchronization point.

Note that the tiling directive and the indicator for its end appear as a comment in ordinary Fortran. This allows its use in a sequential code without changing the semantics in that case.

The iterative method (1.6.21) from Section 1.6.2 (one-dimensional Jacobi iteration) gives a simple illustration of the basic tiling construct. See Program 5.11 for a sequential implementation, together with Program 5.10 which provides some initializations. This can be parallelized easily using tiling as shown in Program 10.1.

10.3.1 Private variables

It is also possible to extend the `parallel do` directive with a list of private variables, such as

```
c$omp parallel do private (a,b,i,j,x,y)
```

The simple example in Program 4.7 can be written as in Program 10.2.

The first part of the code computing the partial sums (1.5.1) in Section 5.4.4 can be written as in Program 10.3. Note that the loop index is used in the subsequent computations and is therefore declared private.

```
c$omp parallel do private (TEMP,I)
      do I = 1,100
        TEMP = I
        A(I) = 1.0/TEMP
      enddo
c$omp end parallel do
```

Program 10.2 OpenMP code with a private directive to eliminate a dependence caused by the use of a temporary variable.

```
c$omp parallel do private (k)
      do k = 0, P-1
        localsum(k) = 0.0
        do i = 1+k*(N/P), (k+1)*(N/P)
          localsum(k) = localsum(k) + x(i)
        enddo
      enddo
c$omp end parallel do
```

Program 10.3 Using tiling to compute partial sums in parallel. The loop index is declared private since it appears in computations.

10.3.2 Decomposition choices

With further optional variables, the tile construct can specify quite complex subdivisions of the iteration space. The directive

```
C$omp parallel do schedule(static)
```

indicates a (static) block decomposition of the iteration space (Section 1.5.1) where the block size is the size of the iteration space divided by the number of processors executing the "parallel do" (more on that number in Section 10.3.5). The directive

```
C$omp parallel do schedule(static, chunksiz)
```

indicates a block decomposition of the iteration space where the block size is given by the variable `chunksiz`. A standard cyclic decomposition of the iteration space (Exercise 1.12) would result from choosing `chunksiz=1`.

One of the main benefits of tiling is the ease with which you can specify different types of dynamic scheduling of parallel loops. For example,

```
C$omp parallel do schedule(dynamic, chunksiz)
```

indicates that chunks of loop indices should be allocated to processors on a first-available basis. This way, if one processor gets bogged down on a particular chunk, it does not slow down the others. And if one processor gets done early, it is immediately assigned more work (if there is some left). If a chunk size is not specified, it is set to one by default.

A more complex form of of dynamic scheduling of parallel loops can be specified by

```
C$omp parallel do schedule(guided, chunksiz)
```

which starts with a system-dependent (large) size for the chunks each processor takes, and then exponentially reduces the chunk size down to `chunksiz`. This allows large segments to be done without interruption initially, with smaller segments scheduled later to improve load balancing.

10.3.3 Explicit synchronization

The beginning and end of a tile construct are implicit barriers (Section 5.4.3) for all the threads executing the tiling construct. Thus synchronization is implicit in the tile construct. More complex `parallel do` constructs [98] may also include barriers and locks. Explicit synchronization can be achieved in OpenMP with the

```
c$omp critical
```

directive, which acts like a guard (see Section 5.4.1) or mutex (see Section 7.3) at the beginning of a critical section. The end of the critical section is marked by the

```
c$omp end critical
```

directive. Thus the code in Program 5.1 can be written as in Program 10.4.

```
c$omp parallel do
      do i=1,n
c$omp critical
        x = x+1
c$omp end critical
      end do
```

Program 10.4 OpenMP code with a critical section.

10.3.4 Reductions

Reductions in OpenMP can be done easily in conjunction with a `parallel do` construct. Suppose that all we want to do is sum a vector of values as is done in the simple reduction statement in **P**fortran code in Program 2.1 (or in the MPI "allreduce" command in Program 2.2). The code in Program 10.5 does this. If you leave out the "reduction" line of code, it will still execute, but give unpredictable (and wrong) results (cf. Exercise 10.7). Reductions can also be done using explicit critical sections (cf. Exercise 10.8).

```
c$omp parallel do private (I)
c$omp+ reduction(+:totals)
      do I = 1,100
        totals = totals + localsum(I)
      enddo
c$omp end parallel do
```

Program 10.5 OpenMP code with a reduction.

10.3.5 How many

So far, we have not said how many processors might be devoted to a tiled loop. This could be done on different systems in a variety of ways. The number of processors (or threads, cf. Section 7.3) can be designated either at the system level or via the function

```
call omp_set_num_threads(inthreads)
```

where `inthreads` is the desired number. If set at the system level, it can be determined inside the code via the statement

```
nThreads = omp_get_num_threads()
```

In the KSR system it was possible to specify a *team* (see Section 10.4) of processes to be devoted to a particular tiled loop.

10.4 TEAMS

Built into the tile statement is the handling of the different processes (or threads) that will execute the different parts of the iteration space. If nothing else is done, new processes (or threads) will be initiated at each tile statement to execute the parallelized loop. Since this can involve significant overhead, it might be possible to use an existing **team** of processes (or threads) by indicating `team = somename` as a parameter in the tile statement. Here `somename` is the name of the team to be used, but we omit the details required to define a particular team of this name. Implicit in the `team` concept is the number of processes; that is, a given team has a specified number of processes (or processors). This makes it easy to specify the amount of parallelism in a loop as well as to eliminate repeated process (or thread) creation.

The KSR system provided for teams as first-class objects, and since this is an interesting notion, we preserve here some of the key ideas. We will not give specific notation for creating a team, but will just presume that some command exists for defining the **team name** and the **team cardinality** (number of threads or processes or processors) it represents. In practice, differentiating teams by *name* may reduce the overhead for initializing such

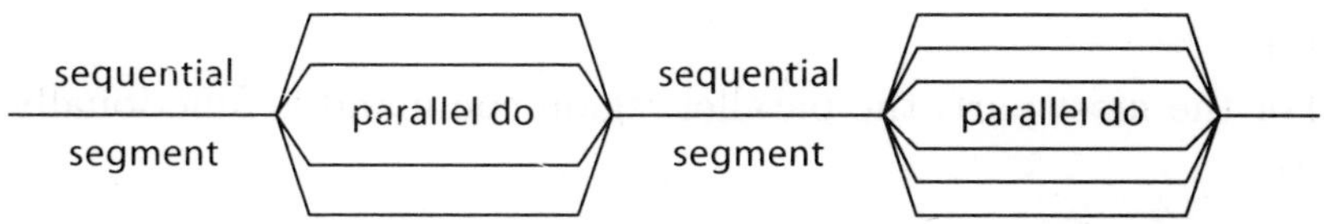

Figure 10.1 The model of execution of tiled (parallel) loops and interleaved sequential regions. In the first parallel loop, four threads are operational, and in the second, six.

a group of entities: teams can be created once and re-used without the overhead of thread or process creation. If no team name is specified in a tile statement, then the statement is executed by a default team with a team cardinality that is specified at the operating system level (before execution of the program).

Team members are numbered from zero to the team cardinality minus one. The team cardinality is always at least one, and when it is more than one, the thread or process invoking the team becomes the **team master** and assumes the role of team member number zero in the team.

We will not emphasize special uses of team names, since this is not universally supported in specific systems. However, we do want to indicate why this might be a useful concept. The initialization of private variables is an interesting question. In [98], the initial values of private variables in a parallel loop are taken to be undefined, no matter how they may have been referenced before. In KSR Parallel Fortran, the value of the private variable in the *master* thread (a particular one that is singled out) will enter the loop with its copy of the private variable initialized to the value it had as a regular variable before entering the loop. The values in the other threads are like typical Fortran variables. If they had values in other loops using the same `team`, then they retain these values.

10.5 PARALLEL REGIONS

The model of execution of tiled (parallel) loops can be visualized in Figure 10.1. This is to be contrasted with, for example, the message passing model in which all "threads" are always operational. This would be represented by a fixed number of horizontal lines in contrast to the more complex picture in Figure 10.1. The style of execution for the message passing model is something that can be of interest even with shared memory. The construct that allows this is called a **parallel region**.

Parallel regions operate like implicit `parallel do` constructs. The syntax in OpenMP is similar to that of parallel do statements as well, being of the form

```
c$omp parallel
```

to start the region and

```
c$omp end parallel
```

to end it.

For the most part, the parallel region command is functionally equivalent to

```
c$omp parallel do
      do i=1,nProcs
```

where `nProcs` is the number of processors (or threads) which would execute the parallel region. For this reason, we do not go into the notation in more detail for parallel regions. In OpenMP, most of the modifiers of a `parallel do` command can be added to a `parallel` command [30].

10.6 EXERCISES

Exercise 10.1. Write a program to compute simple sums as in Section 1.5.1 using tiling. Determine the performance as a function of N and P as well as the error as a function of N.

Exercise 10.2. Write a program to compute primes using the sieve algorithm in Section 1.5.3 using tiling. Do this for one value of k and print the primes each processor finds as it finds them. Test it with $k = 31$.

Exercise 10.3. Write a program to compute the solution to the ordinary differential equation 1.6.1 using the second order method 1.6.9 using tiling. Run this on one and two processors and determine the speedup and communication time. Do 100 time steps with $\Delta t = .01$. Let $f(x)$ be determined by the code in Program 8.19. Let a and b be typed as floating point numbers, and set $a = 2.0$ and $b = 1.0/a$. How does the two-processor speedup depend on the choice of k?

Exercise 10.4. Do the two-dimensional case of the Jacobi iteration (Section 8.1.7, (1.6.21), and Section 1.6.2) using tiling. The original sequential code reads as in Program 8.21.

Exercise 10.5. Modify the one-dimensional Jacobi iteration in Program 10.1 to specify a block size.

Exercise 10.6. Consider the code in Program 10.6 which uses loop tiling to do Gaussian elimination. Which processors work with the j-th column on the k-th iteration? Explain why that might cause excessive data transfer between processor caches.

Exercise 10.7. Remove the "reduction" line in Program 10.5 and compare it to the original code including the reduction. Run the new code many times. Do you always get the same answer?

```
    do k=1,n-1
c$omp parallel do private (j) schedule (static,1)
      do j=k+1,n
        do i=k+1,n
          a(i,j) = a(i,j) -    (a(i,k)/a(k,k))* a(k,j)
        end do
      end do
c$omp end parallel do
    end do
```

Program 10.6 Gaussian elimination via OpenMP tiling.

Exercise 10.8. Remove the "reduction" line in Program 10.5 but replace it with

```
c$omp critical
c$omp end critical
```

commands around the appropriate statement. Compare it to the original code including the reduction. Do you always get the same answer?

Exercise 10.9. Combine the code in Program 10.3 and Program 10.5 without the specific blocking as a single parallel code. Compare the performance with the combination of codes in Program 10.3 and Program 10.5. Check that you get the same answer.

Chapter Eleven
Matrix Eigen Analysis

> Plan any woodworking project from the final coat of paint in.
> —*An unknown carpenter*

This chapter pulls together algorithmic and language ideas from earlier chapters toward the development of a complete parallel implementation of a common computational problem: finding eigenvalue/eigenvector pairs. We give an extended example for a population modeling system based on the Leslie matrix. Owing to the simplicity of the Leslie matrix model, one chapter is sufficient to cover the derivation of the model (Section 11.1), the basic concepts from linear algebra and the power method, a standard algorithm for solving the eigenvalue problem inherent to the Leslie matrix method (Section 11.2), and program requirements and implementation (Section 11.3).

The main computational kernel of the power method is a matrix-vector product; parallelizing this is studied in Section 11.4. Further applications of eigen analysis are presented in Section 11.5. In addition, we introduce some basic concepts from *software engineering*, as we are now transitioning from small problems to large projects. One key concept here is the need to develop *requirement specifications* before any code is written.

The problem addressed in this chapter is quite simple. However, the software development approach used here should be applied in the projects developed in later chapters.

11.1 THE LESLIE MATRIX MODEL

The Leslie matrix [102, 103] is a simple linear model used to predict population growth of flora and fauna from trees and humans down to insects. Through some straightforward analysis of the linear system, one can determine whether a stable population exists, predict population counts at a given time, and determine final population sizes if they exist. The Leslie matrix is a type of compartment model where populations are divided into discrete age groups each spanning some number of years. The age categories are viewed as connected compartments between which individuals move as they age. More complex compartment models can be treated by the same techniques we develop here.

11.1.1 Compartment models and discrete transfers

The population in an n-compartment model is modeled as quantities of material in each of n compartments at some time t. We write this as the vector

$$X(t) = [x_1(t),\ x_2(t), \ldots, x_n(t)]^T,$$

where the state of the system is given as $X(t)$.

The flow rate from compartment i to j, $r_{ji}(t)$, depends on the compartment properties. Example units include grams/minute, joules/sec, and animals/month. The *transfer coefficient*, a_{ji}, is a percentage of the rate of change of material from i to j, where

$$a_{ji}(t) = r_{ji}(t)/x_i(t).$$

In discrete transfer models, material is exchanged between compartments at discrete intervals

$$t_1 = \Delta t,\ t_2 = 2\Delta t, \ldots.$$

We are interested in finding the distribution of material at some time $t+k\Delta t$. This is just the material in the compartments at time t, $X(t)$, plus the amount entering and leaving in the interval $[t, t+k\Delta t]$; we can calculate these amounts using the transfer coefficients

$$\begin{aligned} x_i(t+\Delta t) &= x_i(t) + \text{amount entering} - \text{amount leaving} \\ &= x_i(t) + \Delta t \sum_{j \neq i} a_{ij}\, x_j(t) - \Delta t \Big(\sum_{j \neq i} a_{ji} \Big)\, x_i(t) \\ &= x_i(t) + \Delta t \sum_{k=1}^{n} a_{ik} x_k(t), \end{aligned} \tag{11.1.1}$$

where we assume that the transfer coefficient into a compartment from itself is reduced by the flow out of that compartment, that is, $a_{ii} = -\sum_{j\neq i} a_{ji}$. We write (11.1.1) in matrix form

$$X(t+\Delta t) = X(t) + \Delta t\ \mathbf{A}\ X(t), \tag{11.1.2}$$

where $\mathbf{A} = [a_{ij}]$.

11.1.2 The model

Let us assume a population divided into $n+1$ groups (compartments), each group of length k time units as follows

$$\begin{aligned} G_0 = [0,\ k-1], G_1 = [k,\ 2k-1],\ G_2 = [2k,\ 3k-1],\ \ldots, \\ G_n = [nk,\ (n+1)k-1]. \end{aligned} \tag{11.1.3}$$

Let $X(t)$ give the age structure of the population

$$X(t) = [x_1(t),\ x_2(t), \ldots, x_n(t)]^T,$$

where $x_i(t)$ represents the number of species in age group G_i at time t. For a human population, one might choose $k = 4$ and $n = 20$, with the unit being years. On the other hand, if one wanted to study monthly population variation, one could pick $k = 1$ and $n = 960$, with the unit being months.

The Leslie matrix model in its simplest form takes into account only the females, their reproductive rate, and their survival rate from one age group to the next. Other details, such as population pressure effects, number of males, and environmental effects, are ignored. The parameter F_k represents the average number of female offspring born to an individual in age group k that survive into the next time period; S_k gives the probability of an individual surviving from age class k into age class $k+1$; and $x_k(t+\Delta t)$ is the group population at time t, where Δt is chosen to suitably sample species events.

Using this model, we can write the following system of equations for all age groups:

$$\begin{aligned}
x_0(t+1) &= F_0 x_0(t) + F_1 x_1(t) + \cdots + F_n x_n(t),\\
x_1(t+1) &= S_0 x_0(t),\\
x_2(t+1) &= S_1 x_1(t),\\
&\ \vdots\\
x_n(t+1) &= S_{n-1} x_{n-1}(t),
\end{aligned}$$

where we represent the time interval Δt as a unit time interval from now on. In matrix form

$$X(t+1) = \mathbf{P}\ X(t) \tag{11.1.4}$$

with the population matrix

$$\mathbf{P} = \begin{pmatrix} F_0 & F_1 & F_2 & \ldots & F_n \\ S_0 & 0 & 0 & \ldots & 0 \\ 0 & S_1 & 0 & \ldots & 0 \\ \vdots & \vdots & \vdots & & \vdots \\ 0 & 0 & 0 & S_{n-1} & 0 \end{pmatrix} \tag{11.1.5}$$

An example of the complete matrix equation for an eight-group model is given in Figure 11.1.

11.1.3 Stable populations

We recall some basic concepts from linear algebra. The most important is the idea of an **eigenpair** (X, λ) for a matrix $\mathbf{A}$, which consists of an **eigenvector** $X \neq 0$ and an **eigenvalue** λ which satisfy $\mathbf{A}X = \lambda X$. Let $\mathbf{I}$

$$\begin{bmatrix} x0 \\ x1 \\ x2 \\ x3 \\ x4 \\ x5 \\ x6 \\ x7 \end{bmatrix} = \begin{bmatrix} F0 & F1 & F2 & F3 & F4 & F5 & F6 & F7 \\ S0 & 0 & 0 & 0 & 0 & 0 & 0 & 0 \\ 0 & S1 & 0 & 0 & 0 & 0 & 0 & 0 \\ 0 & 0 & S2 & 0 & 0 & 0 & 0 & 0 \\ 0 & 0 & 0 & S3 & 0 & 0 & 0 & 0 \\ 0 & 0 & 0 & 0 & S4 & 0 & 0 & 0 \\ 0 & 0 & 0 & 0 & 0 & S5 & 0 & 0 \\ 0 & 0 & 0 & 0 & 0 & 0 & S6 & 0 \end{bmatrix} \begin{bmatrix} x0 \\ x1 \\ x2 \\ x3 \\ x4 \\ x5 \\ x6 \\ x7 \end{bmatrix}$$

Figure 11.1 Diagrammatic representation of the Leslie matrix equation matrix, **P**, modeling eight population groups.

denote the identity matrix whose ij entry is one if $i = j$ and zero otherwise. Then λ is an eigenvalue of $\mathbf{A}$ if and only if the matrix $\mathbf{A} - \lambda\mathbf{I}$ has a (nonzero) null vector X (a corresponding eigenvector), and this happens if and only if the determinant of the matrix $\mathbf{A} - \lambda\mathbf{I}$ is zero.

The determinant of the matrix $\mathbf{A} - \lambda\mathbf{I}$ is a polynomial in λ of degree at most n, the dimension of $\mathbf{A}$, and the coefficients of this polynomial are themselves polynomial expressions in the coefficients of $\mathbf{A}$. The eigenvalues are the roots of this polynomial. Even for matrices with coefficients that are real numbers, we must allow for eigenpairs which have entries that are complex numbers, although the eigenvalues will appear in pairs: if λ is a complex eigenvalue then so is it complex conjugate $\overline{\lambda}$. In general, an $n \times n$ matrix will have n eigenvalues (although multiplicities can occur), and we can thus order them from largest (in complex modulus) to smallest. If the largest (in complex modulus) is real, it is called the **dominant eigenvalue**.

We state without proof the following theorem regarding the Leslie matrix. Its proof can be found implicitly in Section 11.2.

Theorem 11.1.1. If **P** has a dominant eigenvalue, λ_0, with eigenvector

$$E^0 = [e_0,\ e_1, \ldots,\ e_n]^T,$$

then, for almost all starting vectors, each age class will eventually grow exponentially at the rate of λ_0 per time period. Moreover, the *stable age distribution* of the population, S, is given by

$$S = E^0/\|E^0\|_1 = [e_0,\ e_1,\ \ldots,\ e_n]^T \ / \ \|E^0\|_1, \qquad (11.1.6)$$

where the scalar $\|E_0\|_1 = |e_1| + |e_2| + \cdots + |e_n|$ is called the ℓ^1-norm of E^0.

An equation for the eigenvalues of the the population matrix (11.1.5) can be derived from

$$
\begin{aligned}
0 = \det(\mathbf{P} - \lambda\mathbf{I}) &= \begin{pmatrix} F_0 - \lambda & F_1 & F_2 & \dots & F_n \\ S_0 & -\lambda & 0 & \dots & 0 \\ 0 & S_1 & -\lambda & \dots & 0 \\ \vdots & \vdots & \vdots & \vdots & 0 \\ 0 & 0 & 0 & S_{n-1} & -\lambda \end{pmatrix} \\
&= (F_0 - \lambda)(-\lambda)^n - F_1 S_0 (-\lambda)^{n-1} + F_2 S_0 S_1 (-\lambda)^{n-2} \\
&\quad - F_3 S_0 S_1 S_2 (-\lambda)^{n-3} + \cdots \qquad (11.1.7) \\
&= (-\lambda)^n \left(F_0 + \sum_{i=1}^{n} F_i \lambda^{-i} \prod_{j=0}^{i-1} S_j - \lambda \right) \\
&= (-\lambda)^n \left(\sum_{i=0}^{n} F_i \lambda^{-i} \prod_{j=0}^{i-1} S_j - \lambda \right),
\end{aligned}
$$

where we make the convention that $\prod_{j=0}^{-1} S_j := 1$ in the last step, to simplify notation. In the derivation, we also assumed that $\lambda \neq 0$; see Exercise 11.3. Thus an eigenvalue λ must satisfy the equation

$$\sum_{i=0}^{n} F_i \lambda^{-i} \prod_{j=0}^{i-1} S_j = \lambda. \qquad (11.1.8)$$

By inspection, we can see that the corresponding eigenvector is given by

$$[1,\ S_0/\lambda,\ S_0 S_1/\lambda^2, \dots,\ S_0 S_1 \cdots S_{n-1} \lambda^{-n}]^T \qquad (11.1.9)$$

since (11.1.8) holds. We can rewrite (11.1.8) as a polynomial in $\xi := \lambda^{-1}$ (again, if $\lambda \neq 0$) as

$$p(\xi) := \sum_{i=1}^{n+1} \alpha_i \xi^i = 1 \quad \text{where} \quad \alpha_{i+1} = F_i \prod_{j=0}^{i-1} S_j \quad \text{for} \quad i = 0, \dots, n. \qquad (11.1.10)$$

The smallest root(s) of this equation (see Exercise 11.5) correspond to the largest eigenvalue(s). Since the coefficients α_i are real numbers, the roots are either real numbers or complex conjugate pairs. The two most likely scenarios are (1) the smallest root is real, so that there is a dominant eigenvalue and (2) the smallest roots are complex conjugate pairs.

This first case was addressed in Theorem 11.1.1. Under fairly simple conditions, we can guarantee that this holds for the Leslie matrix. We assume that the coefficients S_i are always positive; otherwise there is a zero probability of survival from one age group to another. In addition, if F_n is positive, then the directed graph associated with the matrix $\mathbf{P}$ is strongly connected (see Exercise 11.2), and hence $\mathbf{P}$ is irreducible [20]. Thus the Perron-Frobenius theorem implies that $\mathbf{P}$ has a dominant eigenvalue.

If $F_n = 0$, it is easy to interpret the way in which $\mathbf{P}$ is "reducible" by noting that the growth of the n-th age cohort is completely determined by the younger cohorts. The number in the n-th cohort is just given by the number in cohort $n-1$ adjusted by the survival rate S_n. There is no feedback if there are no offspring from the n-th cohort. In general, if $F_i = 0$ for $i = k, \dots, n$ then all of the i-th cohorts are determined for $i = k, \dots, n$ from cohort $k-1$, simply by the survival rates. Thus there is no loss of generality in assuming that $F_n \neq 0$ in the Leslie model, and therefore that $\mathbf{P}$ is irreducible.

Example 11.1.2. Consider some population with three age groups, where one-tenth of G_0 females survive into G_1, and one-half of G_1 females survive into G_2. The species reproduces in G_1 and G_2 at the rate of five and three individuals per female, respectively. Accordingly, we set up the Leslie matrix

$$\mathbf{P} = \begin{pmatrix} 0.0 & 5.0 & 3.0 \\ 0.1 & 0.0 & 0.0 \\ 0.0 & 0.5 & 0.0 \end{pmatrix}$$

Let the initial population be

$$x(0) = (20, 10, 5)$$

and consider what happens if we apply the iteration in (11.1.4). For one thing, we expect from Theorem 11.1.1 that the population may grow exponentially, and only the age *distribution* may tend to a limit. Thus we should normalize the resulting population values, e.g., by the total population, which is $\|x(t)\|_1$ at time t, or by the Euclidean norm $\|x(t)\|_2$, where $\|z\|_2 := \left(\sum_{i=1}^{n} z_i^2\right)^{1/2}$. In Table 11.1 we list the results of the model for ten time steps normalized by the Euclidean norm.

An eigenvector corresponding to the dominant eigenvalue ($\lambda = 1.9911$) is

$$E^0 = (0.9857, 0.1634, 0.0410)$$

which has been normalized to have $\|E^0\|_2 = 1$. The population tends to a stable distribution consistent with this eigenvector after about eight generations.

11.2 THE POWER METHOD

The **power method** is an iterative method for finding the dominant eigenvalue and the corresponding eigenvector of a matrix $\mathbf{A}$ [56]. It is very similar in spirit to our simulation of the Leslie model in Example 11.1.2. Suppose that $\mathbf{A}$ is an $n \times n$ matrix, and write it in Jordan canonical form, i.e., such that $\mathbf{X}^{-1}\mathbf{A}\mathbf{X} = \Lambda$, where Λ is the bidiagonal matrix with diagonal entries $\lambda_1, \dots, \lambda_n$. Furthermore, let us assume that the eigenvalues are numbered

time	Group_0	Group_1	Group_2
t_0	0.8729	0.4364	0.2182
t_1	0.9985	0.0439	0.0333
t_2	0.9235	0.3828	0.0255
t_3	0.9954	0.0809	0.0508
t_4	0.9707	0.2385	0.0293
t_5	0.9908	0.1270	0.0473
t_6	0.9816	0.1876	0.0364
t_7	0.9876	0.1505	0.0436
t_8	0.9845	0.1709	0.0395
t_9	0.9863	0.1593	0.0419
t_{10}	0.9854	0.1656	0.0405

Table 11.1 Population distribution in individuals for three groups and ten time steps determined using the Leslie matrix model.

so that $\mid \lambda_1 \mid \geq \mid \lambda_2 \mid \geq \cdots \geq \mid \lambda_n \mid$. It is easy to see what happens if we define a sequence of vectors by repeatedly multiplying by $\mathbf{A}$, viz.,

$$Y^{n+1} = \mathbf{A}Y^n,$$

namely, by induction we have $Y^n = \mathbf{A}^n Y^0$. Using the Jordan form, we find

$$\mathbf{A}^n = \mathbf{X}\Lambda^n\mathbf{X}^{-1}. \tag{11.2.1}$$

If $\mathbf{A}$ is a diagonalizable matrix (it is not clear that the Leslie matrix is diagonalizable since it is not normal), then Λ would be diagonal, and Λ^n would be the diagonal matrix with entries λ_i^n. But this gives the correct impression of what happens in the general case: $|\lambda_1|^n$ dominates the behavior. Note that if $\mathbf{A}X \approx \lambda X$ and $\|X\|_2 = 1$, then $X^T\mathbf{A}X \approx \lambda$.

Given an initial guess $g^{(0)} \in R^n$, the power method produces a sequence of approximate eigenvectors $g^{(k)}$ and corresponding approximate eigenvalues $\lambda^{(k)}$ as follows

$$\begin{aligned} &\textit{for } k = 1, 2, \ldots \\ &\quad z^{(k)} = A\, g^{(k-1)} \\ &\quad \lambda^{(k)} = [g^{(k-1)}]^T\, z^{(k)} \\ &\quad g^{(k)} = z^{(k)}/\|z^{(k)}\|_2 \\ &\textit{end} \end{aligned} \tag{11.2.2}$$

where $\|z\|_2 := \left(\sum_{i=1}^n z_i^2\right)^{1/2}$ denotes the Euclidean norm of z. Note that $z^T z = \|z\|_2^2$ and that $g^{(k)}$ in (11.2.2) is defined so that $\|g^{(k)}\|_2 = 1$ for $k \geq 1$.

Theorem 11.2.1. If $\mathbf{P}$ has a dominant eigenvalue, λ_0, with eigenvector

$$E^0 = [e_0,\ e_1, \ldots,\ e_n]^T,$$

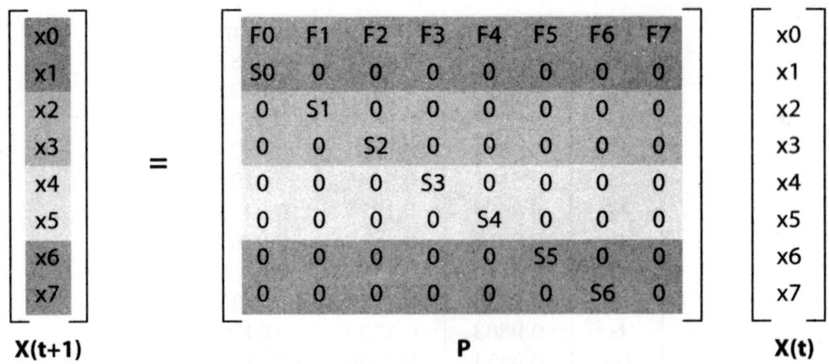

Figure 11.2 Diagrammatic representation of a row-wise distribution of the Leslie matrix, **P**, modeling eight population groups. The parallel implementation is shown for four processes; the data for each process is shaded. The calculation is also shown to be distributed by rows as indicated by the distribution of the resultant vector, $X(t+1)$.

then the power method will converge for almost all initial vectors: $\lambda^k \to \lambda_0$ and $z^{(k)} \to \alpha E^0$ for some scalar α.

It is easy to see that, if the power method converges, it converges to an eigenpair, as follows. If $g^{(k)} \to g$, then also

$$z^{(k)} \to z := Ag$$

by continuity of matrix-vector multiplication, and the continuity of the norm implies that $g = \|z\|_2^{-1} z$. Similarly, continuity of the vector-vector dot product implies that

$$\lambda^{(k)} \to \lambda := g^T z = [\frac{1}{\|z\|_2} z]^T z = \|z\|_2.$$

Thus $z = \lambda g$ and $Ag = z = \lambda g$.

The vectors $g^{(k)}$ are always of length one, but they do not need to converge to anything in general. They can oscillate back and forth if, for example, the largest eigenvalue(s) are a complex pair. In fact, we see by the proof above that convergence of the power method implies that the limiting λ is a positive real number.

It is theoretically possible to start the power method with an initial vector $g^{(0)}$ that is orthogonal to E^0, and have the resulting vectors stay orthogonal to E^0. However, any small perturbation that moves the vectors away from the orthogonal subspace will restore the basic behavior of the power method.

11.3 A PARALLEL LESLIE MATRIX PROGRAM

In this section we develop the design for a parallel program implementing the basic Leslie matrix model. First, we outline the *requirement specification*, which is independent of the implementation, and independent of whether the implementation is serial or parallel. With a requirement specification and the algorithmic details behind us, we proceed to specify the implementation details.

With a solid understanding of the underlying theory, one might be tempted to shortcut this step and jump to a favorite editor to write a program by the seat of one's pants. Indeed, this method will work for some tasks, but the time one ultimately spends on implementation design will almost always return the favor in a better product brought to fruition more quickly than with less planning. The time one *should* spend at the design phase, however, depends on a number of factors such as software size and complexity, and the software engineering team size. Certainly there are diminishing returns from over-design, but this is not the usual problem.

11.3.1 Program requirements (specifications)

A requirement specification is typically a contract between programmers and some customer. It is not uncommon to iterate over the requirements and ensuing design numerous times. Of the numerous methods used for designing software (see, e.g., [87, 106]), it is not our intention to cover any of them. However, for all but the most trivial project, it is advisable to have a software goal independent of an implementation, with a clear picture of both.

We will design a Leslie matrix program to address the requirements:

i) Determine whether some population stabilizes.

ii) Determine what is the stable population distribution if it exists.

iii) Determine what is the population at some time, t.

We assume as input:

i) number of population groups, N,

ii) population group fecundity rates, F_k, $0 \leq k < N$,

iii) survival rates from group i to j, S_{ji}, and

iv) the initial population of the groups.

In effect there are an infinite number of implementations that would satisfy our design goals. One such implementation, for example, would require only one routine that performs all tasks and outputs the results. That approach is undesirable for a number of reasons. For one, a single routine makes it practically impossible for more than one programmer to work on the project. Such an approach is contrary to sustainable and flexible software as the tightly coupled functionality makes it problematic to modify select portions and to incorporate other routines, such as a matrix multiplication. In the next section we outline a modular implementation.

11.3.2 Program implementation

Our implementation will compartmentalize the following functionality:

- Leslie functions
  - Input and Output
  - FindStablePopulation
  - ProjectPopulation
- Utility functions
  - Matrix multiplication
  - Eigensolver

This separation of functionality permits us to plug in utility functions for matrix multiplication and eigensolvers that are part of various libraries; in addition, we can supply our own. The matrix multiplication routine can take advantage of the special case here, that is, multiplying a matrix, represented only by two arrays, by a *vector* presented in Section 11.4. We know that the Leslie matrix is positive definite and is therefore invertible, so we can use the power method described in Section 11.2.

11.3.2.1 Input

An I/O scheme is outlined here for implementing the Leslie matrix program outlined in Section 11.3.1. The specification allows for implicit representation of zeros; that is, the Leslie matrix parameters may be expanded into the corresponding zero-filled matrix. Also note that the specification calls for functionality to select for *block* or *cyclic* distribution of the Leslie matrix rows.

The input to the program will consist of a free format tableau of numbers on separate lines for

line:	*input_type*	*distribution_type*	*number_timesteps*
block:	*Leslie_matrix*		
block:	*initial_population*		

where a **block** may consist of one or more lines. The input in detail:

input_type selects the format of the Leslie matrix in the input text file. For *input_type =1* the program inputs the Leslie matrix *parameters* only; the zero positions are not explicitly input. For *input_type = 2* the program inputs the Leslie matrix fully represented (zero-filled); this option will be useful for accessing small test cases without Leslie matrix structure for testing various subroutines.

distribution_type selects between *block contiguous* and *cyclic* distributions of rows, for values *1* and *2*, respectively.

Leslie matrix with input_flag=1 is input with implicit zeros from a text file which contains the *real* values in the following two lines:

$$\begin{array}{llllllll} F_0 & F_1 & F_2 & F_3 & \ldots & F_{n-1} & F_n \\ S_0 & S_1 & S_2 & S_3 & \ldots & S_{n-1} & \end{array}$$

If $n > 7$, break the number of elements into 8 elements per row. For example, for $n = 9$,

$$\begin{array}{lllll} F_0 & F_1 & F_2 & \ldots & F_7 \\ F_8 & F_9 & & & \\ S_0 & S_1 & S_2 & \ldots & S_7 \\ S_8 & S_9 & & & \end{array}$$

Full matrix with input_flag=2 is input with all values including explicit zeros from a text file which contains the real values:

$$\begin{array}{lllll} a_1 & a_2 & a_3 & \ldots & a_N \\ a_{N+1} & a_{N+2} & a_{N+3} & \ldots & a_{2N} \\ \vdots & \vdots & \vdots & \ldots & \vdots \\ a_{N^2-N+1} & a_{N^2-N+2} & a_{N^2-N+3} & \ldots & a_{N^2} \end{array}$$

where for $N > 8$, break the number of elements into 8 elements per row as described above. Here, N corresponds to $n + 1$ where n is the index specific to the Leslie matrix.

initial population, X, is a vector of length N and of type *real.* It is fully represented for both *input_type 1* and *2.* For $N > 8$, break the number of elements into 8 elements per row as described above.

11.3.2.2 Output

The Leslie matrix and population vector are output exactly as they are input with the exception that each row is labeled with the owning process. For example, the matrix output for Example 11.1.2, cyclically distributed, is

$$\begin{array}{llll} p_0 & 0.00 & 5.00 & 3.00 \\ p_1 & 0.10 & 0.00 & 0.00 \\ p_0 & 0.00 & 0.50 & 0.00 \end{array}$$

11.3.2.3 Largest eigenvalue by the power method

This *function* determines the largest eigenvalue of $\mathbf{P}$ and the corresponding eigenvector $\mathbf{E_0}$ using the *power method.* Your program should use a *maximum* of n processes, where n is the dimension of the matrix $\mathbf{P}$. Any norm may be chosen with the appropriate convergence criteria. The program should handle nonconverging cases with a *warning message.* Use the subsequent *matrix multiplication* and *convergence criteria* functions.

11.3.2.4 Matrix multiplication

This *function* computes the product of a matrix and a vector, to be used in the power method.

11.3.2.5 Convergence criteria

This *function* determines whether an iterative method for approximating eigenpairs has converged, by comparing subsequent eigenvalue $(\lambda^{(k+1)} - \lambda^{(k)})$ and eigenvector $(g^{(k+1)} - g^{(k)})$ approximants. Assume that the $g^{(k)}$'s are normalized but consider the need to normalize the $\lambda^{(k)}$'s. Used by the power method.

11.3.2.6 Stable age population

This *function* determines the stable age population using (11.1.6) and the algorithm from Section 11.3.2.3, given $\mathbf{X(0)}$ and $\mathbf{P}$. This routine will observe the fact that $\mathbf{P}$ is distributed by row either cyclically or blockwise, and $\mathbf{X(0)}$ is replicated. This calls the power method routine.

11.3.2.7 Project population

This *function* evaluates (11.1.4) for *number_timesteps* steps. This routine will print the population *distribution* at each time step. For an example output format, see Table 11.1.

11.3.2.8 Main program

This calls *Input* and calls the routines *Stable age population* or *Project population* (or both) and then calls *Output.*

11.3.3 A parallel version

A straightforward parallelization of the implementation specification in Section 11.3.2 can be achieved with a *block distribution of rows* of the Leslie matrix followed with the same distribution of the matrix multiplication and the eigensolver. Figure 11.2 diagrams a row-wise distribution for four processes. With this method communication takes place

- prior to the *power method* to seed uniformly the *g vector*;
- for matrix multiplication to collect the distributed portions of the *g vector*—called on each iteration of the power method;
- and for input and output.

The row distributed by blocks can easily allow for a cyclic distribution of rows of the Leslie matrix.

A space-efficient distribution will use at most

$$(\lceil N/\mathtt{nProc}\rceil\ + 1) \times \text{size}(\mathtt{REAL})$$

space for inputting and storing an $N \times N$ matrix $\mathbf{P}$. As a first approximation, a parallel code can replicate the vector X across processes using space N at each process, since the leading space term is the matrix $\mathbf{P}$ with `nProc` processors. However, a truly scalable implementation would need to distribute X as well as $\mathbf{P}$.

11.4 MATRIX-VECTOR PRODUCT

The basic operation in the power method (Section 11.2) and the Jacobi iteration (Section 1.6.2 and Section 5.6) is the multiplication of a matrix times a vector. In the examples in Section 1.6.2 and Section 5.6, the matrix in question was tri-diagonal. The Leslie matrix has a similarly special structure. It is also of interest to have algorithms for multiplication of a matrix times a vector when the matrix is a full matrix. We consider some algorithms for this as well.

The formula for multiplying a matrix **a** times a vector **x** is

$$y_i = \sum_{j=1}^{n} a_{ij}x_j \quad \forall i = 1, \ldots, n. \tag{11.4.1}$$

In matrix notation, we would write only `Y=AX`.

A sequential algorithm for a matrix-vector product (for a full matrix) is shown in Program 11.1. There are various ways to parallelize this operation. For simplicity, we will consider the case that the number of processors $P = n$.

```
do i=0,n-1
   y(i) = a(i,1)*x(1)
   do j=1,n-1
     y(i) = y(i) + a(i,j)*x(j)
   enddo
enddo
```

Program 11.1 Sequential computation of matrix-vector product.

We will be interested in parallelizations of Program 11.1 in which the matrix-vector operation could be repeated, as, for example, occurs in the Jacobi iteration (Sections 1.6.2 and 8.1.7). In the first two algorithms, each processor starts with all of the vector **x** and at completion has all of the vector **y**. This means that some results may have to be combined by a reduction (Chapter 6) after they have been computed in a distributed fashion.

There are two different parallelizations of Program 11.1 that are in a sense dual to each other. In one, shown in Program 11.2, each processor computes only one entry `y(myProc)`, and then these are combined via a reduction. In this code, each processor only needs one row of the matrix a.

```
y(myProc) = a(myProc,0)*x(0)
do j=1,n-1
  y(myProc) = y(myProc) + a(myProc,j)*x(j)
enddo
call vcombin{y,n}
```

Program 11.2 Parallel computation of matrix-vector product with each processor computing one entry. Assumes $n = P$ and presumes that the subroutine `vcombin` has been defined as in Program 8.8 or Program 6.8.

In the other parallelization of Program 11.1, shown in Program 11.3, each processor computes only part of the contribution but to all of the entries of y, and then these are combined via a reduction. In this code, each processor only needs one column of the matrix a.

```
do i=0,n-1
  y(i) = a(i,myProc)*x(myProc)
enddo
y=+{y}
```

Program 11.3 Parallel computation of matrix-vector product with each processor computing part of all entries. Assumes $n = P$.

These two codes both require only part of the matrix a, and they require $\mathcal{O}(n)$ computation and $\mathcal{O}(n)$ communication. Since one requires a row of a and the other a column of a, it is natural to ask if there is some compromise involving something in between.

Suppose for the moment that $P = n^2$. Consider the code shown in Program 11.4. Here we achieve in some sense the maximum possible parallelism: every processor computes just one multiply. The reduction in the do j loop in Program 11.2 is equivalent (see Exercise 11.14) to the reduction in Program 11.4.

```
do i=0,n-1
  y(i) = 0.0
enddo
i = myProc/n
j = mod(myProc,n)
y(i) = a(i,j)*x(j)
y=+{y}
```

Program 11.4 Parallel computation of matrix-vector product with each processor computing only one multiply. Assumes $P = n^2$.

Although Program 11.4 displays major parallelism, there is a big shortcoming. The "reduction" step requires putting zero in all of the entries, and the operation `y=+{y}` may not have the optimal communication properties. The reduction could be split in two parts. First, the processors for which `i=myProc/n` for a given `i` would all sum their values, say to processor `i*n`. Then these processors would combine values and perhaps distribute them back to all other processors. However, such an algorithm would still be very communication intensive. Where the algorithm in Program 11.4 becomes interesting is when it is applied to matrices with $n = k\sqrt{P}$ for $k > 1$. Such a generalization is quite easy if we use block operations.

Any $n \times n$ matrix, if n can be factored as $n = k \cdot \ell$, can be written as a $k \times k$ matrix of $\ell \times \ell$ blocks (or vice versa). The formula for multiplying a block matrix times a (block) vector (we block the vector in the corresponding way) looks the same as (11.4.1), but we must interpret terms like $a_{ij}x_j$ themselves as multiplication of a matrix (a_{ij}) times a vector (x_j). Moreover, the summation is a summation of vectors, not scalars. With this interpretation, the single multiplication in Program 11.4 becomes the multiplication of an $\ell \times \ell$ matrix times a vector of length ℓ. It requires ℓ^2 MAPs, where MAPs stands for **multiply-add pairs**. Note that now $P = k^2$. Presumably, even the simple algorithm of putting zeros in all n entries of the product vector `y`, and the simple reduction step `y=+{y}` may be sufficiently efficient, if ℓ^2 is large compared with n. Observe that

$$\ell^2/n = \ell/k = n/k^2 = n/p,$$

so the block version of Program 11.4 is efficient for large blocks, as would be intuitive. We leave to Exercise 11.11 the details of the implementation. For more information see [49].

The BLAS (basic linear algebra subroutines) provide optimized routines to perform matrix-vector products [97, 104].

11.5 POWER METHOD APPLICATIONS

The need to compute eigenvalues and eigenvectors arises in diverse situations. We began with a biological model, based on the Leslie matrix concept, but there are other examples where the matrices in question are inherently much larger. In this section, we describe just two of them.

11.5.1 Modes of fluctuation

Many physical models are described by differential equations, and their corresponding eigenvalues and eigenvectors describe their fundamental frequencies and modes of fluctuation. These eigenvalues and eigenvectors can be approximated by discretizing the differential equations. In Section 1.6.2, we introduced a linear system to approximate a second order differential operator with coefficients (compare (1.6.17))

$$b_i = \frac{-1}{h_i}, \qquad a_i = \frac{1}{h_i} + \frac{1}{h_{i+1}} \tag{11.5.1}$$

based on a discretization mesh where h_i is defined in (1.6.15). The $N \times N$ matrix for the system is of the form

$$\mathbf{P} = \begin{pmatrix} a_1 & b_1 & 0 & \dots & 0 & 0 \\ b_1 & a_2 & b_2 & \dots & 0 & 0 \\ 0 & b_2 & a_3 & \dots & 0 & 0 \\ \vdots & \vdots & \vdots & \vdots & \vdots & \vdots \\ 0 & \dots & 0 & b_{N-2} & a_{N-1} & b_{N-1} \\ 0 & \dots & \dots & 0 & b_{N-1} & a_N \end{pmatrix} \tag{11.5.2}$$

The power method can be used to compute the largest eigenvalue and eigenvector of $\mathbf{P}$ (in this case, $\mathbf{P}$ is symmetric and positive definite so there is a unique largest eigenvalue).

Difference (or finite element) methods generate matrices with structure very similar to (11.5.2), with N limited only by the size of memory. For a problem of this size, it is clear that a parallel version of the power method may be essential. We leave as Exercise 11.9 to modify the Leslie matrix code of Section 11.3 to deal with the special structure of these matrices.

11.5.2 Implicit rankings

There are many situations in which it is desired to estimate rankings of related objects based on relationships among the objects. Suppose that we want to measure popularity. One way to do that is to see how many people keep your phone number in their personal digital assistants. If there are many such people, then you must be popular. But you are surely more popular if the people who keep your number are themselves popular. So a better way to rank would be to keep track of not only how many people list you but also their rankings. For example, your ranking might be defined to be a simple multiple of the sum of all rankings of people who list you. However, this is a circular definition. How can you define your ranking until you know all other rankings? And how can you define them since presumably some of them must depend on your own?

The way out of this dilemma is to write the relationships using matrices and then observe that it leads to an eigenvalue problem, as follows. Let $\lambda > 0$ denote an unknown parameter for the moment which represents the constant of proportionality for rankings. Let $\mathbf{A} = (a_{ij})$ denote the matrix with the property that $a_{ij} = 1$ if and only if the j-th person lists the i-th person's phone number, and zero otherwise. Then the i-th ranking x_i can be determined from other rankings (x_j) by the relationship

$$x_i = \frac{1}{\lambda} \sum_{\{j\,:\,a_{ij}\neq 0\}} x_j. \tag{11.5.3}$$

This just says that the i-th ranking is proportional to the sum of the rankings of the entities that point to it, with constant of proportionality given by $1/\lambda$. Using properties of the definition of the matrix $\mathbf{A} = (a_{ij})$, we thus see that for all i

$$\lambda x_i = \sum_{\{j\,:\,a_{ij}\neq 0\}} x_j = \sum_j a_{ij} x_j = (\mathbf{A}X)_i\,. \tag{11.5.4}$$

This says that X and λ are eigenpairs: $\mathbf{A}X = \lambda X$. If the matrix $\mathbf{A}$ is irreducible [20], then there is a non-negative eigenpair, where λ is the dominant eigenvalue. In this case, the power method can be used to approximate X and λ. Note that rankings, like eigenvalues, only can be meaningfully defined to within a constant factor. That is, absolute rankings make no sense; only rankings relative to others are useful.

Computing popularity of people based on phone number tabulation may be a silly example. But it is prototypical of other uses which are more realistic. The use of **link popularity** for search engines for the World Wide Web is an example. Instead of phone numbers, we record links to web pages. The above ideas carry over immediately and provide a model of rankings of web pages based on the links that point to them and their rankings. Current web search engines compute the corresponding eigenvalue problem for the entire web each day, with the order of a billion web pages ranked currently.

11.6 EXERCISES

Exercise 11.1. Give sufficient conditions that guarantee that a Leslie matrix is positive definite. (Hint: try proof by contradiction.)

Exercise 11.2. For an $n \times n$ non-negative matrix (a_{ij}), we define the associated directed graph with vertices consisting of the integers $1, \ldots, n$ and edges $i \to j$ if $a_{ij} > 0$. We say that the graph is strongly connected if for any pair of integers $i, j = 1, \ldots, n$ there is a path in the graph from i to j. Prove that the associated directed graph for the Leslie matrix is strongly connected if and only if $F_n > 0$. (Assume that all the $S_i > 0$.)

Exercise 11.3. Under what condition is a Leslie matrices invertible? (Hint: use the derivation (11.1.7) to consider what it would mean to have $\lambda = 0$.)

Exercise 11.4. The roots of the polynomial $\xi^2 - 1$ are ± 1 and correspond to the case $\alpha_2 = 1,\ \alpha_1 = 0$ in (11.1.10). This is the case of a two-compartment model with $F_0 = 0$ and $S_0 \cdot F_1 = 1$. Investigate the behavior of the Leslie model in this simple case. (Hint: it suffices to scale the equations by a scalar multiple, so you can assume that $S_0 = F_1 = 1$.)

Exercise 11.5. Recall that the polynomial $p(\xi)$ in (11.1.10) has positive coefficients. Prove that it is strictly increasing for $\xi > 0$, unless $p \equiv 0$. Using this and the fact that p is zero at $\xi = 0$, prove there is a unique $\xi > 0$ where $p(\xi) = 1$. Moreover, show that there is no $\zeta < 0$ with $p(\zeta) = 1$ such that $-\zeta < \xi$. (Hint: for the last inequality, show that the odd order terms can only make p smaller, i.e., $p(-x) \leq p(x)$.)

Exercise 11.6. Calculate the communication and computation costs for the row-wise Leslie matrix implementation in Section 11.3.2. What is the computation-to-communication ratio? What are the spatial requirements?

Exercise 11.7. Describe an implementation that uses a column-wise distribution of the Leslie matrix, $\mathbf{P}$. Perform the same performance calculations from Exercise 11.6. What are the spatial requirements?

Exercise 11.8. a. Develop a design specification and implementation specification for the Leslie matrix based on Section 11.3. Complete the specification wherever it appears incomplete. For your implementation design, specify an application program interface (API).

b. Implement a sequential version using your specification and API.

c. Implement a parallel version using the method described in Section 11.3.3. You may use a parallel implementation of your choosing, but justify your choice.

d. With a class meeting, using the design specification and APIs developed individually, arrive at a design and API. Divide the class into groups, with each group responsible for coding one of the Leslie components

- input and output
- matrix multiplication
- power method and stopping criterion
- high-level Leslie routines
- driver

See Section 11.3.2.

e. Assign a leader for each group who together with other group leaders assembles and tests the components. Evaluate the process.

f. In a separate document (outside the code itself)

Describe the parallel algorithms you used. If you reuse a parallel algorithm for different parts of the program, you should describe the parallel algorithm once, and indicate where it is used.

Estimate the space requirements of the program.

State all important assumptions.

g. Programming style issues: The programming style is up to you; however, below are strong guidelines for this exercise that are largely program readability and maintainability. Your program will be evaluated for *readability*, in addition to *correctness* and *performance*.

Pass parameters through subroutine interfaces. Common blocks may be used, but only *occasionally*.

Use meaningful names for variables.

(This applies to Fortran.) *Type* all variables explicitly and use *implicit none*.

Comment your program to assist in readability.

Avoid gotos.

Indent blocks.

Exercise 11.9. Implement the Leslie matrix code of Section 11.3 to deal with the special structure of the matrices in Section 11.5.1. Test this on the special case in which the mesh size in (1.6.15) is a constant, namely, $h = (b - a)/(N + 1)$. In this case, the matrix is

$$\mathbf{P} = \begin{pmatrix} 2 & -1 & 0 & \dots & 0 \\ -1 & 2 & -1 & \dots & 0 \\ 0 & -1 & 2 & \dots & 0 \\ \vdots & \vdots & \vdots & & \vdots \\ 0 & 0 & 0 & -1 & 2 \end{pmatrix} \tag{11.6.1}$$

Compute the largest eigenvalue and corresponding eigenvector as a function of N. As N becomes large, do these tend to a limiting form?

Exercise 11.10. Implement the Leslie matrix code of Section 11.3 to deal with the special structure of the matrices in Section 11.5.2. All that need be stored are the links $i \leftarrow j$. As a subtask, write a routine to multiply such a matrix times a vector. (Hint: use a neighbor list, cf. Section 13.4.)

Exercise 11.11. Give the block version of Program 11.4 described on page 251.

Exercise 11.12. Modify the program in Program 11.2 to allow the case $n = Pk$ for $k \geq 1$. Use **P**fortran or **P**C. (Hint: use a "block" representation of matrix operations, cf. Exercise 11.11.)

Exercise 11.13. Modify the program in Program 11.3 to allow the case $n = Pk$ for $k \geq 1$. Use **P**fortran or **P**C. (Hint: use a "block" representation of matrix operations, cf. Exercise 11.11.)

Exercise 11.14. Prove that the program in Program 11.2 is equivalent to the program in Program 11.5.

```
do i=0,n-1
   y(i) = 0.0
enddo
do j=0,n-1
   y(myProc) = y(myProc) + a(myProc,j)*x(j)
enddo
y=+{y}
```

Program 11.5 Equivalent program for matrix-vector product with each processor computing one entry showing one combination strategy. Assumes $n = P$.

Chapter Twelve
Linear Systems

> In scientific computing, performance is a constraint, not an objective—*one of the authors*

One of the most basic numerical computations is the solution of linear equations by direct methods. Gaussian[1] elimination is the familiar technique of adding a suitable multiple of one equation to the other equations to reduce to a smaller system of equations. Done repeatedly, this eventually produces a triangular system that can be solved easily. We consider basic algorithms for parallelizing Gaussian elimination and solution of triangular systems of equations.

The solution of triangular systems represents one of the greatest challenges in parallel computing, especially for the sparse matrix case. We analyze several algorithms in part to provide some more challenging examples of parallel codes. The inner loops of these codes will be seen to be of the type that can be executed efficiently by the BLAS (basic linear algebra subroutines) [97, 104].

12.1 GAUSSIAN ELIMINATION

We consider parallelization of the fundamental algorithm for the solution of linear equations based on Gaussian elimination. We begin by reviewing the sequential algorithm and its dependences. Then, using information gleaned from the latter, we describe two of the many ways of deriving a parallelization.

12.1.1 Dependences in Gaussian elimination

Consider a system of equations

$$\sum_{j=1}^{n} a_{ij}x_j = f_i \quad \forall i = 1, \ldots, n. \tag{12.1.1}$$

[1]Johann Carl Friedrich Gauss (1777–1855) was one of the giants of mathematics and indeed of all science. Gauss developed least squares approximation, the concept of complex numbers, and gave the first proof of the fundamental theorem of algebra, to list just three topics from a remarkable range of contributions.

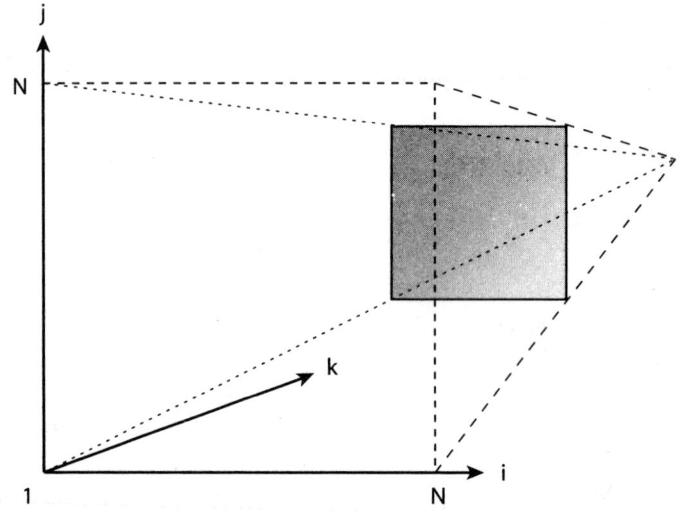

Figure 12.1 The iteration space for the standard sequential algorithm for Gaussian elimination forms a trapezoidal region with square cross-section in the i, j plane. Within each square (with k fixed) there are no dependences.

Code for the standard sequential algorithm for Gaussian elimination is shown in Program 12.1. The corresponding iteration space for this code is depicted in Figure 12.1.

```
do k=1,n-1
   do i=k+1,n
     l(i,k) = a(i,k)/a(k,k)
   enddo
   do j=k+1,n
     do i=k+1,n
       a(i,j) = a(i,j) - l(i,k) * a(k,j)
     enddo
   enddo
enddo
```

Program 12.1 Sequential Gaussian elimination [86].

Gaussian elimination reduces the system (12.1.1) to a pair of triangular systems

$$\begin{aligned} \sum_{j=1}^{i} \ell_{ij} y_j &= f_i \quad \forall i = 1, \ldots, n, \\ \sum_{j=1}^{i} u_{ij} x_j &= y_i \quad \forall i = 1, \ldots, n. \end{aligned} \tag{12.1.2}$$

The matrix L is the lower triangular matrix computed in Program 12.1 (which determines the values below the diagonal) with ones placed on the diagonal [86]. The system (12.1.2) can be solved by the algorithm shown in Program 12.4. Gaussian elimination performs a **matrix factorization**

$$A = LU, \tag{12.1.3}$$

where U is the upper triangular part of the matrix A at the end of Program 12.1. The solutions of (12.1.2) can be determined by algorithms analogous to Program 12.4 (see Exercise 12.18).

The dominant part of the computation in solving (12.1.1) is the factorization Program 12.1 in which L and U are determined. The triangular system solves in (12.1.2) require less computation. For this reason, we focus first on the parallelization of Program 12.1, returning to triangular systems in Section 12.2.

There are no loop-carried dependences in the innermost two loops (the `i` and `j` loops) in Program 12.1 (see Exercise 12.1). Therefore these loops can be decomposed (Definition 1.5.5) in any desired fashion. We now consider two different ways of parallelizing Program 12.1.

12.1.2 Standard parallelization of Gaussian elimination

The algorithm in Program 12.1 for Gaussian elimination can be parallelized using a message-passing paradigm as depicted in Program 12.2. It is based on decomposing the matrix column-wise, and it corresponds to a decomposition of the middle loop (the `j` loop) in Program 12.1. A typical decomposition would be cyclic, since it provides a good load balance (see Exercise 12.3).

```
do k=1,n-1
  if( " I own column k " )
    do i=k+1,n
      l(i,k) = a(i,k)/a(k,k)
    enddo
    "broadcast" l(k+1 : n)
  else "receive" l(k+1 : n)
  endif
    do j=k+1,n ("modulo owning column j")
      do i=k+1,n
        a(i,j) = a(i,j) - l(i,k) * a(k,j)
      enddo
    enddo
enddo
```

Program 12.2 Standard column-storage parallelization Gaussian elimination [51].

We can estimate the time of execution of the standard Gaussian elimination algorithm as follows. For each value of k, $n-k$ divisions are performed in computing the multipliers `l(i,k)`; then these multipliers are broadcast to all other processors. Once these are received, $(n-k)^2$ multiply-add pairs (as well as some memory references) are executed, all of which can be done in parallel. Thus the time of execution for a particular value of k is

$$c_1(n-k) + c_2\frac{(n-k)^2}{P}, \tag{12.1.4}$$

where the constants c_i model the time for the respective basic operations. Here, c_2 can be taken to be essentially the time to compute a "multiply-add pair" $a = a - b * c$ for a single processor. The constant c_1 can measure the time both to compute a quotient and to transmit a word of data.

For many systems, the time to transmit a word of data far exceeds the time required to perform a floating point operation, even a division. For simplicity, we will assume therefore that c_1 is simply the time required to transmit a word of data in a broadcast. Summing over k, we find that the total time of execution is (approximately)

$$\sum_{k=1}^{n-1}\left(c_1(n-k) + c_2\frac{(n-k)^2}{P}\right) \approx \tfrac{1}{2}c_1 n^2 + \tfrac{1}{3}c_2\frac{n^3}{P}. \tag{12.1.5}$$

The time to execute this algorithm sequentially is correspondingly (approximately)

$$\tfrac{1}{3}c_2 n^3 \tag{12.1.6}$$

since there is no need for communication. Therefore, the speedup for the standard column-storage parallelization of the Gaussian elimination algorithm is

$$S_P = \left(\frac{3\gamma}{2n} + \frac{1}{P}\right)^{-1} \tag{12.1.7}$$

where $\gamma = c_1/c_2$ measures the ratio of communication time to computation time. Thus the efficiency is

$$E_P = \left(\frac{3\gamma P}{2n} + 1\right)^{-1} \approx 1 - \frac{3\gamma P}{2n}. \tag{12.1.8}$$

In particular, this implies that the efficiency will be the same for values of P and n which have the same ratio P/n. In Table 12.1, we see this behavior exhibited in the columns marked "standard GE" for which the above analysis is applicable. We can state this formally in the following result.

Theorem 12.1.1. The algorithm Program 12.2 is scalable; we can take $P_n = \epsilon n$ and have a fixed efficiency of

$$\frac{1}{\frac{3}{2}\gamma\epsilon + 1} \tag{12.1.9}$$

for n arbitrarily large.

The algorithm in Program 12.2 is not scalable with respect to memory (Definition 2.4.6). The total storage in the Gaussian elimination algorithm is n^2 words, and $M(n,P) = n^2/P + \mathcal{O}(n)$ for the standard column-storage parallelization, leading to $\mathcal{O}(n)$ storage per processor in the case that we take the number of processors proportional to n. Thus, it is not scalable with respect to memory (see Exercise 12.14 for a formal proof). From a practical point of view, it is not the memory that limits the size of n for most current and future computers since the execution time with $P = \mathcal{O}(n)$ is $T_P = \mathcal{O}(n^2)$. That is, the algorithm tends to be more time-constrained than memory-constrained.

Example 12.1.2. Consider the choice $P = n/\gamma$ which corresponds to an efficiency of 40%. Then to a first approximation, the memory usage per processor is γn and the execution time is $T_P = \frac{1}{3}c_2\gamma n^2 = \frac{1}{3}c_1 n^2$. If we consider the memory constrained case, and M is the number of words a single node can store, then we have $M = \gamma n$ and hence

$$T_P = \tfrac{1}{3}c_1 MP \quad \text{and} \quad P = \frac{M}{\gamma^2}.$$

(Note that the quantity $c_1 M$ is the amount of time it takes to communicate the entire memory.) The execution time grows with both M and P, whereas the number of processors we can use effectively is strongly diminished by the size of γ.

Suppose we were able to bring together 10^4 processors with $M = 10^8$ words of memory each, and with suitable communication speed so that $\gamma = 10^2$ (hence $P = M/\gamma^2$ is satisfied). Suppose the computing power of each processor is 10^8 FLOPS, or $c_2 = 10^{-8}$. (Note that $\gamma = 10^2$ and $c_2 = 10^{-8}$ imply that the communication system can send 10^6 words per second, which is reasonable even over carefully constructed Ethernet systems.) Then this corresponds to $T_P = 10^6$ seconds with $n = 10^6$; 10^6 seconds corresponds to over eleven days of computing time.

As the memory limit M continues to increase, so does the expected execution time for the largest computation we could do. So from a practical point of view, this algorithm is scalable with respect to realistic amounts of memory, even if it is not scalable in the sense of Definition 2.4.6.

12.1.3 Overlapped Gaussian elimination

Since the major cause of inefficiency in the standard parallel version of the Gaussian elimination algorithm is the communication cost, it is natural to seek a variant that allows communication and computation to be overlapped. This can be done as shown in Program 12.3.

The main idea of Program 12.3 is to compute the “multipliers” `l(i,k)` as soon as it is possible to do so, and then to broadcast them to all other

```
first processor computes l(2:n,1) & "broadcasts"
do k=1,n
  unless("I own column k") "receive" l(k+1:n,k)
  if( " I own column k+1 " )
    do i=k+1,n
      a(i,k+1) = a(i,k+1) - l(i,k) * a(k,k+1)
      nextl(i,k+1) = a(i,k+1)/a(k+1,k+1)
    enddo
    "broadcast" nextl(k+2 : n)
  endif
  do j=k+2,n ("modulo owning column j")
    do i=k+1,n
      a(i,j) = a(i,j) - l(i,k) * a(k,j)
    enddo
  enddo
enddo
```

Program 12.3 Overlapped (column-storage) parallel Gaussian elimination.

	16 processors		64 processors	
matrix size	standard	overlapped	standard	overlapped
$n = 128$	57%	69%		
$n = 256$	77%	87%	42%	50%
$n = 512$	91%	96%	64%	79%
$n = 1024$	95%	98%	79%	89%
$n = 2048$			93%	98%

Table 12.1 Efficiencies for two versions (standard and overlapped) of Gaussian elimination for factoring full $n \times n$ matrices on an Intel iPSC.

processors. On systems with separate communications processors (such as the Intel iPSC), this can provide enhanced performance, as indicated in Table 12.1. The performance is more difficult to model in this case since the overlap is not necessarily perfect. For this reason, we do not attempt a precise model of the performance of the overlapped algorithm.

12.2 SOLVING TRIANGULAR SYSTEMS IN PARALLEL

Gaussian elimination reduces a square system of equations to a triangular one (see Section 12.1.1). The latter is (sequentially) trivial to solve, if one starts at the correct end of the triangle [86]. An algorithm for a lower triangular system (with matrix `a` like the matrix `l` generated in Program 12.1) is in Program 12.4. There are now loop-carried dependences in both the `i` and `k` loops (see Exercise 12.17), although the inner loop is a reduction. These loops cannot easily be parallelized, but we will see in Section 12.2.1

that they can be decomposed in a suggestive way (see Figure 12.2).

```
x(1)=f(1)/a(1,1)
do i=2,n
   x(i)=f(i)
   do j=max(1,i-w), i-1
      x(i) = x(i) - a(i,j)*x(j)
   enddo
   x(i)=x(i)/a(i,i)
enddo
```

Program 12.4 Sequential solution algorithm for a banded lower triangular system [86].

For generality, we have presented the code for a banded triangular system in Program 12.4 where `w` is the bandwidth. If `w` = `n` then we have the full matrix case. See Exercise 12.4 for the algorithm for banded Gaussian elimination.

Solving a triangular system appears to be essentially sequential at first. In fact, solving an ordinary differential equation (e.g., (1.6.1)) by a difference method (e.g., (1.6.6)) is quite similar to Program 12.1 when f in (1.6.1) is a linear function of u and independent of t. There are several situations of interest for triangular systems. Let us consider some different cases to provide motivation for what is to come.

We could be interested in solving a triangular system just once. Typically this occurs when the triangular system arises via matrix factorization. Since the time required for a single triangular system solve is minor compared with matrix factorization (compare Exercise 12.5 and Exercise 12.19), the cost of the triangular system is negligible. Only modest efforts at parallelization may be useful.

We could also be interested in solving a triangular system with many right-hand sides, all available at one time. For example, (12.2.12) is an example of this type. Due to the large amount of data (the right-hand sides), there are special opportunities for parallelism which make triangular solution appear similar in character to the factorization problem. Since this has already been considered in Section 12.1, we will not study this case in any depth (see Exercise 12.25).

We could also be interested in solving a triangular system with many right-hand sides, only one of which is available at a time, and which depend nonlinearly on each other. This occurs when solving time-dependent problems or nonlinear problems in which the triangular system is part of an inner loop. The right-hand side changes as the outer loop progresses as a function of the solution determined in the inner loop. In this case, any initial preprocessing of the triangular system can be amortized. The issue is just producing a solution of the triangular system as quickly as possible. This is perhaps the most challenging situation to parallelize efficiently, and

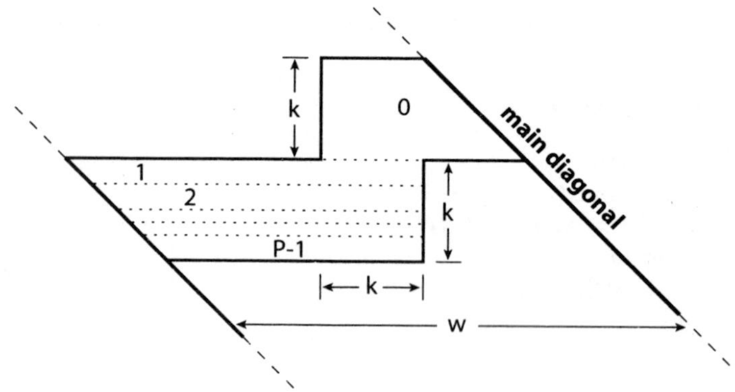

Figure 12.2 Schematic of "toy duck" parallelization of a banded triangular matrix equation solution algorithm.

therefore we will concentrate on this case.

12.2.1 The "toy duck" algorithm

Let us begin by considering a straightforward parallelization of the standard algorithm shown in Program 12.4. We will compute the same arithmetic operations in the same order, but we will organize them in a way that presents independent tasks that can be done in parallel. We begin by describing the ℓ-th stage for $\ell > 1$ assuming all needed information has been initialized. We describe the initialization stages $\ell = 0, 1$ subsequently. Figure 12.2 depicts the various computations done at this stage. We assume that k is a parallelization parameter that will be specified later. It will be a positive integer less than $\frac{1}{2}w$. At the ℓ-th step, we assume that all x_i's for $i \leq k\ell$ have already been computed and distributed to each processor. At each step, solution values x_i will be computed for k new indices i and distributed to each processor.

Processors 1 through $P - 1$ compute

$$b_i = b_i^{(\ell)} := \sum_{j=\max(i-w,1)}^{k\ell} a_{i,j} x_j \quad \forall i = 1 + k(\ell+1), \ldots, k(\ell+2). \qquad (12.2.1)$$

In the simplest case (as we now assume) we will have

$$k = \nu(P - 1) \qquad (12.2.2)$$

for some integer $\nu \geq 1$, so that each processor simply computes ν different b_i's. Note that this requires access to the (previously computed) values x_j for $j \leq k\ell$, and it is facilitated if it is stored row-wise. Simultaneously, processor 0 computes $x_{k\ell+1}, \dots, x_{(k+1)\ell}$ by the standard algorithm, namely,

$$x_i = a_{i,i}^{-1} \left(f_i - b_i^{(\ell-1)} - \sum_{j=(\ell-1)k+1}^{i-1} a_{i,j} x_j \right) \quad \forall k\ell < i \leq (\ell+1)k. \tag{12.2.3}$$

We can assume that $a_{i,i}^{-1}$ has been precomputed and stored, if desired. At the end of this step, processor 0 sends $x_{k\ell+1}, \dots, x_{(k+1)\ell}$ to the other processors, and the other processors send $b_{(k+1)\ell+1}, \dots, b_{(k+2)\ell}$ to processor 0. This completes the ℓ-th step for $\ell > 1$. For $\ell = 0, 1$, we simply let processors $1, \dots, P-1$ be idle. These steps involve a total of $2k^2$ MAPs (multiply-add pairs). The last step also has processors $1, \dots, P-1$ idle, as processor 0 finishes the final trapezoid of computation.

Load balance in (12.2.1) can be achieved in a number of ways. If $\nu = 2$, then perfect load balance is achieved by having processor 1 doing the first and last row, processor 2 doing the second and penultimate row, and so on. The total number of operations to compute (12.2.1) is

$$k(w-k) - \tfrac{1}{2}k^2 = kw - \tfrac{3}{2}k^2 \text{MAPs}. \tag{12.2.4}$$

Thus the time estimate for (12.2.1) is proportional to

$$\left(w - \tfrac{3}{2}k\right) \frac{k}{P-1} \tag{12.2.5}$$

time units, where the unit is taken to be the time required to do one multiply-add pair. Processor zero does $\frac{3}{2}k^2$ MAPs, and thus the total time for one stage of the program is proportional to

$$\max\left\{ \tfrac{3}{2}k^2, \left(w - \tfrac{3}{2}k\right) \frac{k}{P-1} \right\}. \tag{12.2.6}$$

These are *balanced* if

$$\tfrac{3}{2}k^2 = \left(w - \tfrac{3}{2}k\right) \frac{k}{P-1}, \tag{12.2.7}$$

which reduces to having

$$P = \frac{2w}{3k}. \tag{12.2.8}$$

Recalling our assumption (12.2.2), we find that

$$P(P-1) = \frac{2w}{3\nu}. \tag{12.2.9}$$

Note that the optimal P depends only on the bandwidth w and not on n. Thus the algorithm is not scalable in the usual sense (Definition 2.4.3) if w remains fixed independently of n.

The total amount of data communicated at each stage is $2k$ words. Since (12.2.7) implies that the computational load is proportional to k^2, it is clear that this algorithm is scalable if $w \to \infty$ as $n \to \infty$ (Exercise 12.20). The case of a full matrix corresponds to $w = n$. The "toy duck" algorithm has substantial parallelism in this case. For fixed ν, (12.2.9) implies that P is proportional to $\sqrt{w}$, and this in turn implies that k is proportional to $\sqrt{w}$. The amount of memory per processor is directly proportional to the amount of work per processor, so this is proportional to k^2, and hence w, in the balanced case (12.2.7).

12.2.2 A block inverse algorithm

The following algorithm can be found in [127]. Let us write the lower triangular matrix L as a block matrix. Suppose that $n = ks$ for some integers k and s.

$$\begin{pmatrix} L_1 & 0 & 0 & 0 & 0 & 0 \\ R_1 & L_2 & 0 & 0 & 0 & 0 \\ 0 & R_2 & L_3 & 0 & 0 & 0 \\ 0 & 0 & \cdots & \cdots & 0 & 0 \\ 0 & 0 & 0 & R_{k-2} & L_{k-1} & 0 \\ 0 & 0 & 0 & 0 & R_{k-1} & L_k \end{pmatrix} \tag{12.2.10}$$

A triangular matrix is invertible if and only if its diagonal entries are not zero (see [86] or just apply the solution algorithm in Program 12.4). Thus any sub-blocks on the diagonal will be invertible as well if L is, as we now assume. That is, each L_i is invertible, no matter what choice of k we make.

Let D denote the block diagonal matrix with blocks $D_i := L_i^{-1}$. If we premultiply D times L, we get a simplified matrix:

$$DL = \begin{pmatrix} I_s & 0 & 0 & 0 & 0 & 0 \\ G_1 & I_s & 0 & 0 & 0 & 0 \\ 0 & G_2 & I_s & 0 & 0 & 0 \\ 0 & 0 & \cdots & \cdots & 0 & 0 \\ 0 & 0 & 0 & G_{k-2} & I_s & 0 \\ 0 & 0 & 0 & 0 & G_{k-1} & I_s \end{pmatrix} \tag{12.2.11}$$

where I_s denotes an $s \times s$ identity matrix, and the matrices G_i arise by solving

$$L_{i+1}G_i = R_i, \quad i = 1, \ldots, k-1. \tag{12.2.12}$$

The original system $Lx = f$ is changed to $(DL)x = Df$. Note that we can write Df in block form with blocks (or segments) b_i which solve

$$L_i b_i = f_i, \quad i = 1, \ldots, k. \tag{12.2.13}$$

The blocks L_i in (12.2.13) are $s \times s$ lower triangular matrices with bandwidth w (we assume that $s \geq w$), so the band algorithm Program 12.4 is appropriate to solve (12.2.13).

Depending on the relationship between the block size s and the bandwidth w, there may be a certain number of the first columns of the matrices R_i which are identically zero. In particular, one can see (Exercise 12.26) that the first $s - w$ columns are zero. Due to the definition of G_i, the same must be true for them as well (Exercise 12.27). Let $\widehat{G}_i$ denote the rightmost w columns of G_i, let M_i denote the top $s-w$ rows of $\widehat{G}_i$, and let H_i denote the bottom w rows of $\widehat{G}_i$. Further, split b_i similarly, with u_i denoting the top $s-w$ entries of b_i and v_i denoting the bottom w entries of b_i. We may then write the blocks (strips) x_i of the solution vector in two corresponding parts: y_i denoting the top $s-w$ entries of x_i and z_i denoting the bottom w entries of x_i. The notation is summarized in

$$\widehat{G}_i = \begin{pmatrix} M_i \\ H_i \end{pmatrix} \qquad x_i = \begin{pmatrix} y_i \\ z_i \end{pmatrix} \qquad b_i = \begin{pmatrix} u_i \\ v_i \end{pmatrix} \qquad \begin{matrix} \}s-w \\ \}w \end{matrix} \tag{12.2.14}$$

and the dimensions of M_i and H_i are

$$\underbrace{M_i}_{w} \;\; \} \, s-w \qquad\qquad \underbrace{H_i}_{w} \;\; \} \, w \tag{12.2.15}$$

All of these quantities have now simple relationships. First of all we have

$$y_1 = u_1, \quad z_1 = v_1. \tag{12.2.16}$$

We can inductively determine the z_i's by

$$z_{i+1} = v_{i+1} - H_i z_i \quad \forall i = 1, \ldots, k-1. \tag{12.2.17}$$

Then we can separately determine the y_i's by

$$y_{i+1} = u_{i+1} - M_i z_i \quad \forall i = 1, \ldots, k-1. \tag{12.2.18}$$

There are no dependences in (12.2.18), but (12.2.17) appears at first to be sequential. However, if w is sufficiently large, there is an opportunity for parallelism in each iteration of (12.2.17) using the techniques in Section 11.4. Moreover, we show in Section 12.3.1 that (12.2.17) can be written as a lower triangular system itself, and we describe an appropriate parallel solution algorithm.

There are two cases to distinguish in applying the above algorithm. One is the case where a system is solved only once, and the systems (12.2.12) become a major part of the computation. The other is the case where a system is solved many times, and the cost of solving the systems (12.2.12) can be amortized since they need be solved only once.

The primary amount of work in (12.2.13) is

$$k\left(ws - \tfrac{1}{2}w^2\right) = wn - \tfrac{1}{2}\frac{w^2 n}{s} \tag{12.2.19}$$

MAPs, whereas the primary amount of work in (12.2.17) is

$$w^2(k-1) = \frac{w^2(n-s)}{s} \tag{12.2.20}$$

MAPs, and the primary amount of work in (12.2.18) is

$$w(s-w)(k-1) = \frac{w(s-w)(n-s)}{s} = wn - \frac{w^2 n}{s} - w(s-w) \qquad (12.2.21)$$

MAPs. The sum of (12.2.19), (12.2.20), and (12.2.21) is nearly $2nw$, twice the amount of work as in the sequential case (Program 12.4). The amount of parallelism in (12.2.17) is complex to assess (see Sections 11.4 and 12.3.1), but once all the z_i's are computed (and appropriately distributed), (12.2.18) can be done (trivially) in parallel. Moreover, (12.2.13) can also be computed trivially in parallel.

A time estimate for the fully parallel parts of (12.2.13) and (12.2.18) is

$$\widetilde{T}_P \approx \frac{wn}{P}\left(2 - \frac{3}{2}\frac{w}{s} - \frac{s-w}{n}\right). \qquad (12.2.22)$$

If (12.2.17) is computed sequentially, then ignoring communication we have

$$\begin{aligned} T_P &\approx wn\left(\frac{w}{s} - \frac{w}{n} + \frac{1}{P}\left(2 - \frac{3}{2}\frac{w}{s} - \frac{s-w}{n}\right)\right) \\ &= wn\left(\frac{w(P-1)}{n} + \frac{1}{P}\left(2 - \frac{3}{2}\frac{wP}{n} + \frac{w}{n} - \frac{1}{P}\right)\right) \end{aligned} \qquad (12.2.23)$$

if $P = k$ (thus we assume $P \le n/w$ since $s \ge w$ was assumed previously). Therefore

$$E_P^{-1} \approx \frac{wP(P-1)}{n} + \left(2 - \frac{3}{2}\frac{wP}{n} + \frac{w}{n} - \frac{1}{P}\right). \qquad (12.2.24)$$

Theorem 12.2.1. The above algorithm, with (12.2.17) computed sequentially, is scalable with $P \le c\sqrt{n/w}$ for any fixed $c < \infty$.

The proof of this theorem requires that we add in the effect of communication. But in, say, a ring topology this adds only a term of size $wk = wP \le c^2 n/P$ to (12.2.23), and thus a term of size at most c^2/w to the estimate (12.2.24) for E_P^{-1}.

12.2.3 Parallel prefix

The only major sequential step in Section 12.2.2 is the solution of (12.2.17). Parallel prefix provides one parallel solution to problems of this type. Using this to solve (12.2.17) in combination with the remaining algorithms in Section 12.2.2 leads to improved scalability.

Parallel prefix is an algorithm which applies to quite general operations [100], as described in Section 6.2. Let us recall the setting for this algorithm. Suppose we have an operator $\oplus$ that is associative and we wish to compute $g_i := h_i \oplus h_{i-1} \oplus \cdots \oplus h_1$ for $i = 1, \ldots, 2^\kappa$. Using a binary tree, parallel prefix computes this as described in Section 6.2.

The application of parallel prefix to solving a banded triangular linear system provides perhaps the simplest to state parallel algorithm. We assume the lower triangular matrix L is already of the form in (12.2.17), namely,

$$x_i + H_{i-1}x_{i-1} = v_i \quad \forall i = 1, \ldots, 2^\kappa, \tag{12.2.25}$$

where all undefined quantities (H_0, H_1, x_0, etc.) both here and subsequently are set implicitly to zero. This requires a preprocessing stage, as described in Section 12.2.2 or in (12.3.3). Then the relation (12.2.25) between subsequent blocks of the solution x can be written in an extended (specifically, $(w+1) \times (w+1)$) block matrix form as

$$\begin{pmatrix} x_i \\ 1 \end{pmatrix} = \begin{pmatrix} -H_{i-1} & v_i \\ 0_w & 1 \end{pmatrix} \begin{pmatrix} x_{i-1} \\ 1 \end{pmatrix} =: h_i \begin{pmatrix} x_{i-1} \\ 1 \end{pmatrix} \tag{12.2.26}$$

where 0_w denotes a row vector of zeros of length w and h_i denotes the indicated $(w+1) \times (w+1)$ matrix. Applying induction, we thus see that

$$\begin{pmatrix} x_i \\ 1 \end{pmatrix} = g_i \begin{pmatrix} 0_w \\ 1 \end{pmatrix} \tag{12.2.27}$$

where $g_i := h_i \oplus h_{i-1} \oplus \cdots \oplus h_1$ and $\oplus$ is matrix multiplication for $(w+1) \times (w+1)$ matrices. Therefore, we may use parallel prefix to compute the $(w+1) \times (w+1)$ matrices g_i and then recover the solution from (12.2.27).

Parallel prefix requires 2κ steps involving matrix multiplication of two $(w+1) \times (w+1)$ matrices and communication (along edges of a tree) which send a $(w+1) \times (w+1)$ matrix at each step. Thus in the form presented in Section 6.2, the computation is $\mathcal{O}(\kappa w^3)$ and the communication is $\mathcal{O}(\kappa w^2)$, for example, for a ring topology.

In the special case that $s = w$ in the algorithm in Section 12.2.2, the matrices M_i disappear and $G_i = H_i$. We can thus think of (12.2.25) as a special case of (12.2.10). Parallel prefix applied to this problem requires $\mathcal{O}(\kappa w^3)$ time compared with nw time in the sequential case. A speedup of $n/\kappa w^2$ is the largest possible with parallel prefix alone. The efficiency would satisfy (recall that $n = Pw$)

$$E_P^{-1} = \frac{P\kappa w^3}{nw} = \frac{P\kappa w^2}{n} = \kappa w = w \log_2 P \tag{12.2.28}$$

which does not imply scalability. Thus parallel prefix alone is not a scalable triangular solver. However, we now look at combining it with other algorithms.

12.2.4 Combining with parallel prefix

If (12.2.17) is computed by the parallel prefix algorithm, then the time estimate in (12.2.23) becomes

$$T_P \approx wn\left(\frac{w^2}{n}\log_2 P + \frac{1}{P}\left(2 - \frac{3wP}{2n} + \frac{w}{n} - \frac{1}{P}\right) + \gamma\frac{w}{n}\log P\right), \quad (12.2.29)$$

where γ is the ratio of communication to computation time in parallel prefix. Therefore

$$\begin{aligned} E_P^{-1} \approx& \left(\frac{w^2}{n} + \frac{\gamma w}{n}\right) P\log_2 P + \left(2 - \frac{3wP}{2n} + \frac{w}{n} - \frac{1}{P}\right) \\ =& \frac{w^2+\gamma w}{s}\log_2 P + \left(2 - \frac{3w}{2s} + \frac{w}{n} - \frac{1}{P}\right). \end{aligned} \quad (12.2.30)$$

Here we are assuming that $k = P = 2^\kappa$. Taking $P\log_2 P \le cn/(w^2+\gamma w)$ would be required for a scalable algorithm. Note that the leading term in (12.2.30) is smaller than the leading term in (12.2.28) by a factor w/s; s is a parameter (larger than w) under our control. We can collect these results in the following.

Theorem 12.2.2. The algorithm in Section 12.2.2, where (12.2.17) is solved by parallel prefix, is scalable for $P\log_2 P \le cn/(w^2+\gamma w)$ for any fixed $c < \infty$. In particular, we must take $s \ge \max\{w, \epsilon(w^2+\gamma w)\log_2 P\}$ for some $\epsilon > 0$.

The expression $w^2+\gamma w$ in the theorem can be improved to $w^2+\beta w+\lambda$ where λ is the latency and β measures bandwidth.

Note that the original matrices h_i have a special form, but the typical matrices occurring in the parallel prefix algorithm (i.e., $h_i \oplus h_{i-1} \oplus \cdots \oplus h_j$) will not have any special structure. Thus they must be treated as general full matrices. Moreover, repeated solutions of a fixed triangular system follow exactly the same algorithm, without any reduction in work, since the data are represented in the matrices h_i. However, it is possible to modify the second phase of parallel prefix depicted in Figure 6.3 to communicate just the vectors in (12.2.27), reducing the communication and computation cost substantially. With this modification, the work in the second part of the algorithm becomes analogous to odd-even reduction (Section 12.3.3). Alternatively, observe that there is redundant computation in the algorithm presented in Section 6.2, and when w is large it may be cheaper to increase the communication. While the communication and computation in the parallel prefix solution to (12.2.25) are similar in pattern to odd-even reduction (Section 12.3.3), they are larger by a factor w in both cases. Thus it may be possible to improve this performance.

12.3 DIVIDE-AND-CONQUER ALGORITHMS

There are several algorithms that can be based on a strategy of divide-and-conquer. Here we consider three of them.

12.3.1 A divide-and-conquer inverse algorithm

The following is another algorithm found in [127]. We begin by writing the lower triangular matrix L as a block matrix, as in (12.2.10) but with $n = 2^\kappa w$ for some integer κ and w being the bandwidth. Next, we let D denote the block diagonal matrix with blocks $D_i := L_i^{-1}$, and we premultiply D times L to get the simplified matrix shown in (12.2.11) for the case $s = w$. We will introduce slightly different notation for this case, viz.

$$L^{(0)} := DL = \begin{pmatrix} I_w & 0_w & 0_w & 0_w & \cdots & 0_w \\ H_1^{(0)} & I_w & 0_w & 0_w & \cdots & 0_w \\ 0_w & H_2^{(0)} & I_w & 0_w & \cdots & 0_w \\ \cdots & \cdots & \cdots & \cdots & \cdots & \cdots \\ 0_w & \cdots & 0_w & H_{2^\kappa-2}^{(0)} & I_w & 0_w \\ 0_w & \cdots & 0_w & 0_w & H_{2^\kappa-1}^{(0)} & I_w \end{pmatrix} \tag{12.3.1}$$

where I_w denotes an $w \times w$ identity matrix, 0_w denotes an $w \times w$ matrix of zeros, and the matrices $H_i^{(0)}$ arise by solving an equation similar to (12.2.12). The original system $Lx = f$ is changed to $(DL)x = Df$. Let

$$v^{(0)} = Df. \tag{12.3.2}$$

Note that we can compute $v^{(0)} = Df$ in block form with blocks (or segments) $v_i^{(0)}$ of size w which solve

$$L_i v_i^{(0)} = f_i, \quad i = 1, \ldots, 2^\kappa. \tag{12.3.3}$$

So far, we have the same setup as in Section 12.2.2 with $s = w$, resulting essentially in (12.2.17). But now we take a different tack.

Let us give the main idea of the divide-and-conquer algorithm by considering the case $\kappa = 1$, i.e., $n = 2w$. In this case,

$$L^{(0)} = \begin{pmatrix} I_w & 0_w \\ H_1^{(0)} & I_w \end{pmatrix} \tag{12.3.4}$$

and the inverse of $L^{(0)}$ is easily seen to be

$$M := \left(L^{(0)}\right)^{-1} = \begin{pmatrix} I_w & 0_w \\ -H_1^{(0)} & I_w \end{pmatrix} \tag{12.3.5}$$

Thus if we multiply $L^{(0)}$ by M, we get the identity matrix, and we find $x = Mv^{(0)}$.

In the general case (12.3.1), it is not so easy to write down the inverse, but we can approximate it by defining

$$M^{(0)} := \begin{pmatrix} I_w & 0_w & 0_w & 0_w & 0_w & \cdots & 0_w \\ -H_1^{(0)} & I_w & 0_w & 0_w & 0_w & \cdots & 0_w \\ 0_w & 0_w & I_w & 0_w & 0_w & \cdots & 0_w \\ 0_w & 0_w & -H_3^{(0)} & I_w & 0_w & \cdots & 0_w \\ \cdots & \cdots & \cdots & \cdots & \cdots & \cdots & \cdots \\ 0_w & \cdots & 0_w & I_w & 0_w & 0_w & 0_w \\ 0_w & \cdots & 0_w & -H_{2^\kappa-3}^{(0)} & I_w & 0_w & 0_w \\ 0_w & \cdots & 0_w & 0_w & 0_w & I_w & 0_w \\ 0_w & \cdots & 0_w & 0_w & 0_w & -H_{2^\kappa-1}^{(0)} & I_w \end{pmatrix} \tag{12.3.6}$$

If we now multiply $M^{(0)}$ times $L^{(0)}$, we get

$$L^{(1)} := M^{(0)}L^{(0)} = \begin{pmatrix} I_{2w} & 0_{2w} & 0_{2w} & 0_{2w} & \cdots & 0_{2w} \\ \widehat{H}_1^{(1)} & I_{2w} & 0_{2w} & 0_{2w} & \cdots & 0_{2w} \\ 0_{2w} & \widehat{H}_2^{(1)} & I_{2w} & 0_{2w} & \cdots & 0_{2w} \\ \cdots & \cdots & \cdots & \cdots & \cdots & \cdots \\ 0_{2w} & \cdots & 0_{2w} & \widehat{H}_{2^{(\kappa-1)}-2}^{(1)} & I_{2w} & 0_{2w} \\ 0_{2w} & \cdots & 0_{2w} & 0_{2w} & \widehat{H}_{2^{(\kappa-1)}-1}^{(1)} & I_{2w} \end{pmatrix} \tag{12.3.7}$$

where the "hat" matrices are defined via

$$\widehat{H}_\ell^{(1)} = \begin{pmatrix} 0_w & H_{2\ell}^{(1)} \\ 0_w & H_{2\ell+1}^{(1)} \end{pmatrix} = \begin{pmatrix} 0_w & H_{2\ell}^{(0)} \\ 0_w & -H_{2\ell+1}^{(0)}H_{2\ell}^{(0)} \end{pmatrix} \tag{12.3.8}$$

for all $\ell = 1, \ldots, 2^{\kappa-1} - 1$, and where we set $H_0^{(0)} := I_w$.

The original system $Lx = f$ is changed to

$$L^{(1)}x = v^{(1)} := M^{(0)}v^{(0)}. \tag{12.3.9}$$

The computation of $v^{(1)} = M^{(0)}v^{(0)}$ can be done trivially in parallel. In particular, $v^{(1)}$ can be computed in block form via

$$\begin{aligned} v_{1+2\ell}^{(1)} &= v_{1+2\ell}^{(0)} \qquad \text{and} \\ v_{2+2\ell}^{(1)} &= v_{2+2\ell}^{(0)} - H_{1+2\ell}^{(0)}v_{1+2\ell}^{(0)} \quad \forall \ell = 0, \ldots, 2^{\kappa-1} - 1. \end{aligned} \tag{12.3.10}$$

where the block size of $v^{(1)}$ is the same (w) as the block size of $v^{(0)}$.

Now $L^{(1)}$ has the same form as $L^{(0)}$, but with the value of κ reduced by one. So we can continue the transformation. We multiply $M^{(1)}$ times

$L^{(1)}$ to get $L^{(2)} := M^{(1)}L^{(1)}$, where

$$M^{(1)} := \begin{pmatrix} I_{2w} & 0_{2w} & 0_{2w} & 0_{2w} & 0_{2w} & \cdots & 0_{2w} \\ -\widehat{H}_1^{(1)} & I_{2w} & 0_{2w} & 0_{2w} & 0_{2w} & \cdots & 0_{2w} \\ 0_{2w} & 0_{2w} & I_{2w} & 0_{2w} & 0_{2w} & \cdots & 0_{2w} \\ 0_{2w} & 0_{2w} & -\widehat{H}_3^{(1)} & I_{2w} & 0_{2w} & \cdots & 0_{2w} \\ \cdots & \cdots & \cdots & \cdots & \cdots & \cdots & \cdots \\ 0_{2w} & \cdots & 0_{2w} & I_{2w} & 0_{2w} & 0_{2w} & 0_{2w} \\ 0_{2w} & \cdots & 0_{2w} & -\widehat{H}_{2^\kappa-3}^{(1)} & I_{2w} & 0_{2w} & 0_{2w} \\ 0_{2w} & \cdots & 0_{2w} & 0_{2w} & 0_{2w} & I_{2w} & 0_{2w} \\ 0_{2w} & \cdots & 0_{2w} & 0_{2w} & 0_{2w} & -\widehat{H}_{2^\kappa-1}^{(1)} & I_{2w} \end{pmatrix} \qquad (12.3.11)$$

This yields

$$L^{(2)} = \begin{pmatrix} I_{4w} & 0_{4w} & 0_{4w} & 0_{4w} & \cdots & 0_{4w} \\ \widehat{H}_1^{(2)} & I_{4w} & 0_{4w} & 0_{4w} & \cdots & 0_{4w} \\ \cdots & \cdots & \cdots & \cdots & \cdots & \cdots \\ 0_{4w} & \cdots & 0_{4w} & \widehat{H}_{2^{(\kappa-2)}-2}^{(2)} & I_{4w} & 0_{4w} \\ 0_{4w} & \cdots & 0_{4w} & 0_{4w} & \widehat{H}_{2^{(\kappa-2)}-1}^{(2)} & I_{4w} \end{pmatrix} \qquad (12.3.12)$$

where

$$\widehat{H}_\ell^{(2)} = \begin{pmatrix} 0_{2w} & \widehat{H}_{2\ell}^{(1)} \\ 0_{2w} & -\widehat{H}_{2\ell+1}^{(1)}\widehat{H}_{2\ell}^{(1)} \end{pmatrix} \quad \forall \ell = 1, \ldots, 2^{\kappa-2} - 1. \qquad (12.3.13)$$

The product matrix in (12.3.13) can be evaluated

$$\widehat{H}_{2\ell+1}^{(1)}\widehat{H}_{2\ell}^{(1)} = \begin{pmatrix} 0_w & H_{4\ell+2}^{(0)} \\ 0_w & -H_{4\ell+3}^{(0)}H_{4\ell+2}^{(0)} \end{pmatrix} \begin{pmatrix} 0_w & H_{4\ell}^{(0)} \\ 0_w & -H_{4\ell+1}^{(0)}H_{4\ell}^{(0)} \end{pmatrix}$$
$$= \begin{pmatrix} 0_w & -H_{4\ell+2}^{(0)}H_{4\ell+1}^{(0)}H_{4\ell}^{(0)} \\ 0_w & H_{4\ell+3}^{(0)}H_{4\ell+2}^{(0)}H_{4\ell+1}^{(0)}H_{4\ell}^{(0)} \end{pmatrix} \qquad (12.3.14)$$

Therefore

$$\widehat{H}_\ell^{(2)} = \begin{pmatrix} 0_w & 0_w & 0_w & H_{4\ell}^{(2)} \\ 0_w & 0_w & 0_w & H_{4\ell+1}^{(2)} \\ 0_w & 0_w & 0_w & H_{4\ell+2}^{(2)} \\ 0_w & 0_w & 0_w & H_{4\ell+3}^{(2)} \end{pmatrix} = \begin{pmatrix} 0_w & 0_w & 0_w & H_{4\ell}^{(0)} \\ 0_w & 0_w & 0_w & -H_{4\ell+1}^{(0)}H_{4\ell}^{(0)} \\ 0_w & 0_w & 0_w & -H_{4\ell+2}^{(0)}H_{4\ell+1}^{(0)}H_{4\ell}^{(0)} \\ 0_w & 0_w & 0_w & H_{4\ell+3}^{(0)}H_{4\ell+2}^{(0)}H_{4\ell+1}^{(0)}H_{4\ell}^{(0)} \end{pmatrix} \tag{12.3.15}$$

for all $\ell = 1, \ldots, 2^{\kappa-2} - 1$. Again, x solves $L^{(2)}x = M^{(1)}v^{(1)}$.

The computation of $v^{(2)} := M^{(1)}v^{(1)}$ can be done in block form via

$$\begin{aligned} \begin{pmatrix} v_{1+4\ell}^{(2)} \\ v_{2+4\ell}^{(2)} \end{pmatrix} &= \begin{pmatrix} v_{1+4\ell}^{(1)} \\ v_{2+4\ell}^{(1)} \end{pmatrix} \\ \begin{pmatrix} v_{3+4\ell}^{(2)} \\ v_{4+4\ell}^{(2)} \end{pmatrix} &= \begin{pmatrix} v_{3+4\ell}^{(1)} \\ v_{4+4\ell}^{(1)} \end{pmatrix} - \begin{pmatrix} H_{1+2\ell}^{(1)} \\ H_{2+2\ell}^{(1)} \end{pmatrix} v_{2+4\ell}^{(1)} \end{aligned} \tag{12.3.16}$$

for $\ell = 0, \ldots, 2^{\kappa-2} - 1$, where the block size has remained w, the block size of $v^{(0)}$.

The general rule is now clear:

$$\begin{aligned} \begin{pmatrix} v_{1+2^r\ell}^{(r)} \\ v_{2+2^r\ell}^{(r)} \\ \cdots \\ v_{2^{r-1}+2^r\ell}^{(r)} \end{pmatrix} &= \begin{pmatrix} v_{1+2^r\ell}^{(r-1)} \\ v_{2+2^r\ell}^{(r-1)} \\ \cdots \\ v_{2^{r-1}+2^r\ell}^{(r-1)} \end{pmatrix} \\ \begin{pmatrix} v_{1+2^{r-1}+2^r\ell}^{(r)} \\ v_{2+2^{r-1}+2^r\ell}^{(r)} \\ \cdots \\ v_{2^r(\ell+1)}^{(r)} \end{pmatrix} &= \begin{pmatrix} v_{1+2^{r-1}+2^r\ell}^{(r-1)} \\ v_{2+2^{r-1}+2^r\ell}^{(r-1)} \\ \cdots \\ v_{2^r(\ell+1)}^{(r-1)} \end{pmatrix} - \begin{pmatrix} H_{1+2^{r-1}+2^r\ell}^{(r-1)} \\ H_{2+2^{r-1}+2^r\ell}^{(r-1)} \\ \cdots \\ H_{2^r(\ell+1)}^{(r-1)} \end{pmatrix} v_{2^{r-1}+2^r\ell}^{(r-1)} \end{aligned} \tag{12.3.17}$$

for $\ell = 0, \ldots, 2^{\kappa-r} - 1$, where

$$H_{i+2^r\ell}^{(r)} = \pm \prod_{j=0}^{i-1} H_{j+2^r\ell}^{(0)}. \tag{12.3.18}$$

Here, the formula for the sign alternation is left as Exercise 12.33. The computation of (12.3.17) for each ℓ requires 2^{r-1} matrix-vector products, hence $2^{r-1}w^2$ MAPs. The total computational work in (12.3.17) for each r is thus $2^{\kappa-1}w^2$ MAPs $= \frac{1}{2}nw$ MAPs. In addition, the matrices (12.3.18) would need to be computed, but this could be done only once if we were solving problems with multiple right-hand sides. Note that the matrices (12.3.18) can be computed inductively, reducing the amount of work required (see Exercise 12.32).

Observe that (12.3.17) can be simplified by writing

$$\begin{aligned} v_{i+2^{r-1}+2^r\ell} \leftarrow v_{i+2^{r-1}+2^r\ell} \; - \; & H^{(r-1)}_{i+2^{r-1}\ell}\, v_{2^{r-1}+2^r}, \\ i = 1,\ldots,2^{r-1}, \quad & \ell = 0,\ldots,2^{\kappa-r}-1 \end{aligned} \tag{12.3.19}$$

for $r = 1,\ldots,\kappa$. Note that $v_{i+2^r\ell}$ does not change at the r-th iteration for $i = 1,\ldots,2^{r-1}$. Thus $x_i = v_i = v_i^{(r)}$ for $i = 1,\ldots,2^{r-1}$ after the r-th iteration.

After κ steps of (12.3.17), we find $x = v^{(\kappa)}$. The κ steps of (12.3.17) require a total of

$$\tfrac{1}{2}\kappa n w \text{ MAPs}. \tag{12.3.20}$$

(Recall that $\kappa \geq 2$ has been assumed.) This is to be compared with the sequential work of only nw MAPs.

The significant advantage of (12.3.17) is the extensive amount of (convenient) parallelism. However, $\kappa = \log_2(n/w)$ steps are required, and this leads to significant inefficiency for large n. But this algorithm can be combined with that of Section 12.2.2 to advantage. In particular, (12.2.17) is an equation of the form (12.3.1), but with n reduced to $kw = n(w/s)$. Choosing s large has little detrimental effect on the parallel efficiency of (12.2.13) or (12.2.18). However, it decreases the absolute dimension of (12.2.17). Since the algorithm (12.3.17) is a smaller part of the overall computation, it can be used to advantage.

We now turn to a detailed analysis of parallel efficiency of the combined algorithms.

12.3.2 Divide, conquer, and combine

Using (12.3.17) to solve (12.2.17) requires

$$\widetilde{T}_P = \tfrac{1}{2}w^2 \log_2 P \tag{12.3.21}$$

time in view of (12.3.20). (Recall $k = P$ in this case.) This improves on parallel prefix (Section 12.2.3) by a simple factor of w, but it assumes that some preprocessing (involving this extra factor of w time) has been done.

If (12.2.17) is computed by the divide-and-conquer algorithm, then the time estimate in (12.2.23) becomes

$$T_P \approx wn\left(\frac{w}{2n}\log_2 P + \frac{1}{P}\left(2 - \frac{3wP}{2n} + \frac{w}{n} - \frac{1}{P}\right)\right) \tag{12.3.22}$$

and therefore

$$\begin{aligned} E_P^{-1} \approx & \frac{w}{2n} P\log_2 P + \left(2 - \frac{3wP}{2n} + \frac{w}{n} - \frac{1}{P}\right) \\ = & \frac{w}{2s}\log_2 P + \left(2 - \frac{3wP}{2n} + \frac{w}{n} - \frac{1}{P}\right) \end{aligned} \tag{12.3.23}$$

Again, we are assuming that $k = P = 2^\kappa$.

Theorem 12.3.1. Ignoring communication costs, the algorithm in Section 12.2.2, with (12.2.17) solved by divide-and-conquer, is scalable for $P\log_2 P \le cn/w$ for any fixed $c < \infty$. In particular, we must take $s \ge \max\{w, \epsilon w\log_2 P\}$ with $\epsilon > 0$.

Note that the first step of the divide-and-conquer algorithm involves k triangular solves (12.3.3) and the second step involves $k/2$ independent multiplications of a $w \times w$ matrix times a vector of length w. Thus we can take P to be a divisor of $k/2$ and get a load balanced parallelization. We leave as an exercise to determine the communications costs for various networks (see Exercises 12.28 and 12.29).

12.3.3 Odd-even reduction

Odd-even reduction is usually thought of as a solution method for a tridiagonal matrix [100]. It is straightforward to extend it to the case of a block tridiagonal matrix. However, we will restrict to the case of a lower triangular band matrix, which we write as a bidiagonal block matrix. We again assume the lower triangular matrix L is of the form in (12.2.10) but with $n = 2^\kappa w$ for some integers κ and w being the bandwidth. Further, we also assume that L has been converted into the form (12.3.1). The original system $Lx = f$ is changed to $(DL)x = Df$. Let $v^{(0)} = Df$ as in (12.3.2) which we can compute in block form via (12.3.3). Specifically, we can write (12.2.10) as

$$x_i + H_{i-1}^{(0)} x_{i-1} = v_i^{(0)} \quad \forall i = 1, \ldots, 2^\kappa, \tag{12.3.24}$$

where all undefined quantities ($H_0^{(0)}$, $H_1^{(0)}$, x_0, etc.) both here and subsequently are set implicitly to zero.

The main idea of odd-even reduction is to eliminate the odd-numbered equations in (12.3.24) in favor of the even-numbered ones. That is, we write

$$x_i = v_i^{(0)} - H_{i-1}^{(0)} x_{i-1} \tag{12.3.25}$$

for i odd, and substitute into (12.3.24). The even terms then satisfy

$$x_{2i} + H_{i-1}^{(1)} x_{2i-2} = v_i^{(1)} \quad \forall i = 1, \dots, 2^{\kappa-1}, \tag{12.3.26}$$

where

$$\begin{aligned} H_i^{(1)} &:= - H_{2i}^{(0)} H_{2i-1}^{(0)} \quad \forall i = 2, \dots, 2^{\kappa-1}, \\ v_i^{(1)} &:= v_{2i}^{(0)} - H_{2i}^{(0)} v_{2i-1}^{(0)} \quad \forall i = 1, \dots, 2^{\kappa-1}. \end{aligned} \tag{12.3.27}$$

At this stage there are some similarities to the algorithm in Section 12.3.1. However, the main difference is that subsequently odd-even reduction now proceeds recursively on the system (12.3.26), defining $x_i^{(1)} := x_{2i}$.

The general form of the odd-even reduction is then a matrix definition step

$$H_i^{(r)} := -H_{2i}^{(r-1)} H_{2i-1}^{(r-1)} = (-1)^r \prod_{j=0}^{2^r-1} H_{2^r-j}^{(0)} \quad \forall i = 2, \dots, 2^{\kappa-r} \tag{12.3.28}$$

followed by a vector update

$$v_i^{(r+1)} := v_{2i}^{(r)} - H_{2i}^{(r)} v_{2i-1}^{(r)} \quad \forall i = 1, \dots, 2^{\kappa-1}. \tag{12.3.29}$$

For repeated triangular solutions with the same matrix, only the vector update (12.3.29) needs to be repeated once the H's have been computed.

Once the recursion (or iteration) performs κ steps, there is only one equation in one unknown $x_n = x_1^{(\kappa)}$. This is solved and the result is used to determine $x_{n/2}$ from (12.3.25), and so forth, that is,

$$x_{2i+1}^{(r-1)} = v_{2i-1}^{(r)} - H_i^{(r)} x_i^{(r)} \quad \forall i = 1, \dots, 2^{\kappa-r}. \tag{12.3.30}$$

Thus odd-even reduction takes 2κ steps. After the H's have been computed via (12.3.28), each step involves only multiplication of a $w \times w$ matrix times a vector of length w. The algorithm in Section 12.3.1 involved only κ steps of this type. On the other hand, for the algorithm in Section 12.3.1 there is a fixed number of such operations, and in odd-even reduction the number of such operations is halved at each step. Thus odd-even reduction does less work but has more steps, and the algorithm in Section 12.3.1 has half the steps and a more even load balance.

12.4 EXERCISES

Exercise 12.1. Prove there are no loop-carried dependences in the inner-most two loops (the `i` and `j` loops) of Program 12.1 that performs Gaussian elimination.

Exercise 12.2. Determine the dependence distance vectors (Definition 4.2.6) for the triple loop shown in Program 12.5 that performs Gaussian elimination. Show that the carrier index (Definition 4.2.5) is one in each case. (Hint: just write the dependence distance vectors in terms of `i`, `j`, and `k`.)

Exercise 12.3. Determine the load balance (Definition 1.5.7) for both cyclic and block decompositions of the `j` loop in Program 12.2.

Exercise 12.4. Modify the code shown in Program 12.1 to perform Gaussian elimination for a banded system of equation with bandwidth $w \geq 1$. That is, assume a system where $a_{ij} \equiv 0$ whenever $|i-j| > w$. (Hint: just change the loop limits, cf. Program 12.4.)

Exercise 12.5. Show that the amount of work done to perform Gaussian elimination for a banded system of n equations (cf. Exercise 12.4) with bandwidth $w \geq 1$ is $\mathcal{O}(w^2 n)$.

Exercise 12.6. Parallelize Program 12.1 using the row-oriented algorithm in [51]. Write this using "message passing" as your parallel programming language.

Exercise 12.7. Parallelize Program 12.1 using "tiling" (Chapter 10) instead of "message passing" (cf. Program 12.2) as your parallel programming language. Compare the data movement for a "modulo" decomposition of the `for j` loop versus a "block" decomposition.

Exercise 12.8. Parallelize Program 12.1 by "tiling" (Chapter 10) the `for i` loop (cf. Exercise 12.7), where first you interchange the `i` and `j` loops. Compare this with the row-oriented algorithm in [51] (see Exercise 12.6).

Exercise 12.9. Give a performance prediction graph which is based on the model in (12.1.5), with the parameters $c_1 = 10^{-6}$, $c_2 = 10^{-8}$, and $n = 10^6$.

Exercise 12.10. Code the algorithm shown in Program 12.2 to perform a column-oriented parallelization of Gaussian elimination using the parallel language of your choice. Give a performance prediction graph which isolates the times for the main computation from the computation and communication of the pivots.

Exercise 12.11. Modify the code shown in Program 12.2 to perform a column-oriented parallelization of banded Gaussian elimination (cf. Exercise 12.4). (Hint: just change the loop limits, cf. Program 12.4.) Determine the scalability properties of this algorithm.

Exercise 12.12. Modify the code shown in Program 12.1 to perform Gaussian elimination with *pivoting* [86].

Exercise 12.13. Modify the code shown in Program 12.2 to perform a column-oriented parallelization of Gaussian elimination with *pivoting* (see Exercise 12.12).

Exercise 12.14. Give a formal proof that Program 12.2 is not scalable with respect to memory. (Hint: if the local memory size is bounded by M, then $n^2 \le MP$. Use this to show that $P/n \to \infty$ as $n \to \infty$.)

Exercise 12.15. In Section 1.6.1, we observed that a difference method for a linear ordinary differential equation gives rise to a linear recurrence relation. Show that such a system corresponds to solving a banded triangular system.

Exercise 12.16. Determine the number of memory references in Program 12.1 (it is sufficient to determine the leading term for large n). Compare this with a **compact factorization** algorithm

$$\begin{aligned} u_{kj} :=& a_{kj} - \sum_{p=1}^{k-1} \ell_{kp} u_{pj}, \quad j = k, \ldots, n, \\ \ell_{ik} :=& \frac{1}{u_{kk}} \left(a_{ik} - \sum_{p=1}^{k-1} \ell_{ip} u_{pk} \right), \quad j = k+1, \ldots, n, \end{aligned} \tag{12.4.1}$$

where we loop (12.4.1) for $k = 1, \ldots, n$ and define $\ell_{kk} = 1$ for all k. In particular, determine the number of memory references in (12.4.1) for $k = 1, \ldots, n$ and show that the total is half of what is in Program 12.5 (for large n).

Exercise 12.17. Determine the dependence distance vectors (Definition 4.2.6) for the code shown in Program 12.4 that solves triangular systems.

Exercise 12.18. Give an algorithm analogous to Program 12.4 to solve an upper triangular system such as in (12.1.2).

Exercise 12.19. Show that the amount of work done to solve an upper triangular system (12.1.2) of size n with bandwidth $w \ge 1$ is $\mathcal{O}(wn)$. (Hint: see the derivation of (12.1.5).)

Exercise 12.20. Consider the "toy duck" algorithm in Section 12.2.1 and suppose it is balanced as indicated in (12.2.7). Prove that it is scalable (Definition 2.4.3) if the bandwidth $w = w(n)$ depends on n in such a way that $w = w(n) \to \infty$ as $n \to \infty$. Is it scalable with respect to memory (Definition 2.4.6) in this case? Apply your results to the non-banded case ($w = n$).

Exercise 12.21. Parallelize Program 12.4 using a simple column distribution analogous to the distribution used and produced by the column-oriented parallelization (Program 12.2) of Gaussian elimination. Determine the scalability properties of this algorithm. Compare this algorithm with the "toy duck" algorithm in Section 12.2.1.

Exercise 12.22. Parallelize Program 12.4 using a row distribution analogous to the distribution used and produced by the row-oriented parallelization (Exercise 12.6) of Gaussian elimination. Compare this program with the "toy duck" algorithm in Section 12.2.1.

Exercise 12.23. Program the "toy duck" algorithm in Section 12.2.1 in the case $\nu = 1$ in the parallel language of your choice.

Exercise 12.24. Program the "toy duck" algorithm in Section 12.2.1 in the case $\nu = 2$ in the parallel language of your choice in such a way as to ensure load balance among processors $1, \ldots, P-1$.

Exercise 12.25. Determine the speedup for solving triangular systems with k right-hand sides by the "toy duck" algorithm in Section 12.2.1.

Exercise 12.26. Prove that the first $s-w$ columns in the blocks R_i in (12.2.10) are zero. (Hint: draw a picture and count.)

Exercise 12.27. Prove that the first $s-w$ columns in the blocks G_i in (12.2.11) are zero. (Hint: apply Exercise 12.26 and write the definition (12.2.12) of G_i as s systems of equations for the columns of G_i.)

Exercise 12.28. Determine a minimal (i.e., as small as you can find) communications network that allows the combined algorithm for banded triangular matrix equation solution in Section 12.3.2 to execute without contention.

Exercise 12.29. Determine the speedup for the combined algorithm for banded triangular matrix equation solution in Section 12.3.2, including computing all the required matrices in (12.3.18), assuming that all communications can execute without contention. Assume that γ floating point operations can be done in the time to communicate one word (ignore latency).

Exercise 12.30. Write a program to solve (12.2.17) by parallel prefix. Test it for both correctness and scalability. What is the execution time as a function of the size of the matrix and number of processors (give a model and compare with your timing data)? (Hint: first test the matrix multiplication routine separately, then take H_i to be k_i times the matrix of all ones. Choose the k_i to be primes so that you can uniquely identify what products have been computed at each step.)

Exercise 12.31. Using parallel prefix to solve (12.2.17) may not be advantageous. Give conditions on P, n, w, and s that indicate when parallel prefix is beneficial. In particular, show that it will not be unless $P \geq w$, but give more complete conditions as well.

Exercise 12.32. Show how the matrices defined in (12.3.18) can be defined inductively, requiring at most $\mathcal{O}(w^3)$ MAPs for each $H^{(r)}_{i+2^r\ell}$. What is the total amount of work required to compute all of them?

Exercise 12.33. Determine a formula for the sign in (12.3.18).

```
do k=1,n-1
  do j=k+1,n
    do i=k+1,n
      a(i,j) = a(i,j) - (a(i,k)/a(k,k))*a(k,j)
    enddo
  enddo
enddo
```

Program 12.5 Condensed version of Gaussian elimination code.

12.5 PROJECTS

The following projects require extensive testing and performance analysis. They build on the exercises and provide a chance to develop more serious computational systems. Moroever, the projects are not "stand alone" but build on each other. By combining appropriate ones, larger projects can be constructed.

One simple test matrix is $A = LU$, where $L = U^t$ and L is a (possibly banded) matrix of all ones. It is easy to see the pattern in A. In the full matrix case, the i-th row is of the form $1\ 2\ 3\ \ldots\ i$ up to the diagonal, and then is constant from then on (equal to i). This matrix provides a convenient test for factorization codes.

Project 12.1. Implement the combined algorithms of Section 12.2.4. (Hint: see Exercise 12.30.)

Project 12.2. Implement the combined algorithms of Section 12.3.2. (Hint: see Exercises 12.32 and 12.33.)

Project 12.3. Do Projects 12.1 and 12.2 and compare the software systems by testing them for banded triangular systems. For what values of w, n, and P is one better than the other for your implementation?

Project 12.4. Implement the "toy duck" algorithm in Section 12.2.1 for general $\nu \geq 1$ (cf. Exercises 12.23 and 12.24). Compare this with the systems developed in Projects 12.1 and 12.2. For what values of w, n, and P is one better than the other for your implementation?

Project 12.5. Develop a system to factor a matrix using Program 12.2 (see Exercise 12.10) and to solve the resulting triangular systems using the code in Project 12.1. What transformation has to be done on the triangular factors to get them from the format produced by Program 12.2 to the one consumed by Project 12.1?

Project 12.6. Develop a system to factor a matrix using Program 12.2 (see Exercise 12.10) and to solve the resulting triangular systems using the code in Project 12.2. What transformation has to be done on the triangular factors to get them from the format produced by Program 12.2 to the one consumed by Project 12.2?

Project 12.7. Parallelize the compact factorization algorithm (12.4.1) to factor a matrix and solve the resulting triangular systems using the code in Project 12.2. What transformation has to be done on the triangular factors to get them to the one required by Project 12.2?

Project 12.8. Complete the analysis of the odd-even reduction algorithm presented in Section 12.3.3 and see how it would compare with those of Section 12.2.4 and Section 12.3.1. Implement odd-even reduction and see how it compares with the systems developed in Projects 12.1 and 12.2 for banded triangular systems. For what values of w, n, and P is one better than the other for your implementation?

Project 12.9. Implement the partitioned inverse approach to parallel sparse triangular solution [76] and compare it to the other methods discussed in this chapter.

Chapter Thirteen
Particle Dynamics

The Force will be with you, always—*Obi-Wan Kenobi in "Star Wars"*

Particle dynamics models are used in disciplines as diverse as astrophysics, biophysics, and fluid dynamics.

The "particles" in questions may represent atoms in a molecular dynamics simulation,[1] or clusters of galaxies in astrophysics. They are an abstraction that can be divided further in a more accurate model (an atom can be subdivided and modeled using quantum mechanics), but in the particle model the individual particles are autonomous and indivisible.

Only the simplest codes for particle dynamics have intrinsic parallelism of any substantial amount. Thus the primary objective in this chapter will be to modify basic algorithms to achieve parallelism. Often this can be done in ways that provide equivalent results (e.g., ones that are identical if the arithmetic were exact). The result of such restructuring will be code with loops with no dependences. For simplicity, we will say that a loop can be "tiled" (see Chapter 10) if there are no loop-carried dependences (Definition 4.2.3). By this we mean that the loop may be parallelized using tiling (Chapter 10) in a shared memory programming style, but the same property means that the loop can be parallelized easily by any other programming style as well. It would be equivalent to say that the loop is trivially parallel. We choose the shared memory programming terminology in part because we will also use it as a way to describe the effect of various decompositions of the loop, and the choice of tiling "strategy" (Chapter 10) provides appropriate terminology for this. However, any decomposition that can be achieved by a given tiling strategy can also be achieved in other programming styles, as we will indicate explicitly as appropriate.

Particle dynamics provides a computational problem with irregular data structures. Previous problems we have considered involving matrices have typically been more regular. Irregularity is a common feature of more challenging parallel computation. Particle dynamics also provides an example of some of the largest simulations [125, 124]. The ideas that we introduce

[1] Aneesur Rahman (1927–1988) worked at Argonne National Laboratory and was a pioneer of molecular dynamics. He studied properties of liquid argon [123] using the Lennard-Jones potential (13.9.4) on a system containing 864 atoms and a CDC 3600 computer. The Aneesur Rahman Prize was established in 1992 to recognize work in computational physics.

in this chapter can be applied in many other contexts.

13.1 MODEL ASSUMPTIONS

Consider the simulation of many-particle systems governed by Newtonian mechanics,

$$\mathbf{F} = m\mathbf{a}.$$

We assume that there is a function $\mathbf{f}(\mathbf{x},\mathbf{y})$ which describes the force between two particles at positions $\mathbf{x}$ and $\mathbf{y}$. Let $\mathbf{x}_i =$ denote the position of the i-th particle in the system, with $i = 1, \ldots, N$.

We assume that the total force on the i-th particle is given by the sum of pairwise forces, namely,

$$\mathbf{F}(\mathbf{x}_i) := \sum_{i\neq j=1}^{N} \mathbf{f}(\mathbf{x}_i,\mathbf{x}_j) = \sum_{j=1}^{i-1} \mathbf{f}(\mathbf{x}_i,\mathbf{x}_j) + \sum_{j=i+1}^{N} \mathbf{f}(\mathbf{x}_i,\mathbf{x}_j). \tag{13.1.1}$$

This is a strong assumption, or model of reality, and it is subject to some error in most systems. However, we will ignore such issues here. Note that the forces $\mathbf{f}$ and $\mathbf{F}$ and the positions $\mathbf{x}_i$ are vectors in three-dimensional space $I\!R^3$.

The motion of the system of particles is then governed by the system of ordinary differential equations

$$\mathbf{F}(\mathbf{x}_i) = m_i \frac{d^2\mathbf{x}_i}{dt^2}, \tag{13.1.2}$$

where m_i denotes the mass of the i-th particle.

To simplify notation in the code, the pairwise force function $\mathbf{f}$ will be denoted by `ourforce` and written as if it were a scalar quantity, even though this representation may need to be expanded in languages not supporting vector types.

13.1.1 Computing the force

The dominant computation in particle dynamics is the force calculation. This can be done in a simple double loop shown in Program 13.1. This is trivially parallel: each `F(I)` is independent of all others. Note that the forces `F` and the positions `X` are vectors in $I\!R^3$. The `I` loop can be "tiled" to realize this parallelism (see Exercise 13.1), and a variety of decomposition strategies will balance the load (see Exercise 13.9).

Once forces have been computed, e.g., as described in Program 13.1, they can be used together with (13.1.2) to move particles forward in time. A popular way to do this [108] is a time-stepping scheme known as the Verlet algorithm:

$$\mathbf{x}_i^{k+1} = 2\mathbf{x}_i^k - \mathbf{x}_i^{k-1} + \Delta t^2 \mathbf{F}(\mathbf{x}_i^k)/m_i, \tag{13.1.3}$$

```
do I=1,N
  F(I)=0
  do J=1,N
    F(I)=F(I) + ourforce( X(I) , X(J) )
  enddo
enddo
```

Program 13.1 Particle dynamics force calculation. The function `ourforce` computes the force f in (13.1.1).

where Δt is the time step (some small positive number) and $\mathbf{x}_i^k$ denotes the position of the i-th particle at the k-th time step. If we start this process at $t_0 = 0$, then the k-th time step is at time $t_k = k\Delta t$. The Verlet algorithm is more generally known as a "leap-frog" scheme [108].

The time-stepping scheme (13.1.3) is trivially parallel: a loop over the index variable i can be decomposed arbitrarily and executed in parallel with no dependences. Thus particle dynamics in its simplest form can be parallelized easily in a scalable fashion. However, the amount of work grows quadratically in the number of particles, and this has inspired people to modify the basic algorithm to decrease the basic amount of work being done without destroying the basic physics being represented. We now turn to a discussion of typical modifications that are used in practice.

13.1.2 Modifications of the model

Computing the solutions of the system (13.1.2) of equations is quite simple if N is small, but the computational effort grows like N^2, due to the need to evaluate (13.1.1) at each time step. For large N the computational effort becomes prohibitive and several simplifications are utilized to reduce the cost, as follows.

- Newton's Third Law $\mathbf{f}(\mathbf{x}_i, \mathbf{x}_j) = -\mathbf{f}(\mathbf{x}_j, \mathbf{x}_i)$ can cut the amount of computation in half.
- A *cutoff radius* can be used to simplify the force calculation.
- Constraints can be used to coerce groups of particles to move together.

Changes such as these to the basic algorithm make it feasible to compute with larger numbers of particles, but they greatly complicate the parallelization of the code. We now discuss them in some detail.

13.2 USING NEWTON'S THIRD LAW

Newton's Third Law $\mathbf{f}(\mathbf{x}_i, \mathbf{x}_j) = -\mathbf{f}(\mathbf{x}_j, \mathbf{x}_i)$ can cut the computation in half. This "law" (really, just a modeling assumption) is appropriate for all of the applications described at the beginning of the chapter. It implies that the self-force must be zero: $\mathbf{f}(\mathbf{x},\mathbf{x}) = -\mathbf{f}(\mathbf{x},\mathbf{x})$ means $\mathbf{f}(\mathbf{x},\mathbf{x}) = 0$. It further allows us to restrict the summation over the second particle index `J` in Program 13.1 to be greater than the first particle index `I`, as implemented in Program 13.2. Recall that the pairwise force function $\mathbf{f}$ is denoted by `ourforce`. See Exercise 13.12 regarding the equivalence of Program 13.1 and Program 13.2.

```
do I=1,N
  F(I)=0
  do J=I+1,N
    tmpforce = ourforce( X(I) , X(J) )
    F(I)=F(I) + tmpforce
    F(J)=F(J) - tmpforce
  enddo
enddo
```

Program 13.2 Program segment to compute particle dynamics forces using Newton's Third Law.

13.2.1 Dependences in the force calculation

When we did *not* use Newton's Third Law, it was simple to parallelize the force calculation by tiling the `I` loop in Program 13.1. Now, tiling the `I` loop in Program 13.2 may give the wrong answer due to dependences in the force calculation resulting from the following possibilities.

- We may have `I=J(I')`, where `J(I')` stands for the value of `J` in the `I'` iteration of the outer loop.
- We might also have `J(I)=J(I')` for different iterations of the outer loop.

Both of these would be a possible source of error (see Exercise 13.5).

13.2.2 Parallelizing by force replication

The following is a way to parallelize the code for computing the force using Newton's Third Law. We make a copy of `F` local to each process(or); hence the name **replication** for this parallelization technique. (More precisely, we will refer to it as the **force replication** parallelization approach.) This will be seen as a fundamental limitation to the scalability of the parallelization, but its simplicity is a key virtue and it has been quite successful in practical computations.

Each local copy of `F` will hold the value of the force on all particles due to interactions only with a *selected subset of particles.* These subsets need to form a decomposition of all particles: each particle must be in one subset, and none should appear in more than one subset. Now we will see that the separate force contributions can be computed independently, but at the end of this phase all we have is P different partial sums. We then have to sum the separate contributions at the end of the loop. The fact that we can divide the computation in this way is a simple result of the fact that the total force is a sum (13.1.1) of individual forces.

The first part of the replication algorithm, namely, the computation of the partial forces, can be done using tiling by adding a second index, as shown in Program 13.3. We use the notation FF to denote the partial force array, which has an additional array index. Here the division of the particles is a simple cyclic subdivision. This has been chosen to enhance the load balance (see Section 13.5.5 for more discussion of this). We can tile the outermost loop on K in Program 13.3. A Pfortran implementation makes F local automatically; more details will be discussed in Section 13.5.2.

```
do K=1,P
  do I=1,N
    FF(I,K)=0
  enddo
  do I = K, N, P
    do J=I+1,N
      tmpforce = ourforce( X(I) , X(J) )
      FF(I,K)=FF(I,K) + tmpforce
      FF(J,K)=FF(J,K) - tmpforce
    enddo
  enddo
enddo
```

Program 13.3 Replication to parallelize computation of particle forces using Newton's Third Law with a cyclic subdivision of particles. FF is the array of partial forces.

```
do I=1,N
  F(I)=0
  do K=1,P
    F(I)=F(I)+FF(I,K)
  enddo
enddo
```

Program 13.4 Program segment to combine partial forces FF computed in the replicated algorithm implemented in Program 13.3.

13.2.3 Global reduction step

Due to the nature of the replication technique, at the end of the loop no processor has fully computed F. It is necessary to accumulate all the values, as

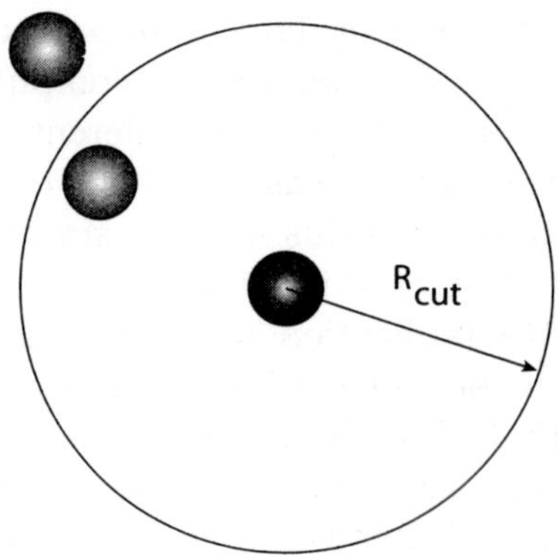

Figure 13.1 Cutoff radius. One atom is inside and one atom is outside the cutoff radius around the darker-shaded atom.

indicated in Program 13.4. (See Exercise 13.4 regarding its possible tilings.) This step requires significant communication and becomes the barrier to scalability in many particle dynamics codes (cf. Theorem 13.6.1). However, in the simple cases considered so far, in which we work with all of the atoms in determining the particle forces, the communication time is swamped by the computation time for large N (see Exercise 13.6).

13.3 FURTHER CODE COMPLICATIONS

Particle dynamics codes are further complicated by the use of many different techniques, depending in part on the particular application domain [36]. Here we limit discussion to two more frequently used techniques, namely, the use of a cutoff radius and the imposition of constraints. We address these two effects briefly here. We will consider the effect both of these techniques have on the development of a parallel code for particle dynamics. Other types of complications include the use of charge groups in molecular dynamics codes [36].

13.3.1 Using a cutoff radius

A *cutoff radius* R is used to split the force $\mathbf{F}(\mathbf{x}_i)$ into two parts:

$$\mathbf{F}(\mathbf{x}_i) := \sum_{|\mathbf{x}_i - \mathbf{x}_j| < R} \mathbf{f}(\mathbf{x}_i, \mathbf{x}_j) + \sum_{|\mathbf{x}_i - \mathbf{x}_j| \geq R} \mathbf{f}(\mathbf{x}_i, \mathbf{x}_j). \tag{13.3.1}$$

This is depicted in Figure 13.1.

The part of the force arising from particles outside the cutoff radius is updated less frequently, reducing the computational cost per time step from $\mathcal{O}(n^2)$ to

$$\mathcal{O}(nR^3 + \epsilon n^2).$$

From a practical point of view, this force computation is essentially linear in N. However, for large enough N, the quadratic term will eventually be dominant. *Fast summation* techniques can be used to avoid this quadratic dependence on N [43, 44].

When a cutoff radius is used, the key requirement is a **neighbor list** or **pair list** of particles which indicates which particles are within the cutoff radius of a given particle. The type of data structure used for this list is a matter of choice. It should be chosen to make it efficient both to generate and to use the pair or neighbor list. In Section 13.4, we consider a linear data structure frequently used to represent this information, together with approaches for parallelizing its generation. In Section 13.5, we study how forces can be calculated in parallel using a pair list. In Section 13.6.3, we present a performance analysis of a particular implementation of a molecular dynamics code which uses these ideas.

13.3.2 The SHAKE algorithm

Another simplifying technique is to constrain certain particles to move as a group, rather than separately. Such an example might be the three particles comprising a water molecule. This turns the system (13.1.2) into differential algebraic equations and complicates the code significantly, but it allows much larger time steps to be utilized in many cases. In molecular dynamics, this technique is known as the **SHAKE** algorithm. This can be parallelized with considerable success by different techniques [35, 39]. Here we describe only the basic form that such an algorithm takes.

Once forces have been computed, e.g., as described in the combination of Program 13.3 and Program 13.4, they can be used together with (13.1.2) to move particles forward in time, e.g., using the Verlet algorithm (13.1.3). When constraints are imposed on the relative positions of particles, the constraints would have to be imposed together with a time-stepping scheme such as (13.1.3). For example, in molecular dynamics the hydrogen bond lengths are frequently fixed, since these bond lengths would be the most rapidly fluctuating mode in the system and the variations in length have little overall effect on the chemistry of the system. Constraining the bond lengths allows significantly larger time steps to be taken without degrading the stability of time-stepping schemes such as (13.1.3) [108]. Mathematically, bond length constraints would appear as

$$|\mathbf{x}_j^k - \mathbf{x}_i^k| = d_{ij}, \tag{13.3.2}$$

where $|\mathbf{x}|$ denotes the Euclidean length of $\mathbf{x}$, and d_{ij} is the length of the bond between atoms i and j. In the case of hydrogen bonds, we would have $d_{ij} = d$ for all i and j, with d a constant.

The SHAKE algorithm is a clever way to achieve (13.3.2) while still keeping the spirit of (13.1.3). It loops over all bond pairs i, j, adjusting the positions of both $\mathbf{x}_j^k$ and $\mathbf{x}_i^k$ such that (13.3.2) holds and such that the

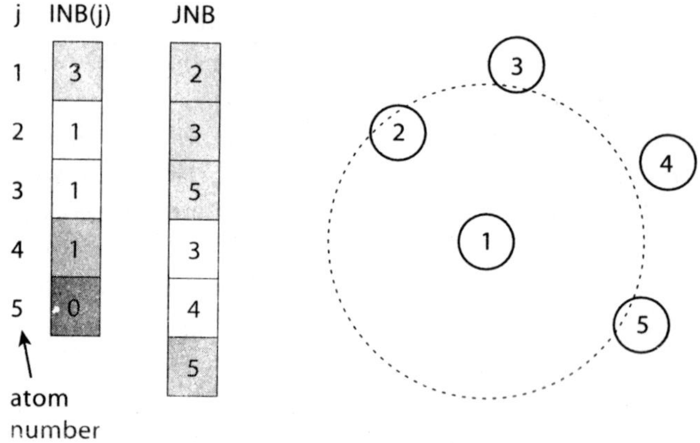

Figure 13.2 The pair list. The INB array lists the number of neighbors of each atom, and the JNB array lists the atom numbers for all of the neighbors. Different shadings in the JNB array indicated the neighbor groupings for each different atom. Listed are the neighbors having atom index *larger* than the atom itself, taking advantage of Newton's Third Law (Section 13.2).

center of mass of $\mathbf{x}_j^k$ and $\mathbf{x}_i^k$ remains the same. That is, the positions are adjusted along the line joining $\mathbf{x}_j^k$ and $\mathbf{x}_i^k$, weighted by the respective masses m_j and m_i (one of these would be the mass of a hydrogen atom in the case of hydrogen bonds, the other the mass of the atom to which it is bonded). If the bond sets are disjoint, one pass through all of the bond pairs i, j is sufficient to enforce (13.3.2). However, typically, one atom will be bonded to more than one hydrogen atom, such as in a water molecule, in which one oxygen atom is bonded to two hydrogen atoms. Thus, the SHAKE algorithm iterates over all bond pairs i, j, creating a sequence of atom positions $\mathbf{x}_i^{k,\ell}$ which hopefully converges as $\ell \to \infty$ [40].

Although the basic time-stepping computation (13.1.3) is trivially parallel, there is a strong coupling (dependence) in the SHAKE algorithm in the loop over the bond pairs i, j. Therefore, the SHAKE algorithm requires a clever parallelization. Two approaches that have been utilized are pipelining [39] (see Section 4.6.2) and a spatial decomposition [35]. It is beyond our scope to address this in detail here. Rather, we leave it as an example of the further complications that can appear in real particle dynamics codes.

13.4 PAIR LIST GENERATION

Using a cutoff radius (Figure 13.1) requires that a "pair list" (JNB in the following) of neighboring particles within the cutoff radius (Figure 13.2) be determined. Different techniques can be used to store and access this information, but we will focus on one very simple one which uses a *linear* data structure for the pair list.

13.4.1 Pair list data structures

In the simple approach we study here, the `JNB` array lists all neighbors in a linear data structure that is very efficient to use. The array `INB` records the numbers of particles within the cutoff radius for each particle. This is depicted in Figure 13.2. The arrays `INB` and `JNB` can be computed using the code shown in Program 13.5. We omit coding required for a full implementation in Fortran required to handle multidimensional positions **x**, computation of Euclidean distances, and so forth.

```
J0 = 0
JJ = 0
do I = 1, N
  do J = I+1, N
    if( | X(I) - X(J) | < R ) THEN
      JJ = JJ + 1
      JNB(JJ) = J
    endif
  enddo
  INB(I) = JJ - J0
  J0 = JJ
enddo
```

Program 13.5 Pair list computation: original version. The notation `| X |` is pseudo-code for the Euclidean length of the vector `X`.

Additional arrays, `start` and `finish`, are needed in order to access the `JNB` array, as computed in Program 13.6. The neighbors of particle `I` are to be found in positions `start(I)` to `finish(I)` in the pair list,

```
JNB(start(I):finish(I))
```

and are accessed sequentially in this range.

```
start(1)=1
finish(1)= INB(1)
do I = 2, N
   start(I)= finish(I-1) + 1
   finish(I) = finish(I-1) + INB(I)
enddo
```

Program 13.6 Additional arrays needed to access the `JNB` array.

13.4.2 Parallelizing pair list generation

The critical difficulty with parallelizing this algorithm is the dependence (Chapter 4) in the `JNB` array on previous iterations of the `for I` loop. This dependence could not be dealt with by existing compiler techniques. However, the dependence occurs not in the *values* of JNB but rather in the *locations* of the values. The values of JNB are independent of each other, but the locations of the values are dependent on other locations, which are computed at the same time as the values in the code above.

13.4.3 Parallelizing with a scratch space

We may compute the iterations separately and figure out later where to put the data generated from them. By introducing the notion of a "scratch space" JNBL we can easily remove the dependences as can be computed using the code shown in Program 13.7.

```
do I = 1, N
   JL = 0
   do J = I+1, N
     if( | X(I) - X(J) | < R ) THEN
       JL = JL + 1
       JNBL(JL,I) = J
     endif
   enddo
   INB(I) = JL
enddo
```

Program 13.7 Pair list computation: transformed version. The notation | X | is pseudo-code for the Euclidean length of the vector X.

Observe that for each I there is potential dependence of JNB on previous iterations, so we make separate copies of the JNB array, one for each I. Now each iteration of the I loop is independent of the others and can be computed in parallel. The I loop can be "tiled" to realize this parallelism. However, we need to choose the "strategy" carefully to assure load balancing.

This approach requires extra memory, namely,

$$N \times \max\{\texttt{INB(I)} \ : \ \texttt{I} = 1, \ldots, N\} \tag{13.4.1}$$

whereas the sequential case requires only

$$\sum_{\texttt{I}=1}^{N} \texttt{INB(I)}. \tag{13.4.2}$$

Each processor needs

$$\frac{N}{P} \times \max\{\texttt{INB(I)} \ : \ \texttt{I} = 1, \ldots, N\} \tag{13.4.3}$$

words of memory.

If necessary, the JNBL values could be collected as computed using the code shown in Program 13.8, but in practice they would probably be left distributed.

```
do IALL = 1, N
  JNB( start(IALL) : finish(IALL) ) = JNBL( 1:INB(IALL) , IALL)
enddo
```

Program 13.8 Code to collect JNBL values.

Note that this parallelism in the JNB computation has been created at the expense of subsequent communication and possibly of increased storage. One difficulty in doing this automatically is that there is no a priori bound on the size of the scratch copies.

13.4.4 Pfortran implementation

The above approach translates directly into the model needed in Pfortran. Each processor will compute a collection of the iterations, ISTART@p $\leq$ I $\leq$ IEND@p. (In the following code, we will assume this information is in the arrays ISTART(p) and IEND(p), known at all processors.)

The number may depend on p due to the triangular shape of the double loop.

Each processor will have a (local) copy of part of the JNB array.

The original code can be used, the only exception being that it may be preferable to keep the local INB array distinct. This is depicted in the code shown in Program 13.9.

```
J0 = 0
JJ = 0
do I = ISTART(myProc), IEND(myProc)
  do J = I+1, N
    if( | X(I) - X(J) | < R ) THEN
      JJ = JJ + 1
      JNB(JJ) = J
    endif
  enddo
  INB(I) = JJ - J0
  J0 = JJ
enddo
```

Program 13.9 Pair list computation: Pfortran version. The notation | X | is pseudo-code for the Euclidean length of the vector X.

The Pfortran approach requires less memory; namely, each processor needs

$$M := \max \left\{ \sum_{\mathtt{I=ISTART}(p)}^{\mathtt{IEND}(p)} \mathtt{INB(I)} \;:\; p = 0, \ldots, P-1 \right\} \qquad (13.4.4)$$

whereas for the "scratch space" technique each processor needs

$$\frac{N}{P} \times \max \{ \mathtt{INB(I)} \;:\; \mathtt{I} = 1, \ldots, N \}. \qquad (13.4.5)$$

We will see that the optimal *load balancing* strategy, to equalize the work load, will be to make

$$M \approx \frac{\sum_{\mathtt{I}=1}^{N} \mathtt{INB(I)}}{P} \qquad (13.4.6)$$

which is the amount of memory required in the sequential case divided by P. Thus the optimal work load strategy is also the optimal memory strategy.

Since `JNB` is the largest data structure in the problem, it is likely that it would not ever be collected in one place, but rather left distributed. However, it would be essential for load balancing to know the values of `INB`, which could be collected in **P**fortran as follows.

```
      DO 1 p = 0, nProc - 1
1       INB(ISTART(p):IEND(p))=INB(ISTART(p):IEND(p))@p
```

This exchange of information is much less than optimal in terms of communication. See the code in Section 8.2.1 on ranges of variables for concatenating an array (called `ithere` in that example).

It is possible to parallelize using tiling with less scratch space. We can simulate the **P**fortran implementation using the replication technique, as indicated in Program 13.10. The `K` loop in Program 13.10 can be "tiled" (see Exercise 13.8).

```
do K = 1, P
  do I = 1, N, P
        JL = 0
        do J = I+1, N
          if( | X(I) - X(J) | < R ) THEN
            JL = JL + 1
            JNBL(JL,K) = J
          endif
        enddo
        INBL(I,K) = JL
  enddo
enddo
```

Program 13.10 Pair list computation: replicated version.

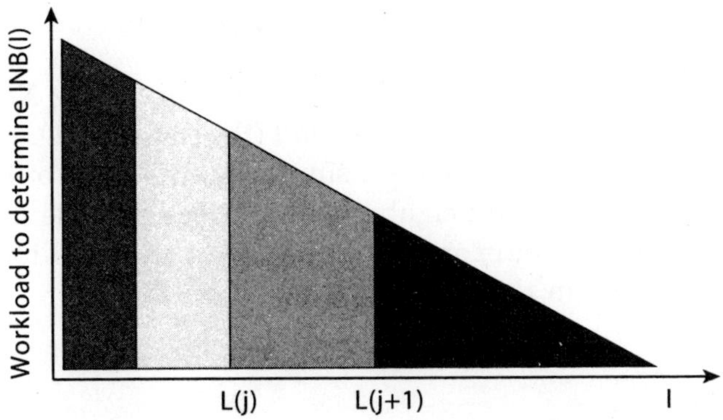

Figure 13.3 The work distribution in constructing the pair list. The shaded areas indicate a load balanced distribution.

13.4.5 Load balancing the pair list computation

The computation of the pair list is substantial. In the construction of the pair list each pair needs to be considered only once because of the interaction symmetry that follows from Newton's Third Law. This reduces the number of computations and the size of the data structure storing the pairs. This use of the interaction of the force on particle `I` by particle `J` for the force on particle `J` by particle `I` results in a triangular iteration space for the doubly nested loop as illustrated in Figure 13.3. The inner `J` loop involves evaluation of `N-I` "distance" evaluations in floating point arithmetic, plus some indexing and memory references for each neighbor. This pair list computation must be load balanced to achieve good performance.

On average, we expect the number of neighbors `J` of particle `I` (with `J>I`) to decrease linearly with `I`. Thus the amount of work to be done can be approximated by a triangle. Load balancing a triangular work load can be done by dividing the `I` loop so that the resulting work is the same in each subset. In the IPfortran code, each subset in the `I` loop corresponds to a trapezoidal subset of the work triangle, as shown in Figure 13.3. We must assure that all trapezoids have the same area. A formula (Exercise 13.10) can be derived that gives such a subdivision of the `I` loop. *If the number of neighbors* `J>I` *decreases linearly with* `I`*, then* `JNB` *will be equally distributed.*

We can also achieve load balancing in the replicated algorithm by other techniques. We can divide the work in the triangle using a "modulo" strategy. Again, if the number of neighbors `J>I` decreases linearly with `I`, then the work in calculating `JNBL` will be equally distributed. Also, under this assumption, the memory requirements for `JNBL` will be equally distributed. Note that the replicated algorithm requires the introduction of a replication of the `INB` array (P copies of a vector of length N).

13.5 FORCE CALCULATION WITH A PAIR LIST

The sequential form of the particle force calculation, using Newton's Third Law (Section 13.2) and the neighbor list `JNB` (Section 13.4.1), can be written as shown in Program 13.11, which is a simple modification of Program 13.2. The `JNB` array points only to neighbors with larger particle index, to avoid duplicate calculations of `ourforce`. Recall again that the force `F` and the positions `X` are vectors in three-dimensional space $I\!R^3$.

```
do I=1,N
  F(I)=0
  do J=start(I), end(I)
    tmpforce = ourforce( X(I) , X(JNB(J)) )
    F(I)=F(I) + tmpforce
    F(JNB(J)) = F(JNB(J)) - tmpforce
  enddo
enddo
```

Program 13.11 Particle force calculation.

13.5.1 Parallelizing the force calculation

When we did *not* use Newton's Third Law, it was simple to parallelize the force calculation by tiling the `I` loop. Now, tiling the `I` loop may give the wrong answer. The following two conditions express the two types of dependences described in Section 13.2.1 in the case the pair list `JNB` is used.

- We may have `I=JNB(J(I'))`, where `JNB(J(I'))` stands for the value of `JNB(J)` in the `I'` iteration of the `I` loop.
- We might also have `JNB(J(I))=JNB(J(I'))` and this would be a possible source of error.

We again consider the replication approach to parallelizing the force calculation (compare with Section 13.2.2) when both a pair list and Newton's Third Law are used. As before, we make a local copy of the entire force array `F` and have each processor compute only the part of the force that is related to a particular subset of atoms. After all these partial forces have been calculated, we then sum up all of the separate contributions at the end of the loop. The **P**fortran implementation makes `F` local to each process automatically. This can be done using tiling by adding a second index to the force array `F` (see Section 13.5.4).

13.5.2 The force calculation in Pfortran

Here we give the details of the implementation in **P**fortran. Once the processor has the relevant data, it simply does the computation shown in Program 13.12. New names (**startL, endL**) are introduced only to clarify the fact that they refer to the local copy of the JNB array.

```
do I = 1,N
   F(I)=0
enddo
do I = Istart(myProc),Iend(myProc)
  do J = startL(I), endL(I)
    tmpforce = ourforce( X(I) , X(JNB(J)) )
    F(I) = F(I) + tmpforce
    F(JNB(J)) = F(JNB(J)) - tmpforce
  enddo
enddo
```

Program 13.12 The force calculation in IPfortran.

Note: we do not store the entire JNB array locally. The neighbor list is the largest data structure in this code and is distributed uniformly over P processors.

13.5.3 Global reduction step

Due to the nature of the above algorithm, at the end of the loop no processor has fully computed F. It is necessary to accumulate all the values, which is easily done in IPfortran via the reduction operation

```
F = +{F}
```

or in many message passing systems by a vendor-supplied subroutine call. Note that the sequential semantics of the original code have not been kept, since the order of summation may be different.

At this point the positions X can be updated via a time-stepping scheme, e.g., (13.1.3), for the system (13.1.2). In addition, the SHAKE algorithm (Section 13.3.2) could be used to preserve any constraints if desired.

13.5.4 The replicated force calculation using tiling

A similar algorithm can be obtained using replication (and tiling on K), as shown in Program 13.13 (cf. Program 13.3). To distinguish the original force array F from the replicated force array, we have again named the latter FF. A reduction must be applied to FF to obtain the complete force vector F:

$$\mathtt{F(I)} := \sum_{k=1}^{P} \mathtt{FF(I,}k\mathtt{)}.$$

The code to implement this is identical to Program 13.4.

```
do 3 K=1,P
  do I = 1,N
    FF(I,K)=0
  enddo
  do I = K, N, P
    do J = startL(I,K), endL(I,K)
      tmpforce = ourforce( X(I) , X(JNBL(J,K)) )
      FF(I,K)=FF(I,K) + tmpforce
      FF(JNBL(J,K),K)=FF(JNBL(J,K),K) - tmpforce
    enddo
  enddo
enddo
```

Program 13.13 The replicated force calculation using a neighbor list.

13.5.5 Balancing the work in the force calculation

The force computation must be load balanced to achieve good performance. The code for the force computation can be paraphrased as

```
do I=1,N
     "do C × INB(I) units of work"
enddo
```

for some constant C, since `INB(I)=end(I)-start(I)+1`. Once we know `INB` (which may change in an outer loop), we can schedule the separate tasks appropriately.

In the **P**fortran implementation, we balance the work by making

$$\sum_{\mathtt{I}=\mathtt{ISTART}(p)}^{\mathtt{IEND}(p)} \mathtt{INB(I)}$$

the same for all p. This, in turn, ensures that the memory, as indicated by (13.4.2), is also balanced.

With tiling, we depend on the "modulo" strategy in Program 13.13 to keep the load balanced [26]. This simple "modulo" strategy will not necessarily be load balanced. But, if the number of neighbors J>I decreases linearly with I, then the work will be equally distributed. If the distribution is more complex, a load imbalance could occur, but this is also the case with the **P**fortran implementation.

13.5.6 Coding details

In the **P**fortran implementation of UHGROMOS [32], a molecular dynamics code, all of the `INB` array is kept at each processor. Each processor then participates in the load balancing step, determining a contiguous set of indices

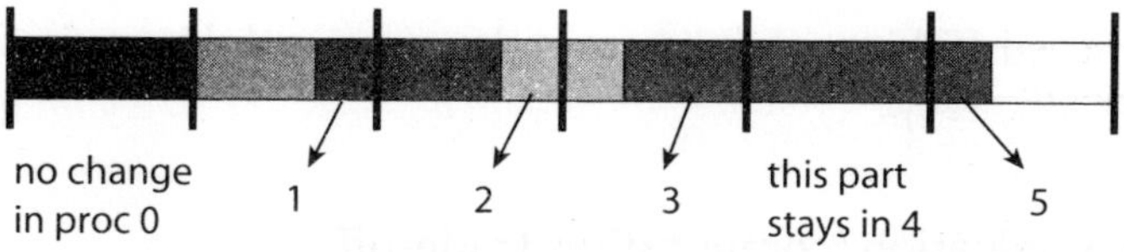

Figure 13.4 The JNB array, $P = 6$, in the case of a typical load distribution. The arrows indicate the movement of data between processors.

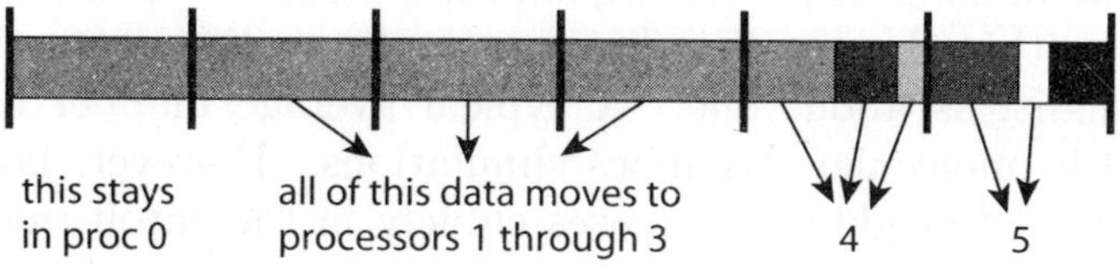

Figure 13.5 The JNB array, $P = 6$, in the case of a bad load distribution. The arrows indicate the movement of data between processors.

```
Istart(myProc):Iend(myProc)
```

for which to compute the above.

The most time-consuming step in the load balancing is the exchange of the JNB array values for these I. The time required to carry out this exchange is not predictable a priori.

There is a one-to-one correspondence between the work to be done and the elements of the JNB array. The exchange of the JNB array is described in Figure 13.4. The basic algorithm is to line up all the work (JNB) in a row, divide the length of the row roughly equally into P parts, and then push jobs (parts of JNB) in either direction as necessary to achieve a balance.

Only a qualitative analysis of the JNB exchange can be made, due to the arbitrariness of the distribution of data. If the distribution of the JNB is nearly balanced, then the above algorithm does not involve much data movement. If a ring topology is supported in the architecture of the memory system, then the data exchanges can be done with no contention in many cases. However, there is no a priori bound that can be given on the amount of data movement.

An arbitrarily large amount of data may have to be moved arbitrarily far, as depicted in Figure 13.5.

13.6 PERFORMANCE OF REPLICATION ALGORITHM

The parallel implementation of particle dynamics using replication is communication intensive because the forces are not computed locally. However, it avoids duplicate force computations in keeping with the spirit of the sequential algorithm when using Newton's Third Law. The experience with the UHGROMOS code parallelized in this way indicates that the communication overhead is tolerable for modest numbers of processors. But, for large numbers of processors, the cost of collecting F exceeds the cost of computing it in a distributed fashion. A more complex approach is required for a truly scalable code [35, 120].

13.6.1 Communication/computation trade-off

It can be shown that the communication overhead equals the computational time when the number of processors is proportional to the average number of neighbors within the cutoff radii. For the Intel *i*PSC/860, the constant of proportionality is about one. A typical average number of neighbors is about 100 in molecular dynamics simulations. However, note that the average number of neighbors increases cubicly in the cutoff radius, so that the break-even number of processors increases cubicly with the cutoff radius.

The communication cost can be analyzed as follows [33]. Both the computation of `F` and the collection of `F` scale linearly with N:

- the time required for `F=+{F}` is $\mathcal{O}(N)$
- the time for (load balanced) force computation is (Exercise 13.11)

$$\frac{\sum_{i=1}^{N} \mathtt{INB}(i)}{P} = \frac{N \times \mathtt{INB}\mathrm{ave}}{P}, \tag{13.6.1}$$

where

$$\mathtt{INB}\mathrm{ave} := \frac{1}{N}\sum_{i=1}^{N} \mathtt{INB}(i) \tag{13.6.2}$$

is the average number of neighbors within the cutoff radius. Therefore we have proved the following theorem.

Theorem 13.6.1. For the replicated force algorithm, the ratio of computation cost to communication cost for P processors is proportional to

$$\mathtt{INB}\mathrm{ave}/P,$$

where $\mathtt{INB}\mathrm{ave}$ is defined in (13.6.2) and the constant of proportionality c is independent of N. Thus (2.3.10) implies that the speedup is at most $\mathtt{INB}\mathrm{ave}/c$, independent of N.

For fixed $\mathtt{INB}\mathrm{ave}$, the cost of communication will dominate for large P, independent of N. The constant of proportionality c in Theorem 13.6.1 depends on

- the machine's rate of computation,
- its communication speed, and
- the amount of work done in computing the force on a pair of particles.

In the experiments with the molecular dynamics code GROMOS parallelized in this way, for $\texttt{INB}_{\text{ave}}$ about 100, the crossover point, at which communication time is equal to computation time, occurs near 100 processors on the Intel *i*PSC/860 [33]. This implies that c was near one for this system.

13.6.2 Scalability

$\texttt{INB}_{\text{ave}}$ increases cubicly in the cutoff radius, R, so that the "break-even" number of processors, where the communication time is equal to computation time, given by $P \propto \texttt{INB}_{\text{ave}}$, also increases cubicly with the cutoff radius. In the limit of having an infinite cutoff radius (that is, no cutoff at all), we have $\texttt{INB}_{\text{ave}} = N$ (see Exercise 13.6) and the communication costs are swamped by the computational cost: the algorithm is fully scalable as N increases. However, for a fixed cutoff radius, the replicated algorithm is not scalable.

One way to achieve a scalable code for a fixed cutoff radius is to abandon the use of Newton's Third Law and to allow each processor to compute *all* contributions to *part* of `F`, to eliminate the global reduction operation `F=+{F}` [64]. This is done by having `JNB` include *all* neighbors, not just those with larger particle index. This eliminates the assignment

```
F(JNB(J))=F(JNB(J)) - ourforce( X(I) , X(JNB(J)) )
```

as well as the communication cost of the reduction `F=+{F}`, but at the expense of *doubling* the amount of computation.

Note that the **P**fortran implementation mixes the ownership of the force array `F`. Any part of the array may be computed by a large number of processors. The simple reduction

```
F = +{F}
```

is not at all optimal for large P, since most of the local entries of `F` will be zero in that case. If it were possible to know in advance which entries of `F` would be nonzero, we could schedule a reduction in a scalable way.

13.6.3 Analysis of a parallelization of the GROMOS code

We now apply performance analysis (Section 2.5.1) to a parallelization of the GROMOS code using replication of the force array. Figure 13.6 depicts the data on different components of the computation and communication in a parallelized version of the GROMOS code.

The two parallelized parts of the particle dynamics code, the force calculation and the pair list construction, decrease nearly linearly. The cost of the global reduction operation is increasing slightly because an algorithm was used that requires $\mathcal{O}(n \log P)$ time (see Section 6.6). It is clear that the time to do the reduction will equal the time for the force calculation for $P \approx 100$. The cost of load balancing is varying a bit, but the absolute cost is

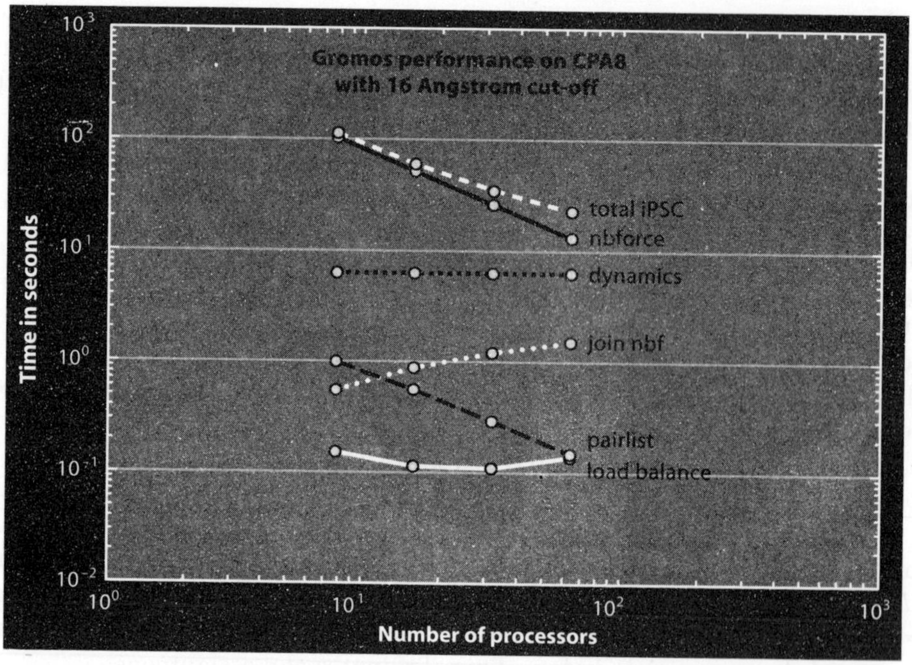

Figure 13.6 Logarithmic performance prediction graph for the UHGROMOS code.

insignificant (remember, this is a logarithmic scale). In this implementation, the time-stepping (which included SHAKE) was not parallelized at all.

13.7 CASE STUDY: PARTICLE DYNAMICS IN HPF

We now illustrate HPF concepts in the context of particle dynamics. The specific topics addressed include data alignment, data distributions, irregular accesses, and subroutine interfaces.

13.7.1 The spatial decomposition

Models for particle dynamics and other physical phenomena typically involve some spatially near-neighbor interactions requiring communication between logical neighboring processes. A spatial decomposition reflects physical reality, segmenting the discretized space into contiguous chunks, which, in turn, are assigned to processing elements. A spatial decomposition turns out to be the decomposition of choice in many particle dynamics models since the locality it retains results in a minimum amount of data movement between processing elements.

Figure 13.7 illustrates four spatial decompositions distributed onto logical process arrays of varying dimensions. We make the simplifying assumption that data dependences are present between the neighboring pro-

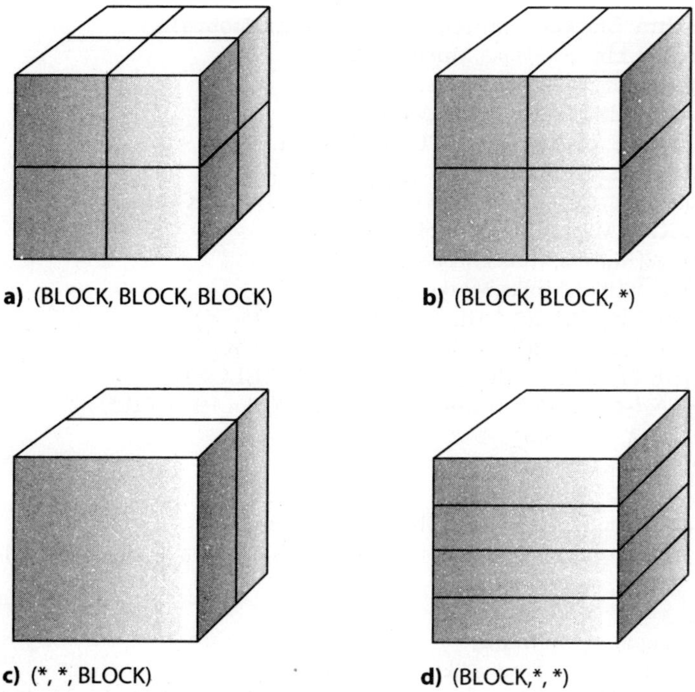

Figure 13.7 Some decompositions and distributions for the array $A(N, N, N)$ illustrating a) `blockwise` for $P = 8$; b) `columnwise` for $P = 4$; c) `slicewise` for $P = 2$; d) `slicewise` for $P = 4$.

cess domains only.[2] (*Process domains* refer to the portion of the array assigned to a processing element.) How best to aggregate and map space onto processing elements depends on numerous issues including the range of the particle interactions, the size of the simulated space, the number of processing elements, and so on. To minimize communication, the general rule is to minimize the surface-to-volume ratio of the processor domains. For a detailed discussion of this topic interested readers are referred to [70, 35].

Initially, each particle (or atom) is assigned to the spatial region that spans the particle's coordinate. After initialization, the particles undergo dynamics according to the model at hand. The particle coordinates are checked at intervals to determine if the recent displacements have resulted in atoms moving out of their currently assigned spatial block.

An HPF subroutine that performs the reassignment of displaced atoms to the proper spatial regions is given in Program 13.14. The simulation space is represented by the last three dimensions of the coordinate array, `blkX`, and the charge array, `blkQ`; each of these arrays can contain up to `Matms` atoms. Space is partitioned among processes by the blockwise distribution of `blkX`, `blkQ`, and `nAtomsBlk` (lines 5–7). Atoms are distributed by mak-

[2]With this constraint, the size of spatial domains must be greater than or equal to a cutoff radius, thereby limiting the number of processes that can be used.

```
   subroutine BlockDecomposition(blkX,blkQ,nAtomsBlk)
 2 real blkX(3,Matms,Mblks,Mblks,Mblks)
   real blkQ(Matms,Mblks,Mblks,Mblks)
 4 real nAtomsBlk(Mblks,Mblks,Mblks)
   DISTRIBUTE blkX(*,*,BLOCK,BLOCK,BLOCK)
 6 DISTRIBUTE blkQ(*,BLOCK,BLOCK,BLOCK)
   DISTRIBUTE nAtomsBlk(BLOCK,BLOCK,BLOCK)
 8 real blkX2(3,Matms,Mblks,Mblks,Mblks)
   real blkQ2(Matms,Mblks,Mblks,Mblks)
10 real nAtomsBlk2(Mblks,Mblks,Mblks)
   DISTRIBUTE blkX2(*,*,BLOCK,BLOCK,BLOCK)
12 DISTRIBUTE blkQ2(*,BLOCK,BLOCK,BLOCK)
   DISTRIBUTE nAtomsBlk2(BLOCK,BLOCK,BLOCK)
14 call duplicate(blkX,blkQ,nAtomsBlk,blkX2,blkQ2,nAtomsBlk2)
   do zold = 1, Nblks(3)
16   do yold = 1, Nblks(2)
       do xold = 1, Nblks(1)
18       do iatm = 1, nAtomsBlk2(xold,yold,zold)
           blkInd(1:3) = Coord_to_Index(blkX2(1,iatm,xold,yold,zold))
20         xnew = blkInd(1)
           ynew = blkInd(2)
22         znew = blkInd(3)
           jatom = nAtomsBlk(xnew,ynew,znew)
24         blkX(1:3,jatom,xnew,ynew,znew) = blkX2(1:3,iatm,xold,yold,zold)
           blkQ(1:3,jatom,xnew,ynew,znew) = blkQ2(1:3,iatm,xold,yold,zold)
26         nAtomsBlk(xnew,ynew,znew) = jatom + 1
         enddo
28     enddo
     enddo
30 enddo
   call duplicate(blkX2,blkQ2,nAtomsBlk2,blkX,blkQ,nAtomsBlk)
32 return
   end
```

Program 13.14 The input coordinate array contains the coordinates for atoms that have undergone some dynamical motion. Thus, these atoms may have moved out of their present "block" of space. `Subroutine BlockDecomposition` remaps the atoms to their new spatial elements, if necessary. Statements 24, 25, and 26 could involve interprocess data movement. A prescriptive interface has been chosen for the parameters.

ing assignments to the distributed coordinate array `blkX` and charge array `blkQ`. Suppose, for example, that atom 9 in block (3,7,5) has moved to block (2,7,5). Then for the assignment

```
blkX(1:3,jatom,2,7,5) = blkX2(1:3,iatom,3,7,5)
```

process p owning spatial element (3,7,5) will send the coordinates and other data to process q owning (2,7,5).[3] Arrays for replicating input parameters (lines 2–4) are declared (lines 11–13) and defined (line 14) on each invoca-

[3] Language and runtime support for irregular accesses are areas of ongoing research [71, 68].

tion of subroutine `BlockDecomposition` so that the left-hand assignments (lines 24–26) do not overwrite the right-hand side data.

The particle-simulation dynamics limit what can be accomplished at compile time. Since the new index `blkInd(1:3)` into the blockwise distributed coordinate array is an unknown until it is calculated (line 19), interprocess data exchange cannot be determined ahead of time. Furthermore, the correspondence between the left-hand side assignments to `blkX` and `blkQ` and the loop indices cannot be determined until the loop is executed (foiling attempts to apply loop bounds reduction). The data-parallel compiler can address this problem by generating code that makes a "dry run" through the loop with an inspector. The inspector determines what data processes own, establishing a communication schedule [67].

```
     program ParticleDynamics
 2   real blkX(3,Matms,Mblks,Mblks,Mblks)
     real blkF(Matms,Mblks,Mblks,Mblks)
 4   real blkQ(Matms,Mblks,Mblks,Mblks)
     real nAtomsBlk(Mblks,Mblks,Mblks)
 6   DISTRIBUTE blkX(*,*,BLOCK,BLOCK,BLOCK)
     DISTRIBUTE blkF(*,*,BLOCK,BLOCK,BLOCK)
 8   DISTRIBUTE blkQ(*,BLOCK,BLOCK,BLOCK)
     DISTRIBUTE nAtomsBlk(BLOCK,BLOCK,BLOCK)
10     call Intialize(blkX,blkQ,nAtomsBlk,nSteps)
       do istep = 1, nSteps
12       call BlockDecomposition(blkX,blkQ,nAtomsBlk)
         call InteratomicForcesShort(blkX,blkQ,nAtomsBlk,blkF)
14       call InteratomicForcesLong(blkX,blkQ,nAtomsBlk,blkF)
         call MoveParticles(blkX,blkQ,nAtomsBlk,blkF)
16     enddo
     end
```

Program 13.15 A simplified a particle dynamics program. The first subroutine call (line 12) enforces the spatial decomposition; particles move in response to inter-particle forces (calculated at lines 13 and 14). `MoveParticles` (line 15) calculates displacements from the calculated forces.

13.7.2 The force calculation and data distribution

The main program skeleton for our particle dynamics Program 13.15 consists of variable declarations (lines 2–5), data distribution directives (lines 6–9), and data initialization (line 10). The rest of the program iterates over time steps with a subroutine call to relocate atoms with the spatial decomposition (line 12; see Program 13.14); calls to calculate the interaction forces (lines 13 and 14; see Program 13.16); and a call to calculate the new atom positions (line 15). We next consider the short- and long-range interactions.

Calculating short- and long-range interactions

The short-range interactions are calculated using a cutoff radius as described in Section 13.3.1. A key point is that interprocess data movement to satisfy data dependences benefits from the locality resulting from the spatial decomposition: For any given particle, neighboring particles will be either in or adjacent to the particle's spatial volume.

For the long-range interaction we use the particle mesh Ewald (PME) method. PME is a variant of the well-known Ewald method [119, 79] used to model particle interactions in systems with periodic boundary conditions. The method treats short- and long-range interactions separately. The short-range interactions are computed as usual with a cutoff radius truncating interactions beyond a certain distance; the short-range interactions are referred to as the *real part*. The long-range interactions are computed in the finite *reciprocal space* corresponding to the real-space component from immediately outside the cutoff radius to infinity. The transform into and out of reciprocal space is achieved with a Fast Fourier Transform (FFT).

We consider a system of particles modeled as a collection of charges residing in an infinitely periodic system formed by replicating the central "box" containing the explicit particles.[4] A regular mesh superimposed over the central box is used as the framework for a charge distribution derived from the particles in the central box; the charge distribution is also periodic. The principal steps in the PME method are:

i) Extrapolate the charges onto the mesh: In this step point charges are "smeared" onto the charge mesh using, e.g., the "triangular charge cloud" (TSC) method [79].

ii) Take the 3D FFT of the smeared charge mesh.

iii) For each of three dimensions:

- Take convolution of FFT'ed charge mesh with Green's function and k-vector for this dimension.
- Take inverse 3D FFT of mesh resulting from previous step.
- Calculate reciprocal force for this dimension for each atom using mesh in previous step.

We have argued that a spatial decomposition takes advantage of the (real) space locality for calculating the short-range force. In the long-range force calculation, however, a 3D FFT is calculated. Let us assume that the FFT is calculated with a series of 1D FFTs, the usual case for FFTs in scientific subroutine libraries. Consequently, inter-process data movement can be reduced in the FFT routines with columnwise distribution of data; a slabwise distribution (Figure 13.7 c and d) is better yet.

---

[4]Periodic boundary conditions result in an infinite simulation box.

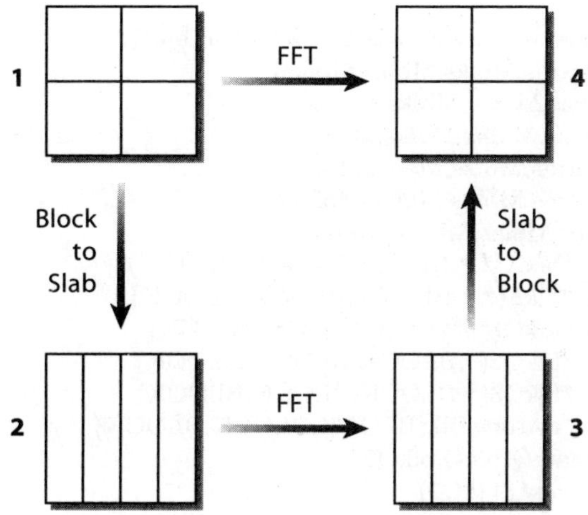

Figure 13.8 A graphical representation of alternate methods to calculate the long-range force component from a blockwise decomposition at state 1. On path 1,4, no remapping occurs from the blockwise decomposition; the FFT is performed on blockwise distributed data. On path 1,2,3,4 a remapping from blockwise to slabwise occurs going from state 1 to state 2, with a remapping from slabwise to blockwise going from state 3 to state 4.

We assume that a blockwise spatial distribution is used by the particle simulation outside of the long-range interaction code. Thus, it makes sense to use a descriptive interface for the formal parameters in subroutine `InteratomicForcesLong` (Program 13.16) to assert that data redistribution need not take place; in other words, the long-range force routine only needs to concern itself with the blockwise spatial decomposition. For the FFT routine, however, the programmer must determine the more effective mapping: 1) no distribution; 2) blockwise (Figure 13.7 a,b); 3) slabwise to facilitate the FFT operations (Figure 13.7 c and d).

If the cost to redistribute from a blockwise distribution to a slabwise distribution is offset by the savings in data movement in the course of performing the 3D FFTs, then $\mathrm{FFT}_{\mathrm{slab}}$, Program 13.18 is preferable. Put another way, in Figure 13.8 is the cost to traverse path 1,2,3,4 less than the cost to traverse path 1,4? If not, then Program 13.17 is preferable. With HPF the programmer can test the two distribution methods simply by changing the distribution statements in the long-range force routines. To test the distribution in this case amounts to changing the distributions in the FFT and *convolution* routines as shown in Program 13.17 and Program 13.18.

13.8 EXERCISES

Exercise 13.1. Can the `I` loop in Program 13.1 be "tiled" (and yield correct code)? Same question about the loop on `J`?

Exercise 13.2. Can the `I` loop in Program 13.2 be "tiled" (and yield

```
subroutine InteratomicForcesLong(blkX,blkF,blkQ)
real blkX(3,Matms,Mblks,Mblks,Mblks)
real blkF(Matms,Mblks,Mblks,Mblks)
real blkQ(Matms,Mblks,Mblks,Mblks)
real blkQ2(Matms,Mblks,Mblks,Mblks)
real blkQ3(Matms,Mblks,Mblks,Mblks)
real nAtomsBlk(Mblks,Mblks,Mblks)
DISTRIBUTE *blkX(*,*,BLOCK,BLOCK,BLOCK)
DISTRIBUTE *blkF(*,*,BLOCK,BLOCK,BLOCK)
DISTRIBUTE *blkQ(*,BLOCK,BLOCK,BLOCK)
DISTRIBUTE *blkQ2(*,BLOCK,BLOCK,BLOCK)
DISTRIBUTE *blkQ3(*,BLOCK,BLOCK,BLOCK)
DISTRIBUTE *nAtomsBlk(BLOCK,BLOCK,BLOCK)
  call ExtrapolateQ(blkQ,blkQ2)
  call FFT(+1,blkQ,blkQ2)
  do idim = 1, 3
    call Convolution(idim,blkQ,blkQ2)
    call FFT(-1,blkQ2,blkQ3)
    call InteratomicForcesLong(idim,blkX,blkQ,blkQ3,nAtomsBlk,blkF)
  enddo
end
```

Program 13.16 `LongRangeForce` calculates the reciprocal space component for the PME method. Formal parameter mappings in this routine are descriptive.

```
program FFTblock(fftType,Qin,Qout)
real Qin(Matms,Mblks,Mblks,Mblks)
real Qout(Matms,Mblks,Mblks,Mblks)
DISTRIBUTE *Qin(*,BLOCK,BLOCK,BLOCK)
DISTRIBUTE *Qout(*,BLOCK,BLOCK,BLOCK)
 call 3D_FFT_as_series_of_1D_FFTs
```

Program 13.17 Descriptive mappings for formal parameters in FFT component of PME. `FFTblock` *describes* a blockwise decomposition for the input array Qin. (See text for details.)

correct code)? Same question about the loop on `J`?

Exercise 13.3. Can the `K` loop in Program 13.3 be "tiled" (and yield correct code)? Same question about the loop on `I`? Same question about the loop on `J`?

Exercise 13.4. Can the `I` loop in Program 13.4 be "tiled" (and yield correct code)? Same question about the `K` loop?

Exercise 13.5. Describe the type of dependence (forward, backward, etc.) implied by the relations `I=J(I')` and `J(I)=J(I')` in Section 13.2.1 (see the discussion following Definition 4.1.3 for terminology).

```
program FFTslab
real Qin(Matms,Mblks,Mblks,Mblks)
real Qout(Matms,Mblks,Mblks,Mblks)
DISTRIBUTE Qin(*,*,*,BLOCK)
DISTRIBUTE Qout(*,*,*,BLOCK)
 call 3D_FFT_as_series_of_1D_FFTs
```

Program 13.18 Prescriptive mappings for formal parameters in FFT component of PME. **FFTslab** *prescribes* a slabwise decomposition (xy slabs) for the input array Qin. (See text for details.)

Exercise 13.6. Consider the replicated force algorithm implemented in the combination of codes given in Program 13.3 and Program 13.4. Prove that the ratio of computation to communication is $\mathcal{O}(N)$ (give references to algorithms used for the communication and a full description of the operation counts). (Hint: show that the communication in the reduction in Program 13.4 can be $\mathcal{O}(N)$, cf. Section 6.6, versus a minimum of $\mathcal{O}(N^2)$ computation in Program 13.3.)

Exercise 13.7. Prove that Program 13.2 is equivalent to using Program 13.3 followed by Program 13.4, ignoring roundoff errors. (Hint: compare both of these with Program 13.19.)

```
do I=1,N
  F(I)=0
enddo
do K=1,P
  do I = K, N, P
    do J=I+1,N
      tmpforce = ourforce( X(I) , X(J) )
      F(I)=F(I) + tmpforce
      F(J)=F(J) - tmpforce
    enddo
  enddo
enddo
```

Program 13.19 Sequential computation of particle forces using Newton's Third Law in a cyclic order.

Exercise 13.8. Prove that the `K` loop in Program 13.10 can be "tiled" (and yield correct code).

Exercise 13.9. Prove that tiling Program 13.1 with either a block or a cyclic strategy will be load balanced.

Exercise 13.10. Derive the formula that gives such a subdivision of the `I` loop into uniform work units (see Section 13.4.5).

Exercise 13.11. Prove the formula (13.6.1).

Exercise 13.12. Suppose that Newton's Third Law holds: $\mathbf{f}(\mathbf{x},\mathbf{y}) = -\mathbf{f}(\mathbf{y},\mathbf{x})$. Prove that Program 13.1 and Program 13.2 produce the same "force" array `F` as a result (ignoring roundoff errors), where the function `ourforce` computes the value of $\mathbf{f}(\mathbf{x},\mathbf{y})$.

Exercise 13.13. Suppose that Newton's Third Law holds: $\mathbf{f}(\mathbf{x},\mathbf{y}) = -\mathbf{f}(\mathbf{y},\mathbf{x})$. Let `INB(I)` = `N - I` for all `I`, and let `JNB(Q(I)+1:Q(I)+INB(I))` = `(I+1:N)`, where $Q(I) = \sum_{j=1}^{I-1} N - I$. Prove that Program 13.2 and Program 13.11 produce the same "force" array `F` as a result (ignoring roundoff errors), where the function `ourforce` computes the value of $\mathbf{f}(\mathbf{x},\mathbf{y})$.

Exercise 13.14. Perform a simulation of liquid argon [123] using the Lennard-Jones potential on a system containing 864 atoms. Do not use a cutoff radius.

Exercise 13.15. Improve the statement of Theorem 13.6.1 to show that speedup is at most

$$\left(\frac{1}{P} + \frac{c}{\mathrm{INB}_{\mathrm{ave}}}\right)^{-1}.$$

(Hint: use (2.3.10).)

13.9 PROJECTS

The following projects develop molecular dynamics simulations for simple model systems. When the number of atoms is large, it will be necessary to compute some simple functionals of the motion to get a feeling whether or not things are going according to plan. Temperature is defined by

$$T(t) := \frac{1}{3Nk_B} \sum_{i=1}^{N} m_i |\mathbf{v}_i(t)|^2, \tag{13.9.1}$$

where $\mathbf{v}_i = \frac{d\mathbf{x}_i}{dt}$. Here k_B is Boltzmann's constant[5] and m_i is the mass of the i-th atom. The unit of energy used frequently in molecular dynamics is kilo-Joules per mole (kJ/mol). For example, the oxygen molecule O_2 has a bond

[5]Austrian Ludwig Boltzmann (1844–1906) was a developer, together with American Josiah Willard Gibbs (1839–1903), of the field of statistical mechanics, in which macroscopic properties of large systems can be explained based on microscopic behavior. Gibbs received the first doctorate in engineering in the United States, from Yale in 1863; however, he did not publish his first paper until he was 34 years old.

(or dissociation) energy estimated at approximately 490 kJ/mol (kiloJoules per mole), where a mole of O_2 contains Avogadro's number of molecules in an approximately 32 g sample. The energy of a hydrogen bond is much smaller, around 20 kJ/mol depending on the environment of the bond. The Boltzmann constant $k_B \approx 8.314 \times 10^{-3}$ kJ/mol^{-1}K^{-1} provides a conversion factor between energy and temperature.

Energy is a derived unit, based on our choice of length, time, and mass. The atomic mass unit (amu) is conceptually equal to one gram divided by Avogadro's number. If we use the amu for mass, the nanosecond for time and the nanometer for space, then the energy unit is kJ/mol. These are natural units to use at the molecular scale. The weight of an atom in amu's is approximately the number of neutrons and protons in its nucleus.

Temperature can be monitored as the simulation evolves using the correspondence of kinetic energy and atomic velocities as shown in (13.9.1). Similarly the diffusion coefficient can be determined from

$$\begin{aligned} D &:= \lim_{t\to\infty} \frac{1}{6N}\frac{d}{dt}\sum_{i=1}^{N} |\mathbf{x}_i(t) - \mathbf{x}_i(0)|^2 \\ &= \lim_{t\to\infty} \frac{1}{3N}\sum_{i=1}^{N} \mathbf{v}_i(t)\cdot(\mathbf{x}_i(t) - \mathbf{x}_i(0)), \end{aligned} \tag{13.9.2}$$

and one can investigate how D might depend on the temperature T.

The most time consuming part of a molecular dynamics simulation is the nonbonded force calculation consisting of electrostatic and van der Waals interactions. The former interaction plays no direct role for a noble gas like argon; the latter can be modeled by the well-known Lennard-Jones potential

$$V(r) := 4\epsilon\left(\left(\frac{\sigma}{r}\right)^{12} - \left(\frac{\sigma}{r}\right)^{6}\right). \tag{13.9.3}$$

This potential energy function has a minimum (most favorable interaction) at an interatomic distance $r = \sqrt[6]{2}\sigma$. The force field parameters ϵ and σ depend on the types of atoms involved, and can differ for the repulsive and attractive terms.

Project 13.1. For simulations with atoms of only one mass, it can be convenient to choose units of mass, length, and energy so that $m = 1$, $\sigma = 1$, and $\epsilon = 1$. Verify that using reduced units the unit of time is $\sqrt{\sigma^2 m/\epsilon}$ and the unit of temperature is ϵ/k_B. Calculate the unit of time for argon based on reduced units given the parameters $m = 6.69 \times 10^{-26} kg$, $\sigma = 3.405$ Ångstroms, and $\epsilon = 1.654 \times 10^{-21}$Joules. The interaction between two atoms using reduced units for (13.9.3) is

$$V(r) = 4\left(\frac{1}{r^{12}} - \frac{1}{r^6}\right). \tag{13.9.4}$$

verify that the force ∇V acting on the atom at $\mathbf{x}_i$ due to the atom at $\mathbf{x}_j$ is

$$\mathbf{F}_{ij} = \frac{24(\mathbf{x}_i - \mathbf{x}_j)}{|\mathbf{x}_i - \mathbf{x}_j|^2}\left(\frac{2}{|\mathbf{x}_i - \mathbf{x}_j|^{12}} - \frac{1}{|\mathbf{x}_i - \mathbf{x}_j|^6}\right). \tag{13.9.5}$$

Note that $\mathbf{F}_{ij} = -\mathbf{F}_{ji}$.

Project 13.2. Perform a simulation of liquid argon [123] atoms modeled with the Lennard-Jones potential and parameters given in Project 13.1 without a cutoff radius. Begin with atoms spaced on a lattice of size $\sqrt[6]{2}\sigma$ and initial velocities of magnitude $\sqrt{3k_BT/m}$ determined by a random number generator that uniformly distributes the directions over the unit sphere. Start with T=94.4 K. Choose $n = k^3$ atoms, where k is the number of lattice points in each direction. Using timesteps of 10 femtoseconds, see how the observed temperature defined in (13.9.1) varies as a function of time. See to what extent your results depend on k and the size of the time step. (See Exercise 13.14.)

Project 13.3. A useful structural property to calculate is the radial distribution function, $g(r)$, which can be estimated using the number $n(r)$ of distances $|\mathbf{x}_i - \mathbf{x}_j| \in [r, r + \Delta r]$ between atoms in a single atom simulation. Then $g(r)$ is defined to be

$$g(r) := \lim_{\Delta r \to 0} \frac{V}{N}\frac{n(r)}{4\pi r^2 \Delta r}, \tag{13.9.6}$$

where V is the volume occupied by the material. Since $g(r)$ is known for many liquids it can be used to test a simulation. Note that V is just a scaling factor and would not affect the location of the peaks and valleys of $g(r)$. For the liquid argon simulation in Project 13.2 determine $g(r)$ from a distance of 1 to 8 Ångstroms. Note that the size of the slice, Δr, needs to be determined for adequate sampling. Another property expected is that the magnitude of the velocities squared will become randomly distributed around the mean value of $3k_BT/m$ according to the Maxwell-Boltzmann distribution. Investigate the evolution of the distribution of velocities in your simulations.

Unfortunately, argon and other materials will drift off into space in a vacuum. Computer simulations are often carried out in a fixed volume that is cubic or rectilinear. In order to overcome edge effects an infinite volume is simulated through the virtual periodic replication of the central simulation box surrounded by replica images of itself. The surrounding images are manifest by permitting interactions to penetrate from one side of a box to the other side. Also, when an atom leaves one side of a box it enters the other side with identical velocity. In order to minimize the effects of the crystal-like artificial boundaries, atoms are restricted from interacting with an atom and its image. This is achieved by insisting that the cutoff radius be less than one half the simulation box size in any dimension.

Project 13.4. Periodic boundary conditions for a rectilinear volume with edge lengths e_1, e_2, and e_3 are implemented by wrapping atom coordinates x_i, y_i, and z_i when the atom leaves the central volume so that the atom enters the opposite side. Determine pseudo code to implement a translation of atomic coordinates keeping atoms in the central, computational box.

Project 13.5. Assume periodic boundary conditions for a rectilinear volume as in Project 13.4. Determine pseudo code for detecting pairwise nonbonded interactions for a cutoff radius r_{cut} and atom pairs with coordinates x_i, y_i, z_i and x_j, y_j, z_j.

Project 13.6. Repeat Project 13.2 using periodic boundary conditions and using a cutoff radius of 8 Ångstroms. How do the results differ?

Project 13.7. Perform a simulation of two isotopes of argon [123] using the Lennard-Jones potential on a periodic system using an 8 Ångstrom cutoff radius. (Hint: Just change the masses.) Compute the diffusion coefficients for each component and for relative diffusion [148, 147].

Project 13.8. Perform a simulation of a mixture of argon and krypton [148, 147] using the Lennard-Jones potential on a periodic system using an 8 Ångstrom cutoff radius. Check for convergence of the diffusion coefficients as $n \to \infty$. (Hint: plot the diffusion coefficients as a function of n and see if you think it is tending to a limit.)

Project 13.9. Simulate liquid argon (and/or krypton) to determine how the diffusion coefficient (13.9.2) depends on the temperature (13.9.1). See how the results depend on the cutoff radius.

Chapter Fourteen
Mesh Methods

> Do you guys know what you are doing, or are you just hacking?—*Unknown*

Many computations in science and engineering are based on **meshes** (or **grids**) of one sort or another. The term "grid computing" has taken on a new meaning: computing using resources distributed over the planet [48]. Parallel computing is essential to "grid computing," but in this chapter "grids" mean just meshes. We will attempt to use the term "mesh" whenever possible, but the term "multigrid" is so well established that we are compelled to continue with it. The term "multimesh" just does not sound right, even though it would mean the same thing.

These computations can be done with finite difference, finite element, or many other types of discretizations. However, all of these methods have similarities with respect to parallelization. We try to indicate the key ideas with a simple one-dimensional problem on a regular mesh. Multidimensional problems on regular meshes are of course more complex, and we give a brief introduction to the issues here. Irregular meshes just make it harder. But many of the key ideas do appear in the simple case considered here. Finally, we consider scalable algorithms for initial value problems.

14.1 BOUNDARY VALUE PROBLEMS

In Section 1.6.2, we considered solving ordinary differential equations of second order, with data values specified at each end of the interval of definition of the solution, called the *boundary values.* We consider a different set of boundary values from those in Section 1.6.2. In particular we consider for simplicity the boundary value problem

$$\begin{aligned} -\frac{d^2u}{dx^2} =& f(x) \quad \forall x \in [0,1], \\ u'(0) = 0,& \quad u(1) = 0 \end{aligned} \tag{14.1.1}$$

(compare (1.6.11) and (1.6.12)). This has the special property that the exact solution can be written as

$$u(x) = \int_x^1 \int_0^t f(s)\, ds\, dt. \tag{14.1.2}$$

To begin with, suppose we have a regular mesh defined by $x_i = (i-1)\Delta x$ with $\Delta x = 1/N$ for some integer N, with $1 \le i \le N+1$. Using a finite difference approximation such as (1.6.13) or a finite element approximation, we arrive at a simple system of linear equations to solve. For completeness, we explain briefly the finite element approach [25]. It is based on the **variational formulation**

$$\int_0^1 u'(x)\phi_i'(x)\,dx = \int_0^1 f(x)\phi_i(x)\,dx \quad \forall i = 1,\ldots,N, \tag{14.1.3}$$

where the functions ϕ_i are piecewise linear "hat" functions that are one at the i-th node x_i and zero at all other nodes. For general functions f, it is further necessary to introduce an approximation scheme to evaluate $\int_0^1 f(x)\phi_i(x)\,dx$. One natural method is the trapezoidal rule:

$$\int_{x_i}^{x_{i+1}} f(x)\,dx \approx \frac{\Delta x}{2}\left(f(x_i) + f(x_{i+1})\right). \tag{14.1.4}$$

With this approximation for the integral on the right-hand side of (14.1.3), it simplifies to (1.6.13) for $2 \le i \le N-1$. Introducing the boundary value $u_{N+1} = 0$ makes (1.6.13) correct in the case $i = N$. For $i = 1$, the variational formulation helps to identify the correct equation. Now there is only one interval of integration, and the equation becomes

$$u_1 - u_2 = \frac{\Delta x^2}{2} f(x_1). \tag{14.1.5}$$

A set of equations can be derived on an arbitrary mesh $0 = x_1 < x_2 < \cdots < x_n < \cdots < x_{N+1} = 1$; cf. Exercise 14.2.

14.1.1 A matrix factorization

The finite difference or finite element matrix A for solving the equation (14.1.1) has a simple tridiagonal form

$$A = \begin{pmatrix} 1 & -1 & 0 & 0 & \cdots & 0 \\ -1 & 2 & -1 & 0 & \cdots & 0 \\ 0 & -1 & 2 & -1 & \cdots & 0 \\ \cdots & \cdots & \cdots & \cdots & \cdots & \cdots \\ 0 & \cdots & -1 & 2 & -1 & 0 \\ 0 & \cdots & 0 & -1 & 2 & -1 \\ 0 & \cdots & 0 & 0 & -1 & 2 \end{pmatrix} \tag{14.1.6}$$

where the linear system is of the form

$$AU = F \tag{14.1.7}$$

with $F_1 = \frac{1}{2}\Delta x^2 f(x_1)$ and $F_i = \Delta x^2 f(x_i)$ for $i = 2,\ldots,N$. The matrix A has an explicit factorization $A = LL^t$ into a product of a lower bidiagonal matrix L and its transpose L^t (which is an upper bidiagonal matrix):

$$
\begin{aligned}
L &:= \begin{pmatrix} 1 & 0 & 0 & 0 & \cdots & 0 \\ -1 & 1 & 0 & 0 & \cdots & 0 \\ 0 & -1 & 1 & 0 & \cdots & 0 \\ \cdots & \cdots & \cdots & \cdots & \cdots & \cdots \\ 0 & \cdots & -1 & 1 & 0 & 0 \\ 0 & \cdots & 0 & -1 & 1 & 0 \\ 0 & \cdots & 0 & 0 & -1 & 1 \end{pmatrix} \\
L^t &= \begin{pmatrix} 1 & -1 & 0 & 0 & \cdots & 0 \\ 0 & 1 & -1 & 0 & \cdots & 0 \\ 0 & 0 & 1 & -1 & \cdots & 0 \\ \cdots & \cdots & \cdots & \cdots & \cdots & \cdots \\ 0 & \cdots & 0 & 1 & -1 & 0 \\ 0 & \cdots & 0 & 0 & 1 & -1 \\ 0 & \cdots & 0 & 0 & 0 & 1 \end{pmatrix}
\end{aligned}
\tag{14.1.8}
$$

The factorization $A = LL^t$ provides a discrete analogue of the integral representation (14.1.2). Using the factorization, the solution to $AU = F$ can be obtained [86] by the simple algorithm shown in Program 14.1. It involves an auxiliary vector Y which solves $LY = F$, in which case U satisfies $L^tU = Y$. The components of the vector Y corresponds to the values $u'(x_i)$ which are represented by the inner integral in (14.1.2).

```
y(1) = f(1)
do i = 2, N
 y(i) = y(i-1) + f(i)
enddo
u(N) = y(N)
do i = N-1,1,-1
 u(i) = u(i-1) + y(i)
enddo
```

Program 14.1 Forward and backward solution with simple bidiagonal factors.

14.1.2 Parallel direct triangular solver

In Section 12.2, we introduced direct methods to solve banded triangular systems suitable for a small bandwidth w. For the system (14.1.8), we have $w = 1$. Let us consider the algorithm from Section 12.2.2 in detail in this case.

We write the lower triangular matrix L as a $P \times P$ block matrix whose entries are $s \times s$ blocks, where $n = Ps$ for some integers P and s. We multiply L by a block diagonal matrix D to obtain the form

$$DL = \begin{pmatrix} I_s & 0 & 0 & 0 & 0 & 0 \\ G_s & I_s & 0 & 0 & 0 & 0 \\ 0 & G_s & I_s & 0 & 0 & 0 \\ 0 & 0 & \cdots & \cdots & 0 & 0 \\ 0 & 0 & 0 & G_s & I_s & 0 \\ 0 & 0 & 0 & 0 & G_s & I_s \end{pmatrix} \tag{14.1.9}$$

where I_s denotes an $s \times s$ identity matrix, and the $s \times s$ matrix G_s satisfies $L_s G_s = R_s$ with R_s of the form

$$R_s = \begin{pmatrix} 0 & 0 & 0 & 0 & 0 & -1 \\ 0 & 0 & 0 & 0 & 0 & 0 \\ 0 & 0 & 0 & 0 & 0 & 0 \\ \cdots & \cdots & \cdots & \cdots & \cdots & \cdots \\ 0 & 0 & 0 & 0 & 0 & 0 \\ 0 & 0 & 0 & 0 & 0 & 0 \end{pmatrix} \tag{14.1.10}$$

(cf. (12.2.10) and following). By inspection, G_s is an $s \times s$ matrix of the form

$$G_s = \begin{pmatrix} 0 & 0 & 0 & 0 & 0 & -1 \\ 0 & 0 & 0 & 0 & 0 & -1 \\ 0 & 0 & 0 & 0 & 0 & -1 \\ \cdots & \cdots & \cdots & \cdots & \cdots & \cdots \\ 0 & 0 & 0 & 0 & 0 & -1 \\ 0 & 0 & 0 & 0 & 0 & -1 \end{pmatrix} \tag{14.1.11}$$

The rightmost column of G_s is a vector we denote by $-\mathbf{1}_s$; the matrix $\hat{G}_i$ in (12.2.14) is in this case just the vector $-\mathbf{1}_s$. Therefore the matrix M_i in (12.2.14) is the vector $-\mathbf{1}_{s-1}$ and H_i is just a scalar (1×1 matrix) equal to -1.

The original system $Lx = f$ is changed to $(DL)x = b := Df$, where b can be written in block form with blocks b_i defined by solving

$$L_s b_i = f_i \tag{14.1.12}$$

and f_i denotes the i-th block of f. Further, split b_i with u_i denoting the top $s-1$ entries of b_i and v_i denoting the bottom entry of b_i. We may then write the blocks x_i of the solution vector in two corresponding parts: y_i denoting the top $s-1$ entries of x_i and z_i denoting the bottom entry of x_i.

The z_i's satisfy (see (12.2.14) and following)

$$\begin{aligned} z_1 &= v_1, \\ z_{i+1} &= v_{i+1} + z_i \quad \forall i = 1, \ldots, P-1. \end{aligned} \tag{14.1.13}$$

Then we can separately determine the y_i's by

$$\begin{aligned} y_1 &= u_1, \\ y_{i+1} &= u_{i+1} + z_i \mathbf{1}_{s-1} \quad \forall i = 1, \ldots, P-1. \end{aligned} \tag{14.1.14}$$

If we solve (14.1.13) by parallel prefix (Section 12.2.3), then the time estimate for the full algorithm (including (14.1.12)) is

$$T_P \approx \frac{2c_1 n}{P} + 2c_2 \log_2 P, \tag{14.1.15}$$

where c_1 is the time to do one floating point addition and c_2 is the time to do one step of the parallel prefix algorithm with 2×2 matrices. Therefore

$$E_P^{-1} \leq 2 + \frac{2\gamma P \log_2 P}{n}, \tag{14.1.16}$$

where $\gamma = c_2/c_1$.

Theorem 14.1.1. The above algorithm is scalable with $P \log_2 P \leq \mu n$ for any fixed $\mu < \infty$ with efficiency bounded below by

$$E_P \geq \frac{1}{2 + 2\gamma\mu}. \tag{14.1.17}$$

14.2 ITERATIVE METHODS

The solution of the system (14.1.7) can be done by a variety of iterative methods. We will consider a sequence of techniques, starting with stationary methods and progressing from less efficient to more efficient, ending with multigrid methods. One of the simplest is the Jacobi iteration (1.6.19) or equivalently (1.6.20). For our simple problem to solve the equations (14.1.1) with a regular mesh, it takes the form

$$\begin{aligned} u_1^{k+1} &= u_2^k + \tfrac{1}{2} h^2 f(x_1), \\ u_n^{k+1} &= \tfrac{1}{2}\left(u_{n+1}^k + u_{n-1}^k + h^2 f(x_n)\right) \quad \forall n = 2, \ldots, N, \end{aligned} \tag{14.2.1}$$

where $h := \Delta x$ and we define $u_{N+1} = 0$ for simplicity (recall that there is a boundary condition $u(1) = 0$ and $x_{N+1} = 1$).

The data-parallel version of the Jacobi iteration depicted in Figure 1.14 has a high degree of parallelism, but one shortcoming of the implementation is that the vectors $\left(u_n^k : n = 1, \ldots, N\right)$ and $\left(u_n^{k+1} : n = 1, \ldots, N\right)$ have to be segregated. The Gauss-Seidel variant avoids this by defining

$$\begin{aligned} u_1^{k+1} &= u_2^k + \tfrac{1}{2} h^2 f(x_1), \\ u_n^{k+1} &= \tfrac{1}{2}\left(u_{n+1}^k + u_{n-1}^{k+1} + h^2 f(x_n)\right) \quad \forall n = 2, \ldots, N, \end{aligned} \tag{14.2.2}$$

where the computation of u_n^{k+1} proceeds with n in increasing order. Happily, Gauss-Seidel converges faster than Jacobi, as well as reducing memory traffic and/or complexity in coding. It can be written in "assignment" notation as

$$\begin{aligned}&u_1 \leftarrow u_2 + \tfrac{1}{2}h^2 f(x_1)\\&\text{For } n = 2, \ldots, N\\&\quad u_n \leftarrow \tfrac{1}{2}\left(u_{n+1} + u_{n-1} + h^2 f(x_n)\right).\end{aligned} \tag{14.2.3}$$

Unfortunately, there are now strong dependences (see Definition 4.1.3) within each Gauss-Seidel iteration. The simple data parallelism of the Jacobi iteration is lost. Moreover, although the Gauss-Seidel method converges eventually, to get accuracy comparable to the accuracy of the discrete equations, one still has to take $\mathcal{O}(N^2 \log N)$ iterations, and each iteration itself takes $\mathcal{O}(N)$ work. A solution can be obtained by the factorization method in only $\mathcal{O}(N)$ total work, in the serial case.

14.2.1 Parallel iterative methods

Parallelization of the Jacobi iteration (14.2.1) was considered in Chapter 1 as the prototype data-parallel computation, as depicted in Figure 1.14. The Gauss-Seidel variant (14.2.2) or equivalently (14.2.3) cannot be parallelized by such a simple approach. A radical alteration of the algorithm is required.

Perhaps the simplest in concept is to follow the data-parallel approach, simply breaking the dependences. Suppose $N = rP$. Consider the iteration

$$\begin{aligned}u_1^{k+1} &= u_2^k + \tfrac{1}{2}h^2 f(x_1),\\u_{ri+1}^{k+1} &= \tfrac{1}{2}\left(u_{ri+2}^k + \underline{u_{ri}^k} + h^2 f(x_{ri+1})\right) \quad \forall i = 1, \ldots, P-1,\\u_{ri+n}^{k+1} &= \tfrac{1}{2}\left(u_{ri+n+1}^k + u_{ri+n-1}^{k+1} + h^2 f(x_{ri+n})\right)\\&\qquad \forall n = 2, \ldots, r \qquad \forall i = 0, \ldots, P-1,\end{aligned} \tag{14.2.4}$$

where we have underlined the term that differs from (14.2.2). By breaking the dependences of u_{ri+1}^{k+1} on u_{ri}^{k+1} in (14.2.2), we get P parallel tasks. This algorithm has been studied extensively in [128]. Unfortunately, it does not have good scalability as a solver, although it can be used effectively as a "smoother" in multigrid (cf. the discussion following (14.3.8) below). In a message passing style, this is easily coded as a variant of (14.2.3), as depicted in Program 14.2. For simplicity, we have added the variable `u(0)`≡`u(1)` to simplify the logic for the first step. This is only needed at processor zero, and at the highest-numbered processor, the boundary value `u(1+N/P)=0` is applied.

14.2.2 Different orderings

A more efficient parallelization of Gauss-Seidel involves a complete reordering of the iterations. Note that following (14.2.2) we specified that the computation of u_n^{k+1} proceeds with n in increasing order. Suppose instead

```
do j=1,jiters
   if (myProc .eq. 0) u(0)=u(1)
   if (myProc .eq. nProc−1) u(1+N/P)=0
   do i = 1, N/P
      u(i) = 0.5*(u(i+1) + u(i−1)) + f(i)
   enddo
   u(0) = u(N/P)@mod(myProc−1,nProc)
   u(1+N/P) = u(1)@mod(myProc+1,nProc)
enddo
```

Program 14.2 Pfortran code implementing simple data-parallel modification of Gauss-Seidel. Note: this is only correct for two or more processors due to the way the boundary values are updated.

that we take a different ordering. For example, suppose we computed with all odd n first, followed by the even values. That is,

$$\begin{aligned} u_1^{k+1} &= u_2^k + \tfrac{1}{2}h^2 f(x_1), \\ u_{2n-1}^{k+1} &= \tfrac{1}{2}\left(u_{2n-2}^k + u_{2n}^k + h^2 f(x_{2n-1})\right) \quad \forall n = 2, \ldots, N/2, \end{aligned} \tag{14.2.5}$$

where for simplicity we assume N is even. This computation of the odd values is followed by computing the even values:

$$u_{2n}^{k+1} = \tfrac{1}{2}\left(u_{2n+1}^{k+1} + u_{2n-1}^{k+1} + h^2 f(x_{2n})\right) \quad \forall n = 1, \ldots, N/2. \tag{14.2.6}$$

This is not at all the same algorithm, and it is somewhat remarkable that it has such similar convergence properties [145]. However, it clearly has the same type of data parallelism as the Jacobi algorithm. In fact, the implementation can be written to look just like two interleaved Jacobi iterations:

$$\begin{aligned} & u_1^o \leftarrow u_1^e + \tfrac{1}{2}h^2 f(x_1) \\ & \text{For } n = 2, \ldots, N/2 \\ & \quad u_n^o \leftarrow \tfrac{1}{2}\left(u_{n+1}^e + u_n^e + h^2 f(x_{2n+1})\right). \\ & \text{For } n = 1, \ldots, N/2 \\ & \quad u_n^e \leftarrow \tfrac{1}{2}\left(u_{n+1}^o + u_n^o + h^2 f(x_{2n})\right). \end{aligned} \tag{14.2.7}$$

Here u^e denotes the even-indexed entries of (14.2.6) and u^o denotes the odd-indexed entries.

The general approach taken in (14.2.6) or equivalently (14.2.7) is a **coloring** of the index set. Here the coloring is odd-even, typically called **red-black coloring** due to the resemblance of the generalization to two dimensions with a chess board. In (14.2.7), the approach is clear. The index set is divided into two sets, and the iteration computes the two different sets in sequence. In general, there could be more than two "colors" that divide the index set. The key point is that when computing one color of indices, the values on the right-hand side come from another color. The different colors are not computed in parallel. Rather, the computation of each color displays maximal data parallelism. Each of the entries can be computed independently of all of the others.

Although it is far from obvious that arbitrary index colorings would be a good idea, one can at least contemplate other colorings that might have better properties with regard to parallelism. Let us look at the variant of Program 14.2 depicted in Program 14.3. This has been written in a message passing style to emphasize the opportunity to overlap communication and computation. The coloring scheme involves two colors, but the values `U(K)` communicated to the neighbor with a greater processor number comprise one group. The rest, the variables `U(1),..., U(K-1)`, comprise the other. To see this, observe that a type of pairwise barrier exists just before the computation of `U(K)`. All processors (at least those less than `nnodes()-1`) will wait until the `rcv` has been completed. This will only happen once the matching processor has executed the `snd` before the `DO i` loop.

```
k=N/P
tagl= 1
if (nodeid() .lt. nnodes()-1) call snd(tagl, u(k), 8, nodeid()+1, 1)
do j=1,jiters
   if (nodeid() .gt. 0) call rcv(tagl, u(0), 8, nodeid()-1, 1)
   if (nodeid() .eq. 0) u(0)=u(1)
   u(1) = 0.5*(u(2) + u(0)) + f(1)
   tagr=2*j
   if (nodeid() .gt. 0) call snd(tagr, u(1), 8, nodeid()-1, 1)
   do i = 2, k - 1
      u(i) = 0.5*(u(i+1) + u(i-1)) + f(i)
   enddo
   if (nodeid() .lt. nnodes()-1) call rcv(tagr, u(k+1), 8, nodeid()+1,1)
   if (nodeid() .eq. nnodes()-1) u(k+1)=0
   u(k) = 0.5*(u(k+1) + u(k-1)) + f(k)
   tagl=2*j + 1
   if (nodeid() .lt. nnodes()-1) call snd(tagl, u(k), 8, nodeid()+1, 1)
enddo
```

Program 14.3 Code implementing (in message passing) another modification of Gauss-Seidel which overlaps communication and computation.

14.3 MULTIGRID METHODS

The solution of the system (14.1.7) by multigrid methods is simple in concept but tedious in detail [25]. A basic building block is the the Jacobi iteration (14.2.1) or the Gauss-Seidel iteration (14.2.2). But rather than iterate to convergence, such iterative schemes are halted after a few iterations, and the problem is then transferred to a coarser mesh (or "grid" as we will prefer to call it in this section). This process is then repeated, recursively.

Let us introduce some notation. Suppose there are $K > 1$ **multigrid levels**, by which we mean several things. First of all, we suppose that we begin with a **coarse grid** $x_i = (i-1)\Delta x$ with $\Delta x = 1/N$ for some integer N, with $1 \le i \le N+1$. We call this the **level-zero grid**. The level-one grid is obtained from the level-zero grid by subdividing. We could number the resulting grid points in various ways, but let us number them via

$$\begin{aligned} x_{N+2i} &= x_i \quad \forall i = 1, \ldots, N+1, \\ x_{N+2i+1} &= \tfrac{1}{2}(x_i + x_{i+1}) \quad \forall i = 1, \ldots, N. \end{aligned} \tag{14.3.1}$$

Note that we have defined the level-one grid abstractly in terms of the level-zero grid points, even though we have defined the latter as a uniform grid for simplicity. If the level-zero grid was nonuniform, (14.3.1) would still be the correct definition of the level-one grid.

The general k-th level grid can be defined in terms of the previous level by

$$\begin{aligned} x_{N_k+2i-1} &= x_{N_{k-1}+i} \quad \forall i = 1, \ldots, \nu_{k-1}, \\ x_{N_k+2i} &= \tfrac{1}{2}(x_{N_{k-1}+i} + x_{N_{k-1}+i+1}) \quad \forall i = 1, \ldots, \nu_{k-1}-1, \end{aligned} \tag{14.3.2}$$

where ν_k is the number of points in level k (with $\nu_0 = N+1$) and N_k is the number of points in all previous levels ($N_0 \equiv 0$ and $N_1 = N+1$). By induction,

$$\begin{aligned} \nu_k &= 2\nu_{k-1} - 1, \\ N_{k+1} &= N_k + \nu_k \end{aligned} \tag{14.3.3}$$

for all $k \ge 0$.

The grid points themselves play a background role compared to the values of the approximate solution at the corresponding points. Suppose that $U_{N_{k-1}+1}, \ldots, U_{N_k}$ denote these values for level $k-1$. Then we can view these values as defining a piecewise linear function on the grid for level $k-1$, namely

$$u^{k-1}(x) = \sum_{i=1}^{\nu_k} U_{N_{k-1}+i}\phi_i^{k-1}(x), \tag{14.3.4}$$

where the "hat" functions $\phi_i^{k-1}(x)$ are the same as in (14.1.3) for the grid (14.3.1) on level $k-1$. Since the grids are nested, $u^{k-1}(x)$ is also naturally a piecewise linear function on the k-th level grid. Its values at the k-th level grid points can be determined by interpolation:

$$\begin{aligned} U_{N_k+2i-1} &= U_{N_{k-1}+i} \quad \forall i = 1, \ldots, \nu_{k-1}, \\ U_{N_k+2i} &= \tfrac{1}{2}(U_{N_{k-1}+i} + U_{N_{k-1}+i+1}) \quad \forall i = 1, \ldots, \nu_{k-1}-1. \end{aligned} \tag{14.3.5}$$

In some cases, it will be appropriate to also apply the boundary condition

$$U_{N_k} = 0 \quad \forall k \ge 1. \tag{14.3.6}$$

Note that if $U_{N_k} = 0$ then (14.3.5) implies that $U_{N_{k+1}} = 0$ (see Exercise 14.8). It will also be necessary to transfer information from a finer grid to a coarser grid. Here the transformation is not so obvious. A good choice appears [25] to be the transpose of the coarse-to-fine operator (14.3.5), which works out to be

$$U_{N_{k-1}+i} = \tfrac{1}{2}U_{N_k+2i-1} + \tfrac{1}{4}\left(U_{N_k+2i-2} + U_{N_k+2i}\right) \quad \forall i = 1, \ldots, \nu_{k-1}. \tag{14.3.7}$$

14.3.1 The V-cycle

The basic Gauss-Seidel iteration can be applied on any grid level. Let us assume that the vector F has been assigned the correct values for each grid, namely, $F_{N_k+i} = h_k^2 f(x_{N_k+i})$ for $i > 1$ and $F_{N_k+1} = \frac{1}{2}h_k^2 f(x_{N_k+1})$. The iteration (14.2.3) becomes

$$\begin{aligned} & U_{N_k+1} \leftarrow U_{N_k+2} + F_{N_k+1} \\ & \text{For } n = 2, \ldots, \nu_k \\ & \quad U_{N_k+n} \leftarrow \tfrac{1}{2}\left(U_{N_k+n+1} + U_{N_k+n-1} + F_{N_k+n}\right). \end{aligned} \tag{14.3.8}$$

This will converge to the solution of an equation on the k-th level grid, which we write for clarity as

$$A^k U^k = F^k. \tag{14.3.9}$$

While the Gauss-Seidel iteration (and other iterations) does not move the approximation very quickly toward its ultimate goal, it does have the effect of smoothing out the error between the approximation and the solution. For this reason, (14.3.8) is known as a **smoothing step** in multigrid methods.

Let us describe what we will call the **k-th level iteration**. We assume that $k \geq 1$ in the general case; if $k = 0$, we will apply some other method, such as Gaussian elimination or just lots of smoothing steps. We start with the smoothing step, i.e., iteration (14.3.8), being done m_k times on level k. The residual error

$$R^k := F^k - A^k U^k$$

on the k-th level mesh can be defined by

$$\begin{aligned} & R_{N_k+1} \leftarrow F_{N_k+1} - U_{N_k+1} + U_{N_k+2} \\ & \text{For } n = 2, \ldots, \nu_k \\ & \quad R_{N_k+n} \leftarrow F_{N_k+n} - 2U_{N_k+n} + U_{N_k+n+1} + U_{N_k+n-1}. \end{aligned} \tag{14.3.10}$$

The error $E = \widetilde{U} - U$, where $\widetilde{U}$ denotes the exact solution to $A\widetilde{U} = F$, satisfies the **residual equation**

$$A^k E^k = R^k, \tag{14.3.11}$$

where we add superscripts to indicate the grid level for clarity. The point is that

$$\widetilde{U}^k = U^k + E^k. \tag{14.3.12}$$

However, solving (14.3.11) is equivalent in complexity to solving the original equation. But the key point is that the solution of (14.3.11) is "smooth" on the current mesh, thanks to the smoothing step (14.3.8), so we can try to approximate it on a coarser mesh. Thus we define

$$R_{N_{k-1}+i} = \tfrac{1}{2} R_{N_k+2i-1} + \tfrac{1}{4}\left(R_{N_k+2i-2} + R_{N_k+2i}\right) \qquad (14.3.13)$$

for all $i = 1, \ldots, \nu_{k-1}$. We now "solve" (14.3.11) on level $k-1$. What is a bit complex about multigrid is that the solution on level $k-1$ is done recursively, that is, we apply the process we are defining (the k-th level iteration) on level $k-1$. We have not finished defining it, but suppose this makes sense (which it does inductively since we defined what to do for $k = 0$); then we take the "solution" and add it to U to produce the result of the k-th level iteration. To do so, we need to use the coarse-to-fine transfer (14.3.5). And for symmetry, it may be useful to apply another m_k smoothing steps starting with the augmented vector.

To summarize, the k-th level iteration is a function that takes an input vector (the right-hand side) and produces an approximate solution on the k-th level grid. In part of its definition, this function is called (recursively, or at least inductively) on level $k-1$. As we have described it, the k-th level iteration involves working down the grid levels to zero, then working back up the grids. This is called a **V-cycle** since plotting the levels used in sequence results in something like a "V."

14.3.2 Full multigrid

The basic V-cycle iteration matrix for the problem we are considering has a spectral radius bounded strictly less than one, independent of the level k. Thus simply repeating the V-cycle on a given level will converge to an accuracy of $\mathcal{O}(\Delta x^2)$ in $\mathcal{O}(|\log \Delta x|)$ iterations. However, there is more to be gained from the multigrid approach. To be precise, let us start by solving (14.3.9) on the level-zero mesh. For simplicity, let us assume this is solved exactly for $U^0 = (U_1, \ldots, U_{N+1})$. Then using the coarse-to-fine transfer (14.3.5), we can define an initial approximation to U^1. We use this as the beginning of a level-one iteration (which does smoothing, solves a level-zero residual equation, uses the coarse-to-fine transfer again, and follows by more smoothing). The level-one iteration is repeated r times in this manner. When done, we use (14.3.5) again to define an initial approximation to U^2, and so on. By doing r repetitions of the k-th level iteration at each level, we complete what is know as the **full multigrid** V-cycle. It can be shown that it will converge to an accuracy of $\mathcal{O}(\Delta x^2)$ in $\mathcal{O}(1)$ iterations. That is, for r a sufficiently large constant, each k-th level iteration will solve (14.3.9) to an accuracy of $\mathcal{O}(\Delta x_k^2)$. For example, $r = 10$ is usually sufficient.

14.3.3 Parallel multigrid

Multigrid is easily parallelized in much the same way the Jacobi iteration or variants of the Gauss-Seidel iteration. Indeed, there are simply two parts: smoothing and inter-grid transfers. The smoother is a standard iterative method, possibly modified for parallel computation. The inter-grid transfers have a similar structure in that only data at the ends of the local arrays need by transferred.

The time spent in computation in a basic V-cycle can be estimated by

$$T^s{}_P \approx \sum_{k=0}^{K-1} \frac{c_1 N 2^{-k}}{P}, \tag{14.3.14}$$

where c_1 is the time to do basic floating point operations in the smoothing step, and K is the number of levels.

The communication in multigrid involves just sending data at each end of the data interval in each processor at each step in the V-cycle, so it is proportional to K, with the primary contributor to the constant being the latency time λ. What is left is to "solve" on the coarse grid at level K. There are $N2^{-K}$ unknowns at this level, and we could simply solve redundantly at each processor. However, it would be necessary to collect the right-hand side at each processor, which could also be done in time proportional to $N2^{-K}$. Let c_2 denote this constant of proportionality (coming mainly from bandwidth constraints if $N2^{-K}$ is large). Thus we can estimate the time for the overall algorithm to be

$$T_P \approx \frac{2c_1 N}{P} + \lambda K + c_2 N 2^{-K}. \tag{14.3.15}$$

Equating the first and last terms, we find $P = 2^{K+1}/\gamma$ where $\gamma = c_2/c_1$. With this choice of P, we find

$$T_P \approx \frac{4c_1 N}{P}. + \lambda \log_2(P\gamma/2). \tag{14.3.16}$$

This implies an efficiency of

$$E_P^{-1} \approx 4 + \frac{\lambda P \log_2(P\gamma/2)}{c_1 N}. \tag{14.3.17}$$

Theorem 14.3.1. The parallel V-cycle algorithm is scalable with

$$P \log_2 P \leq \mu n$$

for any fixed $\mu < \infty$ with efficiency asymptotic (for P large) to

$$E_P \approx \frac{1}{4 + \lambda\mu/c_1}. \tag{14.3.18}$$

14.4 MULTIDIMENSIONAL PROBLEMS

In Program 8.21, the Jacobi method applied to a two-dimensional approximation of Laplace's equation was presented as an exercise. Here we develop this type of application in more detail, starting with the derivation of the discrete equations from the differential equation.

In Section 14.1, we considered solving boundary value problems in one dimension for ordinary differential equations of second order. Here we generalize this to multiple dimensions. For simplicity, we give details only in the two-dimensional case for the boundary value problem

$$-\frac{\partial^2 u}{\partial x^2} - \frac{\partial^2 u}{\partial y^2} = f(x) \quad \forall x, y \in [0,1], \tag{14.4.1}$$

where for simplicity we assume that $u = 0$ on the boundary of the square $\{(x,y) : x, y \in [0,1]\}$.

Again suppose we have a regular mesh defined by $x_i = y_i = (i-1)\Delta x$ for $1 \le i \le N+1$ with $\Delta x = 1/N$ for some integer N. Using a finite difference approximation such as (1.6.13) or a finite element approximation, we arrive at a simple system of linear equations to solve. (A set of equations can also be derived on a more general mesh $0 = x_1 < x_2 < \cdots < x_n < \cdots < x_{N+1} = 1$, $0 = y_1 < y_2 < \cdots < y_n < \cdots < y_{N+1} = 1$, cf. Exercise 14.3.) That is, the mesh points are of the form (x_i, y_j) which is often called the "tensor product" mesh because the corresponding basis functions in a finite element approximation on such a mesh can be viewed as the tensor product of the one-dimensional bases.

The finite difference or finite element matrix A for the equations (14.1.1) on a regular tensor product mesh has a simple block tridiagonal form

$$A = \frac{1}{\Delta x^2}\begin{pmatrix} B_N & -1 & 0 & 0 & \cdots & 0 \\ -I_N & B_N & -I_N & 0 & \cdots & 0 \\ 0 & -I_N & B_N & -I_N & \cdots & 0 \\ \cdots & \cdots & \cdots & \cdots & \cdots & \cdots \\ 0 & \cdots & -I_N & B_N & -I_N & 0 \\ 0 & \cdots & 0 & -I_N & B_N & -I_N \\ 0 & \cdots & 0 & 0 & -I_N & B_N \end{pmatrix} \tag{14.4.2}$$

where I_N denotes the $N \times N$ identity matrix and B_N is of the form

$$B_N := \begin{pmatrix} 4 & -1 & 0 & 0 & \cdots & 0 \\ -1 & 4 & -1 & 0 & \cdots & 0 \\ 0 & -1 & 4 & -1 & \cdots & 0 \\ \cdots & \cdots & \cdots & \cdots & \cdots & \cdots \\ 0 & \cdots & -1 & 4 & -1 & 0 \\ 0 & \cdots & 0 & -1 & 4 & -1 \\ 0 & \cdots & 0 & 0 & -1 & 4 \end{pmatrix}. \tag{14.4.3}$$

A is an $N^2 \times N^2$ matrix, with bandwidth N for the ordering of mesh points given above. Thus even the toy-duck algorithm of Section 12.2.1 can be used effectively for large N, with $P = \epsilon N$ processors. However, the ordering of mesh points given above is known not to be optimal in the sequential case, so the picture is not so simple.

Better mesh orderings do not reduce the bandwidth in the sense that there are still points $\mathcal{O}(N)$ away from the diagonal for an optimal ordering, but what is achieved is a reduction of the average bandwidth. To take advantage of such structure, more general sparse matrix algorithms are needed.

Iterative methods for solving $AX = F$ do not care much about the ordering of the mesh points, and in particular, multigrid can be applied in the multidimensional case with little change in concept.

14.5 INITIAL VALUE PROBLEMS

In Section 1.6.1, we considered a simple initial value problem for an ordinary differential equation and observed that it exhibits a limited kind of natural parallelism. However, we will now try to paint a different picture in order to discover a scalable parallel algorithm. What can provide the increasing data size needed for such scalability is a long time interval of integration. Indeed, there are many simulations in which the primary interest is a very long time of integration. For example, answering the age-old question of the potential nature of the "star of Bethlehem" as a conjunction of planets [82, 111] requires such a simulation.

We will only consider a very simple example here motivated by a swinging pendulum. To a first approximation, the position $u(t)$ of the pendulum satisfies a differential equation

$$\frac{d^2u}{dt^2} = f(u) \tag{14.5.1}$$

with initial conditions provided at $t = 0$:

$$u(0) = a_0,\ u'(0) = a_1 \tag{14.5.2}$$

for some given data values a and a_1.

The variable u can be taken to denote the angle that the pendulum makes compared with the direction of the force of gravity. Then $f(u) = mg \sin u$, where g is the gravitational constant and m is the mass of the weight at the end of the pendulum. (We are ignoring the mass of the rod that holds this weight.)

We can approximate via a difference method (see Section 14.1 or Section 1.6.2, in particular (1.6.13)) to get a recursion relation

$$u_{n+1} = 2u_n - u_{n-1} - \tau f(u_n), \tag{14.5.3}$$

where $\tau := \Delta t^2$.

If the displacements of the pendulum position from vertical are small, then we can use the approximation $\sin u \approx u$ to get a linear equation

$$\frac{d^2u}{dt^2} = mgu. \tag{14.5.4}$$

In this case, the difference equations become a linear recursion relation of the form

$$u_{n+1} = (2 - \tau mg)\, u_n - u_{n-1}. \tag{14.5.5}$$

The initial conditions (14.5.2) provide starting values for the recursion. For example, we can take

$$u_0 = a \quad \text{and} \quad u_{-1} = a_0 - a_1 \Delta t. \tag{14.5.6}$$

This allows us to solve (14.5.5) for $n \geq 0$.

The recursion (14.5.5) corresponds to a banded lower triangular system of equations of the form

$$LU = b, \tag{14.5.7}$$

where the bandwidth of L is $w = 2$, the diagonal and subsubdiagonal terms of L are all one, and the subdiagonal terms of L equal $\tau mg - 2$. The right-hand side g is of the form

$$b_1 = (1 - \tau mg)\, a_0 + a_1 \Delta t \quad \text{and} \quad b_2 = -a_0 \tag{14.5.8}$$

and $b_i = 0$ for $i \geq 3$. Thus we can solve this by the scalable parallel algorithms of Sections 12.2 and 12.3.

When f is not linear, the algorithms of Sections 12.2 and 12.3 do not appear to be directly applicable. We can formulate a set of equations to define the entire vector of values u_i as an ensemble, but it is no longer a linear equation. We can write it formally as

$$F(U) = 0, \tag{14.5.9}$$

where F is defined by

$$F(U) = L^0 U + \tau mg \phi(U) - b \tag{14.5.10}$$

with L^0 the same as L above with $\tau = 0$, that is, L^0 is a lower triangular matrix with bandwidth $w = 2$, the diagonal and subsubdiagonal terms of L^0 are all one, and the subdiagonal terms of L^0 equal -2. The function ϕ thus contains all of the nonlinearity and has the simple form

$$\phi(U)_{ij} = \delta_{j,i-1} \sin u_{i-1}, \tag{14.5.11}$$

where $\delta_{i,j}$ is the Kronecker delta.

14.5.1 Newton's method

Nonlinear equations can vary in difficulty in ways that are hard to characterize, and there are many different solution methods that can be appropriate in different settings. However, one of the most powerful methods available is the Newton-Raphson[1] method. We begin by describing how it works in a simple, one-dimensional setting. We assume that the problem to be solved is of the form in (14.5.9), where now U denotes a single variable. Thus we are seeking a point where the graph of F crosses the U axis. If we are given a particular guess U^n, a natural way to find a nearby zero-crossing of F would be to draw the tangent line to the curve from the point $(U^n, F(U^n))$ and find the point U^{n+1} where this tangent line goes through the axis. Remembering that the slope of the tangent is $F'(U^n)$ at that point, we get the equation

$$\frac{0 - F(U^n)}{U^{n+1} - U^n} = F'(U^n). \tag{14.5.12}$$

This can be written in a more algorithmic form as

$$U^{n+1} = U^n - \frac{F(U^n)}{F'(U^n)}. \tag{14.5.13}$$

If we start close to a solution, this algorithm has the remarkable property of squaring the error at each step (some restrictions apply [86]), your experience may vary), namely,

$$|U^{n+1} - U^n| \approx C|U^n - U^{n-1}|^2 \tag{14.5.14}$$

which means that the number of correct digits in the answer doubles at each iteration. Thus, once you get close, you converge very rapidly.

The multidimensional version of the Newton-Raphson method is a bit more complex to derive, but it is formally equivalent. First, note that (14.5.13) can be written

$$F'(U^n)\left(U^{n+1} - U^n\right) = -F(U^n). \tag{14.5.15}$$

We have to understand what $F'(U^n)$ should mean in the multidimensional context, but it is simply the Jacobian matrix of all partial derivatives of F with respect to the vector U:

$$J_F(U)_{i,j} := \frac{\partial F_i(U)}{\partial u_j}. \tag{14.5.16}$$

Then the multidimensional version of the Newton-Raphson method is

$$J_F(U^n)\left(U^{n+1} - U^n\right) = -F(U^n). \tag{14.5.17}$$

It helps to write this in two steps as follows. First we solve the linear system

$$J_F(U^n)V = -F(U^n), \tag{14.5.18}$$

[1] Joseph Raphson (1648–1715) added substantial clarification to a method proposed by his contemporary Newton, which in turn was based on an ancient heritage [54] of algorithms for finding roots of equations. Raphson's less well-known name is often dropped to give an abbreviated name for the method.

and then we set

$$U^{n+1} = U^n + V \tag{14.5.19}$$

and repeat the process until convergence.

To see how this works, let us return to the pendulum problem. In the case of the pendulum, we have F defined by (14.5.10). It takes a careful look at the definition, but it is not hard to see that the Jacobian matrix for a linear function of the form $U \to L^0 U$ is the matrix L^0. Thus $J_F(U) = L^0 + \tau mgJ_\phi(U)$. With ϕ of the form (14.5.11), it can be shown that

$$J_\phi(U)_{ij} = \delta_{j,i-1}\phi'(u_{i-1}) = \delta_{j,i-1}\cos u_{i-1}. \tag{14.5.20}$$

The Jacobian has the same form as the original matrix L. In fact, if F is linear, Newton's method is equivalent to just solving the system (14.5.7) and converges in one step.

14.5.2 Linearized initial value problem

There is another way to interpret the Newton algorithm for solving the initial value problem. Suppose that we have an approximate solution u to (14.5.1) which satisfies the initial conditions (14.5.2), and define the residual $R(u)$ by

$$R(u) := \frac{d^2u}{dt^2} - f(u) \tag{14.5.21}$$

which is a function of t defined on whatever interval u is defined on. Now suppose that we try to add a perturbation v to u to get it to satisfy (14.5.1) (more) exactly. We use a Taylor expansion to write

$$f(u+v) = f(u) + vf'(u) + \mathcal{O}(v^2). \tag{14.5.22}$$

Thus the sum $u+v$ satisfies an initial value problem of the form

$$\frac{d^2(u+v)}{dt^2} - f(u+v) = \frac{d^2v}{dt^2} - vf'(u) + R(u) + \mathcal{O}(v^2). \tag{14.5.23}$$

With (14.5.23) as motivation, we now *define* v by solving the initial value problem

$$\frac{d^2v}{dt^2} = vf'(u) - R(u) \tag{14.5.24}$$

with initial conditions provided at $t = 0$:

$$v(0) = 0,\ v'(0) = 0. \tag{14.5.25}$$

Newton's method (14.5.17) can now be seen as just a discretization of the initial value problem (14.5.24).

14.5.3 Getting Newton started

Newton's method (14.5.17) converges rapidly once you get close to a solution, as indicated in (14.5.14), but how do you get close in the first place? This question does not have a good answer in general, but we can indicate one type of approach here. Suppose that we had a simplified approximation $\tilde{f}$ to f and we solved

$$\frac{d^2u}{dt^2} = \tilde{f}(u) \tag{14.5.26}$$

exactly, together with the initial conditions (14.5.2). For example, with $f(u) = \sin u$ we might have $\tilde{f}(u) = u$ as an approximation. This makes (14.5.26) linear, and in this simple case we can even solve the equation in closed form (in terms of sines and cosines). It is much faster to evaluate $\tilde{f}(u)$ than $f(u)$ in this case, so the computation of the initial guess would be much less costly.

If we use the solution u to (14.5.26) as the starting guess for Newton's method, then the initial residual $R(u)$ has a simple interpretation. We can express it simply as

$$R(u) = \frac{d^2u}{dt^2} - f(u) = \tilde{f}(u) - f(u). \tag{14.5.27}$$

Thus the size of the residual is simply related to the error in approximation of f by $\tilde{f}$. Since the first Newton step v satisfies (14.5.24), we can bound the size of v in terms of $R(u)$, and hence $f - \tilde{f}$. More precisely, (14.5.24) becomes

$$\frac{d^2v}{dt^2} = vf'(u) - \left(\tilde{f}(u) - f(u)\right). \tag{14.5.28}$$

Since v is zero at the start (see (14.5.2)), it will be small for at least some reasonable interval of time. The size of v can be predicted as u is computed, and the process can be stopped if the prediction gets too large. Thus there is a natural way to control the size of the Newton step in this case.

14.5.4 Other methods

It would be possible to approximate on a coarser mesh as well. That is, we could use a larger Δt in (14.5.3) (recall that $\tau = \Delta t^2$). It would then be necessary to interpolate onto a finer mesh to define the residual appropriate for (14.5.24) (or equivalently in (14.5.18) in the discretized case). In this way, a multigrid approach could be developed in the time variable. See [11] (and references therein) for an example of this idea. This paper presents as well a different approach to solving nonlinear initial value problems in parallel via domain decomposition in the time domain.

Wave-form relaxation [105, 108] is a quite different approach suitable for a system of ordinary differential equations. It uses a domain decomposition of the system, not of the time domain.

14.6 EXERCISES

Exercise 14.1. Prove that applying the trapezoidal rule (14.1.4) in (14.1.3) yields (1.6.13) for interior mesh points on a uniform mesh.

Exercise 14.2. Derive the general equations corresponding to a finite element approximation (14.1.3) using the trapezoidal rule (14.1.4). Compare with (1.6.14) and (1.6.16).

Exercise 14.3. Derive the general equations corresponding to a two-dimensional finite element approximation (cf. (14.1.3) and (14.1.4)) on the "tensor product" mesh in Section 14.4. Compare with (14.1.6) and (14.4.3).

Exercise 14.4. Prove that the formula (14.1.2) gives the solution to (14.1.1). (Hint: first show that $u'(t) = -\int_0^t f(s)\,ds$.)

Exercise 14.5. Prove that the factorization $A = LL^t$ holds, where (14.1.7) defines A and (14.1.8) defines L (and L^t).

Exercise 14.6. Implement the algorithm in Section 14.1.2.

Exercise 14.7. Implement the code in Program 14.2.

Exercise 14.8. Suppose that $U_{N_k} = 0$. Prove that (14.3.5) implies that $U_{N_{k+1}} = 0$.

Exercise 14.9. Prove that $\nu_k = 2^k N + 1$ for $k \geq 0$, where ν_k is given in (14.3.2). (Hint: use induction on k as suggested in (14.3.3).)

Exercise 14.10. Prove that $N_k = N(2^k - 1) + k$, where N_k is given in (14.3.2). (Hint: use induction on k as suggested in (14.3.3) and Exercise 14.9.)

Exercise 14.11. Implement the multigrid algorithm described in Section 14.3 in the one-dimensional case.

Exercise 14.12. Implement the algorithms in Section 14.5 with $f(u) = mg \sin u$. Integrate for 1000 periods of oscillation.

Exercise 14.13. The loop-carried dependences in Program 14.1 prevent fast execution on the typical (pipeline) processors available today. The algorithm in Section 14.1.2 provides a way to do the equivalent of "loop splitting" (recall Program 4.4). Use this observation to write a faster sequential solver for a bidiagonal system. Compare with the standard algorithm in Program 14.1 to see how the change in order of arithmetic operations changes the results in floating point.

14.7 PROJECTS

The following projects require extensive testing and performance analysis. They build on the exercises and provide a chance to develop more serious computational systems. Moreover, the projects are not "stand alone" but build on each other. By combining appropriate ones, larger projects can be constructed.

To test your codes in the following projects, take any function u that satisfies the boundary conditions, for which you can easily compute (analytically) the function f defined by

$$f := -\frac{\partial^2 u}{\partial x^2} - \frac{\partial^2 u}{\partial y^2}. \tag{14.7.1}$$

For example, the quartic polynomial $u(x,y) = x(1-x)y(1-y)$ would be appropriate (f is a quadratic polynomial in this case).

Project 14.1. Implement the direct methods in Chapter 12 in the two-dimensional case for the matrix (14.1.6).

Project 14.2. Implement the multigrid algorithm described in Section 14.4 in the two-dimensional case.

Project 14.3. Certain models [23] for surface waves on deep water take the form

$$u_t - u_{xxt} + u_x + uu_x = 0, \tag{14.7.2}$$

where u denotes the wave height, x is the direction of propagation of the wave, and t is time. Equations of this form can be approximated easily by writing them in the form

$$(1 - \partial_{xx})\, u_t = -\left(u_x + uu_x\right). \tag{14.7.3}$$

Use multigrid to approximate the solution of

$$(1 - \partial_{xx})\, u_t = F(u) := -\left(u_x + uu_x\right) \tag{14.7.4}$$

and use your favorite time-stepping scheme to advance in time. Consider what happens when two solitary waves [23] collide.

Project 14.4. Apply the techniques of Section 14.5 to one of the molecular dynamics projects such as Project 13.2. Compare this with the technique of [11].

Chapter Fifteen
Sorting

To find a form that accommodates the mess, that is the task of the artist now—*Samuel Beckett*

This chapter surveys some basic parallel sorting algorithms. Sequential sorting methods are recalled in Section 15.1, and are then extended to parallel sorting in Section 15.2. Two parallel sorting methods, *bitonic sort* and *odd-even transposition sort*, are presented in Sections 15.2.1 and 15.2.2. In Section 15.3 examples from particle dynamics (Chapter 13) illustrate application of the methods. Parallel sorting and collective data movement, especially reductions (Chapter 6), draw from some similar principles. Data movement methods akin to those used in implementing parallel reduction operations are a fundamental component to efficient parallel sorting algorithms. In addition, we present in this chapter reduction operations employed to implement data structures that maintain sorted conditions as part of their specification.

15.1 INTRODUCTION

Sorting is an indispensable counterpart to many numerical methods where sorted data structures can reduce the complexity of algorithms downstream. Tasks such as finding a median value are effectively approached by first sorting a list. In Section 1.5.3, we saw that parallelizing sequential algorithms can introduce the need to reorder data computed in parallel by different processes back into a canonical form (see also Exercise 15.12). A more challenging example in this chapter maintains a spatial sort of particles in a limited interaction range n-body simulation to reduce the cost of determining interacting pairs and to reduce the amount of data communicated between processes. The parallel method for this problem formulated in Chapter 13 relied on an all process reduction of n force data, which can be performed in time $\mathcal{O}(n + \log p)$. That approach in its simplicity did not exploit the spatial locality inherent to the problem. In this chapter we present several algorithms that use sorting to maintain and exploit spatial coherence.

Sorting methods are generally either of the type where there is a comparison and exchange, for example, *quicksort* and *bubblesort* (see Program 15.1), or methods that use the key value to frisk the input in some spe-

```
procedure BubbleSort(n, list)
integer n, list(*), i, tmp
logical more
data more/.true./

tmp = list(1) + 1
do while (tmp.NE.list(1))
  tmp = list(1)
  do i = 2, n
     if (list(i-1).GT.list(i)) then
       tmp = list(i)
       list(i) = list(i-1)
       list(i-1) = tmp
     endif
  enddo
enddo

return
end
```

Program 15.1 Code implementing sequential **bubblesort**.

cial, predetermined way, such as with *bucket sort*. It can be shown that any comparative sorting algorithm requires at least $\mathcal{O}(n \log n)$ steps to sort n elements in the worst case. *Quicksort* has an average complexity of $\mathcal{O}(n \log n)$, and a worst case running time of $\mathcal{O}(n^2)$; the worst case time can be reduced by randomizing the input, leading to *randomized quicksort*. Both *heapsort* (see Program 15.3) and *mergesort* are asymptotically optimal (see [37]).

In cases where the sorted order can be determined by means other than comparing elements, the lower bound of comparative sorting can be surpassed. A sort of elements directly into an array – similar to histograms – can be performed with $\mathcal{O}(n)$ operations. However, extra memory, proportional to the *range* of data values, not just the *number* of them, may be required. A spatial bin sort is used in the particle interaction algorithm presented in Section 15.3. In addition to running time, an important sorting algorithm property to consider is the required memory. The algorithms bubblesort, insertion sort, quicksort, and heapsort sort *in place*; that is, the memory used in addition to the input list is bounded by a constant factor. This is an especially important consideration for many parallel sorting applications where multiple processors are harnessed to accommodate memory requirements through judicious distribution of data.

Motivated by theoretical and practical interest, many algorithms have been developed for sorting Not surprisingly, trade offs abound. Even the better overall performers – for example, randomized quicksort – may be outdone in special cases by less sophisticated algorithms. For example, for an already sorted list of n elements, quicksort will require $\mathcal{O}(n \log n)$ steps

```
subroutine InsertionSort(n, list)
integer n, list(*), i, tmp
logical more
data more/.true./

do i = 2, n
  tmp = list(i)
  j = i
  do while (tmp.LT.list(j−1))
     if (list(i−1).GT.list(i)) then
       list(j) = list(j−1)
       j = j − 1
     endif
  enddo
  list(j) = tmp
enddo

return
end
```

Program 15.2 Code implementing sequential **insertion sort**. Insertion sort is similar to sorting a bridge hand, one card at a time into a growing sorted sub-hand. With fewer instructions in the inner loop, insertion sort is preferable to bubblesort for most applications.

whereas bubblesort will require only $\mathcal{O}(n)$ steps (Program 15.1). The best sorting method for an application depends on issues including the frequency of sorting, the disorder of the list, available memory, and the practical performance needs of the application. This holds for sequential and parallel applications, where in general, parallelism complicates matters with additional concerns and trade offs.

15.2 PARALLEL SORTING

Parallel processing brings to sorting the possibility to perform numerous operations, such as comparisons, exchanges, binning, and counting, simultaneously in a given time interval. The optimal running time for comparative-based sorting of *n items* with *n processors* is $\mathcal{O}(\log n)$, which one might expect from the optimal serial complexity. Such algorithms have been found, for example, the parallelizable $\mathcal{O}(n \log n)$ *Hungarian* sorting algorithm. A look at the constant factors in the analysis, however, shows that the algorithm has limited practicality [2].

To adapt a serial algorithm for efficient parallel execution is not always easy, although straightforward parallel adaptation of simple algorithms can yield good speedup. For example, *odd-even transposition sort* in Program 15.4, a parallel analog of sequential bubblesort, is bounded above and below by $\mathcal{O}(n)$, for n elements and n processes [65]. Thus, assuming unit

```
      subroutine heapSort(n,in)
      logical more
      integer n, in(*), tmp, k, m, i, ink
      m = n
      do k = m/2, 1, -1
        ink = k
        call mkheap(ink,m,in)
      enddo
      more = .true.
      do while (more)
        tmp = in(1)
        in(1) = in(m)
        in(m) = tmp
        m = m - 1
        call mkheap(1,m,in)
        if (m.LE.1) more= .false.
      enddo
      return
      end
      subroutine mkheap(k,n,in)
      integer k, n, in(*), j, root
      logical more
      more = .true.
      root = in(k)
      do while (more)
        j = 2*k
        if (j.LT.n) then
          if (in(j).LT.in(j+1)) then
            j = j+1
          endif
        else if (j.GT.n) then
            return
        endif
        if (root.LT.in(j)) then
          in(k) = in(j)
          k = j
          in(k) = root
          more = .true.
        else
          more = .false.
        endif
      enddo
      return
      end
```

Program 15.3 Sequential heapsort. This routine is applied serially at each process to sort the local list. Serial heapsort is attractive due to its $\mathcal{O}(n \log n)$ operation count and since it sorts in place.

interprocess data movement costs (more on this below) the speedup for n processes could reach

$$S(n) = \frac{t_{bubble}^{sequential}}{t_{oddeven}^{parallel}} = \frac{An^2}{Bn} = \mathcal{O}(n)$$

for a parallel efficiency of A/B. To develop an *n-way* parallel algorithm with $\log n$ operations from a sequential algorithm with $n \log n$ operations is more challenging. In general inefficient sequential algorithms have excessive computational fat to trim, and as a result may realize impressive speedup in a parallel version.

Parallel sorting algorithms can be structured for specialized sorting networks, such as comparator networks, where one node houses a single datum and compares two. Such algorithms, for example, *bitonic sort* (Section 15.2.2), will likely require augmentation for scientific applications where typically one node houses many data. The complexities of sorting networks and algorithms that evolved from such network models are often presented in terms of operation counts alone (e.g., comparisons) since stated assumptions usually provide for a data transfer into and out of a node in one cycle. Typically, data movement phases will not be negligible to the overall running time.

In the parallel methods following, we consider 1) the cases with a single datum at each process, so $p = n$, and 2) the case where $n > p$, and p divides n to simplify the presentation. The input to the algorithms is a list of data elements

$$a_0, a_1, \ldots, a_{m-1}, a_m$$

which are evenly distributed across processes. The sorted list is a permutation of the input list

$$a_{i_0}, a_{i_1}, \ldots, a_{i_{m-1}}, a_{i_m}$$

such that for some comparison relation denoted by "<"

$$a_{i_0} < a_{i_1} < \cdots < a_{i_{m-1}} < a_{i_m},$$

where a_{i_j} is *owned* by (local to) process p_j. For $n > p$, a_i represents a sublist of data, and $a_i < a_j$ means that the comparison relation holds for all elements in the respective sublists.

15.2.1 Odd-even transposition sort

Bubblesort derives its name from elements *bubbling* upward through the list (in the inner loop). Odd-even transposition sort resembles bubblesort in the way elements *percolate* upward through the list. A single iteration consists of two phases – odd-even and even-odd – where data can move two positions if necessary, that is, across two processes, since each process holds a single datum in our simplified presentation (we relax this restriction below). A schematic of data-exchanging partners for odd-even sort on ten processes

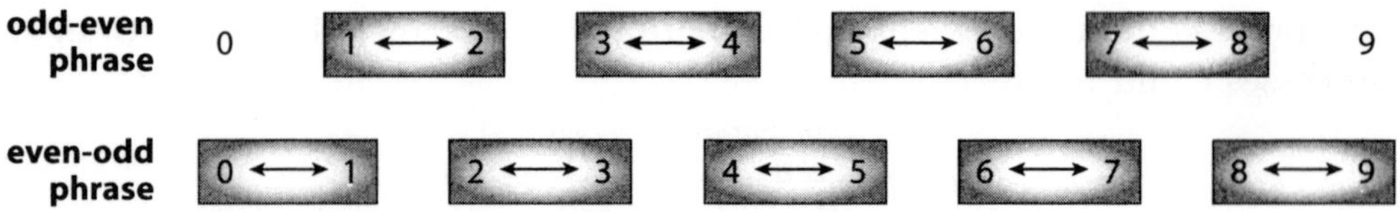

Figure 15.1 The exchange partners pictured here for odd-even sort are for a ten-process system. See Program 15.4 for an implementation.

is shown in Figure 15.1. The interprocess data exchange imposes a one-dimensional array (i.e., a ring), without wraparound, on the processes. The operation count for odd-even sort is bounded by $\mathcal{O}(n)$, for n elements and $p = n$ processes. More precisely, the algorithm is guaranteed to terminate after $n/2$ iterations [65].

Consider the implementation of odd-even sort transposition in Program 15.4. An odd-even sort iteration consists of an *odd-even phase* and an *even-odd phase*. The two phases are:

odd-even phase: the odd processes, p_i, access the value held by the logical neighbors, p_{i+1}, while the even processes, p_{i+1}, access the value held at the odd processes, p_i (Program 15.4, line 10). The odd processes discard the high value; the even processes discard the low value (Program 15.4, lines 11–15).

even-odd phase: the even processes, p_i, access the value held by the odd neighbor, p_{i+1}, while the odd processes, p_{i+1}, access the value held by the even neighbor, p_i (Program 15.4, line 17). The even processes discard the high value; the odd processes discard the low value (Program 15.4, lines 18–22).

The address calculations are calculated by the functions *OddEven* and *Even-Odd* as shown in the right column in Program 15.4.

The **P**fortran data exchange statements utilize the *functions of* `myProc` feature introduced in Section 8.4.3 to express in a single statement the bidirectional data exchange between neighboring nodes. This statement enables the compiler to generate node code that can perform the exchanges simultaneously.

15.2.2 Bitonic sort

Bitonic sort has a natural structure for parallel computation on hypercube networks. The method operates by successively exchanging items on families of hypercubes with members of increasing dimension (Figure 15.2). Knuth elaborates the general concept in [91] where a number of bitonic sorting networks are given. The sort algorithm diagrammed in Figure 15.2 is implemented in the code of Program 15.5 for the case in which each of p processes holds only one value. The number of independent phases in bitonic sort is bounded by $\mathcal{O}(\log^2 n)$.

```
      subroutine OddEvenSort(elmnt)
      integer elmnt, oddeven, evenodd, i, tmp, n
      logical ODD,EVEN
      ODD =(myProc-(myProc/2)*2.EQ.1)
      EVEN = .NOT.ODD
      n = nProc
      do i = 1, n/2
c   odd-even exchange
        tmp = elmnt@oddEven(myProc)
        if (ODD) then
          elmnt = MIN(tmp,elmnt)
        else
          elmnt = MAX(tmp,elmnt)
        endif
c   even-odd exchange
        tmp = elmnt@evenOdd(myProc)
        if (EVEN) then
          elmnt = MIN(tmp,elmnt)
        else
          elmnt = MAX(tmp,elmnt)
        endif
      enddo
      return
      end
      integer function oddEven(me)
      integer me, b
       b = MOD(me,2) + me
       if (me.EQ.0.OR.me.EQ.nProc0) then
         oddEven = me
       else
         oddEven = b - MOD(me+1,2)
       endif
      return
      end
      integer function evenOdd(me)
      integer me, b
         b = MOD(me+1,2) + me
         evenOdd = b - MOD(me,2)
      return
      end
```

Program 15.4 **P**fortran code implementing odd-even transposition sort, a parallel derivative of the sequential bubblesort algorithm.

The routine in Program 15.5 is hard-coded for a number of processes equal to a power of two, but can be generalized for any number of processes (see Exercise 15.6). Rather involved hypercube-based methods have been developed for sorting n items on n processes in $\mathcal{O}(\log n)$ steps. The interested reader is referred to [100].

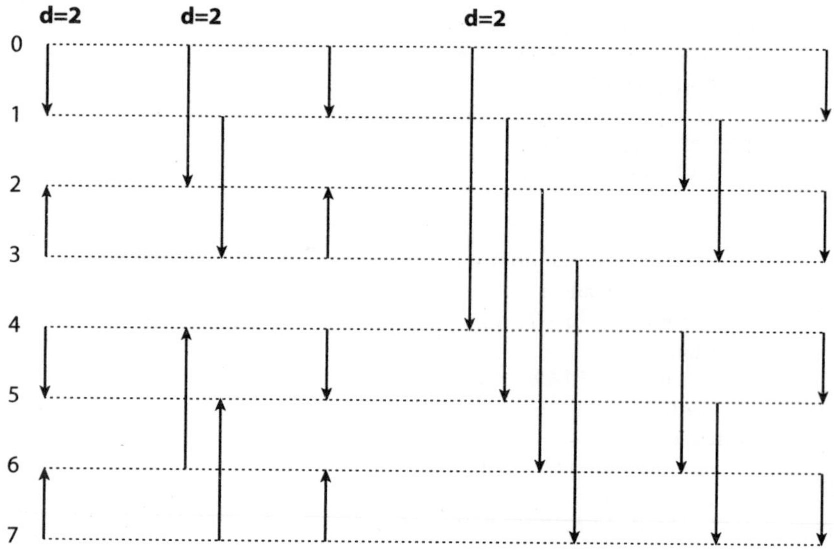

Figure 15.2 Bitonic sort exchanges for $p = 8$ processes are performed on three successive families of hypercubes with dimension *one*, *two*, and *three* [91].

The code given in Program 15.7 provides a simple test of parallel sort routines. It uses a random number generator to define a sequence

$$n_0, n_1, \ldots, n_{p-1}$$

in a method that can be used to test both the bitonic sort and the odd-even sort. For sorting a list with multiple data elements at each process, a practical strategy sorts the individual sets on each processor initially and after each exchange step.

15.3 SPATIAL SORTING

The presentation in Chapter 13 showed the $\mathcal{O}(n^2)$ pairwise force calculation reduced to $\mathcal{O}(n)$ complexity by using a cutoff radius. The cost to form the list of interacting pairs, however, was $\mathcal{O}(n^2)$. An improved variant for pair list construction for serial execution can be performed with a sorted atom list that retains the spatial locality of particles. The pair list extraction and force calculation from the sorted list can be performed in time $\mathcal{O}(n)$. As shown in Section 15.1, the sorting phase can be performed with comparative methods having worst-case running times with a lower bound of $\mathcal{O}(n \log n)$. In addition to comparative sorting of lists, data structures can be used to retain a spatial sort and improve the running time. The spatial decomposition described in [35] uses a three-dimensional array where each array element represents a spatial volume to bin atoms; a linked list associated with each volume element contains the atoms resident there. The pairwise interactions

```
      subroutine BitonicSort(n)
      integer x,i,j,d,ldim,n,iswch
      ldim = 1
      cubedim = log2(nProc)
      ipadr = myProc
      do 1000 j = 0, cubedim-1
        d = ldim
        ldim = ldim*2
        do 100 i = 0, j
          notd = minot_(d)
          ieven = miand_(ipadr,notd)
          iodd = mior_(ipadr,d)
          x@ieven = n@iodd
          x@iodd = n@ieven
          iswch = mod((ibit(myProc,ldim)+ibit(myProc,d)),2)
          if( iswch .EQ. 1 ) then
            n = MIN(x,n)
          else
            n = MAX(x,n)
          endif
          d = d/2
100     continue
1000  continue
      return
      end
c following are routines written in C

  int minot(int *mask) {
    return(~*mask);
  }
  int miand(int *mask,int *nask) {
    return(*mask&*nask);
  }
  int mior(int *mask,int *nask) {
    return(*mask|*nask);
  }
  int ibit(int *m, int *d) {
     return ( *m & *d );
  }
```

Program 15.5 The **bitonic sort** algorithm in **P**fortran. Each process begins with a single datum, n. The code uses the C bit-manipulation routines given at the right: `mior`, `minot`, and `miand` for the logical "or", "not," and "and" functions, respectively. Note the underscore after the C function names in the Fortran code, a widespread naming convention used by compilers and linkers for C routines called from Fortran.

are subsequently picked off directly from the data structure. Only particles within some spatial proximity interact using the nearest-neighbor model, so memory locality and cache utilization are enhanced with spatially coherent organizations. In the following sections, three methods that use spatial ordering are discussed for particle methods: the spatial decomposition [35], the monotonic Lagrangian grid [24], and Bentley's divide-and-conquer neighbor-list construction [19].

15.3.1 Spatial binning and the shift algorithm

A spatial decomposition for distributing particles and the computations associated with them improves interprocess locality, which in turn increases scalability and reduces data exchange costs. Consider a two-dimensional spatial decomposition with uniformly square process domains. These constraints can be extended straightforwardly for three-dimensional decompositions of nonuniform rectilinear domains, but presently simplify the discussion. Particles are assigned to domains based on particle coordinates, where particle k with coordinate (x_k, y_k) is assigned to the domain (i, j) that spans the coordinate intervals

$$[x_{i,j},\ x_{i,j+1}) \quad \text{and} \quad [y_{i,j},\ y_{i+1,j})$$

so that

$$x_{i,j} \ \le\ x_k \ <\ x_{i,j+1} \quad \text{and} \quad y_{i,j} \ \le\ y_k \ <\ y_{i+1,j}.$$

Binning particles into domains consists of a simple range check and assignment, an $\mathcal{O}(n)$ operation for n particles.

Figure 15.3 illustrates an application space subdivided into forty-nine domains, (i, j), seven domains in each dimension, with each domain assigned to a process. Each domain is *shadowed* by surrounding domains within the interaction distance, r. The highlighted central domain in Figure 15.3 is surrounded by twenty-four shadow domains that are marked with diagonal hashes. The following discussion is from the vantage point of this central domain, noting that all domains function independently as a central domain in addition to their roles as neighboring domains.

In many particle applications accesses to shadow regions for information such as particle coordinates are performed at every time step. Consequently, the application benefits from a tailored method for these accesses. One such method is the *shift algorithm* [35]. In the shift algorithm, all shadow region data are obtained from the four orthogonally adjacent domains in two dimensions and the six orthogonally adjacent domains in three dimensions, where we are assuming one domain per process. The exchange is performed in three *phases*: first along the x axis, then along the y axis, and finally along the z axis. Phase d (dimension d) consists of k_d subphases, $k_d = \lceil r_d/u_d \rceil$, where u_d and r_d are the domain extent and the interaction radius, respectively, for dimension d. A subphase consists of an exchange with

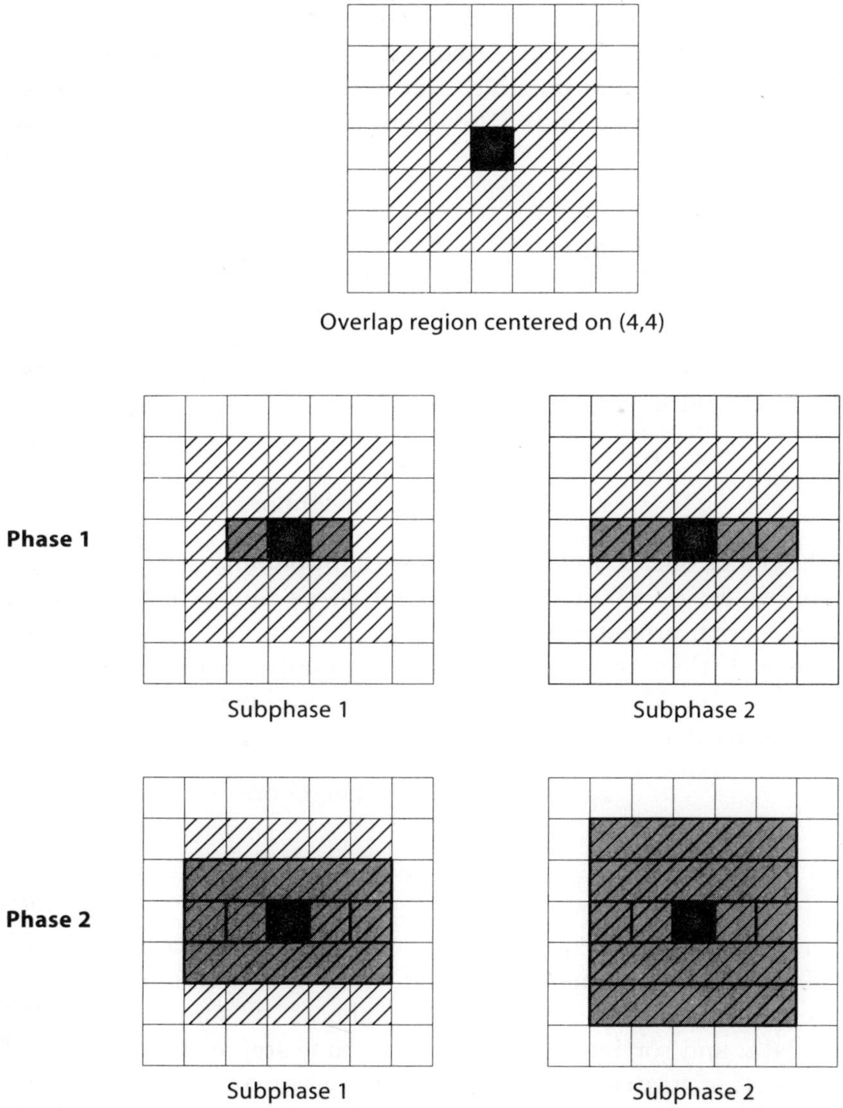

Figure 15.3 Two-dimensional shift communication viewed from the region centered on domain (4,4) with $k_1 = k_2 = 2$. The diagonal hashed regions in the topmost representation show the domains required by (4,4) to perform its calculation, sometimes called *shadow regions*. As the algorithm proceeds (see text for details), those regions buffered by (4,4) by communicating with *adjacent* neighbors are shaded.

the two neighbor processes along the axis of the current phase. Within each phase, the first subphase will shift all data received in all previous phases; within phase one, this will be the set of local atoms. For all subphases after the basis, a process will communicate to each of its two neighbors the data received in the immediately preceding subphase from the opposing neighbor [35]. A natural network topology for the shift algorithm is a three-dimensional mesh where communication could proceed simultaneously without link contention. Other efficient embeddings and algorithms for the data exchange are possible. Detailed discussions of embeddings are outside the scope of this book (the interested reader may consult [100] for an introduction).

15.3.2 Nearly sorted data

A characteristic of many sorting problems in scientific computing is the need to sort data that are only slightly out of order. Consider for the moment a fictitious application in which we start with a sorted list of numbers $x_0 < x_1 < \cdots < x_n$ and repeat an iteration of the form

$$\begin{aligned} &for\ i = 1, n-1 \\ &\qquad x_i \leftarrow \text{average of its neighbors} \pm \epsilon \end{aligned} \tag{15.3.1}$$

where the choice of $\pm$ is done randomly with probability $p(x_i)$, where $p(x) := 1 - x$ and we fix $x_0 = 0$ and $x_n = 1$. That is, we choose + with probability $p(x_i)$ and $-$ with probability $1 - p(x_i)$.

If $\epsilon = 0$, then the iteration (15.3.1) rapidly converges to $x_i = i\Delta x$, where $\Delta x = 1/n$. Moreover, without the random perturbation, the points stay ordered so that

$$x_i \leftarrow \text{average of its neighbors}$$

means

$$x_i \leftarrow (x_{i-1} + x_{i+1})/2. \tag{15.3.2}$$

However, when $\epsilon/\Delta x$ becomes large enough, there is a certain probability that points will become unordered, and things get more interesting.

Computation of the "average of neighbors" is simple via (15.3.2) for ordered data, and sorting the data at each time step can ensure this. However, the sorting strategy is quite different in the case when you suspect the data may already be sorted, or nearly so. The first question to ask is what method can be used to determine if data *are* sorted.

One algorithm that is simple to state begins by checking neighbors (in a ring topology) to see if the local data are sorted. This is the basic step in either the bitonic sort or the odd-even sort. At this step each processor has a Boolean variable `sorted` which is true if the data are sorted locally. More precisely, processors i and $i-1$ exchange data, and processor i sets `sorted=TRUE` if the datum at $i-1$ precedes that of i. This is done for $i = 1, \ldots, P-1$, and processor 0 sets `sorted=TRUE`. Then we compute a simple reduction to take the logical "and" of all the values. This can be done in IPC (Section 8.5) via

$$\texttt{sorted} = \texttt{miand}\{\texttt{sorted}\}\,; \tag{15.3.3}$$

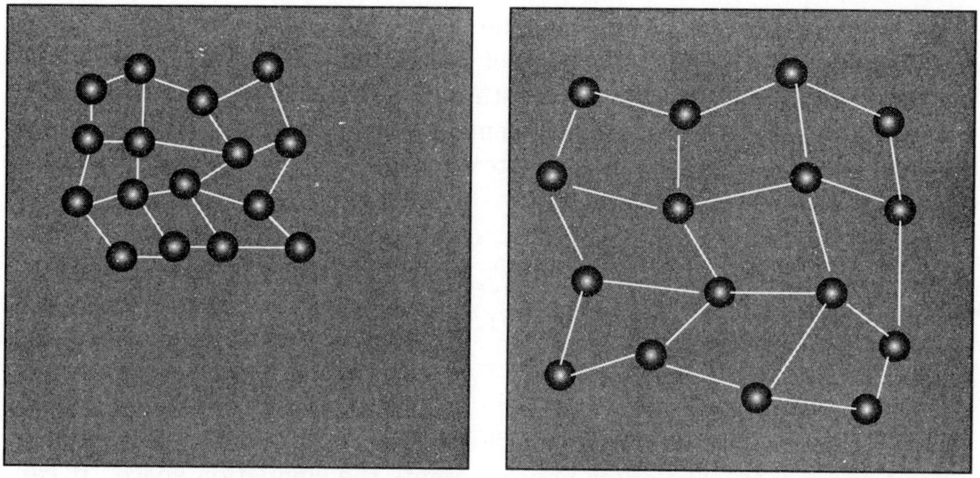

Figure 15.4 A 16-cell, two-dimensional MLG for a 16 particle system at times t and $t + \delta t$. It can be seen that the MLG follows particle motion, assuming that particle positions within the MLG are unchanged.

where `miand` is the C function defined in Program 15.5. We thus find out (in $\log P$ steps on a ring) at all processors if all the data are sorted.

If data are not sorted, then a sort algorithm needs to be used to sort the data. But again, it makes sense to pick an algorithm which has the chance to terminate early if data get sorted early. Odd-even sort can be modified to have this property. One simple implementation would be to do one step of odd-even sort, which involves exchanging local data and merging if the data are not already in sorted order. If the data are sorted we set `sorted=TRUE` (and otherwise `sorted=FALSE`), and then we compute the reduction in (15.3.3). If the amount of data transferred in each exchange step is large, this can be an efficient solution. However, if only a small amount of data is being exchanged, the extra cost of (15.3.3) at each step may be too much to bear; see Exercise 15.13.

15.3.3 Monotonic Lagrangian Grid

The presentation in Section 15.3.1 described inserting particles into bins where the bins corresponded to a fixed volume of space. To decompose the problem for distributed processing, the space (implemented as a two-dimensional array) was decomposed into contiguous, rectilinear sections of bins. That approach, where spatial elements are fixed and moving particles migrate among spatial elements, is an Eulerian approach, borrowing terminology from classical mechanics. The complementary Lagrangian approach has no fixed grid, and everything moves along with particles.

The underlying method of the Monotonic Lagrangian Grid (MLG) associates particles to positions rather than spatial extents.We use the MLG to refer to either the method or the data structure of the method. The word "grid" here just means a mesh, not the world-wide computational grid [48]; see Chapter 14 for a brief discussion of the latter. The MLG retains spatial integrity with a sort using keys consisting of particle coordinates. We define a mesh, $G(\mathrm{nx}, \mathrm{ny}, \mathrm{nz})$, where each element of the mesh, (i, j, k), holds one particle with the Cartesian coordinate $< x, y, z >$. We say that the mesh, G, is in MLG order provided that

$$\begin{aligned} x(i,j,k) \leq & x(i+1,j,k), \quad 1 \leq i < \mathrm{nx}, \\ y(i,j,k) \leq & y(i,j+1,k), \quad 1 \leq j < \mathrm{ny}, \\ z(i,j,k) \leq & z(i,j,k+1), \quad 1 \leq k < \mathrm{nz}. \end{aligned} \tag{15.3.4}$$

A two-dimensional MLG for 16 particles in Figure 15.4 shows the system at times t and $t + \delta t$. The outer box represents the simulation space. It can be seen that the MLG automatically follows the particles. The evolution pictured in the figure could be representative of, for example, a liquid argon simulation where the atoms expand into a vacuum. It should be clear from the MLG conditions that a displacement in particle coordinates need not result in a movement of particles within the MLG, but it may.

The MLG was proposed by Jay Boris to facilitate effective use of vector processors for n-body (particle dynamics) simulations with limited range potentials, such as molecular dynamics with a cutoff radius [24, 96].[1] The interacting pairs can be extracted from the MLG in linear time using a **near neighbor template** (NNT). The NNT is applied by first selecting a *focal node*; a focal node is just an element of the MLG, and consequently, corresponds to a particle. Applied like a stencil, the NNT is centered on a node with the interacting particles (near neighbors) masked and read from the mesh. For example, the function in Program 15.6 implements an NNT with dimensions: $2r+1, 2s+1$, and $2t+1$. The code fragment uses an MLG, G, where a unique particle identifier, *gan*, is stored at each MLG position (i, j, k); a list of *gans* is returned in the data structure, *PairList*, for the particle at (i, j, k).

The NNT provides neighbors within some spatial volume with some probability. To use the MLG successfully, the application must take into account the relationship of the NNT and MLG with application space, so as, for example, to acquire with 100% probability all particles within some desired interaction radius, r. The following construction for establishing MLG order further illustrates the relationship of the MLG to application space.

[1]Bentley mentions an approach in a 1975 report which uses super-keys composed of coordinates, which can be seen to resemble the MLG approach; proposed by Edward McCreight in a private communication [18]. It appears, however, that Boris first formalized and investigated the method.

```
function NNT3D(G,i,j,k,r,s,t,PairList)
integer G(*,*,*),i,j,k,r,s,t,PairList(*),ip

ip = 0
do ik = k-2*t, k+2*t
  do ij = j-2*s, j+2*s
    do ii = i-2*r, i+2*r
      ip = ip + 1
      PairList(ip) = G(ii,ij,ik)
    enddo
  enddo
enddo

return
end
```

Program 15.6 Code implementing the NNT of dimension $2r+1, 2s+1, 2t+1$ for focal node i, j, k. Note that the focal atom is also returned to simplify the loop; the calling routine can adjust for this.

15.3.3.1 Constructing an MLG

An MLG can be established for a collection of particles with a series of sorts thereby satisfying the MLG conditions in (15.3.4). The outline for the procedure is:

i) Sort the entire MLG in order of increasing *z coordinate*, where the traversal order is fastest in the *x index*, next in the *y index*, and slowest in the *z index*.

ii) Using sort order from previous step, sort each *xy plane* (constant z) independently in order of increasing *y coordinate*, where the traversal order is fastest in the *x index* and slowest in the *y index*.

iii) Using sort order from previous two steps, sort each *x row* (constant y) independently in order of increasing *x coordinate*, where the traversal order is over the *x index*.

Each sort phase operates on a one-dimensional list: in the first phase, the list threads through the entire MLG; in the second phase, there are nz lists each threading through a single *xy plane*; in the third and final phase, there are ny × nz lists, each sorted independently. The entire sort can be performed in $\mathcal{O}(n \log n)$ time, where $n = \text{nx} \times \text{ny} \times \text{nz}$, using heapsort in Program 15.3, for example.

After MLG order is established, particle motion makes it necessary periodically to reorder the MLG, or to check the mesh at least. For initially establishing MLG order it is a good idea to use a generally robust sorting algorithm such as heapsort or randomized quicksort. What method one selects for reestablishing MLG order on a previously ordered mesh, however,

Initialize application
Decompose and distribute data
`Establish MLG order`
    `Interprocess sort using bitonic sort`
    `Local sort using heapsort`
Repeat
    Perform application specific tasks
    Extract neighbors from MLG using NNT
    Redistribute data for MLG ordering if necessary
    `Reestablish MLG order`
        `Interprocess sort using insertion sort`
        `Local sort using insertion sort`
    `Exchange boundary data`
    Redistribute data for application if necessary
    Perform application specific tasks
Until done
Exit application

Figure 15.5 An application utilizing an MLG for determining neighbors. *Redistribution steps* are italicized; `MLG related steps` are in typewriter font. Note the choice of sorting algorithms has assumed that the particle motions only slightly perturb the MLG between reordering steps. Should the exchange of boundary data be considered part of MLG overhead?

depends on the application and particle motion. The displacements of atoms in a molecular dynamics simulation of proteins in water are small over, say, several femtosecond time steps; also, the atoms tend to retain approximate relative positions to other atoms in proteins; water molecules tend to migrate, but slowly. An application tracking projectiles and aircraft in space, on the other hand, could confront rapidly changing orientations. The slow moving molecular dynamics particles will result in MLGs only slightly out of order, and therefore a simple sort such as bubblesort or insertion sort could give performance close to linear. For reordering MLGs significantly out of order one is advised to use a sorting algorithm likely to give $\mathcal{O}(n \log n)$ performance.

15.3.3.2 Parallelizing an MLG

We consider the three operations concomitant with parallelizing an application with an MLG:

i) establishing and maintaining MLG order,
ii) exchange of boundary information, and
iii) extracting the neighbors with the NNT.

We have seen in this chapter methods to perform a parallel sort for the first item. To recap, the parallel sort process consists of:

– a parallel method to exchange sublists among processes, and

– a sequential method to merge and sort locally two sublists between interprocess exchanges.

For the purpose of sorting we assume the likely case that a process will hold more than one cell of the MLG. Two methods in this chapter to exchange sublists during a sort are *bitonic sort* (Program 15.5) and *odd-even sort* (Program 15.4). The local, sequential sort could be any number of sorts from *insertion sort* to *quicksort*. The MLG can be decomposed in a number of ways. The decompositions involve various tradeoffs in data movement, which ultimately depend on the application. Some choices for decomposition are by slabs, rows, or blocks. It is likely that each particle will interact with neighbors in x, y, and z. If so, the exchange of boundary information between processes will decrease with a decrease in the *surface-to-volume ratio* (see Section 2.6.5). Accordingly, the decomposition strategies in order of increasing inter-process information exchange are blocks $<$ slabs $<$ rows. For establishing and maintaining MLG order, on the other hand, the preferred decomposition maintains continuity between complete, adjacent rows to minimize inter-process data exchange during the sort. Thus, for the purpose of sorting, the decomposition strategies could differ from the optimal strategy for data exchange. In the final analysis, application and performance parameters determine the favorable decomposition(s).

Nearest neighbors are extracted from the MLG for each particle using the NNT in a fashion outlined in the Fortran function in Program 15.6. Missing MLG boundary data are exchanged at some point after MLG order is established, thereby updating the new particle configuration at MLG nodes. Thus, with buffered boundary data, the cost to extract neighbors with the NNT is linear in the number of particles. It is interesting to speculate whether the cost to exchange boundary data should be considered as part of the MLG overhead. Figure 15.5 gives an outline of an application using the parallel MLG.

15.3.4 Divide-and-conquer for neighbor list construction

In this section we outline Bentley's divide-and-conquer method for determining interacting neighbors for a cutoff-based approach [19]. In contrast to a predefined domain decomposition, this method lends itself to dynamically adapting the size and number of domains to evolving particle distributions. Such an approach could be parallelized using a dynamic thread-based model (see Section 7.3), with threads assigned to domains during the recursive process described below. The method is also an alternative to bin-sorting local atoms described in Section 15.3.1. Consider a collection of n particles in two dimensions, where particles interact within radius r. The method proceeds by first segmenting the space into two subspaces, A and B, then recursively solving the problem again for each subspace. The near-neighbor problem is thereby reduced to finding all pairs with one partner in A and the other in B for each step in the recursion (Figure 15.6).

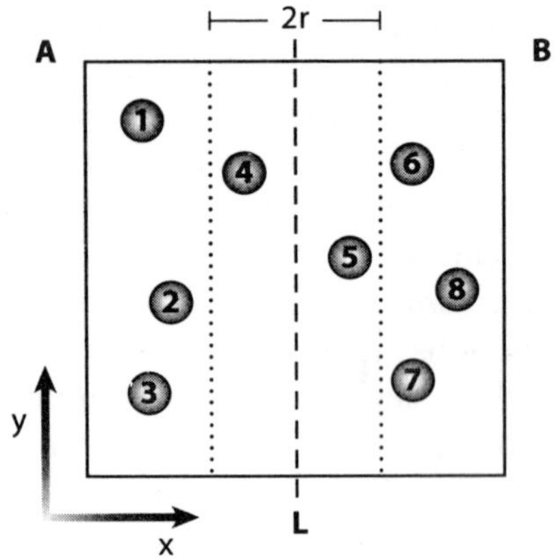

Figure 15.6 Divide-and-conquer neighbors scheme. The problem is halved at each step by the line L, which divides the collection of particles into two subproblems. The neighbor problem is solved at each recursive step within r on either side of L; for the step pictured here, particles 4 and 5 are considered. The next step will solve the problem independently for particle set A $(1, 2, 3, \text{and } 4)$, and set B $(5, 6, 7, \text{and } 8)$. See text for details.

Initially, the list of n particles is sorted in order of increasing x. The bisection of the space into A and B will be along the median x value. The sequential sort for this can be performed in time $\mathcal{O}(n \log n)$. To determine the pairs along the bisector, particles within r of it in A and B are identified and projected onto it (particles 4 and 5 in Figure 15.6). The projection of the particles along the bisector consists of sorting the coordinates into a list in order of increasing y coordinate (note the coordinate sense in Figure 15.6). For each particle i with coordinate (x_i, y_i) in this list, particles in the range $[y_i - r,\ y_i + r]$ are scanned and checked for the proximity distance, r. The total scan complexity is $\mathcal{O}(n)$ provided that the points in each recursive step are sparse along the bisector (see [19]). Thus, the overall scan cost is linear in the number of particles, so that the total running time for n particles is given by the recurrence

$$T(n) = 2T(n/2) + \mathcal{O}(n) \tag{15.3.5}$$

whence $T(n) = \mathcal{O}(n \log n)$ (see Exercise 15.9). Care must be taken in determining the effectiveness of the method for a problem. To see where things can go amiss, consider an extreme case where the extent of each dimensions in a two-dimensional problem space is equal to $r/2$. Then the projection onto the bisector contains all particles, and the scan for pairs on the bisector is not linear in the number of particles, but rather is quadratic in the number. Thus, the method's performance depends in part on the relative size of the cutoff radius with respect to the size of the simulation space. This condition relates to the sparsity condition along the bisector discussed in [19].

```
program TestSort
integer myvalue0,myvalue1
myvalue0 = MOD(17*myProc,63)
write(6,*) myProc,myvalue0
call SortSubroutine(myvalue0)
write(6,*) myProc,myvalue0
stop
end
```

Program 15.7 Code to test parallel sorting routines. Use this with `SortSubroutine` changed to either `OddEvenSort` or `BitonicSort` as appropriate.

15.4 EXERCISES

Exercise 15.1. Determine which function of n in each pair is asymptotically larger: (a.) n or $\log^2 n$? (b.) $n!$ or a^n ? (c.) $n!$ or n^n ?

Exercise 15.2. Implement and run the bitonic sort routine with 2^k processes for various values of k and one datum per process. See Program 15.7 for a test code.

Exercise 15.3. Implement and run the odd-even sort routine with 2^k processes for various values of k and one datum per process. See Program 15.7 for a test code.

Exercise 15.4. Modify the bitonic sort algorithm to sort a list of numbers whose length is m times the number of processors, for some integer m. (Hint: first sort in each processor before exchanging an array of numbers.)

Exercise 15.5. Modify the odd-even sort algorithm to sort a list of numbers whose length is m times the number of processors, for some integer m. (Hint: first sort in each processor before exchanging an array of numbers.) For a test, use the initial values $n = \text{modulo}(131 \times \text{myProc}, 16383)$ (cf. Program 15.7).

Exercise 15.6. Rewrite the bitonic sort routine Program 15.5 in ℙC for any number of processes not necessarily a power of two. Discuss any trade offs in your method. What is the complexity?

Exercise 15.7. The "shift" data exchange method is the counterpart to the sort implemented for spatial decompositions (Section 15.3.1). "Shift" buffers data at processes permitting them to select neighbors from a local data structure. Derive an expression for the data movement costs of "shift" as a function of the data moved and the number of messages; use the parameters α and β, where α is the time to send the null message (latency) and β is the average time to send a datum between two processes. (Hint: use geometric arguments to derive the formula.)

Exercise 15.8. Suppose that the spatial decomposition, $\mathcal{S}$, consists of two-dimensional rectangular regions indexed by pairs of integers (i, j) such that

$$\mathcal{S} = \{(i, j) \mid 1 < i, j < \text{ndomains}\}$$

is constructed as described in Section 15.3.1. For the two-dimensional spatial decomposition $\mathcal{S}$ and the spatial domain (i, j), the set of *k-adjacent* domains is defined to be the set of domains

$$\mathcal{A}_k(i, j) = \{(r, s) \mid \ i - k \le r \le i + k \text{ and } j - k \le s \le j + k\}.$$

For a process to acquire the data in k-adjacent domains is to satisfy k-adjacency. Prove that the shift algorithm described in Section 15.3.1 satisfies k-adjacency. Hint: The shift data exchange method can be viewed as groups of communicating processes where each group satisfies the near-neighbor requirements of a central process (cell). Note that each process is a member of numerous groups and that the group exchanges are intermingled as the shift algorithm unfolds.

Exercise 15.9. The recurrence

$$T(n) = 2T(n/2) + \mathcal{O}(n) \tag{15.4.1}$$

is typical for divide-and-conquer algorithm complexity. Prove that $T(n) = \mathcal{O}(n \log n)$.

Exercise 15.10. Odd-even transposition sort can be used for one datum per process and for lists of data per process.

a. Consider a sequence of integers $a_0, a_i, \ldots, a_n$, and a collection of p processes, where p is equal to the number of data, n. Prove that for any values of a_i odd-even transposition sort results in the sorted list $a'_0, a'_i, \ldots, a'_n$ such that $a'_0 \le a'_1 \le \cdots \le a'_n$.

b. Suppose $n > p$ and that p *divides* n, in other words, that each process, p_i, has a list of elements, s_i, where $|s_i| = |s_j|, \ \forall\ i, j$. Prove that the odd-even exchange pattern results in a sort provided that a local sort and merge is performed.

Exercise 15.11. Code the odd-even transposition sort for lists of data per process. Use heap sort for the initial local sorts.

Exercise 15.12. Augment the prime number sieve code in Section 1.5.3 to implement the sorting/merging necessary to collect the set indicated in (1.5.6).

Exercise 15.13. Derive a variant of odd-even sort which will terminate in $\log P$ steps *after* data have already become sorted. (Hint: one way is to keep track of how much is known to be sorted while doing data exchange. Consider the algorithm for implementing (15.3.3) and see if you can compute something similar while doing data exchange.)

15.5 PROJECTS

The following projects will require some data sets to be sorted. Fortunately, it is easy to check to see if a data set is sorted, so the verification of the programs is relatively easy. There are a number of ways to develop sets of randomly ordered things. For one thing, you can generate random numbers $n_k = (pk \bmod q)$ with p and q large primes (see Program 15.7 and Exercise 15.5). Or you can take a text file such as `/usr/dict/english` (or `/usr/dict/words`) in `Unix` and modify it by deleting the first character of every word.

Project 15.1. Compare bitonic sort and odd-even transposition sort (cf. Exercise 15.11) on a series of large data sets.

Project 15.2. Implement a parallel version of quick sort [126] and apply it to a series of large data sets.

Project 15.3. Compare bitonic sort, odd-even sort, and parallel quick sort (Project 15.2) on a series of large data sets.

Project 15.4. Implement the MLG sorting algorithm and apply it to a molecular dynamics simulation, such as Project 13.2.

Bibliography

[1] Jeanne C. Adams, Walter S. Brainerd, Jeanne T. Martin, Brian T. Smith, and Jerrold L. Wagener. *Fortran 95 Handbook.* MIT Press, 1997.

[2] M. Ajtai, J. Komlos, and E. Szemeredi. Sorting in *c log n* steps. *Combinatorica*, 3(1):1–19, 1983.

[3] F. Allen, G. Almasi, W. Andreoni, D. Beece, B. J. Berne, A. Bright, J. Brunheroto, C. Cascaval, J. Castanos, P. Coteus, P. Crumley, A. Curioni, M. Denneau, W. Donath, M. Eleftheriou, B. Fitch, B. Fleischer, C. J. Georgiou, R. Germain, M. Giampapa, D. Gresh, M. Gupta, R. Haring, H. Ho, P. Hochschild, S. Hummel, T. Jonas, D. Lieber, G. Martyna, K. Maturu, J. Moreira, D. Newns, M. Newton, R. Philhower, T. Picunko, J. Pitera, M. Pitman, R. Rand, A. Royyuru, V. Salapura, A. Sanomiya, R. Shah, Y. Sham, S. Singh, M. Snir, F. Suits, R. Swetz, W. C. Swope, N. Vishnumurthy, T. J. C. Ward, H. Warren, and R. Zhou. Blue Gene: A vision for protein science using a petaflop supercomputer. *IBM Systems Journal*, 40(2):310–327, 2001.

[4] Randy Allen and Ken Kennedy. *Optimizing Compilers for Modern Architectures: A Dependence-based Approach.* Morgan Kaufmann, 2001.

[5] Bowen Alpern, Larry Carter, Ephraim Feig, and Ted Selker. The uniform memory hierarchy model of computation. *Algorithmica*, 12:72–109, 1994.

[6] B. Alpern, L. Carter, and J. Ferrante. Modeling parallel computers as memory hierarchies. In W. K. Giloi, S. Jahnichen, and B. D. Shriver, editors, *Programming Models for Massively Parallel Computers*, pages 116–123. IEEE Computer Society Press, 1993.

[7] Gene M. Amdahl. Validity of the single-processor approach to achieving large scale computing capabilities. In *AFIPS Conference Proceedings*, volume 30, pages 483–485. AFIPS Press, April 1967.

[8] Jennifer M. Anderson, Saman P. Amaraasinghe, and Monica S. Lam. Data and computation tranformations for multiprocessors. In *Proceedings of the Fifth ACM SIGPLAN Symposium on Principles and*

Practice of Parallel Programming, pages 166–178. Assoc. Computing Machinery, July 1995.

[9] G. R. Andrews. Concepts and notations for concurrent programming. *ACM Computing Surveys*, 15:3–69, Jan. 1983.

[10] Eduard Ayguada, Jordi Garcia, and Ulrich Kremer. Tools and techniques for automatic data layout: A case study. *Parallel Computing*, 24(3-4):557–578, 1998.

[11] L. Baffico, S. Bernard, Y. Maday, G. Turinici, and G. Zérah. Parallel-in-time molecular-dynamics simulations. *Phys. Rev. E*, 66:057701, 2002.

[12] Babak Bagheri, Terry Clark, and L. Ridgway Scott. $\mathbb{P}$fortran: a parallel extension of Fortran (the $\mathbb{P}$fortran reference manual). Research Report UH/MD 124, Dept. Math., Univ. Houston, 1992.

[13] Babak Bagheri. *Parallel Programming with Guarded Objects*. PhD thesis, Pennsylvania State Univ., 1994.

[14] B. Bagheri, A. Ilin, and L. R. Scott. A comparison of shared and distributed memory scalable parallel processors: 1. KSR shared memory. In *Proceedings of the Scalable High-Performance Computing Conference*, pages 9–16, Knoxville, Tennessee, May 1994. IEEE Computer Society Press.

[15] B. Bagheri, B. Raghavachari, and L. R. Scott. Sharing variables in parallel programs. Research Report UH/MD 79, Dept. Math., Univ. Houston, 1990.

[16] Siegfried Benkner and Thomas Brandes. Exploiting data locality on scalable shared memory machines with data parallel programs. *Springer Lecture Notes in Computer Science*, 1900:647–657, 2000.

[17] Siegfried Benkner and Hans P. Zima. Compiling High Performance Fortran for distributed-memory architectures. *J. Parallel Comp.*, 25:1785–1825, 1999.

[18] Jon Louis Bentley. A survey of techniques for fixed radius near neighbor searching. Technical Report SLAC-186, STAN-CS-75-513, Stanford Linear Accelerator Center, Stanford Univ., August 1975. Available from National Technical Information Service, U.S. Department of Commerce, 5285 Port Royal Rd., Springfield, VA, 22161.

[19] Jon Louis Bentley. Multidimensional divide-and-conquer. *Comm. of the ACM*, 23(4):214–229, April 1980.

[20] A. Berman and R. J. Plemmons. *Nonnegative Matrices in the Mathematical Sciences*. Academic Press, 1979.

[21] Arthur J. Bernstein. Program analysis for parallel processing. *IEEE Trans. Electronic Computers*, EC-15(5):757–763, 1966.

[22] H. Berryman, J. Saltz, and J. Scroggs. Execution time support for adaptive scientific algorithms on distributed memory machines. *Concurrency: Practice and Experience*, 3(3):159–178, June 1991.

[23] J. L. Bona, W. G. Pritchard, and L. R. Scott. Solitary-wave interaction. *Physics of Fluids*, 23:438–441, 1980.

[24] J.P. Boris. A vectorized "near neighbors" algorithm of order n using a monotonic logical grid. *J. Comp. Phys.*, 66:1–20, 1986.

[25] S. Brenner and L. R. Scott. *The Mathematical Theory of Finite Element Methods, 2nd ed.* Springer-Verlag, 2002.

[26] B. R. Brooks and M. Hodoscek. Parallelization of CHARMM for MIMD machines. *Chemical Design Automation News*, 7:16–22, 1992.

[27] Richard L. Burden and J. Douglas Faires. *Numerical Analysis.* PWS-Kent, 1993.

[28] D. Callahan and K. Kennedy. Compiling programs for distributed-memory multiprocessors. *Journal of Supercomputing*, 2:151–169, October 1988.

[29] Donald L. D. Caspar and Eric Fontano. Five-fold symmetry in crystalline quasicrystal lattices. *Proc. Nat. Acad. Sci.*, 93:14271–14278, 1996.

[30] Rohit Chandra, Leonardo Dagum, Dave Kohr, Dror Maydan, Jeff McDonald, and Ramesh Menon. *Parallel Programming in OpenMP.* Morgan Kaufmann, 2000.

[31] Barbara Chapman, Piyush Mehrotra, and Hans P. Zima. Enhancing openmp with features for locality control. In W. Zwieflhofer and N. Kreitz, editors, *Proc. Eighth ECMWF Workshop on the Use of Parallel Processors in Meteorology "Towards Teracomputing"*, pages 301–313. World Scientific, 1999.

[32] Terry Clark, J. Andrew McCammon, and L. Ridgway Scott. Parallel molecular dynamics. In *Proc. Fifth SIAM Conf. on Parallel Proc. for Sci. Comp., J. Dongarra et al. ed's*, pages 338–344. SIAM, 1992.

[33] Terry Clark, Reinhard von Hanxleden, Ken Kennedy, Charles Koelbel, and L. Ridgway Scott. Evaluating parallel languages for molecular dynamics computations. In *Scalable High Performance Computing Conference*, Williamsburg, VA, 1992.

[34] Terry Clark, Reinhard von Hanxleden, and Ken Kennedy. Experiences in data-parallel programming. *Scientific Programming*, 6:153–158, 1997.

[35] Terry Clark, Reinhard von Hanxleden, J. Andrew McCammon, and L. Ridgway Scott. Parallelizing molecular dynamics using spatial decomposition. In *Proceedings of the Scalable High Performance Computing Conference*, pages 95–102, Knoxville, TN, May 1994. IEEE Computer Society. Available via anonymous ftp from `softlib.rice.edu` as `pub/CRPC-TRs/reports/CRPC-TR93356-S`.

[36] Terry Clark. Attributes of molecular dynamics calculations: Accounting for CPU cycles. In Michael Heath, Virginia Torczon, Greg Astfalk, Petter E. Bjorstad, Alan H. Karp, Charles H. Koelbel, Vipin Kumar, Robert F. Lucas, Layne T. Watson, and David E. Womble, editors, *Proc. Eighth SIAM Conf. on Parallel Proc. for Sci. Comp.*, pages 338–344. SIAM, 1997.

[37] Thomas H. Cormen, Charles E. Leiserson, and Ronald L. Rivest. *Introduction to Algorithms.* MIT Press and McGraw-Hill, 1996.

[38] R. Das, R. v. Hanxleden, K. Kennedy, C. Koelbel, and J. Saltz. Compiler analysis for irregular problems. In *Proceedings of the Fifth Workshop on Languages and Compilers for Parallel Computing*, New Haven, CT, 1992.

[39] Stephen E. DeBolt and Peter A. Kollman. AMBERCUBE MD, parallelization of AMBER's molecular dynamics module for distributed-memory hypercube computers. *J. Comp. Chem.*, 14(3):312–329, 1993.

[40] Xie Dexuan, Tamar Schlick, and L. R. Scott. Analysis of the SHAKE-SOR algorithm for constrained molecular dynamics simulations. *Methods Appl. Anal.*, 7:577–590, 2001.

[41] Edsger W. Dijkstra. Cooperating sequential processes. In F. Genuys, editor, *Programming Languages: NATO Advanced Study Institute*, pages 43–112. Academic Press, 1968.

[42] E. W. Dijkstra. Go to statement considered harmful. *Comm. of the ACM*, 11(3):147–148, March 1968.

[43] Hong-Qiang Ding, Naoki Karasawa, and William A. Goddard III. Atomic level simulations on a million particles: The cell multipole method for Coulomb and London nonbond interactions. *J. Comp. Phys.*, 97(6):4309–4315, 1992.

[44] C. I. Draghicescu. An efficient implementation of particle methods for the incompressible Euler equations. *SIAM J. Numer. Anal.*, 31:1090–1108, 1994.

[45] Jordi Garcia Eduard Ayguada and Ulrich Kremer. Tools and techniques for automatic data layout: A case study. *Parallel Computing*, 24(3-4):557–578, 1998.

[46] R. E. Filman and D. P. Friedman. *Co-ordinated Computing.* McGraw-Hill, 1984.

[47] Message Passing Interface Forum. MPI: A message-passing interface standard. *J. Supercomputer Appl. and High Perf. Comput.*, 8:849–860, 1994.

[48] Ian Foster and Carl Kesselman. *The Grid.* Morgan Kaufmann, 1999.

[49] G. C. Fox, M. Johnson, G. Lyzenga, S. Otto, J. Salmon, and D. Walker. *Solving Problems on Concurrent Multiprocessors.* Prentice-Hall, 1988.

[50] G. A. Geist, Adam Beguelin, Jack Dongarra, Weicheng Jiang, Robert Manchek, and Vaidy Sunderam. *PVM: Parallel Virtual Machine.* MIT Press, 1994.

[51] G. A. Geist and C. H. Romine. LU factorization algorithms on distributed-memory multiprocessor architectures. *SIAM J. Sci. Stat. Comput.*, 9:639–649, 1988.

[52] David Gelernter. Getting the job done. *BYTE Magazine*, 13(November):301–308, 1988.

[53] Kourosh Gharachorloo, Anoop Gupta, and John L. Hennessey. Peformance evaluation of memory consistency models for shared-memory multiprocessors. In *Proceedings of the Fourth International Conference on Architectural Support for Programming Languages and Operation Systems*, April 1991.

[54] Herman H. Goldstine. *History of Numerical Analysis from the 16th through the 19th Century.* Springer-Verlag, 1977.

[55] Herman H. Goldstine. *The Computer from Pascal to von Neumann.* Princeton Univ. Press, 1993.

[56] Gene H. Golub and Charles F. Van Loan. *Matrix Computations, 2nd ed.* John Hopkins Univ. Press, 1989.

[57] Ernesto Gomez. *Single Program Task Parallelism.* PhD thesis, Univ. of Chicago, 2005.

[58] Raymond Greenlaw, H. James Hoover, and Walter L. Ruzzo. *Limits to Parallel Computation.* Oxford, 1995.

[59] William Gropp, Ewing Lusk, and Anthony Skjellum. *Using MPI: Portable Parallel Programming with the Message-Passing Interface, 2nd ed.* MIT Press, 1999.

[60] W. Gropp, E. Lusk, N. Doss, and A. Skjellum. A high-performance, portable implementation of the MPI message passing interface standard. *Parallel Computing*, 22(6):789–828, September 1996.

[61] Emil Grosswald. *Topics from the Theory of Numbers.* Macmillan, 1966.

[62] W. F. van Gunsteren and H. J. C. Berendsen. GROMOS: GROningen MOlecular Simulation software. Technical report, Laboratory of Physical Chemistry, Univ. of Groningen, Nijenborgh, Netherlands, 1988.

[63] John L. Gustafson, Gary R. Montry, and Robert E. Benner. Development of parallel methods for a 1024-processor hypercube. *SIAM J. Sci. Stat. Comp.*, 9(4), 1988.

[64] R. Haacke and B. M. Pettitt. The scaling of molecular dynamics on the KSR-1. In *Proceedings of the Hawaii International Conference on System Sciences*, volume 5, pages 142–152, Maui, HI, 1995.

[65] A. N. Habermann. Parallel neighbor sort. Technical report, Carnegie–Mellon Univ., 1972.

[66] P. Brinch Hansen. The programming language Concurrent Pascal. *IEEE Trans. Software Eng.*, 1:199–207, Jun 1975.

[67] R. v. Hanxleden, K. Kennedy, C. Koelbel, R. Das, and J. Saltz. Compiler analysis for irregular problems in Fortran D. In *Proceedings of the Fifth Workshop on Languages and Compilers for Parallel Computing*, New Haven, CT, August 1992. Available via anonymous ftp from `softlib.rice.edu` as `pub/CRPC-TRs/reports/CRPC-TR92287-S`.

[68] R. v. Hanxleden, K. Kennedy, and J. Saltz. Value-based distributions in Fortran D — a preliminary report. Technical Report CRPC-TR93365-S, Center for Research on Parallel Computation, December 1993. Available via anonymous ftp from `softlib.rice.edu` as `pub/CRPC-TRs/reports/CRPC-TR93365-S`.

[69] R. v. Hanxleden and L. R. Scott. Correctness and determinism of parallel Monte Carlo processes. *J. Parallel Comp.*, 18:121–132, 1992.

[70] R. v. Hanxleden. Parallelizing dynamic processes. Master's thesis, Dept. of Computer Science, Pennsylvania State Univ., 1989.

[71] R. v. Hanxleden. *Compiler Support for Machine-Independent Parallelization of Irregular Problems.* PhD thesis, Rice Univ., December 1994. Available via anonymous ftp from `softlib.rice.edu` as `pub/CRPC-TRs/reports/CRPC-TR94495-S`.

[72] Robert J. Harrison and Ron Shepard. Ab initio molecular electronic structure on parallel computers. *Ann. Rev. Phys. Chem.*, 45:623–658, 1994.

[73] Robert J. Harrison. Portable tools and applications for parallel computers. *Internat. J. Quantum Chem.*, 40:847–863, 1990.

[74] Philip J. Hatcher and Michael J. Quinn. *Data-Parallel Programming on MIMD Computers.* MIT Press, 1991.

[75] M. T. Heath. *Hypercube Multiprocessors 1987.* SIAM, 1987.

[76] N. J. Higham and A. Pothen. The stability of the partitioned inverse approach to parallel sparse triangular solution. *SIAM J. Sci. Computing*, 15:139–148, 1994.

[77] C. A. R. Hoare. Monitors: an operating system structuring concept. *Comm. ACM*, 17:549–557, Oct 1974.

[78] C. A. R. Hoare. *Communicating Sequential Processes.* Prentice-Hall, 1985.

[79] R.W. Hockney and J.W. Eastwood. *Computer Simulation Using Particles.* Institute of Physics Publishing, 1994.

[80] R. W. Hockney and C. R. Jessope. *Parallel Computers.* Adam-Hilger, 1981.

[81] R. W. Hockney and C. R. Jessope. *Parallel Computers 2.* Adam-Hilger, 1988.

[82] David Hughes. *The Star of Bethlehem: An Astronomer's Confirmation.* Walker and Company, 1979.

[83] Kai Hwang and Faye A. Briggs. *Computer Architecture and Parallel Processing.* McGraw-Hill, 1984.

[84] A. Ilin and L. R. Scott. Loop splitting for superscalar architectures. *J. Supercomp. Appl. and High Perf. Comput.*, 10:336–340, 1996.

[85] Intel. *IA-32 Intel Architecture Software Developer's Manual*, volume 1. Intel Corporation, 2003. Order Number 245470-012.

[86] E. Isaacson and H. B. Keller. *Analysis of Numerical Methods.* John Wiley, 1966.

[87] Frederick P. Brooks Jr. *The Mythical Man-month.* Addison-Wesley, 1982.

[88] A. Karp. Gordon Bell Prize for 1997. *NA Digest*, 97(12):226–319, March 1997.

[89] P. Keleher, H. Lu, R. Rajamony, W. Yu, , and W. Zwaenepoel. Treadmarks: Shared memory computing on networks of workstations. *IEEE Computer*, 29(2):18–28, 1996.

[90] Kendall Square Research Corporation. Kendall Square Research technical summary. Technical report, Kendall Square Research, 170 Tracer Lane, Waltham, MA 02154-1379, 1992.

[91] Donald E. Knuth. *Sorting and Searching: The Art of Computer Programming*, volume 3. Addison-Wesley, 1973.

[92] C. Koelbel, D. Loveman, R. Schreiber, G. Steele, Jr., and M. Zosel. *The High Performance Fortran Handbook.* MIT Press, 1994.

[93] N. Koike. NEC Cenju-3: A micro-processor based parallel computer. In *Proceedings of the 8th International Parallel Processing Symposium*, pages 396–401. IEEE Computer Society Press, 1994.

[94] Ed Kushner. Automatic parallelization of grid-based applications for the iPSC/860. Tech. Rep., Intel Corp., 1992.

[95] BBN Laboratories. Butterfly parallel processor overview. BBN Laboratories, Cambridge, Mass., Tech. Rep. 6148, 1986.

[96] S. G. Lambrakos and J. P. Boris. Molecular dynamics simulation of $(N_2)_2$ formation using the Monotonic Lagrangian Grid. *J. Chem. Phys.*, 90:4473–4481, 1989.

[97] C. L. Lawson, R. J. Hanson, D. R. Kincaid, and F. T. Krogh. Basic Linear Algebra Subprograms for Fortran usage. *ACM Trans. Math. Software*, 5(3):308–323, September 1979.

[98] Bruce Leasure. PCF parallel Fortran extensions. *ACM SIGPLAN Fortran Forum*, 10(3):1–57, Sept. 1991.

[99] Peizong Lee and Zvi Meir Kedem. Automatic data and computation decomposition on distributed memory parallel computers. *ACM Trans. Programming Languages and Systems (TOPLAS)*, 24(1):1–50, 2002.

[100] F. Thomson Leighton. *Introduction to Parallel Algorithms and Architectures: Arrays, Trees, and Hypercubes.* Morgan Kaufmann, 1992.

[101] Daniel Lenoski, James Laudon, Kourosh Gharachorloo, Anoop Gupta, and John L. Hennessey. The directory-based cache coherence protocol for the DASH multiprocessor. In *Proceedings of the 17th Annual International Symposium on Computer Architecture*, pages 148–159, 1990.

[102] P. H. Leslie. On the use of matrices in certain population mathematics. *Biometrika*, 33:183–212, 1945.

[103] P. H. Leslie. Some further notes on the use of matrices in population mathematics. *Biometrika*, 35:214–245, 1948.

[104] Xiaoye S. Li, James W. Demmel, David H. Bailey, Greg Henry, Yozo Hida, Jimmy Iskandar, William Kahan, Suh Y. Kang, Anil Kapur, Michael C. Martin, Brandon J. Thompson, Teresa Tung, and Daniel J. Yoo. Design, implementation and testing of extended and mixed precision BLAS. *ACM Trans. Math. Software*, 28(2):152–205, June 2002.

[105] Andrew Lumsdaine and Deyun Wu. Spectra and pseudospectra of waveform relaxation operators. *SIAM J. Sci. Comput.*, 18(1):286–304, January 1997. Dedicated to C. William Gear on the occasion of his 60th birthday.

[106] Robert C. Martin. *Designing Object-oriented C++ Applications using the Booch Method.* Prentice-Hall, 1995.

[107] Yuri Matiyasevich. *Dynamics of Proteins and Nucleic Acids.* MIT Press, Cambridge, 1993.

[108] J. A. McCammon, B. M. Pettitt, and L. R. Scott. Ordinary differential equations of molecular dynamics. *Comput. Math. Appl.*, 28:319–326, 1994.

[109] Piyush Mehrotra, John Van Rosendale, and Hans P. Zima. High Performance Fortran: History, status and future. In *Proc. Fourth Internat. Workshop on Applied Parallel Computing (PARA'98), Umea, Sweden (June 14-17, 1998)*, 1998.

[110] A. A. Michelson. *Studies in Optics.* Dover, 1995.

[111] John Mosley. *The Christmas Star.* Griffith Observatory, Los Angeles, CA, 1987.

[112] Ketan Mulmuley. Lower bounds in a parallel model without bit operations. *SIAM J. Comput.*, 28:1460–1509, 1999.

[113] John Nash. Parallel control. In Harold W. Kuhn and Sylvia Nasar, editors, *The Essential John Nash*, pages 117–125. Princeton Univ. Press, 2001.

[114] J. Nieplocha, R. J. Harrison, and R. J. Littlefield. Global Arrays: A nonuniform memory access programming model for high-performance computers. *J. Supercomput.*, 10:197–220, 1996.

[115] J. Nieplocha, R. Harrison, M. Krishnan, B. Palmer, and V. Tipparaju. Combining shared and distributed memory models: Evolution and recent advancements of the Global Array Toolkit. In G. Bilardi, A. Ferreira, R. Lüling, and J. Rolim, editors, *Proceedings of POOHL 2002 Workshop of ICS-2002, New York City*. Springer-Verlag, 2002.

[116] E. I. Organick, A. I. Forsythe, and R. P. Plummer. *Programming Language Structures*. Academic Press, 1978.

[117] I. Parberry. *Parallel Complexity Theory*. Pitman, 1987.

[118] Henrik G. Petersen and John W. Perram. Molecular dynamics on transputer arrays. *Molec. Phys.*, 67:849–860, 1989.

[119] Henrik G. Petersen. Accuracy and efficiency of the particle mesh Ewald method. *J. Chem. Phys*, 103(9):3668–3679, 1995.

[120] Steve Plimpton. Fast parallel algorithms for short–range molecular dynamics. *J. Comp. Phys.*, 117:1–19, March 1995.

[121] Terrence W. Pratt. *Programming Languages*. Prentice-Hall, 1984.

[122] Charles Radin. *Miles of Tiles*. Amer. Math. Soc., 1999.

[123] Aneesur Rahman. Correlations in the motion of atoms in liquid argon. *Phys. Rev.*, 136:A405–411, 1964.

[124] D. C. Rapaport. Multi-million particle molecular dynamics, II. Design considerations for distributed processing. *Comput. Phys. Comm.*, 62:217–228, 1991.

[125] D. C. Rapaport. Multi-million particle molecular dynamics, I. Design considerations for vector processing. *Comput. Phys. Comm.*, 62:198–210, 1991.

[126] P. Sanders and T. Hansch. On the efficient implementation of massively parallel quicksort. In G. Bilardi, A. Ferreira, R. Lüling, and J. Rolim, editors, *Solving Irregularly Structured Problems in Parallel, LNCS Volume. 1253*, pages 13–24. Springer-Verlag, 1997.

[127] U. Schendel. *Introduction to Numerical Methods for Parallel Computers*. Ellis Horwood, 1984.

[128] L. Ridgway Scott and Dexuan Xie. Parallel linear stationary iterative methods. In Petter Bjørstad and Mitchell Luskin, editors, *Parallel Solution of Partial Differential Equations*, pages 31–55. Springer-Verlag, 2000.

[129] L. R. Scott, J. M. Boyle, and B. Bagheri. Distributed data structures for scientific computation. In M. T. Heath, editor, *Hypercube Multiprocessors 1987*, pages 55–66. SIAM, 1987.

[130] L. R. Scott and Dexuan Xie. The parallel U-cycle multigrid method. In *Proceedings of the 8th Copper Mountain Conference on Multigrid Methods, April 6-11, 1997*, 1997.

[131] Charles L. Seitz. The Cosmic Cube. *Comm. ACM*, 28(1):22–32, 1985.

[132] Ben Shahn. *The Shape of Content.* Harvard Univ. Press, 1957.

[133] Zhiyu Shen, Zhiyuan Li, and Pen-Chung Yew. An empirical study of Fortran programs for parellizing compilers. *IEEE Trans. Parallel and Distributed Systems*, 1(3):356–364, 1990.

[134] D. P. Siewiorek, C. G. Bell, and A. Newell. *Computer Structures: Principles and Examples.* McGraw-Hill, 1982.

[135] Jaswinder Pal Singh, Truman Joe, Anoop Gupta, and John L. Hennessey. An empirical comparison of the Kendall Square Research KSR-1 and the Stanford DASH multiprocessors. In *Proceedings of Supercomputing '93*, 1993.

[136] Marc Snir, Steve W. Otto, Steven Huss-Lederman, David W. Walker, and Jack Dongarra. *MPI: The Complete Reference.* MIT Press, 1995. ISBN 0-262-69184-1.

[137] Neal Stephenson. *Quicksilver.* HarperCollins, 2003.

[138] Harold S. Stone. *High-performance Computer Architecture.* Addison-Wesley, 1987.

[139] G. Strang. *Linear Algebra.* Cambridge-Wellesley Press, 1991.

[140] R. M. Tomasulo. An efficient algorithm for exploiting multiple arithmetic units. *IBM J. Res. and Devel.*, 11:25–33, 1967.

[141] Robert van de Geijn. On global combine operations. LAPACK Working Note 29.

[142] Alan J. Wallcraft. Comparison of Co-Array Fortran and OpenMP Fortran for SPMD programming. *J. Supercomput.*, 22(3):231–250, 2002.

[143] Robert P. Wilson, Robert S. French, Christopher S. Wilson, Saman P. Amarasinghe, Jennifer M. Anderson, Chau-Wen Tseng, Mary W. Hall, Monica S. Lam, and Jonn L. Hennessey. The SUIF compiler system: a parallelizing and optimizing research compiler. Technical Report CSL-TR-94-620, Computer Systems Laboratory, Stanford Univ., 1994.

[144] Michael J. Wolfe. *Optimizing Supercompilers for Supercomputers.* MIT Press, 1989.

[145] D. Xie and L. Adams. New parallel SOR method by domain partitioning. *SIAM J. Sci. Stat. Comp.*, 20:2261–2281, 1999.

[146] Zheng Zhang and Josep Torrellas. Speeding up irregular applications in shared–memory multiprocessors: Memory binding and group prefetching. *Comp. Arch. News*, 23:188–199, May 1995.

[147] Yanhua Zhou and Gregory H. Miller. Green-Kubo formulas for mutual diffusion coefficients in multicomponent systems. *J. Phys. Chem*, 100:5516–5524, 1996.

[148] Yanhua Zhou and Gregory H. Miller. Mutual diffusion in binary Ar-Kr mixtures and empirical diffusion models. *Phys Rev. E*, 53:1587–1601, 1996.

Index

Also Available from PRINCETON Exclusively Published by New Age International Pvt.Ltd.

Asset Pricing Revised Edition
John H. Cochrane
ISBN: 978-81-224-3124-7, Original Edition Price: $99.50, Indian Edition Price: Rs. 495.00

AUCTIONS: Theory and Practice
Paul Klemperer
ISBN: 978-81-224-3125-4, Original Edition Price: $44.00, Indian Edition Price: Rs. 200.00

Advanced In Behaviour Economics
Colin F., Camerer
ISBN: 978-81-224-1720-3, Original Edition Price: $35.00, Indian Edition Price: Rs. 395.00

Advanced International Trade
Feenstra, Robert C.
ISBN: 978-81-224-1719-7, Original Edition Price: $60.00, Indian Edition Price: Rs. 495.00

Advanced International Trade Theory and Evidence
Feenstra, Robert C.
ISBN: 978-81-224-2170-5, Original Edition Price: $60.00, Indian Edition Price: Rs. 295.00

All the News that's Fit to Sell
Hamilton, James T.
ISBN: 978-81-224-1712-8, Original Edition Price: $35.00, Indian Edition Price: Rs. 345.00

A New World Order
Slaughter, Anne-Marie
ISBN: 978-81-224-1879-8, Original Edition Price: $45.00, Indian Edition Price: Rs. 395.00

Behavioral Game Theory
Colin F. Camerer
ISBN: 978-81-224-3126-1, Original Edition Price: $99.50, Indian Edition Price: Rs. 495.00

Credit Risk Pricing, Measurement and Management
Duffie, Darrell
ISBN: 978-81-224-2168-2, Original Edition Price: $75.00, Indian Edition Price: Rs. 295.00

Credit Risk: Pricing Measurement and Management
Duffie, Darrell
ISBN: 978-81-224-1699-2, Original Edition Price: $75.00, Indian Edition Price: Rs. 495.00

Credit Risk Modeling
Lando, David
ISBN: 978-81-224-2172-9, Original Edition Price: $65.00, Indian Edition Price: Rs. 295.00

Credit Risk Modeling Theory and Applications
Lando, David
ISBN: 978-81-224-1696-1, Original Edition Price: $65.00, Indian Edition Price: Rs. 395.00

Comparative Biomechanics
Vogel, Steven
ISBN: 978-81-224-1717-3, Original Edition Price: $60.00, Indian Edition Price: Rs. 695.00

Dynamic Models in Biology
Stephen P. Ellner and John Guckenheimer
ISBN: 978-81-224-3127-8, Original Edition Price: $60.00, Indian Edition Price: Rs. 350.00

Dynamic Asset Pricing Theory
Duffie, Darrell
ISBN: 978-81-224-1695-4, Original Edition Price: $90.00, Indian Edition Price: Rs. 495.00

Entropy
Andreas Greven, Gerhard Keller and Gerald Warnecke
ISBN: 978-81-224-3128-5, Original Edition Price: $87.00, Indian Edition Price: Rs. 399.00

Essays on The Great Depression
Bernanke, Ben S.
ISBN: 978-81-224-1988-7, Original Edition Price: $24.95, Indian Edition Price: Rs. 395.00

Earthquakes in Human History
Boer, Jelle Zeilinga de
ISBN: 978-81-224-1883-5, Original Edition Price: $24.95, Indian Edition Price: Rs. 295.00

Econometrics
Hayashi, Fumio
ISBN: 978-81-224-2122-4, Original Edition Price: $85.00, Indian Edition Price: Rs. 295.00

Econometrics
Hayashi, Fumio
ISBN: 978-81-224-1711-1, Original Edition Price: $85.00, Indian Edition Price: Rs. 695.00

Financial Econometrics Problems, Models, and Methods
Gourieroux, Christian
ISBN: 978-81-224-2171-2, Original Edition Price: $67.50, Indian Edition Price: Rs. 295.00

Financial Econometrics Problems, Models, and Methods
Gourieroux, Christian
ISBN: 978-81-224-1697-8, Original Edition Price: $67.50, Indian Edition Price: Rs. 495.00

Google's Page Rank and Beyond
Amy N. Langville, Carl D. Meyer
ISBN: 978-81-224-3129-2, Original Edition Price: $39.50, Indian Edition Price: Rs. 395.00

Graphic Discovery
Wainer, Howard
ISBN: 978-81-224-1882-8, Original Edition Price: $29.95, Indian Edition Price: Rs. 295.00

Homological Algebra
Cartan, Henri
ISBN: 978-81-224-1997-9, Original Edition Price: $60.00, Indian Edition Price: Rs. 295.00

Hubbert's Peak: The Impending World Oil Shortage
Deffeyes, Kenneth S.
ISBN: 978-81-224-1708-6, Original Edition Price: $16.95, Indian Edition Price: Rs. 175.00

Interest Rate Models An Introduction
Andrew J.G. Cairns
ISBN: 978-81-224-3130-8, Original Edition Price: $49.95, Indian Edition Price: Rs. 200.00

Inflation Targeting
Bernanke, Ben S.
ISBN: 978-81-224-1989-4, Original Edition Price: $19.95, Indian Edition Price: Rs. 395.00

Infinity and the Mind
Rudy Rucker
ISBN: 978-81-224-2110-1, Original Edition Price: $19.95, Indian Edition Price: Rs. 295.00

Irrational Exuberance
Shiller, Robert. J.
ISBN: 978-81-224-1876-7, Original Edition Price: $27.95, Indian Edition Price: Rs. 395.00

Interest & Prices Foundations
Woodford, Michael
ISBN:978-81-224-1718-0, Original Edition Price: $ 75.00, Indian Edition Price: Rs. 795.00

Learning and Expectations in Macroeconomics
Evans, Honkapohja
ISBN: 978-81-224-3131-5, Original Edition Price: $61.00, Indian Edition Price: Rs. 495.00

Local Search in Combinatorial Optimization
Aarts, Emile
ISBN: 978-81-224-1999-3, Original Edition Price: $45.00, Indian Edition Price: Rs. 395.00

Liquid Crystals
Collings, Peter J.
ISBN: 978-81-224-1996-2, Original Edition Price: $42.00, Indian Edition Price: Rs. 395.00

Mathematical Techniques In Finance
Cerny, Ales
ISBN: 978-81-224-1715-9, Original Edition Price: $39.95, Indian Edition Price: Rs. 295.00

Microfoundations of Financial Economics
Lengwiler, Yvan
ISBN: 978-81-224-1698-5, Original Edition Price: $49.95, Indian Edition Price: Rs. 295.00

Neoclassical Finance
Ross, Stephen A
ISBN: 978-81-224-1881-1, Original Edition Price: $35.00, Indian Edition Price: Rs. 195.00

Optimization Insights and Applications
Jan Brinkhuis and Vladimir Tikhomirov
ISBN: 978-81-224-3132-2, Original Edition Price: $94.00, Indian Edition Price: Rs. 595.00

Plasma Physics for Astrophysics
Russell M. Kulsrud
ISBN: 978-81-224-3133-9, Original Edition Price: $60.00, Indian Edition Price: Rs. 295.00

Quadrangular Algebras
Richard M. Weiss
ISBN: 978-81-224-3134-6, Original Edition Price: $47.50, Indian Edition Price: Rs. 150.00

Quantitative Risk Management
Alexander J. McNeil, Rüdiger Frey, Paul Embrechts
ISBN: 978-81-224-3135-3, Original Edition Price: $85.00, Indian Edition Price: Rs. 495.00

Real Analysis Measure Theory, Integration, & Hilbert Spaces
Elias M Stein and Rami Shakarchi
ISBN: 978-81-224-3136-0, Original Edition Price: $70.00, Indian Edition Price: Rs. 495.00

Scientific Parallel Computing
L. Ridgway Scott, Terry Clark, Babak Bagheri
ISBN: 978-81-224-3137-7, Original Edition Price: $64.00, Indian Edition Price: Rs. 395.00

Strange Curves, Counting Rabbits, and other Mathematical Explorations
Ball, Keith
ISBN: 978-81-224-1878-1, Original Edition Price: $29.95, Indian Edition Price: Rs. 295.00

Small Worlds
Watts J. Duncan
ISBN: 978-81-224-1714-2, Original Edition Price: $24.95, Indian Edition Price: Rs. 195.00

The Structure and Dynamics of Networks
Mark Newman, Duncan J. Watts, Albert-Lászlá Barabási
ISBN: 978-81-224-3138-4, Original Edition Price: $69.00, Indian Edition Price: Rs. 595.00

Thermodynamics, A Dynamical Systems Approach
Wassim M. Haddad, V.S. Chellaboina and Sergey G. Nersesov
ISBN: 978-81-224-3139-1, Original Edition Price: $58.00, Indian Edition Price: Rs. 395.00

The Complexity of Cooperation
Axelrod, Robert
ISBN: 978-81-224-1709-8, Original Edition Price: $23.95, Indian Edition Price: Rs. 175.00

The Paradox of Asset Pricing
Bossaerts, Peter
ISBN: 978-81-224-2000-5, Original Edition Price: $32.95, Indian Edition Price: Rs. 295.00

The Econometrics of Financial Markets
Campbell, John Y.
ISBN: 978-81-224-2169-9, Original Edition Price: $95.00, Indian Edition Price: Rs. 395.00

The Econometrics of Financial Markets
Campbell, John Y.
ISBN: 978-81-224-1707-8, Original Edition Price: $95.00, Indian Edition Price: Rs. 595.00

The Future of Money
Cohen, Benjamin J.
ISBN: 978-81-224-1998-6, Original Edition Price: $19.95, Indian Edition Price: Rs. 295.00

The Calculus Gallery
Dunham, William
ISBN: 978-81-224-1880-4, Original Edition Price: $29.95, Indian Edition Price: Rs. 295.00

The Meaning of Relativity
Einstein, Albert
ISBN: 978-81-224-1817-0, Original Edition Price: $14.95, Indian Edition Price: Rs. 95.00

The Challenge of Global Capitalism
Gilpin, Robert
ISBN: 978-81-224-1713-5, Original Edition Price: $24.95, Indian Edition Price: Rs. 195.00

The New Division of Labor
Levy, Frank
ISBN: 978-81-224-1884-2, Original Edition Price: $39.95, Indian Edition Price: Rs. 195.00

The Theory of Incentives
Martimort David
ISBN: 978-81-224-1710-4, Original Edition Price: $34.95, Indian Edition Price: Rs. 295.00

The Company of Strangers A Natural History of Economic Life
Seabright, Paul
ISBN: 978-81-224-1877-4, Original Edition Price: $18.95, Indian Edition Price: Rs. 395.00

The New Financial Risk In the 21st Century Order
Shiller, Robert. J.
ISBN: 978-81-224-1716-6, Original Edition Price: $18.95, Indian Edition Price: Rs. 245.00

Why Stock Markets Crash
Didier, Sornette
ISBN: 978-81-224-1790-6, Original Edition Price: $19.95, Indian Edition Price: Rs. 275.00